Writing on
the Renaissance Stage

University of Delaware Press
Manuscript Competition Winners

Shakespearean Literature
John W. Blanpied, *Time and the Artist in Shakespeare's English Histories*
Robert Ornstein, *Shakespeare's Comedies: From Roman Farce to Romantic Mystery*
Donald W. Foster, *Elegy by W. S.: A Study in Attribution*
David Hoeniger, *Medicine and Shakespeare in the English Renaissance*
Peggy Muñoz Simonds, *Myth, Emblem, and Music in Shakespeare's Cymbeline*
Marvin Rosenberg, *The Masks of* Hamlet
Frederick Kiefer, *Writing on the Renaissance Stage: Written Words, Printed Pages, Metaphoric Books*

Early American Culture to 1840
Daniel D. Reiff, *Small Georgian Houses in England and Virginia: Origins and Development through the 1750s*

Military, Naval, and Diplomatic History
Richard J. Hargrove, *General John Burgoyne*

Eighteenth-Century Studies
Donald T. Siebert, *The Moral Animus of David Hume*
Ruben Quintero, *Literate Culture: Pope's Rhetorical Art*
Lois Bueler, Clarissa's *Plots*
Alexander Pettit, *Illusory Consensus: Bolingbroke and the Polemical Response to Walpole, 1730–1737*

American Art
Rowland Elzea, *John Sloan's Oil Paintings: A Catalogue Raisonné*
Thomas P. Somma, The Apotheosis of Democracy, *1908–1916: The Pediment for the House Wing of the United States Capitol*

Writing on the Renaissance Stage

Written Words, Printed Pages, Metaphoric Books

Frederick Kiefer

Newark: University of Delaware Press
London: Associated University Presses

© 1996 by Associated University Presses, Inc.

All rights reserved. Authorization to photocopy items for internal or personal use, or the internal or personal use of specific clients, is granted by the copyright owner, provided that a base fee of $10.00, plus eight cents per page, per copy is paid directly to the Copyright Clearance Center, 222 Rosewood Drive, Danvers, Massachusetts 01923. [0-87413-595-8/96 $10.00+8¢ pp, pc.]

Associated University Presses
440 Forsgate Drive
Cranbury, NJ 08512

Associated University Presses
16 Barter Street
London WC1A 2AH, England

Associated University Presses
P.O. Box 338, Port Credit
Mississauga, Ontario
Canada L5G 4L8

The paper used in this publication meets the requirements
of the American National Standard for Permanence of Paper
for Printed Library Materials Z39.48–1984.

Library of Congress Cataloging-in-Publication Data

Kiefer, Frederick, 1945–
   Writing on the Renaissance stage : written words, printed pages, metaphoric books / Frederick Kiefer.
     p. cm.
   Includes bibliographical references and index.
   ISBN 0-87413-595-8 (alk. paper)
   1. English drama—Early modern and Elizabethan, 1500–1600—History and criticism. 2. Writing in literature. 3. English drama—17th century—History and criticism. 4. Theater audiences—England—History. 5. Books and reading—England—History. 6. Books and reading in literature. 7. Theater—England—History. 8. Printing in literature. 9. Renaissance—England. 10. Metaphor. I. Title.
PR658.W7K54   1996
822'.309357—dc20   96-10170
                                                                                CIP

PRINTED IN THE UNITED STATES OF AMERICA

For
Muriel Jacques Kiefer

Contents

Acknowledgments	9
Introduction	11

Part One

1. Erasmus, Luther, and the Scriptural Word	21
2. Written Words and Printed Books	44

Part Two

3. Ideology, Printing Press, and Stage	73
4. Writing and Print as Figurative Language	89

Part Three

5. The Book of Conscience	111
6. Conscience on the Stage	124
7. The Book of Nature	163
8. Nature on the Stage	180
9. The Book of Fate	219
10. Fate on the Stage	232
Conclusion	264
Appendix 1: Elizabethan Literacy	268
Appendix 2: Written and Printed Words on the Stage	275
Appendix 3: The Pragmatic Value of Props Involving Writing and Print	283
Appendix 4: Books and Written Materials as Symbols	287
Notes	297
Select Bibliography	347
Index	361

Acknowledgments

THE notes to this book acknowledge those scholars whose work has been instrumental in shaping my own. More difficult to document are debts of a personal kind. The instructors and fellow participants at an NEH institute "Shakespeare in Performance," organized by Homer Swander and Audrey Stanley, led me to consider afresh the significance of theatrical props and onstage action. Meetings of the Shakespeare Association of America provided valuable opportunities to exchange views with other scholars. Particularly helpful was the seminar, "Reading and Writing in Shakespeare," chaired by David Bergeron in 1992. Other colleagues have also assisted me generously: I am especially grateful to Carl T. Berkhout, Roger Dahood, Peter E. Medine, and Richard Hosley. Finally, I have found indispensable the experience of seeing Renaissance plays in performance by the Royal Shakespeare Company and by the National Theatre Company, London.

Parts of this book have appeared previously, in somewhat different form. My treatments of *A Woman Killed with Kindness* and *Pericles* first appeared in *Medieval and Renaissance Drama in England* (1986) and in *The University of Toronto Quarterly* (1991/92), respectively. I am grateful to the editors of both journals for permission to reprint this material.

Quotations of Shakespeare are from *The Riverside Shakespeare,* edited by G. Blakemore Evans (Boston: Houghton Mifflin, 1974). Quotations of the Bible are from *The Geneva Bible: A Facsimile of the 1560 Edition,* with an introduction by Lloyd E. Berry (Madison and Milwaukee: University of Wisconsin Press, 1969).

In quoting from early books and modern original-spelling editions, I have made minor changes: *i/j, u/v,* and long *s* appear as they would in a modern text. Printers' abbreviations have been silently expanded.

Introduction

A visitor to the cathedral of Siena can move from the Middle Ages into the Renaissance by walking through a doorway. From a dark Romanesque church, one steps into a large, light-filled room, decorated with splendid frescoes by Pinturicchio. This room is a library, commissioned by Cardinal Francesco Todeschini Piccolomini to house the books of his uncle, Pope Pius II. That such artistry should be lavished on a library rather than an ecclesiastical structure suggests a new direction of late fifteenth-century culture. Nor is the Piccolomini library unique. No less an architect than Michelangelo designed the Laurentian library in Florence to house books belonging to the Medicis. And according to Castiglione, Federico of Montefeltro, who in 1444 succeeded his brother as ruler of Urbino, "collected many very excellent and rare books in Greek, Latin, and Hebrew, all of which he adorned with gold and silver, deeming these to be the supreme excellence of his great palace."[1] Although the books have long since been removed to the Vatican, Federico's magnificent study, with its trompe l'oeil walls executed in marquetry, remain to dazzle the visitor. Together these three libraries signal the extent to which European culture was becoming increasingly bookish in the late fifteenth and early sixteenth centuries. Erasmus did not exaggerate when he advised princes that the creation of libraries ensured their renown.

In England the new status of books becomes evident in the later fifteenth century. Whereas Edward IV's small collection of books moved from place to place with the rest of the king's baggage, Henry VII established a royal library and in 1492 hired a librarian to help build the collection. When the new Richmond Palace was constructed, it boasted a place for the king's "many goodly, pleasant books of works full delightful, sage, merry and also right cunning."[2] Henry VIII continued this activity, adding books that became available with the dissolution of the monasteries, and creating new libraries at Whitehall, Hampton Court, and Greenwich.[3]

The importance that the written word would possess during the reign of Queen Elizabeth is signaled by her coronation procession through London. At one point the people presented her with an English Bible, which she graciously accepted: "At the receit wherof, how reverently did she with both her handes take it, kisse it, and lay it upon her brest? to the great comfort of the lookers on."[4] Elizabeth's commitment to the written word was not limited to ceremonial occasions. Raphael Holinshed, generalizing about the contents of palaces during her monarchy, notes approvingly, "everie office hath either a bible, or the bookes of the acts and monuments of the church of England, or both, beside some histories and chronicles lieng therein, for the exercise of such as come into the same: whereby the stranger that entereth into the court of England upon the sudden, shall rather imagine himselfe to come into some publike schoole of the universities, where manie give eare to one that readeth, than into a princes palace, if you conferre the same with those of other nations."[5] Although sixteenth-century England may not have produced architecturally magnificent libraries to rank with those that survive in Italy, an Elizabethan created one of the most comprehensive collections of Renaissance Europe. John Dee, who was on cordial terms with Queen Elizabeth, singlehandedly assembled a huge personal library; it included some four thousand books, a thousand of them manuscripts.[6]

What allowed the making, distribution, and collection of books on a scale dwarfing that of the medieval past was an invention of the Renaissance—the printing press using movable type.[7] Books became available in such numbers that they infiltrated people's lives, from their place of work to place of worship. The Reformation, moreover, closely identified the written and printed word with the attainment of salvation, giving a powerful impetus to literacy and education. The effects of the printing press were so startling that it was easy to imagine them the product of supernatural force. Luther's ninety-five theses spread so rapidly in print that the event seemed to contemporaries the work of angels. John Foxe saw in the press nothing less than divine intervention in human affairs, God's answer to the antichrist. A century and a half after Johann Gutenberg set up his press in Mainz, the effects of printing were still so freshly felt that observers continued to exclaim over the press, deeming it as important to the course of history as gunpowder and the mariner's compass.

The logocentric nature of Renaissance culture is revealed not only by the production of books and by the creation of libraries but also by changes in the way people thought and expressed themselves. Increasingly they used metaphors of books when they envisioned abstractions. They spoke, for example, of the book of conscience, the book of nature, and the book of fate. Admittedly, there was a precedent, stretching back to antiquity, for treating concepts in such terms. Metaphoric books, however, were anything but static: the ways in which they were imagined altered, sometimes sharply, as did their prominence, and they flourished in the Renaissance as never before. Although metaphoric books may seem esoteric today, they had an urgency in the sixteenth and seventeenth centuries which they have ceased to enjoy four centuries later. Not only did poets and playwrights invoke them, but so also did theologians, philosophers, and scientists. Metaphoric books, which figured in fierce controversies of the time—over scientific experimentation, medical treatment, astrological prediction, and religious practice—can reveal nothing less than certain directions of Renaissance culture.

Within a culture in which writing and printing were achieving unprecedented ascendancy, it may seem inevitable that playwrights should devote considerable attention to the written word, and indeed the activities of reading and writing appear frequently on the Renaissance stage in England. Letters are penned and sealed, delivered and scrutinized, answered and acted upon, ignored and destroyed. Documents of various kinds are signed and examined, debated and repudiated. Books are carried and consulted, disparaged and dismissed. What Jonas Barish observes of Shakespeare applies no less to his contemporaries: "Shakespeare places a quite extraordinary reliance on *writings* in his plays, even where it almost seems as though he is dragging them in, looking for excuses to insert them. He weaves them deeply and inextricably into the verbal texture of the plays, whether in documents we actually see or those we only hear about, whether they are read out word for word or merely paraphrased, so that graphic communication becomes as natural and inevitable and indispensable a part of the verbal medium as its vocal counterpart."[8]

Despite this deployment Elizabethan and Jacobean playwrights must have held mixed, if not conflicting, attitudes toward writing and printing. Although they belonged to a culture that was ever more literary in character and although they usually depended on printed materials to furnish their plots and on writing to produce their scripts, they earned their living by appealing to audiences that may have been largely illiterate by modern standards.[9] And they wrote plays for performance, not for reading in book form. John Marston, in his address to the reader of *The Malcontent*, laments that "scenes invented merely to be spoken should be enforcively published to be read," and he approves the printing of his tragicomedy because it may revive memories of the play in performance: "the unhandsome shape which this trifle in reading presents may be pardoned for the pleasure it once afforded you when it was presented with the soul of lively action."[10] Ben Jonson begins the epilogue to *The New Inn* with this acknowledgment of the spoken word's importance: "Plays in themselves have neither hopes nor fears, / Their fate is only in their hearers' ears."[11] And John Webster sanctions the printing of *The White Devil* because the play had failed to find "a full and understanding auditory."[12]

The Renaissance theater was the place par excellence of the spoken word, the nature of which is suggested by Erasmus in his *Adages:* "*Viva vox,* The living word, was the term used in old times for anything not written, but taken straight from the mouth of the speaker, lifelike, as it were, and effectual."[13] This definition continues, specifying the deficiency of written words: "Writing is indeed a kind of voice, but as it were an artificial one, somehow mimicking the real voice. Gesture and movement are lacking; in a word, life." Although Erasmus's stark contrast was not formed with the stage in mind, his distinction nonetheless applies to the theater. For what the written word lacks is what an actor supplies: the warmth and emphasis of the spoken word, together with complementary gesture and movement. John Marston, apologizing for publishing *Parasitaster, or The Fawn,* concedes that the life of a comedy "rests much in the actors' voice."[14] John Webster emphasizes the spoken word in his character of "an excellent actor": "Whatsoever is commendable in the grave Orator, is most exquisitly perfect in him; for by a full and significant action of body, he charmes our attention: sit in a full Theater, and you will thinke you see so many lines drawne from the circumference of so many eares, whiles the *Actor* is the *Center*."[15] The very word "audience" by its etymology signals the dependence of theatrical experience on the spoken words heard by listeners.

If playwrights, occupying a place at the intersection of a still vital oral culture and a nascent culture of writing and print, felt any reluctance to dramatize reading and writing, it was because they were attentive to the pragmatic demands of the theater and the expectations of the audience. Shakespeare and his contemporaries knew that reading and writing, in themselves, do not necessarily exert a theatrical appeal. The sight of an actor perusing a book or composing a letter is not likely to engage an audience for long since these are essentially solitary activities and typically require a certain self-absorption on the part of reader or writer. Reading and writing, moreover, are often conducted silently: they will possess a merely pantomimic quality if the reader or writer onstage fails to convert the written word into the spoken. Unless the playwright and actor find ways of making the audience feel the significance of the written word for the character and the dramatic action, writing or reading will constitute a pause in the drama, reducing the energy and momentum of a performance.

This study of the written and printed word on the English Renaissance stage begins by considering the role of writing and printing in Renaissance culture. It focuses on two figures who became especially important in crystallizing opinion about the written and printed word—Erasmus and Luther. Today we associate the one chiefly with editing ancient books, including the New Testament, the other with translating and interpreting Scripture in ways that revolutionized Christianity. Despite their different emphases, however, the written word was at the center of their personal and professional lives. Their careers define the significance that the written and printed word would assume in the later sixteenth century and beyond. Accordingly, this study begins with an examination of their work: what they sought to achieve, what they felt they accomplished, and what actually followed from their endeavors. Although Erasmus and Luther were editors and exegetes rather than playwrights, their work has considerable application here, for they shaped attitudes toward the written word, spurred the proliferation of the printing press, encouraged the growth of literacy, fostered the founding of schools, and invested the written and printed word with a new and enhanced status.

In its middle section this study examines the English accommodation of the forces that Erasmus and Luther helped to set in motion, particularly the implications for the theater. One chapter considers the stage as a site of contention over reading and writing through an examination of religious controversy in Heywood's *If You Know Not Me,* social conflict in the Jack Cade episode of Shakespeare's *2 Henry VI,* and spiritual psychomachia in Marlowe's *Doctor Faustus.* Another chapter, treating figurative language along with related theatrical properties, considers the proliferation onstage of metaphors involving writing or printing, the penchant for describing both the workings of the mind and the interaction of people in these metaphors, and the cultural assumptions that underlie such language.

To explore the relationship of props to language and of both to metaphoric books, this study in its final section looks in detail at selected plays. Each pair of chapters begins with the description of a metaphoric book, suggesting values and attitudes underlying its formulation. The emphasis, however, rests on specific forms that each playwright's invention takes when treating reading and writing. These instances are related to their dramatic context within scenes and within the larger play, for props, like figurative expressions, can have a function transcending their appearance in a single scene. Together they achieve a cumulative impact, one with affective implications: drama in performance engages the emotions more immediately and compellingly than the intellect; a play, after all, is a play, not a document. As Renaissance dramatists knew from practical experience, a play comes fully to life only on a stage, where actors seek a close rapport with their audience. This last section, accordingly, focuses on actions performed and words spoken onstage, together with specific theatrical effects produced by the enactment of reading and writing.

The conviction that dramatic characters are endowed with human traits informs my discussion of the drama. Although some would argue that a character is merely a rhetorical construction within an indeterminate text, theatrical experience suggests that audiences commonly imagine characters as possessing familiar attributes. Whatever the indeterminacies of a script, theatergoers know instinctively that a performance works only when an audience suspends disbelief and imagines the actions and speeches of an actor as proceeding from a person in much the way that words and deeds spring from people we know. If the performance history of plays teaches us anything, it is that we respond to characters on a stage as though they were real people rather than rhetorical constructions. So although a philosophically sophisticated Shakespearean may, for example, be reluctant to assign innocence, say, to Desdemona, the theater is utterly inhospitable to such agnosticism. Indeed, theatrical experience by its very nature encourages—perhaps even compels—us to identify recognizably human traits with the characters who come to life in our presence. If we fail through intellectual inhibition to achieve this identification, then we shall never fulfill the purpose that brings us to a theater in the first place: the desire to be with other people in whose presence we feel and think more deeply than when we are alone.

Writing on
the Renaissance Stage

Part One

1
Erasmus, Luther, and the Scriptural Word

1

In May of 1521, Albrecht Dürer heard that Martin Luther had been betrayed and possibly killed. Stunned by the report, Dürer feared that the incipient reforms within Christianity might be thwarted. Among the possible consequences of Luther's death, one stood out: "It is especially depressing to me to imagine that God should want us to continue listening to the false and blind teachings written and invented by men called 'fathers,' who in many instances have misinterpreted the Word of God or else neglected it."[1] Dürer contemplates the loss of Scripture's champion, the man who insisted upon the supremacy of God's word over the words of church fathers and other theologians whose voluminous commentaries had become, in his view, a barrier between Scripture and the faithful. Should the news of Luther's demise prove accurate, Dürer anticipates a return to prizing the official teachings of the church over the immediate experience of revelation in its written form:

> O God, if Luther is dead, who will henceforth expound the Holy Gospel so clearly? Ah God, what might he have written in the next ten or twenty years? O all you pious Christians, help me to lament this divinely inspired man and pray that another enlightened one be sent us.[2]

In this moment of anguish Dürer ponders the identity of such an "enlightened one," who may step forward:

> O Erasmus of Rotterdam, where will you stand? Do you not see the result of the unjust tyranny of worldly power and of the forces of darkness? Hear, you knight of Christ, ride on beside our Lord Jesus, guard the truth and win the martyr's crown!

That Dürer should think of Desiderius Erasmus as the most logical candidate to continue Luther's work may seem odd to the modern reader, who knows that the Dutch scholar never severed his ties with Rome and that he and Luther eventually became bitter enemies. The linking of the two names, however, would have seemed less curious in the early sixteenth century, for Erasmus helped to make Luther's work possible by recovering the New Testament in Greek and by giving biblical study a new philological emphasis. In fact, Erasmus and Luther shared many of the same assumptions: that the actual words of Scripture are indispensable; that interpreters should know the original languages of Scripture; and that Scripture should be available to every Christian.

Although they came to vilify one another, Erasmus and Luther both contributed to a revaluation of the written word during the sixteenth century. In a culture whose religion venerated the Bible but vested interpretation of that book in the hands of a few, Erasmus and Luther worked to bring Scripture within the reach of every literate person and, by extension, every listener too. By establishing the best possible text and thereby providing the basis for accurate translation and interpretation, Erasmus and Luther enhanced the status of the written word, giving it in practice the importance that it had long held in theory. At the same time, they set in motion a series of developments that would undermine confidence in the written word. The investigation of manuscript transmission and scribal error alerted readers to the potential unreliability of written words. The concern with translation raised questions about how accurate any translation could ever be. The use of the printing press to disseminate Scripture and scriptural commentary disturbed those who saw that the press propagated truth and error alike. So although Erasmus and Luther gave the editing of ancient books a cultural significance that such activity never enjoyed before or since, their endeavor also generated a climate of opinion in which profound skepticism of the written word would ensue.

2

In a portrait, Albrecht Dürer depicts Erasmus's devotion to the written word by showing the scholar at his writing stand, apparently composing a letter. Beneath the letter lies a book, while several other books, one of them open, occupy the foreground of the print.[3] The composition illustrates Erasmus's wide reading and indefatigable activity as a writer. Dürer could not have chosen a more apt pose, for the written word was the culmination of everything that Erasmus learned and thought. In a letter to the Bishop of Liège, who hoped for a face-to-face meeting with the scholar he knew only by reputation, Erasmus said: "There is nothing in me worth seeing; and if there were, it is all expressed in my published work. That is the best part of me, and what remains would be dear at a farthing" (*CWE* 5:271).[4]

Albrecht Dürer's portrait of Desiderius Erasmus at his writing stand. The engraving was made in 1526. Copyright British Museum.

Erasmus's absorption in the written word began early—he describes his upbringing as "bookish" (2:295)—and intensified with his entry into the monastic life. As a monk Erasmus was able to indulge a fascination with literature, particularly that of antiquity. In 1489, two years after joining the Augustinian canons regular at Steyn, he wrote to Cornelis Gerard, "My authorities in poetry are Virgil, Horace, Ovid, Juvenal, Statius, Martial, Claudian, Persius, Lucan, Tibullus, and Propertius; in prose, Cicero, Quintilian, Sallust, and Terence" (1:31). To a certain extent this program of reading was consistent with the institution of monasticism as it had existed since the sixth century, when Cassiodorus, a Roman in the service of the Ostrogothic king Theodoric, founded a religious community at his estate, Vivarium, in southern Italy, charging his followers with the study of Roman classics as well as Scripture; acquaintance with secular writing was intended to help the reader understand sacred writing. The medieval monasteries that spread across Europe continued this enterprise by collecting and copying the works of pagan authors. To some of Erasmus's contemporaries, however, such commingling of the secular and religious seemed dubious. For them pagan literature was, at best, a useless distraction and, at worst, an impediment to spiritual progress. Conscious of this hostility, Erasmus in 1489 defensively justified the reading of Terence's comedies. Detractors, he said, "fail to perceive how much moral goodness exists in Terence's plays, how much implicit exhortation to shape one's life" (1:59). For Erasmus the characters of the Roman playwright are depicted "so that we may first see what is seemly or unseemly in human behaviour and then distribute affection or rebuke accordingly."

The reformation of morals, then, was consistent with the reading of ancient literature, which Erasmus valued for its style as well as its content. He believed that language was essential to the progress of civilization, that a good style was a corollary of spiritual excellence, that the finest style was to be found in ancient writers. Even as a monk Erasmus seemed always to be searching for writers whose latinity transcended what he regarded as the debased literary standard of his time. When he encountered a modern who managed to emulate the stylistic felicity of the ancients, Erasmus was in awe. His reading of Lorenzo Valla's *Elegantiae Linguae Latinae* (ca. 1444) had such an effect: "from that time his mind was gripped by the brilliance of style, the subtle and attractive latinity which clothed the writings of Valla, who grounded them on an erudition applied to their content with cool realism and clear judgment."[5] While still at the monastery Erasmus prepared a paraphrase of Valla's work and, later, when that epitome, in expanded form, found its way into print, Erasmus revised it and oversaw its publication.

As much as he admired the ancients, Erasmus was never slavish in his attitude. In fact when he came to edit Cicero's *De Officiis,* his first annotated edition of a Roman author, Erasmus approached the task with boldness. He suppressed the usual commentaries accompanying *De Officiis,* removed or transposed headings that had unhelpfully divided the work, refined the text itself, and, finally, "reduced the bulk of the volume as far as possible to permit its being carried about always as a pocket handbook" (2:30). This aggressively pragmatic method was in keeping with the attitude toward books that Erasmus had expressed to a friend in 1489: "I consider as lovers of books, not those who keep their books hidden in their store-chests and never handle them, but those who, by nightly as well as daily use, thumb them, batter them, wear them out, who fill up all the margins with annotations of many kinds, and who prefer the marks of a fault they have erased to a neat copy full of faults" (1:58).

Erasmus might well have continued to invest the major part of his energy in editing secular books were it not for a lucky accident in the summer of 1504. While working in the library of the Praemonstratensian abbey of Parc, near Louvain, he came across a manuscript by Lorenzo Valla. It consisted of notes that Valla had prepared when compiling his *Collatio Novi Testamenti,* a collation of Greek and Latin texts of the New Testament, which he had made in the 1440s and 1450s.[6] Reading those notes, Erasmus recognized what he may have intuited all along—that the same expertise needed to collate manuscripts, translate ancient languages, and interpret secular books could be applied to Scripture. To know how manuscripts are transmitted is to have a basis for arriving at a sound text. To know the range of meanings that a word may possess is to read with an understanding denied those who read in a linguistic vacuum. And to know the social circumstances in which a work is produced is to have the context necessary for translation and interpretation. Preparing Valla's notes for the press, Erasmus reached a decision that would change the course of his life. In 1504 he wrote to John Colet, whose lectures on the Pauline Epistles had revolutionized biblical study by examining them as historical documents: "I am now eager, dear Colet, to approach sacred literature full sail, full gallop; I have an extreme distaste for anything that distracts me from it, or even delays me. . . . Hereafter I intend to address myself to the Scriptures and to spend all the rest of my life upon them" (2:86).

Erasmus's endeavor may seem unexceptional in that Christianity had long sought to preserve Scripture as the indispensable link to Christ's life and ministry. From its beginnings Christianity had prized the written word in a way that was exceptional among religions of the Roman empire. Constantine, the first emperor to embrace Christianity, reversed the policies of Diocletian, who had "ordered that all over the empire copies of Christian scriptures should be collected and destroyed."[7] The Christian emperor allowed extant Christian works to be located, safeguarded, and copied.[8] For many centuries manuscripts of religious significance continued to be reproduced by scribes and, in some instances, richly illuminated. Nevertheless, Erasmus's decision to publish Valla's notes was risky, for to copy was one thing; to emend was quite another. What Valla had done was to recognize the faulty state of the Latin Bible and to propose revisions; where discrepancies existed between the New Testament in Greek and in Latin, the earlier Greek wording was preferred. In a letter to Christopher Fisher, an Englishman in the service of the papacy and the person to whom he dedicated his edition of Valla's notes, Erasmus anticipated the reaction of his contemporaries: "They will say it is intolerable presumption in a grammarian . . . to let his impertinent pen loose on Holy Scripture itself" (2:93). For Erasmus, however, Valla was not tampering with Scripture, merely restoring a problematic text: "tell me what is so shocking about Valla's action in making a few annotations on the New Testament after comparing several old and good Greek manuscripts. After all it is from Greek sources that our text undoubtedly comes; and Valla's notes had to do with internal disagreements, or a nodding translator's plainly inadequate renderings of the meaning, or things that are more intelligibly expressed in Greek, or, finally, anything that is clearly corrupt in our texts" (2:93). Having already edited classical books, Erasmus knew well their disposition to textual error. Scripture, he saw, was not immune to the frailty of scribes and translators; the universally used Latin Bible, attributed to St. Jerome, was riddled with mistakes. And, like Valla before him, Erasmus recognized that Christianity was best served by scrupulous fidelity to an accurate text: "if it were possible for the translators of the Old Testament to make mistakes occasionally, especially where the faith is not impugned, could not the translators have done likewise in the New Testament? For Jerome indeed did not translate the latter so much as emend it, though moderately, leaving (as he himself testifies), the words of the text; and it is the words that Valla discusses with particular care" (2:94). This project taught Erasmus that the business of correcting textual corruptions depended on a knowledge of language and grammar.[9] Biblical study was becoming scholarly in a new and rigorous way, for it was now philological as well as theological; philology *was* theology.

The experience of preparing Valla's notes for the press almost certainly inspired Erasmus with the idea for his most important achievement—an edition of the New Testament in Greek, which appeared in 1516. The title Erasmus gave to the work, *Novum Instrumentum,* points to the novelty of his enterprise.[10] He sought to do something unprecedented: to set forth the entire text of the New Testament in its original language, alongside a reliable Latin translation, and to write annotations designed in part to justify his emendations of the traditional Latin.[11] This huge tripartite book proved as disturbing as it was original.[12] Even before publication Erasmus received a letter from Maarten van Dorp, saying, "I should like in the friendliest possible spirit to issue a warning" (3:20). Noting that Lorenzo Valla and Jacques Lefèvre d'Etaples had already experienced opposition to their studies of the New Testament, Dorp urged Erasmus to desist. Any change in the Vulgate would raise the troubling and, to Dorp, unthinkable possibility that the New Testament in use for centuries was defective: "it is not reasonable that the whole church, which has always used this edition and still both approves and uses it, should for all these centuries have been wrong" (3:21). Convinced that Dorp was misguided, Erasmus replied: if there are no errors in the Vulgate, then "why do Jerome and Augustine and Ambrose so often cite a different text from the one we use?" (3:133–34). The evidence suggested to Erasmus that the Latin text was subject to the vicissitude suffered by all written works: "one thing the facts cry out . . . that often through the translator's clumsiness or inattention the Greek has been wrongly rendered; often the true and genuine reading has been corrupted by ignorant scribes, which we see happen every day, or altered by scribes who are half-taught and half-asleep." What an irony, he thought, that a church which venerated the bodies and belongings of the saints should neglect the very basis of Christianity—the written word. In his dedication of the works of Jerome to William Warham, Archbishop of Canterbury, Erasmus observed: "The slippers of the saints and their drivel-stained napkins we put to our lips, and the books they wrote, the most sacred and most powerful relics of those holy men, we leave to lie neglected" (3:257).

Not surprisingly, *Novum Instrumentum* generated hostility in those ignorant of Greek and suspicious of what they did not know; in those accustomed to the Vulgate and fearful of change in so familiar a text; and in those who doubted that philology really had any significant contribution to make to theology. Detractors, for example, seized upon Erasmus's translation of the Greek *logos* in the first verse of John's gospel; instead of the customary *verbum,* Erasmus substituted *sermo,* for which he found precedent in numerous of the church fathers. Anticipating opposition, Erasmus shrewdly held back from making all the changes in the Latin New Testament that he thought warranted; however, "when scholars and friends in high places spurred me on and gave me courage, I introduced them more freely, so as to make the whole New Testament speak in simple, yet proper, Latin. I excepted only certain words and idioms that I considered too entrenched to be changed."[13] Despite such compromises, Erasmus was convinced that the translation of Scripture was properly the work of grammarians: "I do not really believe that Theology herself, the queen of all the sciences, will be offended if some share is claimed in her and due deference shown to her by her humble attendant Grammar; for, though Grammar is of less consequence in some men's eyes, no help is more indispensable than hers" (2:94).

However disturbed some contemporaries were by the implications of his work, Erasmus himself never wavered in the belief that the Bible contained the divine word and that he best served God and church by reconstructing that word in its original form. In the dedication of *Novum Instrumentum* to Pope Leo X, Eramus argued that the reform of Christendom depended upon that written word: "one thing I found crystal clear: our chiefest hope for the restoration and rebuilding of the Christian religion, our sheet-anchor as they call it, is that all those who profess the Christian philosophy the whole world over should above all absorb the principles laid down by their Founder from the writings of the evangelists and apostles, in which that heavenly Word which once came down to us from the heart of the Father still lives and breathes for us and acts and speaks with more immediate efficacy, in my opinion, than in any other way" (3:222). This conviction helps to explain a far-reaching claim about God's word that Erasmus makes in *De Praeparatione ad Mortem,* which he wrote at the bidding of Thomas Boleyn, Earl of Wiltshire, the father of Anne Boleyn. Erasmus asserts that God, upon the crucifixion of Christ, "hath given us his handwriting of grace":

> If ye aske where this chyrograph or handwrytynge that assureth us, remaineth: I answer in the canonicall scriptures, in whiche we rede the wordis of god, not of men. To these no lesse credence is to be youen, than if god had spoken theym unto the, with his owne mouth, yea I dare boldli say somwhat more largely. For if god had spoken unto the by some created lykenes, perchaunce, accordinge to thexample of certayne good men, thou woldest have doubted, whether there were any disceite in the thynge. But al this doubte the perpetuall consent of the catholyke churche, hath cleane take away frome us.[14]

Erasmus seems actually to prefer reading God's written word to hearing that word as it was originally spoken: there is an advantage, he argues, in being separated by centuries from Christ's ministry. To us it may seem that Erasmus makes a virtue of necessity. After all, how else may a Christian come to a certain knowledge of Christ's teachings if not through Scripture? But Erasmus's sincerity cannot be doubted. He remained convinced that Scripture originated in the mind of God and that a scholar could, with reason, knowledge, and skill, ascertain that divine word in written form. This conviction helped to generate a climate of opinion within which the Protestant reformers would flourish.

3

If the temperament and activity of Erasmus are epitomized in Dürer's engraving, those of Martin Luther find expression in a painting by another German artist, Lucas Cranach, some of whose woodcuts illustrate Luther's translation of the Bible into German. In a pulpit Luther preaches to enraptured listeners while he points with his right hand to Christ on the cross, who occupies the center of the composition.[15] With his left hand Luther points to a passage in the Bible that lies open before him. Cranach's painting not only illustrates Luther's allegiance to the scriptural word but also his explication of that word in a forceful, personal appeal to the faithful. Luther's emphasis, then, differs from that of Erasmus, who intended his work chiefly for scholars rather than the laity and who instinctively sought accommodation rather than confrontation.

Despite Luther's differences with Erasmus, the two men had an unmistakable intellectual affinity, something that Dürer recognized when, mistakenly thinking Luther dead, he entertained the hope that Erasmus would continue Luther's work. The careers of Luther and Erasmus, moreover, reveal striking parallels. Like Erasmus, Luther entered the religious life as a young man, joining the Observant Augustinians in Erfurt and, later, in Wittenberg. As a monk Luther began an intensive program of reading, focusing on Scripture; probably for the first time he possessed a copy of the Bible, which he was now able to study with meticulous care. Although not so attentive to the aesthetic claims of the written word as Erasmus, Luther responded powerfully to what he read. In particular he found emotional reassurance in the face of doubts about his own worthiness. One day, pondering St. Paul's Epistle to the Romans, especially the words, "For by it [the Gospel] the righteousnes of God is reveiled, from faith to faith: as it is written, The just shall live by faith" (1:17), Luther arrived at an insight that would provide the foundation of his theology—the significance of faith to salvation. As he told friends years later, "That expression 'righteousness of God' was like a thunderbolt in my heart" (*LW* 54:308–9).[16] If the turning point of Erasmus's life occurred in a monastic library, so apparently did Luther's. There has been much speculation about where in the Augustinian house of Wittenberg Luther's transformation took place, but Steven Ozment persuasively argues that Luther "received his understanding of the righteousness of God after a long period of humble meditation in the tower room—actually the library—of the monastery."[17]

Like Erasmus, Luther disdained the elaborate ceremony of religious life; he sought holiness in personal devotion. The theological counterpart to his search for simplicity was a rejection of the scholasticism that flourished at medieval universities. Of his life as a monk, Luther later told friends, "At that time I dealt with allegories, tropologies, and analogies and did nothing but clever tricks with them" (54:406), a reference (along with the literal meaning) to the fourfold method of interpretation then in vogue. To Luther that had become irrelevant to his life as a Christian: "through the Epistle to the Romans I came to some knowledge of Christ. I recognized then that allegories are nothing, that it's not what Christ signifies but what Christ is that counts" (54:46). For Luther, scholasticism was too imaginative, speculative, theoretical; it was unrelated to the real concerns of ordinary people. What he sought instead was something more direct—a personal confrontation with the actual words of Scripture.

Like Erasmus, Luther believed that there was no substitute for reading Scripture and for doing so, if possible, in the original languages. In 1524 he wrote, "it was not without purpose that God caused his Scriptures to be set down in these two languages alone—the Old Testament in Hebrew, the New in Greek. Now if God did not despise them but chose them above all others for his word, then we too ought to honor them above all others" (45:359). In practice this means that Christians have an obligation to respect the written word of God by preserving, translating, and disseminating it. For Luther, monasticism had failed miserably in this responsibility: "the monasteries and foundations of old . . . established libraries, although there were few good books among them. What a loss it was that they neglected to acquire books and good libraries at that time, when the books and men for it were available, became painfully evident later when, as time went on, unfortunately all the arts and languages declined" (45:373-74).

Luther's esteem for the written word led him to admire those who were able, by analysis of style as well as content, to understand its significance. He was, for instance, impressed by Lorenzo Valla's discovery that the so-called Donation of Constantine to Pope Sylvester, purporting to give broad temporal authority to the papacy, was a forgery. Although Valla had reached this conclusion by 1440, Luther evidently did not learn of it until February 1520, when he read Ulrich von Hutten's edition of Valla's treatise.[18] This had the effect of not only confirming Luther's already low opinion of a materialistic and mendacious papacy but also bolstering his confidence in what a close study of the written word could accomplish.

That confidence was shared by scholars, theologians, editors, and printers in Germany and northern Europe who, because of their common interests, counted both Luther and Erasmus among their friends. Ulrich von Hutten, who eventually joined Luther in opposing Rome, promising to defend him with book and blade, also once called Erasmus "the German Socrates" (*CWE* 3:186). For his part Erasmus wrote to Guillaume Budé in 1518, "I am delighted that you think well of Hutten; to me he has the most delightful nature of anyone I know" (5:306). Johann Lang was a close friend and confidant of Luther, living under the same roof with him at Erfurt and Wittenberg; Erasmus too considered him a friend, calling Lang the "most fairminded of theologians" (6:134). Georgius Spalatinus, who helped gain for Luther the support of the Elector Frederick of Saxony in 1521, was also responsible for translating Erasmus' *Institutio Principis Christiani* and his *Querela Pacis* into German; and Spalatinus wrote to Erasmus in 1516, assuring him that Duke Frederick "has in his ducal library every book of yours that I have been able to find, and intends to buy any others that you may hereafter publish anywhere in the world" (4:167). Both Erasmus and Luther appealed to the same printers too. Johann Froben, who was responsible for printing Erasmus's *Novum Instrumentum,* wrote to Luther in 1519, "Blasius Salmonius, a printer of Leipzig, gave me some of your books, which he had bought at the last Frankfurt Fair, which, as they were approved by all the learned, I immediately reprinted"; and Froben reported to Luther that "We have sold out all your books except ten copies, and never remember to have sold any more quickly."[19] Collectively, such remarks suggest that there existed a community of thinkers transcending national boundaries, who were united by a common concern with the written word in general, with Scripture in particular, and with the religious reforms warranted by Scripture.

So close was the affinity among this group of friends, acquaintances, and correspondents that it is sometimes difficult to distinguish their respective ideas. The early correspondence of Erasmus and Luther, though affected by epistolary convention, suggests an intellectual consanguinity. In his first surviving letter to Erasmus, dated March 1519, Luther wrote: "who is there in whose heart Erasmus does not occupy a central place, to whom Erasmus is not the teacher who holds him in thrall?" (*CWE* 6:281). In May 1519 Erasmus replied, "Your letter gave me great pleasure: it displayed the brilliance of your mind and breathed the spirit of a Christian. No words of mine could describe the storm raised here by your books. Even now it is impossible to root out from men's minds the most groundless suspicion that your work is written with assistance from me and that I am, as they call it, the standard-bearer of this new movement" (6:391). The storm to which Erasmus refers would soon grow more fierce, and he would ever more nervously distance himself from the German reformer. Initially, however, what joined them was greater than what divided them. They were at one, for instance, in their disdain for rituals and indulgences, pilgrimages and monasteries. Both believed that Scripture should be translated and made accessible to every person no matter how humble.[20] Luther was quick to build upon Erasmus's scholarship, which helped to shape his own attitudes toward Scripture. Luther used Erasmus's *Novum Instrumentum* as soon as it became available to him in 1516, and, as Werner Schwarz observes, "Erasmus's influence can be discerned in all the lectures which Luther gave between 1516 and his translation of the New Testament in 1522."[21]

The commonalty existing between Erasmus and Luther is suggested by a woodcut called "The Divine Mill," which appeared on the title page of an anonymous pamphlet entitled *Dyss hand zwen schwytzer puren gemacht;* initially published in Zurich in 1520, the pamphlet went through half a dozen editions. The design depicts Christ emptying his wheat (i.e., his word)—in the form of the evangelists' symbols, along with the image of St. Paul—into the hopper of a mill. Erasmus collects the ground grain (in the form of scrolls), depositing it in a sack over which the dove of the Holy Spirit hovers.[22] Luther then kneads the dough, which takes the form of books. These are subsequently distributed to an unappreciative pope, cardinal, and bishop, who reject the books while above them a bird cries, "Ban, ban," and a peasant wields a flail as if to drive off the clergy. Erasmus and Luther are represented as partners in a common enterprise: the preparation and distribution of God's written word. Perhaps significantly, however, the two men neither face one another nor stand side by side; instead, they literally face in different directions.

Luther's correspondence in the years following the publication of *Novum Instrumentum* suggests that he was growing impatient with Erasmus. As early as March 1517 Luther wrote to Johann Lang, indicating his feeling that the Dutch scholar was not keeping pace with him theologically: "I am reading our Erasmus but daily I dislike him more and more" (*LW* 48:40). In this letter Luther remarks disparagingly that "not everyone is a truly wise Christian just because he knows Greek and Hebrew." Erasmus disappointed him further by failing, he believed, to acknowledge the centrality of God's grace. And Luther was put off by Erasmus's penchant for accommodation. As he wrote to Georgius Spalatinus in September 1521, "in all his writings he is not concerned for the cross but for peace"; and, Luther adds, "The kingdom of God consists in power, says Paul" (48:306). The feisty Luther thought that Erasmus flinched from challenging orthodoxy, even when that challenge was justified by Scripture. In a letter to Johannes Oecolampadius in June 1523, Luther criticized Erasmus for pulling his punches: "He has accomplished what he was called to do: he has introduced among us [the knowledge of] languages, and has called us away from the sacrilegious studies. Perhaps he himself will die with Moses in the plains of Moab, for he does not advance to the better studies (those which pertain to piety)" (49:44). In Luther's

The title page of an anonymous pamphlet entitled *Dyss hand zwen schwytzer puren gemacht,* initially published in Zurich in 1520. By permission of Zentralbibliothek Zurich.

view Erasmus failed to move from a new philology to the new theology toward which it led.

What drove Luther finally to disdain Erasmus and to challenge orthodoxy openly was the peculiarly personal nature of his response to the scriptural word. In 1520 Erasmus wrote to Luther, "I wish you would write a treatise on some part of Holy Scripture, and keep personal feelings out of it" (*CWE* 8:23). Such advice made no sense to Luther for whom biblical interpretation was by definition personal. Tolerating the imposition of nothing between Scripture and his own mind, Luther had little patience with biblical commentary, even of the Greek or Latin fathers whom Erasmus cites so prominently in *Novum Instrumentum*. Nor was Luther concerned with the accumulated teachings of canon law. His innovative approach may be demonstrated by considering a Latin Bible typical of those in use at the beginning of the sixteenth century. Published at Basel in 1498 and again in 1502, this Bible presents the text in the middle of each page, surrounded by glosses, by the *Postillae* of Nicholas of Lyra, and by other explanations. In addition, a gloss printed in small letters appears between the biblical lines. All this commentary is intended to control and direct the reader's response. As Werner Schwarz notes, "The reader is . . . supposed to understand the text in accordance with the tradition which encloses, like a large frame, the official Latin version of the Bible."[23] To Luther this manner of presenting Scripture was anathema: "it is . . . a stupid undertaking to attempt to gain an understanding of Scripture by laboring through the commentaries of the fathers and a multitude of books and glosses" (45:364).

Luther's approach was more immediate; he was most concerned with his own responses, not those of predecessors, however wise or clever. An exegete par excellence, his reading of Scripture was characterized by a combination of intellectual and emotional energy so powerful that it seems almost ferocious. By applying that energy, freed from the constraints of extant commentary, Luther arrived at a new understanding of St. Paul's remark about "righteousness" in the Epistle to the Romans 1:17. Luther came to believe that "righteousness" referred not to God's judgment of sinners but to "the righteousness by which God in his mercy justifies those who have faith."[24]

It was his confidence in the reliability of the written word and in his ability to determine its meaning that led Luther to sever his ties with Rome. At the Diet of Worms, on 18 April 1521, Luther declared to Johann Eck, chancellor to the archbishop of Trier, "Unless I am convinced by the testimony of the Scriptures or by clear reason . . . I am bound by the Scriptures I have quoted and my conscience is captive to the Word of God. I cannot and I will not retract anything, since it is neither safe nor right to go against conscience" (*LW* 32:112). This stance effectively jettisons fifteen hundred years of tradition, institutional and theological. It means in practice that canon law no longer has a claim on the faithful. As Luther wrote in 1520, "it would be a good thing if canon law were completely blotted out, from the first letter to the last, especially the decretals. More than enough is written in the Bible about how we should behave in all circumstances" (44:202). Reliance upon Scripture must be absolute, and anything without scriptural basis must be abandoned. This commitment to Scripture prevented Luther from repudiating his own books, which had been collected and piled on a table at Worms. As Luther explained to the Emperor Charles V, "since I had fortified my little books with clear and intelligible Scripture passages, it does not seem to me right or just to deny the Word of God and revoke my little books in this way, nor could I do it in any way" (48:204). To renounce his treatises would be tantamount, in his mind, to renouncing Scripture, so closely commingled were his words with God's.

Drawing their inspiration solely from Scripture, Luther and the reformers who followed him emphasized with new force God's responsibility for the words of Scripture. The English theologian Richard Hooker, for example, points out how frequently God enjoins his people to write. Hooker traces God's role as author, working through Old Testament prophet and New Testament evangelist alike: "of Moyses it is said, that he *wrote all the wordes of God;* not by his owne privat motion and devise: for God taketh this act to him selfe, *I have written.* Further more were not the Prophetes following commanded also to do the like? Unto the holy Evangelist Saint John how often expresse charge is given, *Scribe, write these thinges?*"[25] Because Scripture has its origin in the mind of God and assumes its form on paper or parchment as a result of his specific instruction, that written word has a unique claim on humankind, its purpose to set forth his design for the world. Through Scripture a Christian attains the most important knowledge of all—how to attain salvation. As Hooker observes, "Readinge doth convey to the minde that truth without addition or diminution, which scripture hath derived from the holie Ghost. And the ende of all scripture is the same which St John proposeth in the writinge of that most divine Gospell, namely *faith,* and through faith *salvation.*"[26]

4

For all its singleminded exaltation of the written word, the Reformation created the conditions for profound anxiety about that word. To be sure, Luther and the other reformers never intended this result, and they probably did not foresee it. Nevertheless skepticism ensued. By following

Erasmus's lead and prizing the written word of God above all else, then devoting themselves to its study with a new exclusivity, the reformers inevitably confronted problems that their predecessors had ignored or perhaps failed to recognize. For example, the more carefully they considered the implications of research on the transmission of manuscripts, the more problematic seemed the continuity of the written word. As they trained their prodigious philological talents on Scripture, they came to recognize that the word of God had been corrupted not only by what they construed as the malice of churchmen but also by the carelessness of scribes. The reformers began to fret about what was and what was not the word of God. They fell to squabbling about how best to render the Greek and Hebrew of Scripture in the vernacular. They also pondered with uncertainty the tools best suited to derive meaning from Scripture. The difficulties they now encountered had, of course, been present all along. But thanks to Valla, Erasmus, and Luther, among others, those problems now required urgent attention.

Before the Reformation the biblical text in its Latin form was considered correct and authoritative, and its translation into the vernacular had a low priority. The church, moreover, taught that an unwritten tradition, with its own authority, survived alongside the written tradition from the time of the apostles, and that the unwritten tradition was available, in the person of the clergy, to resolve difficulties. For such reformers as John Favour, that notion was scandalously wrongheaded: "we wil not devide the word of God into *Scriptum & non Scriptum,* written and not written"[27]; there is only one word of God—the written: "We denie peremptorily that any of these Traditions, which are pretended, and concerne beleefe or manners, are either Christs or his Apostles, if they be not in the Scriptures."[28] The reformers were equally concerned to demolish the church's privileged status as interpreter of Scripture. If Scripture represents the word of God and if believers have access to that word in their own language, then it follows that they may interpret it for themselves and apply it to their own lives. Hence John Calvin's caustic observation: "a most pernicious error widely prevails that Scripture has only so much weight as is conceded to it by the consent of the church. As if the eternal and inviolable truth of God depended upon the decision of men!"[29] The reformers were particularly nettled by what they saw as the church's disparagement of Scripture. John Favour complains: "they must call it an inkie, a blacke Gospell, a mute and dumbe Judge, and such like grosse titles and tearmes as before are out of themselves discovered, and give it no authoritie in respect of the Author principall, which is God."[30] Neglect of Scripture, he contends, "is the very mother of not only superstition but infidelity, it is the ignorance of God."

Close attention to Scripture inevitably generated questions about what was found there. For example, the words of the biblical text sometimes seemed amiss to Luther: "Job didn't speak the way it is written [in his book], but he thought those things. One doesn't speak that way under temptation. Nevertheless, the things reported actually happened. They are like the plot of a story which a writer, like Terence, adopts and to which he adds characters and circumstances" (54:79–80). Luther, then, found a disjunction between the actual words of Scripture and the words as they must have been expressed by the biblical personage. Luther's likening of the scriptural author to an imaginative writer—and a pagan at that—suggests that Scripture was subject to literary convention, that words, though divinely inspired, underwent a change as the spoken words of historical figures took written form.

Luther's doubts extended to Genesis, too. He once told friends, "In my opinion . . . Genesis was not by Moses, for there were books before his time and books are cited—for example, the Book of the Wars of the Lord and the Book of Jashar" (54:373). His study of the Bible also led Luther to question the canonicity of James' Epistle, which had been deemed doubtful before the fourth century: "We should throw the Epistle of James out of this school [i.e., the university in Wittenberg], for it doesn't amount to much. It contains not a syllable about Christ" (54:424). Luther may well have been correct in such suppositions. The effect of his research, however, was to foster doubt about the accuracy and authenticity of what people read when they opened their Bibles.

More than a half century after Luther began challenging the inherited canon, John Donne alluded to the doubts that had been engendered by biblical scholarship: "Next to the eternal and coessential Word of God, *Christ Jesus,* the written Word of God, the Scriptures concern us most; and therefore next to the person of Christ, and his Offices, the Devil hath troubled the Church, with most questions about the certainty of Scriptures, and the Canon thereof."[31] Donne goes on to cite the Book of Esther, which he says was removed from the canon by Bishop Melito a century and a half after Christ's death, a decision ratified by Gregory Nazianzen. Donne's opinion of Esther is not entirely clear: "it is certainly part of that Scripture which is profitable to teach, to reprove, to correct, and to instruct in righteousness."[32] Here Donne asserts the pedagogical utility of the Book of Esther, but is he convinced that it indubitably represents the word of God? The very fact that the question can be asked suggests the quandary that must have faced Donne's contemporaries: how is the ordinary Christian to know with certitude which are the words of God and which are not?

Once the philological analysis of Scripture gained momentum, it was inevitable that textual corruptions would be recognized and require correction. This undoubtedly represented progress; after all, it led to a more reliable text. The process, however, also created doubt, for what trust could a person place in Scripture that changed within his or her own lifetime? Maarten van Dorp anticipated this problem when he chastised Erasmus for proceeding with his New Testament: "a great many people will discuss the integrity of the Scriptures, and many will have doubts about it, if the presence of the least scrap of falsehood in them becomes known . . ." (*CWE* 3:22). The accuracy of Dorp's prediction is apparent in John Calvin's frustration decades later: "they mock the Holy Spirit when they ask: Who can convince us that these writings came from God? Who can assure us that Scripture has come down whole and intact even to our very day?"[33] That Calvin should raise the issue at all indicates the extent to which his contemporaries were vexed. Ironically, the more proficient they became at philology, the more likely they were to entertain doubts of the sort that Calvin describes.

If people began to question the accuracy of available texts, they also pondered a related difficulty: precisely how did the word formulated in God's mind find its way onto the papyrus, parchment, or vellum of Scripture in the first place? Renaissance artists sometimes depict an angel whispering into the ear of St. Matthew. Others depict an angel looking over the writer's shoulder as though checking to see that the writing is accurate. Still others depict an angel actually guiding the hand of the evangelist as he writes.[34] As the diversity of artistic representations suggests, there was no unanimity of opinion about how God's words assumed written form. John Calvin, while professing uncertainty about the exact process, nevertheless declares confidence that the resulting writing is the veritable word of God: "whether God became known to the patriarchs through oracles and visions or by the work and ministry of men, he put into their minds what they should then hand down to their posterity. At any rate, there is no doubt that firm certainty of doctrine was engraved in their hearts, so that they were convinced and understood that what they had learned proceeded from God."[35] Despite his certitude Calvin appears to envision the human writer as intermediary, not merely as recorder; John T. McNeill observes, "the suggestion his language conveys is not of a mechanical verbal dictation, but of an impartation of divine truth that enters the hearts of the Scripture writers."[36]

Even when the modern reader had confidence in the reliability of biblical words, interpretation proved an uncertain business. Deriving meaning from a book written in an ancient language and in a very different culture centuries earlier made considerable demands on that reader. The reformers staked everything on the interpretation of Scripture and, at the same time, stripped away the corporate wisdom of the church, as expressed in decretals and commentary. That left the task of interpretation in the hands of every reader. But what tools was the reader to use?

The reformers typically appealed to faith as the only reliable route to accurate interpretation. Luther, in a letter to Georgius Spalatinus, wrote: "it is absolutely certain that one cannot enter into the [meaning of] Scripture by study or innate intelligence." Indeed, he continues, "You must . . . completely despair of your own diligence and intelligence and rely solely on the infusion of the Spirit" (48:53-54). The problem with this approach to interpretation is that faith, in itself, simply cannot accomplish the job. Linguistic expertise is necessary as well, as Luther himself acknowledged when he described the mistakes of analysis made by Augustine: "How often does not St. Augustine err in the Psalms and in his other expositions, and Hilary [Bishop of Poitiers] too—in fact, all those who have undertaken to expound Scripture without a knowledge of the languages? Even though what they said about a subject at times was perfectly true, they were never quite sure whether it really was present there in the passage where by their interpretation they thought to find it" (45:361). Luther saw that error in interpretation remained a possibility in his own day. He notes, for instance, that a preacher, though possessing faith, may fail to interpret aright what he reads unless he also possesses the requisite linguistic knowledge: "when it comes to interpreting Scripture, and working with it on your own, and disputing with those who cite it incorrectly, he is unequal to the task; that cannot be done without languages" (45:363). Even the most devout preacher will likely botch his analysis for want of expertise: "A saintly life and right doctrine are not enough. Hence, languages are absolutely and altogether necessary in the Christian church . . ." (45:363).

If it cannot compensate for ignorance of language, faith also fails to compensate for ignorance of the general significance of what is read. Philological knowledge and grammar do not themselves ensure accurate interpretation of Scripture. As Luther told friends at table in 1540, "It's not enough to know the grammar [of a biblical passage]. One must observe the sense, for a knowledge of the matters treated brings with it an understanding of the words. Lawyers wouldn't understand the law unless it dealt with matters known to them by experience. Nobody could comprehend the words of Vergil's *Eclogues* unless he was first sure about the contents" (54:375). Without such a context, whether of life or of literature, interpretation will remain problematic. Faith simply cannot provide all the necessary equipment.

Reason, of course, may assist the interpreter: at the Diet of Worms Luther declared that he would not change his opinions unless convinced "by the testimony of the Scriptures or by clear reason" (32:112). Within a religion that accords supreme importance to faith as the requisite for salvation, however, Luther's—and every Christian's—attitude toward reason must remain ambivalent. When asked what significance reason had, Luther replied, "Prior to faith and a knowledge of God, reason is darkness, but in believers it's an excellent instrument" (54:183). Everything hinges, it would seem, on the inner disposition of the individual, as Luther indicated on another occasion when asked about reason's place in theological matters: "I make a distinction. Reason that is under the devil's control is harmful, and the more clever and successful it is, the more harm it does. . . . On the other hand, when illuminated by the Holy Spirit, reason helps to interpret the Holy Scriptures" (54:71). Guided by the Holy Spirit, then, reason is useful; otherwise, not. Luther fails to explain, however, how an individual knows whether an interpreter's reason is controlled by Satan, surely a difficulty for someone listening to a sermon or reading a treatise.

In his remarks on reason, Luther faces a stubborn problem: reason is insufficient without faith, yet faith alone is insufficient to provide a reliable interpretation of Scripture. Unless guided by the Holy Spirit, reason may bring darkness rather than illumination. Yet the whole practice of biblical exegesis will likely be flawed unless supported by the knowledge and reason which faith alone cannot supply. For the Christian of Luther's time, this was more than an intellectual conundrum: Scripture contained the very blueprint for attaining salvation.

Biblical interpretation was not—and could never be—as certain as Luther liked to imagine. In fact, the individual reader can never have absolute confidence in his or her own interpretation. As Gabriel Josipovici explains,

> Luther's questioning of the criterion of authority seems to have raised an unanswerable problem. For no text, whether it is the Book of God or the portrait of Pantagruel's ancestor, is self-explicating. If it means something then that meaning was put into it by someone, but by itself it is dumb to tell what that meaning is. All we can do is to make more or less well-informed inferences and reach a high degree of probability; absolute certainty is inaccessible. So long as there was a community of belief in the Church as to the "real body of Christ" the problem of the criterion did not arise in any acute form.[37]

With the demise of that "community of belief," readers of the Bible confronted an intellectually precarious situation. With every reader becoming his or her own interpreter and without the authority of the church to sanction one interpretation over another, readers found themselves in a world flooded with disparate interpretations. Even Luther's followers disagreed over important doctrinal points.

Michel Foucault relates this phenomenon to a property inherent in language itself: "The function proper to knowledge is not seeing or demonstrating; it is interpreting. Scriptural commentary, commentaries on Ancient authors, commentaries on the accounts of travellers, commentaries on legends and fables: none of these forms of discourse is required to justify its claim to be expressing a truth before it is interpreted; all that is required of it is the possibility of talking about it. Language contains its own inner principle of proliferation."[38] In the century of Erasmus and Luther, the multiplication of commentary achieved unprecedented momentum: "Perhaps for the first time in Western culture, we find revealed the absolutely open dimension of a language no longer able to halt itself, because, never being enclosed in a definitive statement, it can express its truth only in some future discourse and is wholly intent on what it will have said; but even this future discourse itself does not have the power to halt the progression, and what it says is enclosed within it like a promise, a bequest to yet another discourse."[39] Sixteenth-century writers themselves recognized this propensity. Foucault cites Montaigne's musing on the proliferation of interpretations: "It is more of a job to interpret the interpretations than to interpret the things, and there are more books about books than about any other subject: we do nothing but write glosses about each other."[40] Foucault, however, neglects Montaigne's specific remark about biblical commentary only a few paragraphs later: "I have observed in Germany that Luther has left as many divisions and altercations over the uncertainty of his opinions, and more, as he raised about the Holy Scriptures." What Montaigne saw was not merely the propensity for books to be written about other books but also for such writings to result in "divisions" and "uncertainty," thus producing doctrinal fissures within Christendom, with all the attendant misery that Montaigne knew at first hand in France.

It was Erasmus, rather than Luther, who best understood what Foucault calls the "interstice" between a primal text and the infinity of interpretation. Writing to John Colet, Erasmus discusses the range of possibilities inherent in biblical analysis: "the mysteries of scripture can yield different meanings because of their rich abundance, and we must not reject any interpretation so long as it is probable and not contrary to the faith" (*CWE* 1:213). This assertion seems somewhat problematic in that the notion of what is "probable" may vary from one person to another, and what is "contrary to the faith" may depend upon a person's particular convictions. But Erasmus's basic intention is clear: he would include rather than exclude interpretations, for he believes that a single fixed meaning is incompatible with the nature of Scripture and perhaps of all writing. In this, Erasmus parts company with Luther, who believes that Scripture is essentially simple rather than complex, self-explanatory rather than obscure. In *De Servo Arbitrio* Luther mockingly asks Erasmus: "is there any wonder that the Scriptures are obscure, or that with them you can establish not only a free but even a divine choice, when you are allowed to play about with them as if you wanted to make a

Virgilian patchwork out of them? That is what you call solving problems, and removing difficulties by means of an 'explanation.' But it was Jerome and his master Origen who filled the world with such trifles, and set this pestilent example of not paying attention to the simplicity of the Scriptures" (*LW* 33:213). Luther here takes a potshot at Erasmus for devoting so much energy to an edition of Jerome's writings and to editing secular literature as well; interpreting Scripture, Luther argues, is an altogether different endeavor. It was precisely Erasmus's experience as an editor, however, that helps explain his alertness to the multiplicity of meaning. Spending much of his life poring over books of all kinds and reading commentaries on them led Erasmus to conclude that every reader brings something of himself to a text and that the very act of analysis reveals the mind of the reader as well as that of the author. As he notes in *De Libero Arbitrio,* where he assembles biblical passages that appear to support free will and those that seem to disallow it, "since different men have assumed different opinions from the same Scripture, each must have looked at it from his own point of view, and in the light of the end he is pursuing."[41] All interpretation, then, depends to some extent on the habits of mind, cultural assumptions, and personal proclivities of the reader. No one interpretation represents the last word; there is no last word, only additional words each of which contributes something to the interpreter's understanding.

The viewpoints of Erasmus and Luther, so outwardly disparate, ultimately led to much the same end: a disquietude about the reliability of interpretation. Erasmus anticipated the conclusions of other thinkers who came to recognize that reading involves a subtle interplay between the words on the page and the mind of the reader. As Montaigne observes, "An able reader often discovers in other men's writings perfections beyond those that the author put in or perceived, and lends them richer meanings and aspects."[42] As for Luther, his insistence on the literal word, a word accessible to analysis, seemed to promise a certitude that Erasmus could not provide. But Luther's assumption that there exists a world of single, clear meanings was itself undermined by those interpreters who read the same words as he but who drew different conclusions. Sixteenth-century history is replete with individuals claiming to possess a true understanding of Scripture while finding validation in a faith that is singular and subjective. Norman O. Brown observes of Luther, "Literalism combines fetishism of the book with shamanism of the interpreter"; and, he adds, "Luther's method of scriptural interpretation was a combination of grammatical science and soulful intuition."[43] So intensely personal was Luther's approach to Scripture that it could not be universally duplicated. Even though he was supremely confident in his analysis of Scripture, those who read the same words as he but arrived at different conclusions could not possibly share that confidence in his judgments.

Erasmus and Luther based their theological conclusions on the same words in the same book. But where Erasmus built his analysis on a foundation of philology and grammar, Luther gave primacy to what he construed as the overall meaning of Scripture. In short, Luther subordinated exegesis to a conviction about the general significance of a text. This does not mean that Luther was indifferent to philology and grammar, but rather that he appraised their relevance differently. He summarized his approach when discussing with friends his translation of the Old Testament: "if the meaning is ambiguous I ask those who have a better knowledge of the language than I have whether the Hebrew words can bear this or that sense which seems to me to be especially fitting. And that is most fitting which is closest to the argument of the book" (*LW* 54:43). From Erasmus's point of view, this is putting the cart before the horse; for him, translation and interpretation must be strictly grounded in textual analysis. For Luther the letter must give way to the spirit which, with divine help, he intuits. In the sixteenth century those who read both Erasmus and Luther with an open mind must have been led to reflect on the uncertain status of the written word in Christendom. If Christianity was a religion of the book, the words in that book could mean very different things to different people.

In 1521 Albrecht Dürer may have thought that Luther's continued life would ensure the victory of truth by restoring the supremacy of God's word, but history fails to support that belief. As it happened, Luther lived until 1546, but all of the words that he wrote in the twenty-five years following his (falsely) reported death failed to achieve the goal that he and Dürer envisioned. Nor would a century more of life and work have sufficed, for the scriptural word required ever more analysis, explication, and argumentation. No matter how industrious Luther and his followers were, their endeavor never reached completion. Paradoxically, the more they sought to vanquish their opposition, the further did the words of Scripture retreat behind the words of its new champions.

If the meaning of the scriptural word could be so fiercely contested, what written word was immune to misinterpretation and misapplication? Renaissance artists would continue to place books in the hands of saints and of the merely pious, but the identification of the written word with truth and spirituality became ever more tenuous. To some sixteenth-century readers, the written word might convey sanctity, surety, and authority, but to others it was distressingly problematic, a locus of controversy, a source of unease. Nor would this feeling ever deliquesce; it would persist and deepen especially as the phenomenon of print further undermined confidence in the reliability of the written word.

2
Written Words and Printed Books

1

THE rapid dispersal of interpretations and translations, biblical, historical, philosophical, and theological, was made possible by the printing press, developed in the 1440s and 1450s by Johann Gutenberg of Mainz, by his partner the financier Johann Fust, and by Peter Schöffer, Fust's son-in-law.[1] Printing allowed the findings of one scholar to be read and assimilated by others; new texts of old works could be widely circulated, thereby furnishing the basis for new commentary. Virtually every person who could read the printed word could have access to the most recent scholarly discoveries, as the experience of Konrad Peutinger and his wife Margarethe illustrates. Konrad, who served the imperial court, wrote to Erasmus about an incident that occurred on a Sunday in Advent, 1521. At home he was reading the history of the emperors by Tacitus, while Margarethe sat at a nearby table reading Erasmus's Latin translation of the New Testament and comparing it against an old German translation:

> Soon she recalled me from my favourite studies by saying, "I am reading the twentieth chapter of St Matthew, and I see that our friend Erasmus has added something to the text." "What can it be?" I said. She said again, "Why, he gives things which are not in the German either." I soon had Matthew's Gospel, on which that same Jerome wrote a commentary, open before me, and the words "And ye shall be baptized with the baptism that I am baptized with" were not there. I took refuge in your *Annotationes,* from which I was immediately instructed by you that besides Mark these words are also read in Matthew by Origen and Chrysostom and the Vulgate. (*CWE* 8:329)[2]

Although Peutinger relates this incident as a tribute to Erasmus, the account demonstrates also the impact of the printing press, which made both Scripture and scriptural commentary readily available throughout Europe. The revolution wrought by the press happened with extraordinary speed, indeed, within a single generation. In his *Compendium Vitae* Erasmus recounts that his own father, before becoming a priest, made a living as a copyist: "Gerard made his way to Rome. There he earned enough to live on as a copyist, for the art of printing as yet did not exist" (4:404). By the time Gerard's son began his own career, the father's profession had become largely obsolete, at least for the production of books—except for those books given to patrons and prospective patrons, who might be flattered by the effort expended to produce a manuscript book in the age of printing.[3] Printing, however, proved a mixed blessing, especially to Christianity, which fostered it and capitalized on its development, for the press had the effect of intensifying both deference to and anxiety about the written word. Even Erasmus and Luther came to lament certain consequences of the new technology.

2

Although the printing press was a construction of metal and wood, lacking in aesthetic appeal and inert without the application of human muscle, the machine's effect was anything but impersonal: it fostered a spirit of cooperation among the various writers and craftsmen responsible for producing and marketing books. Authors, printers, publishers, binders, and sellers of books were, to a considerable extent, dependent upon one another. Given the capital investment needed for the machinery of the press itself, letter type, and paper, along with the cost of manpower (compositors, inkers, torculators, and proofreaders), and given the complexity of the process, each person in the chain of production had to trust the others to perform ably and honor commitments. In particular, it was in the interest of writers to develop with the men who actually produced their books a relationship transcending that of parties to a contract. Both Erasmus and Luther, who were predisposed by their early experience to see printing as an indispensable tool for doing God's work and their own, had an unusually close affinity with their printers.

Erasmus's attitude toward printing was shaped by his association with the Brethren of the Common Life, a group of Dutch reformers who were in the forefront of the effort to produce books by movable type. The Brethren sprang from the Modern Devotion, a movement founded by Geert Groote (1340–84), a lay preacher of Deventer, who valued simple devotion and the reading of Scripture. Renowned for preaching and pastoral work, especially among schoolboys, the Brethren were particularly identified with the making of books, and they were quick to realize the usefulness of the press in advancing their mission. The press became an extension of the Brethren's traditional work—the reading, copying, illuminating, and binding of books having spiritual import. Confident that their enterprise was compatible with the new machine, they envisioned themselves as "God's priests, teaching not by the spoken word but by the written word."[4] In his formative years Erasmus had close contact with the Brethren: "as a schoolboy . . . [he] boarded with the Brethren in Deventer,"[5] who housed and supervised children attending school; he also lodged for several years at a hostel run by the Brethren in 's-Hertogenbosch. The monastery at Steyn that Erasmus subsequently entered was itself closely connected with the Windesheim Congregation, which had its genesis in the teachings of Geert Groote; the Windesheimers have been called "the most widespread, the most active, the most literary and the most productive of the Modern Devotionalists."[6] The canons regular of St. Augustine, whom Erasmus joined, were themselves indebted to this movement for "their devotion to the exact text of Scripture that derived from their traditional work as copyists."[7]

Martin Luther, too, had an early association with the Brethren: in a letter of 1522 to Claus Storm, the mayor of Magdeburg, Luther records that he had gone to school with the Brethren of the Common Life in that city.[8] This does not mean that Luther actually attended a school run by the Brethren. Instead, like Erasmus, he seems to have lived for a time at one of their hostels, where he would have grown acquainted with their attitudes, especially their valuation of the written word and printing. This common background may help explain why both Erasmus and Luther were so quick to exploit the possibilities offered by the press. It must have seemed the logical extension of the quill pen and thus a means whereby spirituality and knowledge of Scripture might be enhanced.

As a writer Erasmus set out to find the best printers, and he established close ties with several of the most accomplished in Europe. He appears to have had a good working relationship with the Ascensian press of Josse Bade, who printed his edition of Lorenzo Valla's notes on the New Testament in 1505. Erasmus later journeyed to Italy, where he met Aldus Manutius (Aldo Manuzio) in Venice. There Erasmus oversaw the printing of his *Adagiorum Chiliades,* a vastly expanded version of his *Adagiorum Collectanea,* which Bade had printed in 1506. Interestingly, although Erasmus seems to have been indifferent to the art and architecture of Italy, he did appreciate the aesthetic excellence of Aldus' typefaces. Asking Aldus to reprint his Latin translations of Euripides' *Hecuba* and *Iphigenia in Aulis,* Erasmus said, "I should consider that my efforts were given immortality if they were to be published in your type, especially that small fount which is the most elegant of all" (2:132). Erasmus also found the Aldine press congenial for personal as well as aesthetic reasons. He clearly relished the company of Aldus and his associates, who ran an operation described by Martin Lowry as a "mixture of the sweat-shop, the boarding house, and the research institute."[9] That Erasmus lived from January to September 1508 in the household of Aldus's father-in-law and partner, Andrea Torresani of Asola, suggests that theirs was a collaborative enterprise, not merely a business transaction. Later in his career, Erasmus established a similarly close relationship with the Basel printing house run by Johann Froben and the Amerbach brothers. Although Froben may not have been as learned as Aldus, Erasmus admired him for seeking to accomplish in the north what Aldus had brought to fruition in the south: "What Aldus was striving to do among the Italians . . . Froben is trying to achieve on this side of the Alps with no less energy than Aldus, and not without success, although there is no denying that he makes less money by it."[10] Froben's press was indispensable to Erasmus, for it produced *Novum Instrumentum* and the nine-volume works of St. Jerome. As in Italy, Erasmus stayed in the printer's household while his work issued from the press; he became part of the close-knit group that so successfully combined business and scholarship.

Luther, too, developed a symbiotic relationship with the printers responsible for disseminating his interpretations of Scripture. He was, in fact, perhaps the first European to recognize the potential of the press for rapidly shaping public opinion on a national and even an international scale. Luther's ninety-five theses, posted at Wittenberg on 31 October 1517, were intended for academic debate[11] but because they were printed, according to Friedrich Myconius, "hardly fourteen days had passed when these propositions were known throughout Germany and within four weeks almost all of Christendom was familiar with them."[12] This happened so rapidly that, Myconius adds, "It almost appeared as if the angels themselves had been their messengers and brought them before the eyes of all the people." Luther's subsequent treatises appeared quickly and in multiple editions; for instance, "His first great success was the *Sermon on Indulgence and Grace* (1517), which went through twenty-two editions between 1518 and 1520."[13] During these years Luther produced numerous other works which, thanks to the printing press, were widely read: "By the time he was excommunicated in January 1521, as many as one-half million copies of his works may have been in circulation."[14] Luther's translation of the New Testament into German, published in September 1522, also found a huge readership: "Some 5,000 copies were sold within two months, 50 printings in four years, over 200,000 over the course of the next twelve years, and it remains the standard German translation to this day."[15] These figures are all the more astonishing when we consider that at the beginning of the sixteenth century in Germany "2,800 [towns] had populations under 1,000 and only fifteen could boast more than 10,000."[16] If the population was small by modern standards, the number of presses was remarkable: by 1500 "printing presses existed in over 200 cities and towns."[17] The proliferation of presses was made possible, in part, by the modest demands made upon manpower. Martin Lowry observes, "The earliest illustrations show three men—compositor, inker and 'torculator' or operator—at work on each press, so a small company could be run by a nucleus of less than half a dozen all told."[18] The printer's mark of the Ascensian press on Erasmus's *Panegyricus* (ca. 1510),[19] one of the earliest sixteenth-century books to illustrate the workings of a press, depicts the three men described by Lowry. Whether the press was large or small, Luther accommodated his printers by demanding no financial return from them. As he told Wenceslas Link in 1517, "we, too, are very poor as far as money goes, but I make use of a certain modest claim on the printers. Since I take nothing from them for my various works, I occasionally take a copy of a book if I want to" (*LW* 49:167).[20] Luther's strategy paid political and theological dividends. According to Lewis W. Spitz, "perhaps as many as one million copies of his tracts and treatises were in circulation by 1524."[21]

The printing press was, of course, not responsible for Luther's theology, any more than it was responsible for Erasmus's scholarship. But it is difficult to imagine the swift ascendancy of the Reformation without the press. This was apparent even in the sixteenth century. After Luther's death, John Foxe looked back on decades of religious tumult and commented on what printing had wrought. Recounting the history of Jan Hus, who was burned at the stake on 6 July 1415, Foxe sees in the press God's answer to a repressive church: "In this very time so daungerous and desperate, where mans power could do no more, there the blessed wisdome and omnipotent power of the Lord began to worke for his Church, not with sword and tergate to subdue his exalted adversary, but with Printyng, writyng, and readyng, to convince darkenes by light, errour by truth, ignoraunce by learnyng: So that by this meanes of printyng the secret operation of God hath heaped upon that proude kingdome a double confusion."[22] In short, the printing press is God's response to the antichrist. Whatever God's role, no one used the press with more devastating effect than Martin Luther: "Luther made necessary what Gutenberg had made possible: by placing the Scriptures at the centre of Christian eschatology, the Reformation turned a technical invention into a spiritual obligation."[23]

The story of William Maldon of Chelmsford, once intended for inclusion in Foxe's *Acts and Monuments* but omitted, indicates how explosive could be the impact of the printed book on the literate and illiterate alike. When William was a young man, certain townspeople in 1538 purchased a copy of the New Testament in English and on Sundays read it aloud in church for their own edification and that of other listeners. William's father, finding that his son attended these readings, showed up one Sunday and angrily took him away. Predictably, this had the effect of intensifying William's interest, and he decided that he must learn how to read

The title page of Erasmus's *Panegyricus*, printed by the Ascensian press ca. 1510. The printer's mark depicts three men working at a printing press: a compositor, an inker, and a "torculator," or operator. By permission of The British Library (9930.e.35).

so that he could peruse the New Testament without interference. Subsequently, he and his father's apprentice "layed our mony together and bought the Newe Testament in Engelish, and hydde it in our bed strawe, and so exersised it at convenient times. Then shortly after my father set me to the kepyng of a shop of haberdashery and grosary wares, beyng a bowe shott from his howse, and there I plyed my boke."[24] The household might have remained peaceful, if divided, had William not injudiciously reproached his mother one day for venerating the crucifix. Learning of this conversation, his father came up to William's room at night, pulled him out of bed by the hair, beat him savagely, and put a halter around his neck. Only the pleas of William's mother prevented him from suffering further at his father's hands.

The violent contention within the Maldon family points to an unhappy effect of the printing press and the religious movement it helped to advance: printed materials made every town and every home a potential site of conflict. According to Elizabeth L. Eisenstein, "Gutenberg's invention probably contributed more to destroying Christian concord and inflaming religious warfare than any of the so-called arts of war ever did."[25] The distribution of contentious material, moreover, invariably prompted a printed response. Every book or pamphlet deemed theologically objectionable by one side or the other needed to be answered and refuted lest error triumph. Insouciance was never a tactic used in the wars of religion.

Individual writers felt particularly vulnerable when they became the object of attack. Because of a book's potentially wide distribution, any slight in printed form necessitated a reply lest a reputation be permanently besmirched. Hence Erasmus's lengthy scuffle with Jacques Lefèvre d'Etaples, whose second edition of Paul's Epistles (1515) replied to a prior criticism by Erasmus. Attacked in print, Erasmus now felt obliged to counter with his *Apologia ad Iacobum Fabrum Stapulensem* (1517), as well as with various letters. Guillaume Budé, seeing that the controversy was beginning to take on a life of its own, sought to end it in 1517, advising Erasmus that any victory would be pyrrhic: "I hope . . . that, having done battle thus far for the truth, you can pass the thing over in silence for the future; this is important for your reputation, which you have built up by all those thoughtful works of the highest quality" (*CWE* 5:247). Erasmus replied that he had no choice but to continue attacking Lefèvre: "once he had, as I say, published this and plenty more like it, as unfriendly as it was untrue, stuffing the heart of his commentary full of it, and spread it worldwide so that I was the one person who did not know—tell me, what do you think I should do?" (5:309). As Erasmus noted plaintively, "his books are everywhere." The Dutch scholar waged an even more bitter running battle with the Englishman Edward Lee, who disagreed with some of the annotations in *Novum Instrumentum*. Erasmus pestered friends to learn news of Lee's objections and then to obtain a copy of his book. Despite his own stature in Christendom, Erasmus reacted with fury upon reading Lee's attack: "Now at last the work has appeared, and the true nature of the monster is made plain; and even so the wretched man, whose talent is for libel and slander, has hired two or three hack scribblers, in his new annotations and in the more recent *Apologia,* while none the less claiming for himself a certain neatness and elegance of style which he is pleased to call Erasmian. Such is the petty ambition of a worthless wretch!" (7:218).

Far more serious than either of these clashes was the conflict with Luther that developed in the 1520s.[26] This was probably inevitable given the contentious nature of the times. Although Luther's views often coincided with his own, Erasmus fretted about that very similarity. The more controversial Luther became, the more danger Erasmus saw to himself, for as the church stepped up its attack on Luther's books, Erasmus feared that he, too, would become a target. In defense, Erasmus used the only weapon he had at his disposal, the written and printed word, for a preemptive strike. Significantly, he had long conceived of that word as a weapon. In 1515 he wrote of his editions of Jerome and Seneca: "the whole of Jerome and the whole of Seneca had been occupied for many centuries by an infinite army of corruptions, so that nothing was left anywhere that was not held by the enemy. And in this business I had my pen for a sword, the Muses, not Mars, to inspire me, and my battalions were my brains" (3:65). In 1518 Erasmus again used the metaphor, this time imagining himself as wielding a weapon against a person (Jacques Lefèvre) rather than a text: "no one fights more bitterly than he who is dragged into the fray against his will. I only wish my sword might remain buried in the scabbard till it rusts away, or if I must draw it, that I may not be compelled to use it against a friend" (5:286). The very title of Erasmus' *Enchiridion Militis Christiani* (1503) points to the written word as a weapon in the arsenal of the militant Christian, for *enchiridion* means something carried in the hand; it can be translated as either handbook or dagger.[27] Erasmus's language, then, signals the way he looked upon the written word as both a Christian and a scholar. When his estrangement with Luther became increasingly pronounced, Erasmus reluctantly sharpened his weapons and wielded them to inflict damage on the friend who had become an adversary.

Free will became the focus of their conflict. In September 1524 Erasmus published *On the Freedom of the Will,* arguing that people are responsible for their spiritual future and that actions performed out of necessity are devoid of moral value. Luther replied in December 1525 with *On the Bondage of the Will,* maintaining that salvation has nothing to do with the accumulation of merit but rather with the experience of faith, which God in his wisdom grants to some and not others. Luther affirms not the principle of moral responsibility but rather the subjugation of the will. Luther's long, detailed reply to Erasmus befits a theologian well versed in Scripture and used to analyzing the written word with great acuity. Oddly, though, he abandons a reliance upon reason when he addresses Erasmus directly: "your book struck me as so cheap and paltry that I felt profoundly sorry for you, defiling as you were your very elegant and ingenious style with such trash, and quite disgusted at the utterly unworthy matter that was being conveyed in such rich ornaments of eloquence, like refuse or ordure being carried in gold and silver vases" (*LW* 33:16). Such an attack scarcely betokens confidence in an ability to win the day through written argumentation. Indeed, Luther's diatribe sounds like the frustration of someone who subconsciously doubts the validity of his arguments or, more likely in this instance, doubts their efficacy in convincing the opposition. Erasmus' subsequent reply in *Hyperaspistes*, a treatise in two parts (1526 and 1527), abandons the air of calm objectivity that he had maintained in *On the Freedom of the Will* and, if he does not exactly emulate Luther's caustic tone, he does at times bristle with resentment against Luther; perhaps Erasmus realized that victory was not forthcoming through the written and printed word.[28]

Like other theological conflicts of the sixteenth century, that between Erasmus and Luther was inconclusive in the sense that neither man delivered the intellectual equivalent of a knockout blow. This points to a paradox that reliance upon the written and printed word fostered. On the one hand, both Erasmus and Luther saw Scripture as the indispensable foundation of Christian doctrine, a guide to everyday action, the source of knowledge necessary for salvation. Both men were convinced that they understood Scripture and that their arguments, based on the word of God, could advance the cause of truth. On the other hand, the more that Erasmus, Luther, and their contemporaries wrote and published, the clearer it became that error continued to flourish. Printing allowed legions of people to contribute to the wars of truth, but the tracts issuing from the press increased the emotional temperature of the conflict without leading to a clear-cut victory for anyone. Printing had become the single most important vehicle of argumentation, instruction, and propaganda. Alone, however, it could not win the day. Only raw political and military power could accomplish that.

One sign of the growing anxiety about printed materials was the penchant for book burning that seized Europe in the sixteenth century. To be sure, book burning had occurred before the invention of printing; the clergy of Prague, for instance, burned John Wycliffe's works in 1410. But with the advent of printing, what had been isolated incendiary incidents became a conflagration. To their credit both Erasmus and Luther resisted the impulse to join the frenzy of destruction. Erasmus opposed burning the books of Johann Reuchlin, the scholar who sought to revive the study of Hebrew so that the Old Testament could be read in the original language. Erasmus also saw the folly of destroying Luther's works: "The burning of his books will perhaps banish Luther from our libraries; whether he can be plucked out of men's hearts, I am not so sure" (8:72). For someone with Erasmus's confidence in reason, the violence done to books was deeply offensive. Indeed, upon the death of John Colet, Erasmus praised his friend precisely for his willingness to study the arguments of adversaries: "No book was so heretical that he did not read it with attention, saying that he sometimes got more profit from them than from the books of men who define everything in such a way that they frequently pay a fulsome tribute to the leaders of their school, and sometimes to themselves" (8:240–41). Only a year before Erasmus wrote this tribute to Colet, Luther sought to distance himself from his adversaries by saying (August 1520), "We should overcome heretics with books, not with fire, as the ancient fathers did. If it were wisdom to vanquish heretics with fire, then the public hangmen would be the most learned scholars on earth. We would no longer need to study books, for he who overcomes another by force would have the right to burn him at the stake" (44:196–97). Alas, this sensible approach is predicated on a belief in the power of reason to make the truth known and on a willingness to concede the more powerful argument when one encounters it. Most people, then as now, had no such confidence, and they were willing to concede very little. Inevitably, Luther's books became a popular target: they were burned, for example, in Rome (1519), in Cambridge (1520), and in London (1521); Cardinal Wolsey himself presided over the burning at St. Paul's, having had a special platform built from which to witness the spectacle. For their part the reformers were not slow to emulate the practice of their enemies; even Luther succumbed. In a letter to Georgius Spalatinus, Luther reported: "On December 10, 1520, at nine o'clock in the morning, all the following papal books were burned in Wittenberg at the eastern gate . . ." (48:186). He then names the works of canon law consumed by the flames, adding, "This was done so that the incendiary papists may see that it doesn't take much to burn books they cannot refute" (48:187). Into the fire Luther also cast the papal bull condemning him, and the more that he thought about this deed, the more pleased with himself he became. As he wrote to Johann von Staupitz on 14 January 1521, "I have burned the books of the pope and the bull, at first with trembling and praying; but now I am more pleased with this than with any other action of my life, for [these books] are worse than I had thought" (48:192).

Burning books is, of course, only a short step from destroying their authors. In this connection it is interesting that the Council of Constance directed the burning of both Wycliffe's books and bodily remains in 1415: John Foxe remarks that the Council used cruelty "not onelye agaynst the bookes and articles of John Wickliffe, but also in burnyng his body and bones."[29] Authors whose works were condemned while they were still alive were likely to be burned in effigy. Luther told Staupitz on 14 January 1521 that "They have burned me three times [in effigy]: at Louvain, at Cologne, and at Mainz" (48:194). And not only were effigies burned: Luther relates the story of a bookseller in Budapest, who "was burned at the stake, together with his books which were placed around him" (49:91).

In his more confident moments Luther believed that all such outrages were doomed to fail, that an idea, allied to righteousness, would surely prevail. As he said about certain of his manuscripts which he sent to friends but which never reached their destination: "Whoever destroys lifeless paper will not also quench the spirit" (48:351). Luther did not, however, always manage to sustain this confidence. In a treatise of 1523 he urged his followers to retain their books no matter what the threat: "If your prince or temporal ruler commands you to side with the pope, to believe thus and so, or to get rid of certain books, you should say . . . 'if you command me to believe or to get rid of certain books, I will not obey; for then you are a tyrant and overreach yourself, commanding where you have neither the right nor the authority'" (45:111–12). As time went on, Luther seems to have grown ever more uncertain about the survival of the written and printed word. To Georgius Spalatinus, Luther expressed apprehension about the health of his friend Philip Melanchthon: "I implore you not to let Philip stay in Wittenberg if the plague breaks out there. That head must be preserved, so that the Word, which the Lord has entrusted to him for the salvation of souls, may not perish" (48:316). On another occasion Luther worried that his own writings might not survive his demise: "I'm concerned . . . lest the precious gospel may be lost, for it seems to me that I now observe some who first fall into strife and then yield to passions and forget that which is the chief thing in doctrine, with the result that the Word and the glory of God are lost to sight." And, he added, "I'm afraid the same thing will happen after I'm gone" (54:226–27). This is, of course, much the same sentiment that Albrecht Dürer expressed when he heard the false report of Luther's death.

A corollary of consigning books to pyres was making lists of books deemed theologically objectionable and therefore unfit for reading. The censorship of printed books began at Mainz, where printing originated. In 1485 Archbishop Berthold von Henneberg requested that the Frankfurt town council inspect the books to be exhibited at the annual fair and suppress any deemed offensive. "In response to this, the electorate of

Mainz and the imperial city of Frankfurt in 1486 jointly set up the first secular censorship office."[30] Universities also continued their traditional activity of censorship into the era of printing. This enterprise burgeoned following the Diet of Worms and culminated in the *Index Librorum Prohibitorum,* promulgated by Pope Paul IV in 1559 and expanded by Clement VIII in 1596. Ironically, this compilation of titles contained the works of Erasmus, who had dedicated his life to the written word as Christendom's single most important vehicle of truth and reform.

Book banning and burning hardly constitute a sign of confidence in the written word's capacity to advance the cause of truth. In fact, these activities signal suspicion, distrust, and hostility toward the written and printed word. They betoken a fear of the word's power to persuade the unwary, the ignorant, the dull—as well as the prudent, the knowledgeable, and the sophisticated. However satisfying, banning and burning evince the perpetrator's profound, if unacknowledged, doubt about the capacity of his views to prevail in an intellectual contest; those exercises in destruction signal a repudiation of reason. As John Milton wrote in *Areopagitica,* "who kills a man kills a reasonable creature, God's image; but he who destroys a good book, kills reason itself, kills the image of God, as it were, in the eye."[31] The age of the printing press, which had seemed to promise a period of enlightenment, became an age of strife waged by the printed word and by sharper weapons, too. The era of Erasmus and Luther, so hospitable to the production of books in unprecedented numbers, also saw the massive suppression of books. And this was carried out by people who believed that God so valued writing that he entrusted to it the record of his very words.

3

How many books were printed during the Renaissance—from, say, 1450 to 1650? Although the number remains elusive, it must have been huge in relation to the population of Europe. Rudolf Hirsch estimates that in the fifteenth century about 40,000 titles were issued. If one assumes an average run of two hundred fifty copies per title, then the total number of copies before the year 1500 would have been at least ten million.[32] In the first half of the sixteenth century, Hirsch believes, 100,000 separate titles were produced, and if one assumes a somewhat larger number of copies per title, say five hundred, then at least fifty million were produced on European presses by the year 1550.[33] Lucien Febvre and Henri-Jean Martin, using somewhat different assumptions, arrive at even higher figures. They posit the survival of between 30,000 and 35,000 titles between 1450 and 1500, representing 10,000 to 15,000 texts. "Assuming an average print run to be no greater than 500, then about 20 million books were printed *before 1500.*"[34] Febvre and Martin observe that the number of books printed in the sixteenth century was much greater: "some 150,000–200,000 different editions could be shown to have been printed between 1500 and 1600. If we assume, for convenience, 1,000 as an average edition, then between 150–200 million copies were published in the 16th century."[35] Miriam Usher Chrisman, studying the printing trade in Strasbourg between 1480 and 1599, estimates that a typical press run was even larger: "The number of copies printed of any one book could vary from 800 to 2,000. An edition of 1,250 copies was the most efficient use of the press, because a printing team could pull 1,250 sheets off the press in a day."[36] In England most books seem to have been produced in exactly this quantity: "In 1587, the stationers made a regulation limiting editions of all but a few very popular kinds of books to 1,250 copies, ostensibly to protect the employment of journeymen, while allowing runs of 3,000 copies of primers, prayer books, grammars, and almanacs."[37]

Whatever the estimate, book production in the Renaissance so far exceeded medieval output that there can be no real comparison: "More books were printed in the forty years between 1460 and 1500 than had been produced by scribes and monks throughout the entire Middle Ages."[38] In a culture where books had been made one at a time by independent copyists or by monks in scriptoria, the explosion of book production in the fifteenth century had prodigious effects. The sheer number of printed materials meant that books now had a physical presence previously unknown: they became an ever more common feature of churches, universities, schools, and private homes. They stimulated the development of new trades, fostered the growth of literacy, and helped further religious reform. What made all of these developments possible was a simple economic fact: for the first time books were relatively affordable. Prior to the invention of the press, books tended to be expensive and therefore scarce; production of a single Gutenberg Bible on parchment, for instance, "required 170 calf-skins,"[39] a major expense for materials, not to mention labor. Within decades of its invention, the press allowed for the distribution and sale of Bibles and other books to people of modest means. C. S. L. Davies observes, "it had become possible to buy works by Erasmus and Luther at Oxford at about 4*d.* or 6*d.* a copy in 1520. At about a day's wages for a craftsman, this was hardly cheap, but at least it brought books into the purview of the merely comfortably off rather than of the wealthy only."[40]

The ready availability of books was not universally regarded as a boon. In his 1508 *Adages* even Erasmus lamented the number of recently printed books, for they created too many sources of knowledge: "To what corner of the world do they not fly, these swarms of new books? It may be that one here and there contributes something worth knowing, but the very multitude of them is hurtful to scholarship, because it creates a glut, and even in good things satiety is most harmful."[41] Erasmus also fretted over the appearance of books with popular appeal; what he deemed meretricious books were distractions, making it less likely that worthy authors would receive the attention they deserved: "they act as enticing baits, luring the minds of men (flighty and curious of anything new) away from the study of the old authors, which nothing can excel, even though I do not deny that the new-fangled writers may discover some things which escaped the old."[42] Perhaps what Erasmus feared most was the prospect that his books and those of other scholars seeking to recover the culture of antiquity, Christian and pagan, would suffer neglect amid the welter of printed materials that made preposterous claims, stirred up controversy, or attacked people irresponsibly. Of printers he said, "They fill the world with books, not just trifling things (such as I write, perhaps), but stupid, ignorant, slanderous, scandalous, raving, irreligious and seditious books, and the number of them is such that even the valuable publications lose their value."[43] For Erasmus it seemed all too likely that the bad would drive out the good. Thomas M. Greene observes, "Only in a passage such as this can one fully gauge how much power Erasmus and his world attributed to the written and printed word. The vision in fact becomes apocalyptic. The meretricious printer becomes the agent and synecdoche for universal chaos."[44]

The sheer mass of books, moreover, was felt as a psychological weight by those who saw the written word, in either script or print, as becoming too intrusive in people's lives, a source of discontent rather than enlightenment. Pierre de la Primaudaye expresses nostalgia for a time when the written word had not yet gained the status which it had come to enjoy in his own day: "Histories teach us, that when Edicts and decrees were most of all multiplied, then did tyranny gather greatest strength. As it fell out under the tyrant Caligula, who published decrees of all sorts both good and bad, and those written in so small a letter, that men could not read them, to the ende that he might thereby snare those that were ignorant."[45] Montaigne expresses a similar sentiment, linking the corruption and fall of ancient Rome with the proliferation of the written word: "Scribbling seems to be a sort of symptom of an unruly age. When did we write so much as since our dissensions began? When did the Romans write so much as in the time of their downfall?"[46] Godfrey Goodman imagines a lost world of innocence before writing: "O happie was the old world! when all things past by word of mouth, or else a few lines subscribed with the marke of a crosse, and the seale of a tooth did suffice: when in these daies (I am verily perswaded) that, what with writings, conveyances, bils of Chancery, proceedings of Court, the whole land (which we inhabite) might be spread over and covered, as with a garment; yet all will not serve for our securitie."[47] What Goodman and the others lament is the ascendancy of an increasingly disputacious and complicated society wherein the written word proves a detriment more often than not.

The status which the written word achieved sometimes had ludicrous consequences, especially when that word was antique. Erasmus recounts a practical joke played by Pietro Santeramo, who wrote a Latin couplet, gave it a title, "The dying swan before its cave," then found a calligrapher to write the words in such a way that they resembled ancient script. Santeramo went so far as to have the calligrapher omit certain letters from the words so that the couplet would seem to have suffered the ravages of time. Finally, he gave the verses to Fausto Andrelini, who lectured at the University of Paris, telling him that the poem had been discovered among some old relics. According to Erasmus, "Fausto read it over and over again, and it is hard to describe how deeply he was impressed, how he was ravished by it, and almost revered such an accomplished, such an inimitable, piece of antiquity" (3:69).

The combination of plentiful books and admiration for ancient writing could have less amusing results, for the trappings of learning were available with little effort. Erasmus in *De Copia,* a celebration of verbal abundance, cautions that writers and speakers should avoid "the false *copia* which consists in overloading speech or writing with loot from the classics, the result of ignorant and indiscriminate admiration."[48] In his essay "Of the Education of Children," Montaigne complains of those who ransack the writings of antiquity in order to compensate for their own dearth of originality: "The undiscerning writers of our century who amid their nonexistent works scatter whole passages of the ancient authors to do themselves honor, do just the opposite."[49] Montaigne's friend, Pierre Charron, finds that even the most admired books too often represent merely a compilation of ideas by earlier writers rather than genuine creativity: "We see those great, goodly and learned orations, discourses, lectures, sermons, bookes, which are so much esteemed and admired, written by men of greatest learning in this age (I except some few) what are they all, but a heape and collection of allegations, and the labours of other men?"[50] Undeserved deference to anything in writing, especially anything in print, is seen as a modern malady. In his essay "Of Experience" Montaigne asks: "What shall we do with this people that admits none but printed evidence, that does not believe men unless they are in a book, or truth unless it is of competent age? We dignify our stupidities when we put them in print."[51] Similarly, Charron expresses disappointment at the need to justify opinions by citing something printed: "It is . . . imbecillity, and a great & vulgar sottishnes, to run after strange and scholasticall examples, after allegations, never to settle an opinion without testimonies in print, nor to beleeve men but such as are in bookes, nor trueth it selfe but such as is ancient."[52] Such people behave as though the written or printed word were the sole repository of truth, whereas the proliferation of books actually has the baleful result of lending credence to ideas, especially those of a bygone era, simply because they happened to find their way into print.

The sheer abundance of books allowed their accumulation by those interested in stocking a library the way some people furnish a house—for display, not utility. Henry Peacham reproaches the person who possesses books merely to achieve a certain cachet: "Affect not as some doe, that bookish Ambition, to be stored with bookes and have wel furnished Libraries, yet keepe their heads emptie of knowledge: to desire to have many bookes, and never to use them, *is like a childe that will have a candle burning by him, all the while he is sleeping.*"[53] At the other extreme are people so preoccupied with books that their very character becomes warped. More than any other group, scholars are criticized for ransacking the past and losing sight of the distinction between the important and the trivial. Robert Burton complains: "Your supercilious Critickes, Notemakers, Antiquaries find out all the ruines of wit amongst the rubbish of old writers."[54] Sir Thomas Browne notes the unattractive qualities of those who live too exclusively in the world of books: "Schollers are men of peace, they beare no armes, but their tongues are sharper than *Actius* his razor, their pens carry farther, and give a lowder report than thunder; I had rather stand in the shock of a Basilisco than in the fury of a mercilesse Pen."[55]

For every sixteenth-century thinker who finds something to praise in book learning, there is another who challenges its utility. Even so learned a man as Erasmus could, in praising John Colet, remark on his moderation in reading. Colet disdained the laborious reading of all available authors, for "this wore down the natural health and simple vigour of the human mind, and made men less healthy and less adapted to Christian innocence and pure and simple love of others" (8:240). Girolamo Cardano identifies another pitfall when he notes the tendency of book learning to lead people away from the practical and the sensible: "these learned men besyde their Booke, knowe nothing at all, and may easelye be beguiled of any unlearned soule."[56] Francis Bacon decries the propensity of scholars to become too exclusively absorbed in words: "the first distemper of learning, [is] when men studie words, and not matter.... And how is it possible, but this should have an operation to discredit learning, even with vulgar capacities, when they see learned mens works like the first Letter of a Patent, or limmed Booke: which though it hath large flourishes, yet it is but a Letter."[57] Even Martin Luther, among the most studious and prolific writers of the sixteenth century, could tell friends at table in 1532: "The world has now become very sure of itself. It relies on books and thinks that if these are read it knows everything. The devil almost succeeded in getting me, too, to become lazy and secure and to think: 'Here you have the books. If you read them you'll have the answers'" (*LW* 54:163).

Ironically, writers who decried the surfeit of books sometimes themselves exacerbated the problem, and there is no greater exemplar than Luther, whose prodigious output occupies well over a hundred volumes in the modern edition, *D. Martin Luthers Werke* (Weimar 1883–). Luther himself saw a potential moral danger in rampant book production. He worried that the very press which was doing so much to advance the cause of reform would ultimately prove counterproductive: "it is to be feared—and the beginning of it is already apparent—that men will go on writing new and different books until finally, because of the devil's activity, we will come to the point where the good books which are now being produced and printed will again be suppressed, and the worthless and harmful books with their useless and senseless rubbish will swarm back and litter every nook and corner" (45:377). Luther was particularly sensitive to the problem because his reform of the church was intended to focus people's attention on the words of Scripture and banish the accretion of commentary that distanced the Bible from the individual reader. In July 1539 he predicted: "There will be a boundless flood of books, for any and everybody will be writing a book to feed his pride, while others will increase this evil in quest of gain. So the Bible will be buried under a mass of literature about the Bible, and the text itself will be neglected . . ." (54:361). On another occasion when he was despondent, Luther said: "I'd like all my books to be destroyed so that only the sacred writings in the Bible would be diligently read. For one is referred from one book to another, as it happened in the ancient church, when one turned from a reading of the Bible to a reading of Eusebius, then of Jerome, then of Gregory, and finally of the scholastics and philosophers" (54:274–75). The wheel had come full circle. Luther, who began his public career with an effort to bring the Bible to the faithful and to sweep away centuries of commentary, discovered that his own commentary had taken the place of Eusebius, Jerome, and Gregory: "I'd rather that all my books would disappear and the Holy Scriptures alone would be read. Otherwise we'll rely on such writings and let the Bible go" (54:311). Other theologians would, from time to time, continue to lament what the combination of industrious writers and the printing press had wrought—and with just as little effect. John Donne, for instance, reminded his flock: "It is the Text that saves us; the interlineary glosses, and the marginal notes, and the *variae lectiones,* controversies and perplexities, undo us: the Will, the Testment of God, enriches us; the Schedules, the Codicils of men, begger us: because the Serpent was subtiller then any, he would dispute and comment upon Gods Law, and so deceiv'd by his subtilty. The Word of God is *Biblia,* it is not *Bibliotheca;* a Book, A Bible, not a Library."[58]

It was not just the prodigious number of books that proved daunting and depressing but also the fact that the press proved a mixed blessing in that it added a new kind of error to the old. If books in script suffered from inattentive scribes, virtually all printed books suffered from errors made in the print room; and the press, producing multiple copies of every book, made possible the dissemination of mistakes on a previously unimagined scale. As early as 1505 Erasmus lamented the errors that creep into printed Scripture, even when the editor has produced a text that is sound: "what has been corrected can be corrupted once again—unless we are to suppose that in the world of today the self-confidence of the half-educated is less, or command of languages greater, than before; or that the spread of corruption is not facilitated by the art of printing, which all at once expands an isolated error into a thousand copies" (2:95). Erasmus was so disappointed with Josse Bade's printing of his *Adagiarum Collectanea* in 1506 and of his translations of Euripides' *Hecuba* and *Iphigenia in Aulis* the same year that he decided to have Aldus Manutius print the revision of the *Adages* and the two plays. In his 1508 *Adages* Erasmus noted with disapproval the low standards of most printers: "Nowadays the innumerable crowd of printers causes confusion everywhere, especially in Germany. Not everyone may have leave to be a baker, but printing is a trade open to any mortal man."[59] Erasmus's greatest concern was, of course, the accuracy of Scripture, and he fretted, in a 1516 letter to William Latimer, over the unforeseen difficulties of printing his New Testament: "I had to spend much more time than I expected in correcting the printer's copy beforehand and then in reading proof, although two educated men had been hired for the purpose at great expense" (3:299). The following year Erasmus enjoined Wolfgang Lachner, working at the Froben press, "Please warn your proof-reader to learn some more Greek and to be ready to listen to men who know more Greek than he does. You cannot think what harm is done to books by a printer's reader with too good a conceit of himself" (5:187).

Books suffered not only from the honest mistakes of compositors but also from the reluctance of printers to scrap pages in which errors were detected. Every printed page represented an investment in materials (paper and ink) and in manpower; consequently printers, who were first of all businessmen, were loath to destroy sheets containing errors. As a result defective pages were routinely folded and arranged into quires that might otherwise be correct. Modern editors know only too well that no two copies of a Renaissance book are likely to be identical in every detail. Books printed without the knowledge or approval of the author, moreover, were likely to be marred by numerous inaccuracies. Erasmus complained, for instance, that what eventually became his *Colloquia* began as notes for students, one of whom, Augustinus Caminadus, sold a manuscript to Johann Froben. Erasmus savaged the unscrupulous student for the deed: "It was he who put together this book, like Aesop's crow, or rather, like a ballad-seller he strung together his mish-mash as a cook pours his many galley-pots into one, adding names and headings and other bits of his own invention, to make sure that like the ass at Cumae he would give himself away" (6:218). Even the work of the most reliable printers could be compromised when their books were pirated. Erasmus complained about the literary thieves who preyed on Froben: "When anything in the way of a new work comes out which they think will be saleable, two or three of them soon purloin a copy from his printing-house, print it, and sell it cheap" (9:290). All that stood between accuracy and error were the integrity of the printer and the competence of the compositors, as Luther too understood. Seeing his vernacular New Testament pirated by German printers almost immediately after its publication in 1522, Luther sought to alert readers to the distinction between editions that were authorized and those that were not: "He soon had a personal device—the well-known 'Luther rose'—designed and imprinted only on such editions as he had personally overseen."[60]

Unscrupulous printers could also tamper, for political or religious motives, with what they printed. John Favour relates what happened to a work by St. Ambrose, which emerged mangled from the printing house. An eyewitness in Lyons saw two friars delete and insert material where it suited their purpose: "against the full consent of all ancient Copies, [they] blotted out, and put in, at their pleasure, to the great losse of the Printer, the shaming of themselves (but that they are past shame) and to the cosening of all that should buy and trust that corrupted Edition."[61] It is impossible to say whether this report is accurate and, if so, to what extent such chicanery was practiced. It is not unlikely, however, that in time of religious strife every weapon at the disposal of the combatants was used. Even a more or less responsible printer could tamper with an author's work. Johann Froben, who printed Erasmus's edition of Hilary in 1523, produced a new edition in 1535 which contained a treatise that had been issued by another printer. Apparently, Erasmus knew nothing of this additional material, for, according to P. S. Allen, "a note on the verso of the title-page, evidently from the hand of Erasmus, shows that, like the *De duplici martyrio* in the Cyprian of 1530 . . . , it had been set up without his knowledge . . . and that he was quite decided in his mind that it was not genuine."[62]

Most printers were guilty of negligence only, but that was little comfort to authors whose work suffered and who had no recourse. Godfrey Goodman adopted a philosophic stance upon discovering the botched job that printers had made of *The Fall of Man*. In a text littered with omissions, displaced material, and words misread by the compositor, Goodman found additional, unexpected support for his great theme—that the world and everything in it were decaying, falling apart, running to ruin:

> I was very sorrie, to see that, which was so meane in it selfe, should be made worse: but presently I called to mind, that the subject of my booke, was onely to prove a generall corruption, which corruption I should in effect seeme to disprove and denie, unless it might every where appeare, and therefore a necessitie did seeme so to ordaine it, that it should first begin in the author, then in the pen, then in the presse, and now I feare nothing so much as the evill and corrupt exposition of the Reader, for thus there is a generall corruption. How happie was I to make choice of such a subject, which seemes to excuse all the errors of my Pamphlet?[63]

No wonder so many readers in the sixteenth and seventeenth centuries looked askance at printed materials. And their wariness of the printed word inevitably tended to increase distrust of the written word itself.

4

With some justice sixteenth-century thinkers bewailed the shoddy work of printers, the printing of books undeserving of readers, the need to reply to every doctrinal error or personal attack that found its way into print, the deplorable deference of readers toward any printed material, the sheer proliferation of books, and the tendency of books to engender controversy. Nevertheless, they were not universally or consistently disapproving. In fact, their attitude toward the written and printed word could be enthusiastically positive. From the time of Erasmus and Luther to that of Montaigne and Bacon to that of John Milton, writers acknowledged the progress wrought by books. Most felt that the world was, on balance, a better place for the invention of the press, that Scripture was more accessible than it had ever been, that other sources of knowledge—including the wisdom of the ancients—were more widely available, that contemporary translations and treatises could be valuable weapons in the wars of truth, that the very act of reading fostered spirituality, and that the act of writing disciplined the mind. Whatever reservations they had about printers, most Europeans of the Renaissance believed that books were likely to be the most enduring and important artifacts of their civilization.

A culture that looked back to antiquity as often as it looked forward to the New Jerusalem was used to finding testimony to the written word's appeal and power among the ancients. Erasmus in his *Apothegms* approvingly notes the effect of reading on Julius Caesar: "When he read the chronicle of *Alexander* the greate, he could not forbeare to water his plantes."[64] Of Caesar, Pierre de la Primaudaye records: "in the midst of his campe [he] had his Commentaries in his bosome, and that time which he spared from fighting, he bestowed in reading and writing, holding a launce in the left hand, and a pen in the right."[65] Montaigne approvingly cites the penchant of another noble Roman: "I take pleasure in seeing . . . Brutus, with heaven and earth conspiring against him and Roman liberty, stealing some hour of night from his rounds to read and annotate Polybius with complete assurance."[66] The kings of antiquity, moreover, saw the accumulation of books as evidence of their majesty. According to Erasmus, "the most powerful and prosperous monarchs thought no concern more becoming to them than to arrange for the translation of works of outstanding authors into various tongues, that more men might enjoy them. This was, they thought, the way to secure the truest and most lasting renown for themselves and a special ornament for their kingdoms, if they bequeathed to posterity a library equipped with most accurate copies of the very best authors; nor did they think a more serious loss could befall them than the destruction of any of their riches in this kind" (3:255).

Of course, Renaissance authors did not need to search antiquity for evidence that the written word had a salubrious effect. Roger Ascham urged the young to read Castiglione's *Book of the Courtier,* "which book, advisedly read and diligently followed but one year at home in England, would do a young gentleman more good, iwis, than three years' travel abroad spent in Italy."[67] Ascham also generalized that "Learning teacheth more in one year than experience in twenty."[68] For Edward Hall, English history provided models of conduct to emulate or shun: "writyng is the keye to enduce vertue, and represse vice."[69] And Owen Felltham too believed that reading strengthened virtue: "they that turne the *leaves* of the *worthy Writer,* cannot but retaine a *smacke* of their *long-lyv'd Author.* They converse with *Vertues Soule,* which he that writ, did spread upon his *lasting Paper.*"[70] Similarly, John Milton, speaks of books with a reverence befitting religious experience: "a good book is the precious lifeblood of a master spirit, embalmed and treasured up on purpose to a life beyond life."[71]

In *The Advancement of Learning* Francis Bacon sees books as aiding society and its institutions as well as contributing to the knowledge and intellectual development of individuals. Without books, which foster law and religion, he argues, "all thinges dissolve into Anarchie and Confusion."[72] Nor is the beneficial effect of the printed word, Bacon explains, confined to the present: "the Images of men's wits and knowledges re-maine in Bookes, exempted from the wrong of time, and capable of perpetual renovation: Neither are they fitly to be called Images, because they generate still and cast their seedes in the mindes of others, provoking and causing infinit actions and opinions, in succeeding ages. So that if the invention of the Shippe was thought so noble, which carryeth riches, and commodities from place to place, and consociateth the most remote regions in participation of their fruits: how much more are letters to bee magnified, which, as Shippes, pass through the vast Seas of time?"[73]

What had been, during the Middle Ages, the lonely voyages of a few such ships became an armada in the age of printing. With considerable justification sixteenth- and seventeenth-century writers took pride in the invention that allowed books to be produced on a previously unimagined scale. Erasmus, in the commendatory preface to an edition of Livy, pays tribute to the practitioners of the new technology, who provide valuable books at reasonable prices: "If Ptolemy Philadelphus earned an undying name among posterity by his foundation of the library at Alexandria—a famous place indeed and well endowed but yet only one among its kind—what recompense do we not owe to those who daily offer us whole libraries, a whole world so to say of books, in every language and every branch of literature?" (6:253). Later in the sixteenth century Pierre Boaistuau boasted that no previous invention could rival the press: "Among all the workes and doyngs of our Elders and Auncesters, I can find nothing that maye equall or compare to the wonderfull Invention, Utilitie and Dignitie of Printing."[74] Thanks to the press, George Hakewill observes, books are no longer confined chiefly to monastic libraries as they were in the Middle Ages. There are "now more good Authours to bee bought for twenty shillings then could then be purchased for twenty pounds."[75]

So powerful and potentially beneficial was the press that it was deemed the agent of divine providence. John Foxe, in his *Acts and Monuments,* likens the effect of the press to Pentecost: "Notwithstandyng, what man so ever was the instrument, without all doubt God himselfe was the ordainer and disposer therof, no otherwise, then he was of the gift of tounges, & that for a singular purpose. And well may this gift of Printing be resembled to the gift of tongues: for like as God then spake with many tongues, and yet all that would not turne the Jewes, so now, when the holy Ghost speaketh to the adversaries in innumerable sortes of bookes, yet they will not be converted: nor turne to the Gospell."[76] Foxe's paean to printing omits almost nothing: "hereby tounges are knowen, knowledge groweth, judgement increaseth, bookes are dispersed, the Scripture is sene, the Doctours be read, storyes be opened, tymes compared, truth decerned, falsehode detected, and with finger poynted, and all (as I sayd) thorough the benefite of printyng."[77] So spiritually valuable was printing that John Donne, too, could liken the activity of a printer to that of the

Holy Spirit: "when the holy Ghost takes a man into his schoole, he deals not with him, as a Painter, which makes an eye, and an eare, and a lip, and passes his pencill an hundred times over every muscle, and every haire, and so in many sittings makes up one man, but he deales as a Printer, that in one straine delivers a whole story."[78]

The development of printing also allowed writers to achieve goals of a more personal nature: they could contrive what today we call a public image while addressing religious and political issues. They achieved this by making available written materials that would otherwise have remained private—namely, personal letters. Probably no one in the Renaissance wrote more of them than Erasmus,[79] himself the author of a treatise on letter-writing, *De Conscribendis Epistolis*. Early in his career he showed no interest in publishing his letters, but around 1515 he had come to see advantage in their dissemination. Increasingly large collections of his letters appeared between that year and 1521. His letters serve a variety of purposes: they solicit money, express gratitude, ask favors, compliment patrons, answer critics, champion reform. Although Erasmus's motives in approving the printing of such miscellaneous material cannot be known with certainty, we can at least speculate about them, and the dates of publication provide a clue. That Erasmus began to publish his letters as his rift with Luther began to crystallize, especially during the years 1516 to 1521, can hardly be coincidental. During these years Erasmus worried that he would be targeted by those who were growing hostile toward Luther. In October 1519, for instance, Erasmus wrote to Albert of Brandenburg: "Of Luther I know as little as I do of anyone; his books I have not yet found time to read, except for dipping into some of them here and there. If he has written well, none of the credit is due to me; if the reverse, there is nothing that can be laid at my door" (7:110). The writer's apprehension is almost palpable here, and it is interesting that this particular letter should have appeared in eight or more editions even before it was published in his *Epistolae ad Diversos* (1521). His letters may not constitute an entirely consistent stand on controversial issues, but they represented a declaration of orthodoxy in dangerous times; they also demonstrated to contemporaries the breadth of Erasmus's learning, the power of his intellect, the seriousness of his purpose. The letters, then, provided a means of enhancing his reputation and thereby broadening his influence at a time when support for Luther was growing.[80]

A century after Erasmus squared off against Luther, Ben Jonson utilized the printed word to similar effect: he fashioned a public identity that would enhance his personal prestige. Before the publication of Jonson's *Works* in 1616, it was common for authors to affect the pose of an amateur, whose writings somehow found their way into print; an apology often accompanied the appearance of a printed book. With Jonson the authorial presence is forthright, confident, and apparent everywhere, from the title page appropriating the word "works," hitherto reserved chiefly for books of divinity, philosophy, and the like; to the marginalia and notes, demonstrating his vast reading; to the texts of masques, those collaborative enterprises in which the contributions of set and costume designer threatened to overshadow the maker of poetry. By printing masques and plays, Jonson conferred on them a status independent of performance. Printing created an air of permanence and completion, as though his theatrical entertainments did not depend upon actors and audience; it allowed Jonson the opportunity to revise, as he did when he purged *Sejanus* of the "second pen"; it established a community of readers that was quite different from that formed by spectators in a theater or palace; it allowed for reading and re-reading and comment and criticism on the part of that readership; and it even allowed Jonson to shape his career retroactively by excluding early plays and beginning the volume with *Every Man in His Humour,* as though it were his first success.[81] In a brilliant article on Jonson's use of print, Richard C. Newton observes: "In his insistence on the autonomy of his texts, in his creation of his small community of critical readers, and in his confidence in the shape his texts create for reading, Jonson manifests, I believe, a profound realization of what it means to write for print: to write for an audience defined only by the limits of book distribution and the understanding of readers, rather than to perform for a few or to surrender to the whims of copyists, excerpters, and marginal glozers."[82]

Most of Jonson's contemporaries in the theater did not emulate his practice. Thomas Heywood, for example, glances at Jonson while describing the fate of his own scripts: "True it is, that my Playes are not exposed unto the world in Volumes, to beare the title of *Workes,* (as others) one reason is, That many of them by shifting and change of Companies, have been negligently lost, Others of them are still retained in the hands of some Actors, who thinke it against their peculiar profit to have them come into Print, and a third, That it never was any great ambition in me, to bee in this kind Voluminously read."[83] Like Heywood, William Shakespeare seems not to have shared Jonson's ambition to be preserved in print. But he had two friends, Heminges and Condell, willing to gather together and publish the scripts of his plays. Without the 1616 *Works* of Jonson there would have been no precedent for the first folio of 1623, and, without the first folio, half of Shakespeare's plays would have been lost, like so many of Heywood's. Appropriately, it was Ben Jonson who wrote a eulogy for this volume, paying tribute to the deceased dramatist whose work was now being reshaped by the medium of print. David Riggs observes: "The realization that Shakespeare's plays transcended the medium of performance, and belonged in print, bore out Jonson's lifelong contention that plays are (or should be) a serious form of literature. Moreover, the men who prepared the folio for the press (and Jonson may well have been one of them) remade Shakespeare in Jonson's image."[84]

5

Whether they extolled the written and printed word or deplored its influence, writers recognized that books are unlike most other artifacts in being capable of producing the most profound effects on people who may be far removed in time and place from the book's author. Books achieve this by the way in which they engage an individual's psyche. Although a book may exist in many thousands of copies, each reader's confrontation with that book is unique. And such is the psychology of reading that the reader can feel that the words on a page are intended specifically for him or her. Consider, for example, Petrarch's account of his trek up Mont Ventoux, which was inspired by his reading of Livy (the description of Philip of Macedon's ascent of Mount Hemus in Thessaly). Petrarch ascended the mountain with his brother and, upon reaching the summit, drew from his satchel a copy of Augustine's *Confessions*. Opening the volume, Petrarch proceeded to read aloud a passage about men admiring mountains and abandoning themselves. What an observer might construe as fortuitous, Petrarch interprets as providential: "I was sure that what I read had been written for me and for no one else."[85] This claim may seem dubious in the sense that Augustine's words had been written a millennium earlier and perused by generations of readers before Petrarch's birth. But, as any reader knows, the written word can exert the effect that Petrarch describes, no matter how long ago the author lived, for a subtle bond forms between reader and writer, creating a sense of communion; in its most intense form this leads to a feeling that the author is addressing a single reader, a feeling strengthened by the silent reading that was becoming increasingly common in the late Middle Ages and in the Renaissance.[86]

It seems appropriate that Petrarch's experience on Mont Ventoux should involve Augustine, since that patristic author was himself forever changed by words that he read in a book. In his *Confessions* he recounts the day he heard a voice say, "Take up and read, Take up and read." At once he intuited the source of this injunction: "refraining the violent torrent of my tears, up I gat me; interpreting it no other way, but that I was from God himself commanded to open the book, and to read that chapter which I should first light upon."[87] At hand were the Epistles of Paul to the Romans, and the effect of reading just a couple of verses—13:13–14—proved immediate: "No further would I read; nor needed I. For instantly even with the end of this sentence, by a light as it were of confidence now darted into my heart, all the darkness of doubting vanished away."[88] The fulcrum of this conversion is the act of reading; and his sense that the words on the page have special significance for him suffuses Augustine with emotion.

The accounts of Augustine and Petrarch illustrate something that both celebrants and detractors of the written word recognized—that the arrangement of letters on a page can so affect a reader that those words bring about an intellectual, spiritual, and emotional transformation. Although lacking the warmth, inflection, and intonation of speech, the written word nevertheless may achieve what the direct, forceful appeal of another person achieves; and this remains as true of the printed word as of the word in script.

Although they share with people of all ages a certain psychology of reading, Renaissance writers and readers had the capacity to respond to the written and printed word with unusual intensity. Erasmus, for example, felt no disadvantage in being separated from Christ's life by a millennium and a half; after all, he had at hand the written word of the New Testament, which he could read and re-read as often as he wished. Erasmus responded no less forcefully to the writings of contemporaries. In a letter to Guillaume Budé, Erasmus expresses what his friend's missives mean to him: "There is no one whose letters I enjoy as much as yours, and I get profit of all sorts out of them as well as enjoyment" (6:197). Erasmus goes on to say that Budé's written words more than compensate for his friend's absence: "when I read your letters, written with such a high degree of literary skill, I seem somehow to have a more lively impression than if I were listening to you face to face, for all that you are such an entertaining companion in the flesh." It seems clear that Erasmus was able to find in the written word something that most other people find only in the physical presence of another person.

Although this ability to experience a rapport with the author of the written word is hardly confined to the Renaissance, it characterized the most creative minds of that era. Niccolò Machiavelli, for example, couches his feelings for ancient authors in vividly personal terms. In a letter to Francesco Vettori, on 10 December 1513, Machiavelli describes his personal library as a refuge from disappointment, want, and loneliness:

> On the coming of evening, I return to my house and enter my study; and at the door I take off the day's clothing, covered with mud and dust, and put on garments regal and courtly; and reclothed appropriately, I enter the ancient courts of ancient men, where, received by them with affection, I feed on that food which only is mine and which I was born for, where I am not ashamed to speak with them and to ask them the reason for their actions; and they in

their kindness answer me; and for four hours of time I do not feel boredom, I forget every trouble, I do not dread poverty, I am not frightened by death; entirely I give myself over to them.[89]

Michel de Montaigne, too, found respite amid his books: "In my library I spend most of the days of my life, and most of the hours of the day."[90] Within the precincts of his thousand-volume library, Montaigne gained both the pleasure of agreeable company and a sense of power over at least this small part of an inconstant and tumultuous world: "There is my throne. I try to make my authority over it absolute, and to withdraw this one corner from all society, conjugal, filial, and civil." For Montaigne, as for Machiavelli, books take the place of people.[91] Books are not the inert artifacts of other people; in a sense books *are* those people.

Because they responded with such intensity to the written and printed word, sixteenth-century thinkers could fear the dissension engendered by books; they indulged in the suppression of books by banning and burning them; they lamented the explosion of book production in the era of the press; they bewailed the proliferation of biblical interpretations and the controversies that ensued within Christendom; and they worried that absorption in the world of books could detach a person from the realities of ordinary life. But that same powerful response to the word also led sixteenth-century thinkers to prize, study, and edit both Scripture and other books. Thanks to the printing press, moreover, they were able to revive the literature, history, and philosophy of antiquity by presenting the ancients in new and affordable editions. In the work of the greatest writers they were able to find a combination of intellectual and emotional sustenance. As Erasmus told William Warham, those authors "live on for the world at large even after death, and live on in such fashion that they speak to more people and more effectively dead than alive. They converse with us, instruct us, tell us what to do and what not to do, give us advice and encouragement and consolation as loyally and as readily as anyone can. In fact, they then most truly come alive for us when they themselves have ceased to live" (3:256).

Part Two

3
Ideology, Printing Press, and Stage

1

BASED on their reception, Erasmus's works exemplify the far-reaching effects of the written and printed word. That reception was especially enthusiastic in England, which Erasmus visited some half dozen times, teaching at Cambridge, pursuing his scholarship, and befriending Grocyn and Linacre, Colet and More, John Fisher and William Warham. For the English as for other Europeans, Erasmus's achievement as an editor of classical books was inextricably connected with his achievement in biblical study. John Foxe noted that "many were provoked by Erasmus learned workes, to study the Greeke and Latine tongues, who perceivyng a more gentle & ready order of teachyng then before, began to have in contempt the Monkes barbarous and sophisticall doctrine."[1] Not even the ascendancy of the Reformation in England detracted from the respect owed Erasmus.[2] A sign of his continuing importance was the directive, in July 1547, to place his *Paraphrases* of the New Testament in every English church.[3] That work apparently became a part of religious observance: "A Swiss traveller who visited Oxford in 1551 wrote that church services there consisted of a chapter or two from the English Bible and the *Paraphrases* of Erasmus in translation; the rest, he says, was vocal and organ music."[4] Nicholas Udall, in the 1548 edition of the *Paraphrases,* explains its appeal; he contends that Erasmus "is wondreful in comparing of fygures of the olde testamente, in applying of allegories, in declaring of parables, in discussing of doubtful questions, in serching and explicating of profound misteries, wherin he evidently declareth himselfe, that he was a man of an excellent witte, of much study, of exquisite learning, of profounde knowelage, of an exact judgemente, of notable diligence, of woorthy & famous industrie, of singular peinefulnes, of an encomparable memorie, & of an unestimable zele towardes the setting furth of Christes most holy gospel."[5] Perhaps it was knowledge of such admiration that led the citizens of Rotterdam to greet the Earl of Leicester in 1585 by erecting a statue of the Dutch scholar: "The townesmen had made verie memorablie in the middle of the market place the whole proportion of Erasmus in a pulpit, as though he were preaching, holding a booke of the paraphrasis on the gospels in his hand, under whome was written *Erasmus Rotherodame*."[6]

Admittedly, Catholic Erasmus held views different from those of English Protestants, and Alan Sinfield judges the Dutch scholar at odds with what he calls the "puritan humanism" of England: "Humanists like Erasmus proposed that Christians, with the additional inspiration of Jesus, should build on the classical programme of self-sufficient rational virtue. But protestants denied the congruity of pagan and Christian virtue, that people can achieve rational self-determination, and that moral achievement is relevant to salvation."[7] Although I do not contest the gist of this argument, Sinfield depicts too starkly the relationship between Erasmus and English Protestantism. Significantly he omits mention of the *Paraphrases* being placed in English churches and the tributes to Erasmus in Foxe's *Acts and Monuments*, a compilation of Protestant martyrs. He also omits mention of Erasmus's effect on the educational program of European universities, including those of England. Anthony Grafton and Lisa Jardine observe: "In the case of England, in particular, where Henry VIII's quarrel with the canon lawyers in the 1530s made a replacement curriculum an urgent necessity, an Erasmian liberal arts programme was seized upon by the Tudor Establishment (with the support of Thomas Cromwell) as a politically appropriate substitute for scholasticism in the statutes of Oxford and Cambridge."[8] As late as 1600 John Stow, surveying the history of those universities, could approvingly cite Erasmus's praise of English learning: "I have before time rejoiced (saith *Erasmus Roterdam*) that Englande was so well furnished with so manie men of excellent learning, but now I begin to envie her felicitie, for that shee so flourisheth with all kinde of literature, that by taking the commendation therof from other Regions, she doth as it were marvellouslie obscure them."[9] Sinfield also passes over the extraordinary sale of books by Erasmus in England. The survival of an Oxford bookseller's list from 1520 reveals that his "popularity exceeds even that of Aristotle, and his works number some hundred and fifty in a total list of about two thousand items sold."[10] Finally, Sinfield neglects the theatrical evidence, such as it is. In Thomas Drue's *The Life of the Duchess of Suffolk* (ca. 1623), set during the reign of Queen Mary, Erasmus becomes a sympathetically presented character, who assists the Duchess when she flees religious persecution in England.[11]

Whatever their differences with him, the English reformers recognized that Erasmus's attitudes toward the written word—especially his emphasis on Scripture, his confidence in the laity's ability to profit from reading it, and his disparagement of clerical authority—were consonant with their own. And English writers of all kinds, seeking to buttress arguments about biblical translation, moral conduct, and the preservation of written words, frequently invoked his name. For example, William Baldwin, seeking to justify, as a layman, his translation and commentary on the Songs of Solomon, cites the reasoning of Erasmus as set forth in his *Paraphrases:* "I wyl satisfy them with Erasmus his argumentes, whiche they shall fynde in his preface to the Emperour, before his Paraphrase of saint Matthew."[12] Sir Thomas Elyot praises the moral "exhortation" he finds in *The Education of a Christian Prince:* "there was never boke written in latine that in so lytle a portion contayned of sentence, eloquence and vertuous exhortation a more compendious abundaunce."[13] And when John Bale laments the disappearance of early English historical records, he, too, invokes the name of Erasmus: "If we lose the treasure of these authors herin contayned, by the malyce or els slouthfull neglygence of thys wycked age, whych is muche geven to the destruccyon of thynges memorable, we may wele lamente and saye wyth the noble clarke Erasmus of Roterdame. Wyth much payne I absteyne from wepynge (sayth he in a certen Epystle) so oft as I in readynge the cataloges of olde writers, do beholde what profyghtes, yea, what pusaunce, ayde, and confort we have lost."[14]

Erasmus was, of course, not singlehandedly responsible for the developments that transformed English institutions in the sixteenth century, but English historians saw the continuity between Erasmus and the reformers. John Foxe, discussing events in the year 1516, notes the disparaging comments about Rome and the clergy made by people even in the earliest days of the Reformation: "Which thyng, no doubt, was of God, as a secret prophecie, that shortly Religion should be restored: accordyng as it came to passe, about this present tyme when Doct. Martin Luther first began to write, after that Picus Mirandula, and Laurentius Valla, and losse of all, Erasmus Roterodamus, had somewhat broken the waye before, and had shaken the Monkes houses."[15] In a similar vein Foxe remarks, "when Erasmus wrote, and Frobenius Printed, what a blow therby was geven to all Friers & Monkes in the worlde? And who seeth not, that the penne of Luther folowyng after Erasmus and set forward by Printyng, hath set the triple crowne so awrye on the. Popes head, that it is lyke never to be set streight agayne."[16]

To the extent that they insisted on a knowledge of languages, on each individual's reading of Scripture, and on the dissemination of printed books, Erasmus and Luther helped give impetus to the program of writing, translating, analyzing, editing, and publishing that occupied so many English men and women in the sixteenth century. The values championed by Erasmus and Luther contributed to the writing of a vast theological literature; the increase in the number of schools; the growth of literacy;

the success of the printing trade; and the accessibility of books to professionals and ordinary people alike. The work of Erasmus and Luther, despite different emphases, exerted a common effect: it fostered the literary cast of English culture in the sixteenth century, expanding and strengthening the realm of letters.

At the same time, that realm remained in some ways as insecure in the reign of Queen Elizabeth as it had been in the time of Erasmus and Luther. Symptomatic of uncertainty and malaise were the large proportion of newly printed books devoted to religious controversy, as though the gains of the reformers were merely temporary and might be undone by the arguments and arms of Rome; the fractures within English Christendom, made inevitable by the ready access to Scripture and by private responsibility for interpretation; the impulse to censor, betraying a fear that the ideas in books had the capacity to undermine cherished religious and political orthodoxy; expressions of anxiety over the torrent of materials produced by the printing press; and disgust over unscrupulous and incompetent printers. Elizabethan England exhibited much the same inconsistency toward the written and printed word that had marked the era of *Novum Instrumentum* and the ninety-five theses. "Ambivalence" is too mild a term for the amalgam of attitudes involving reading and writing that prevailed in the later sixteenth century.

2

Playwrights, especially in the early and mid-sixteenth century, used the stage to promote spiritual reform. The stage even enjoyed something of the status of the printing press and pulpit as a weapon against Rome. In Foxe's *Acts and Monuments* it is suggested that "preachers, Printers, & players . . . be set up of God, as a triple bulwarke against the triple crowne of the pope, to brynge hym down."[17] Even at the end of Elizabeth's reign the stage could remain a site of doctrinal contention, where old battles over translating the Bible into English and making that Bible available to the faithful were re-enacted. *If You Know Not Me You Know Nobody,* for example, although written and staged ca. 1605, is set in the contentious period when Mary was Queen and England had reverted to Catholicism. The play's alternate title, *The Troubles of Queen Elizabeth,* points to its subject—the plots against Princess Elizabeth, prosecuted by adherents of her sister's regime. From the outset the play dramatizes the ideological gulf separating Mary and Elizabeth, Sir Henry Beningfield complaining of the Princess, "She is a favorite of these heritiques" (l. 97).[18] Embodying a Christianity distinctly different from that of Mary and Philip of Spain, Princess Elizabeth is closely identified with the written word. Her captor, the Constable of the Tower, sneers: "She is my prisoner, and if I durst, / But that my warrant is not yet so strickt, / Ide lay her in a dungeon where her eyes, / Should not have light to read her prayer booke" (ll. 716–19). Later Elizabeth asks for ink and paper so that she "may move my impatient sisters eares, / And urge her to compassionate my woe" (ll. 1031–32). While the Princess writes her letter, Lord Beningfield examines one of her books: "Marry a God. whats here an English bible? / *Sanctum Maria* pardon this prophanation of my hart" (ll. 1039–40). Then almost immediately a dumb show makes visually compelling the supernatural sanction given the English Bible:

> Enter *Winchester, Constable, Barwick,* and *Fryars:* at the other dore 2. *Angels:* the *Fryar* steps to her, offering to kill her: the *Angels* drive them back. *Exeunt.* The *Angel* opens the Bible, and puts it in her hand as she sleepes, *Exeunt Angels, she wakes.* (ll. 1049–53)

Finally, at the end of the play when Mary has died and Elizabeth has succeeded her, the Mayor of London greets the new queen with symbolic gifts: "I from this City London do present, / This Purse and Bible to your Majesty" (ll. 1573–74). Elizabeth acknowledges the gifts, holding in her hands the English Bible:

> We thanke you all: but first this booke I kisse,
> Thou art the way to honor; thou to blisse,
> An English Bible, thankes my good Lord Maior,
> You of our bodie and our soule have care,
> This is the Jewell that we still love best,
> This was our solace when we were distrest,
> This booke that hath so long conceald it selfe,
> So long shut up, so long hid; now Lords see,
> We here unclaspe, for ever it is free.
>
> (ll. 1578–86)

In this exchange between the Mayor and Queen, drama and history converge, for as Alexander Leggatt suggests, the onstage incident recalls the actual coronation procession of Elizabeth almost fifty years earlier, when she received such a Bible, kissed it, and held it to her breast.[19]

3

The changes wrought by the prevalence of the written and printed word, along with the literacy and education it promoted, are manifest not only in the religious conflict of a play like *If You Know Not Me* but also in the way that other social and political conflicts are conceived. The Jack Cade episode of *2 Henry VI* provides an opportunity to witness a playwright's imagination responding to the technology of the printing press and to the developments it helped set in motion. This episode seems intended not simply to affirm one particular view or another (in the manner of *If You Know Not Me*), but to explore the claims of those on either side of the divide separating the literate from their countrymen.

According to Raphael Holinshed, Cade, in fomenting his rebellion, had the wit to assure his compatriots that "the enterprise which he tooke in hand, was both honourable to God and the king, and profitable to the whole realme,"[20] and he succeeded in rallying a force at Blackheath. Confident of victory, he arrived in London where he "cut the ropes of the draw bridge and strooke his sword on London stone" (634). At the guildhall he caused Lord Say to be arraigned and, almost immediately, beheaded. Cade subsequently inspired "open rapine and manifest robberie in diverse houses within the citie" (634). Later, when those heady days were past and he was deserted by his followers, he disguised himself in order to elude his pursuers, but encountered Alexander Eden, who "tooke the said Cade in a garden in Sussex: so that there he was slaine at Hothfield, and brought to London in a cart, where he was quartered" (635). The violence of this story and the prowess of the rebel leader provided Shakespeare with rich opportunities for dramatization. The playwright, however, while preserving the basic story of rebellion and retribution, chose to forgo its more lurid aspects. On the stage Holinshed's overreacher becomes a man sorely aggrieved by the written word and the printing press.

Initially, Shakespeare pits Cade not against the citizenry at London bridge but against the Clerk of Chatham, who has the misfortune to be at the wrong place at the wrong time. The ruffian of *2 Henry VI* asks his captive, "Dost thou use to write thy name? or hast thou a mark to thyself, like a honest plain-dealing man?" (4.2.102–4). In ignorance of his captor's purposes, and with some self-satisfaction, the Clerk affirms his literacy: "Sir, I thank God, I have been so well brought up that I can write my name" (ll. 105–6). What he does not know is that his modest boast will prove his undoing, for Cade proves unremittingly hostile to the written word: "Hang him with his pen and inkhorn about his neck" (ll. 109–10). In this scene the issue is not the Clerk's specific political allegiance but rather his possession of a skill that, in Cade's view, identifies the man with a social hierarchy indifferent or hostile to ordinary folk. Cade's characterization prefigures that of Caliban, who warns Stephano and Trinculo of Prospero, "Remember / First to possess his books; for without them / He's but a sot, as I am" (3.2.91–93). Like people today who are innocent of computers and so scorn the new technology, some spectators at the London theaters must have identified with the sentiments of such characters.

In pitting Cade against Lord Say, Shakespeare considerably amplifies the summary treatment of the chronicle. Holinshed records no words of Lord Say, only his desire to be judged by his peers. In place of this silence, Shakespeare creates nothing less than an ideological justification of the written word. In terms that Erasmus and Luther would surely approve, Lord Say declares:

> Large gifts have I bestow'd on learned clerks,
> Because my book preferr'd me to the King;
> And seeing ignorance is the curse of God,
> Knowledge the wing wherewith we fly to heaven,
> Unless you be possess'd with devilish spirits
> You cannot but forbear to murther me.
>
> (4.7.71–76)

Where the nobleman identifies the written word with the achievement of salvation, Jack Cade sees victimization. Convinced that he has been done in by others' education and literacy, he accuses his adversary:

> Thou hast most traitorously corrupted the youth of the realm in erecting a grammar school; and whereas, before, our forefathers had no other books but the score and the tally, thou hast caus'd printing to be us'd, and, contrary to the King, his crown, and dignity, thou hast built a paper-mill. It will be prov'd to thy face that thou hast men about thee that usually talk of a noun and a verb, and such abominable words as no Christian ear can endure to hear.
>
> (ll. 32–41)

Cade is not wrong in singling out the press for abuse, for it was at the nexus of the developments that we have traced. Printed books had become indispensable to the legal system, as Cade acknowledges when he sends his men "to th' Inns of Court; down with them all" (l. 2). To the illiterate, written and printed records of other kinds, similarly, represented a potential threat to financial security and so Cade directs, "Away, burn all the records of the realm . . ." (ll. 13–14). In contrast to the political authorities, who distributed printed proclamations, which remained mysterious to the unlettered, Cade would revert to the spoken word: "my mouth shall be the parliament of England" (ll. 14–15). With allowance for comic exaggeration on Shakespeare's part, Cade's confrontations have about them the bitter tone of Envy's complaint in *Doctor Faustus:* "I cannot read, and therefore wish all books were burnt" (2.3.133–34).[21]

Shakespeare's rebel appreciates in his dim fashion what another historical figure, Cuthbert Tunstall, Bishop of London, failed to realize: namely, that the phenomenon of books could not be stopped by destroying the books themselves. Elsewhere in his chronicle Holinshed relates what Bishop Tunstall did in 1529 when Miles Coverdale's English Bible was printed and began circulating in London: "minding to prevent that no such bibles should be dispersed within this realme, [he] made inquirie where they were to be sold, and bought them all up; supposing that by this meanes no more bibles would be had: but contrarie to his expectation it fell out otherwise. For the same monie which the bishop gave for these books, was sent over by the merchant unto this Coverdale, and by that meanes he was of that wealth and abilitie, that he imprinted as manie more and sent them over into England" (1309). Whereas Bishop Tunstall purchased books in order to burn them, Jack Cade adopts the sterner strategy of killing those who write them or finance their production. Shakespeare's Cade understands the inexorable nature of the press in a way that the more learned Bishop, who helped Erasmus with the second edition of *Novum Instrumentum*,[22] failed to appreciate.

In dramatizing Jack Cade's rebellion, Shakespeare has profoundly reshaped Holinshed's account. The issue of illiteracy has no role in the chronicle. In fact, Holinshed's rebel prepares "letters of safe conduct" for his followers, sends written instructions to Thomas Cocke concerning the rebellion, and transmits to the king a fifteen-point complaint, which the chronicler dutifully reproduces. However rough Cade may have been, Holinshed presents him as shrewd and, in some ways, sophisticated. When the royal emissaries meet him, they discover a formidable opponent: they "found him sober in talke, wise in reasoning, arrogant in hart, and stiffe in opinion" (634). So clever was the historical figure that, when the king proclaimed a pardon for those who had followed the rebel, Cade argued that "the kings letters of pardon granted to him and them, be not available, nor of none effect, without authoritie of parlement" (635).[23] Clearly, the rebel of the chronicle, whatever the extent of his literacy, was not averse to using the written word when it suited his purpose. By contrast, Shakespeare's rebel is defined by his illiteracy and by the feeling of antagonism that it engenders in him. Few episodes on the Renaissance stage demonstrate so pointedly the extent to which written and printed words had infiltrated people's lives.[24] By presenting the Jack Cade episode in this fashion, Shakespeare is led to his most interesting anachronism: the printing press against which Cade inveighs had not been invented in 1450, the year of his rebellion.

4

The books and documents that appear frequently on the Renaissance stage are nowhere more important than in *Doctor Faustus*, where they become central to the protagonist's moral choices. Even the play's setting, Wittenberg, has particular significance for both writing and printing since that city was home to Martin Luther when he posted his ninety-five theses on a church door, precipitating changes that would confer new status on the written word in European culture. Luther also contributed indirectly to the story of Doctor Faustus, for the German narrative that lies behind Marlowe's play, Michael Keefer observes, is in many respects Lutheran: "its demonology, some of its episodes and many of its turns of phrase are lifted from Martin Luther's writings and table-talk."[25] The development of the printing press, which Luther exploited so brilliantly, may even have contributed to the very name of the wonder-working magician, known historically as Georgius of Helmstadt (a town near Heidelberg). "The name Johann or John Faust may," according to David Bevington and Eric Rasmussen, "represent a confusion with Johann Fust, an early practitioner of that sinister art known as printing."[26]

By coincidence the birth and death dates of the German magician (ca. 1466–ca.1537) match almost exactly those of Erasmus (ca. 1466–1536), and although the two never met, they were alike in some important ways. Like the Dutch scholar, Georgius of Helmstadt was a talented student. He attended the University of Heidelberg, earning a bachelor's degree in 1484 and a master's degree in 1487. If Georgius himself added the Latin *Faustus* to his name, he probably did so to signal his allegiance to humanistic studies; his contemporary, the Italian humanist Andrelini of Forli, who taught at the University of Paris, had already adopted the same name. Like Erasmus, Georgius seems to have felt a special affinity for the written word, though he exuded an arrogance that offended others. According to Johannes Trithemius, a Benedictine abbot, formidable collector of books, and himself the author of *Steganographia,* a work about secret writing, Georgius of Helmstadt "claimed to have acquired such comprehensive wisdom and memory that if all the works of Plato and Aristotle with the whole body of their philosophical thought completely disappeared from the memory of man, he himself, through his genius, like another Ezra, could restore all things with a greater degree of elegance."[27] (The word "elegance" suggests the attention to stylistic felicity common to Erasmus and other humanists seeking to emulate the ancients.) Although Marlowe's protagonist makes no similar claim, he shares a close identification with the written word: he is bookish by temperament and occupation. As *Doctor Faustus* opens, we find the scholar in his study. His first act consists of examining several books from his personal library, and his first speech surveys the fields of knowledge accessible through those books.

The volumes that Faustus examines in the play's opening scene—Aristotle's treatises on logic, Galen's on medicine, Justinian's *Institutes,* and

Jerome's Latin Bible—epitomize traditional subjects of university study, all dependent on the written word, preserved from antiquity and passed down by manuscript to the Renaissance. As befits writings so valuable as to merit transmittal over centuries, the books that Faustus handles would command the respect of most readers. Those books typify methods of inquiry, attitudes, accomplishments, and values regarded as venerable by Marlowe's contemporaries and long represented as such in sixteenth-century drama. Even before Faustus picks up his copy of the Bible, for example, the written word had a specifically religious significance on the stage. A character named the Law of God carries the Ten Commandments in Lewis Wager's *The Life and Repentance of Mary Magdalene*.[28] The written word is also inseparable from divine judgment in John Skelton's *Magnificence,* where Adversity identifies his writing with the will of God: "I am God's prepositor; I print them [write down their names] with a pen" (l. 1942).[29] And in *Lusty Juventus* Good Counsel warns the protagonist, "The terrible plagues which in God's law are written, / Hang o'er thy head both early and late" (ll. 943–44).[30] When Doctor Faustus puts down the Bible and the other books, however, he signals that those fields of study may be seen as deficient. Implicit in his action is a judgment that the written materials supporting theology, philosophy, medicine, and law are similarly lacking. The handling of the books, then, evokes the admiration of a culture for such books while also registering an individual's disgruntlement.

After Faustus rejects the four books, he picks up a very different work: "These metaphysics of magicians / And necromantic books are heavenly, / Lines, circles, signs, letters, and characters— / Ay, these are those that Faustus most desires" (1.1.51–54).[31] As we hear these words, we sense the intoxication with texts promising access to powers once possessed by the ancients but gradually lost with the decline of classical civilization. The 1592 translation of *Historia von D. Johann Fausten* (1587), *The Historie of the damnable life, and deserved death of Doctor John Faustus* by P. F., makes this explicit when it recounts the nature of Faustus's studies: "he accompanied himself with divers that were seen in those devilish arts and that had the Chaldean, Persian, Hebrew, Arabian and Greek tongues, using figures, characters, conjurations, incantations, with many other ceremonies belonging to these infernal arts, as necromancy, charms, soothsaying, witchcraft, enchantment, being delighted with their books, words and names so well, that he studied day and night therein."[32] Intellectually reckless as Faustus may have seemed to Marlowe's contemporaries, his pursuit of knowledge through books containing ancient languages and symbols has a certain logic, for, thanks to Erasmus and Luther, scholars were in fact busy reviving ancient languages, especially

Greek and Hebrew, in order to recover truths recorded in antiquity but subsequently obscured.

What follows Faustus's decision to pursue magic is a battle of the books as one group of characters enjoins him to read Scripture while another urges him to scrutinize magical texts. The Good Angel, for example, says, "O Faustus, lay that damnèd book aside / And gaze not on it, lest it tempt thy soul / And heap God's heavy wrath upon thy head! / Read, read the Scriptures. That is blasphemy" (1.1.72–75). Later when Faustus, seeking a wife, grows angry at the appearance of a devil *dressed like a woman* (2.1.151.s.d.), Mephistopheles placates him with a gift: "Hold, take this book. Peruse it thoroughly. / The iterating of these lines brings gold; / The framing of this circle on the ground / Brings whirlwinds, tempests, thunder, and lightning" (2.1.162–65). Still later, when Faustus begins to fret about the prospect of damnation, Lucifer distracts him with the pageant of the Seven Deadly Sins—followed immediately by the presentation of yet another book: "take this book. Peruse it thoroughly, and thou shalt turn thyself into what shape thou wilt" (2.3.171–73). Such moments prove turning points for Doctor Faustus, confirming his present enterprise and banishing the doubts that might lead in another direction. Indeed, the course of his spiritual career may be charted by the nature of the books he reads and by the use he makes of them.

To the extent that Faustus's salvation or damnation depends upon his own moral choices, that spiritual future hinges upon his skill as a reader of religious texts. *The Historie of the damnable life* reports of Faustus, "without doubt he was passing wise, and excellent perfect in the Holy Scriptures."[33] Marlowe's protagonist also peruses Scripture, at least during his opening soliloquy. As a reader he lacks neither learning nor intelligence, but his interpretation of what he reads is affected by supernatural intervention. Late in the B-text of *Doctor Faustus* Mephistopheles gleefully tells him that his earlier reading of the Bible was subtly influenced by the devils: "When thou took'st the book / To view the Scriptures, then I turned the leaves / And led thine eye" (5.2.99–101)—presumably a reference to the verses about sin and its penalty (Romans 6:23 and 1 John 1–8) that Faustus quotes in part during his first soliloquy (1.1.39–47) in both the A- and B-texts. Thus influenced, Faustus focuses on and cites only parts of the biblical passages, emphasizing the force of damnation and omitting the possibility of divine grace.

To the extent that Marlowe's play is informed by Lutheran and Calvinist theology, Faustus's reading of the Bible is even more problematic, for he lacks the grace that might permit him to read Scripture aright and apply what he reads to his own life. If the deity has not singled him out as one of the elect, then, in a sense, Faustus is already consigned to hell and merely awaits the realization of his destiny.[34] The admonitions of the virtuous figures, while insistent, seem contingent on a divine will favoring the redemption of the protagonist, though the play's existence in two forms complicates the issue. In the A-text the Good Angel says, "Never too late, if Faustus can repent" (2.3.79); in the B-text, the Angel says, "if Faustus will repent" (2.3.80). To Eric Rasmussen, "Whereas the B-text asserts that whether or not Faustus repents is purely a matter of his own volition, the A-text perhaps suggests that he may not be able to repent."[35] The A-text, presumably closer to Marlowe's play in its original form,[36] seems more compatible with Calvinist thought: repentance is possible only if God in his wisdom ordains it. Therefore, Faustus's appearance with the Bible in his hand is rich in irony: he possesses the blueprint for achieving eternal life but is unable to translate those plans into the edifice of his own salvation.

We need not, of course, interpret the dramatic action in such unrelentingly pessimistic terms. Marlowe's dramaturgy, especially by its symmetry pitting Good Angel against Bad, the two virtuous Scholars against Valdes and Cornelius, and the Old Man proffering good advice against Mephistopheles proffering the dagger of despair, suggests that Doctor Faustus stands at a moral crossroads, that his is an ongoing choice, that his decisions are genuine, and that they carry real consequences. In the theater Faustus will likely engage an audience more fully if his situation engenders suspense, if we feel that the outcome is in doubt. Without at least the possibility of redemption, the characterization is flattened; Faustus is reduced to the status of an exemplum; and the dramatic tension tends to drain away.

Whether or not we choose to see *Doctor Faustus* as decisively shaped by Calvin's doctrine of double predestination, the protagonist's bargain with the devil represents the play's crucial theatrical event. Interestingly, that contract seems not to have been part of the Faustus story in its original form. Michael Keefer observes, "Conspicuously absent from the accounts of Doctor Faustus written during his lifetime is any suggestion that he had a pact with the devil."[37] Yet the pact became an essential element of the sixteenth-century narrative. The English translation of the German story even reports that the artifact survived Faustus's death: "certainly this letter or obligation was found in his house after his most lamentable end."[38] Martin Luther's conviction that people actually wrote and subscribed to such contracts undoubtedly helped popularize this aspect of the story. More generally, Luther's preoccupation with the written word, building upon Erasmus's scholarship and coinciding with the proliferation of the printing press, helped create an intellectual milieu within which demonic contracts came to seem entirely plausible.

Although Mephistopheles first proposes the pact, asking for "a deed of gift" (2.1.35), Faustus agrees without hesitation, signing it with his own blood. He willingly does so because he sees the contract not as a hindrance to himself but rather a constraint upon Mephistopheles. It is Faustus who writes out the terms of the agreement, specifying the devil's obligations to him:

> Here, Mephistopheles, receive this scroll,
> A deed of gift of body and of soul—
> But yet conditionally that thou perform
> All articles prescribed between us both.
>
> (2.1.89–92)

His eagerness signals his supreme confidence in the efficacy of the written word. And why should he not be confident? His reading allows him to conjure the devil in the first place: "I see there's virtue in my heavenly words" (1.3.28). Those words include the Latin incantation which he has found in a book, presumably the very one he holds on the title page of the 1616 edition when the devil first appears to him. Despite the experience of twenty-four years, Faustus's confidence in writing and books never really flags—until his final moments. Shortly before his death, when Mephistopheles threatens him for speaking of repentance, Doctor Faustus resorts to the written word once again. As before, he does so in order to wrest some advantage from a superhuman power:

> Sweet Mephistopheles, entreat thy lord
> To pardon my unjust presumption,
> And with my blood again I will confirm
> My former vow I made to Lucifer.
>
> (5.1.70–73)

The impulse to sign anew makes sense not only psychologically as the personal proclivity of a scholar, a man for whom the written word is oxygen, but also culturally as the expression of a society increasingly literate, increasingly disposed to value writing as a guide to action, increasingly dependent upon the written word for transactions of all kinds.

The character who writes out, signs, and later confirms a contract with the devil, who by his reading ranges through the accumulated knowledge of his civilization, who pursues magical texts despite the risks, is the same individual who, near his demise, confesses to a scholar, "O, would I had never seen Wittenberg, never read book!" (5.2.20–21); and still seeking some escape from his predicament as the devils advance on him, he proposes, "I'll burn my books" (l. 123). Perhaps no other character on the Renaissance stage expresses more sharply contrasting attitudes toward written materials. He accepts them, examines them, uses them, and finally repudiates them. Those books occupy the center of his secular

The title page of Christopher Marlowe's *Doctor Faustus*, depicting Faustus conjuring the devil. The woodcut first appeared in the 1616 edition. Faustus has a conjurer's wand in one hand, an open book in the other. By permission of The British Library (C.34.d.27).

and spiritual life. Angels and devils alike do battle for his soul by enjoining him to read one or another book. The mighty opposites who play out their struggle in this tragedy's psychomachia are at one only in their common recognition that the written word can have the most profound consequences for one's soul.

5

Although all three plays examined in this chapter were unquestionably popular, they are not exactly typical of the dramatic handling of the written word on the Elizabethan and Jacobean stage. Among Shakespeare's plays the Jack Cade episode in *Henry VI* is virtually unique in treating at such length the social upheaval exacerbated by the printing press and in making the spiritual value of books crucial to an onstage confrontation (between Lord Say and Cade). Among Marlowe's plays *Doctor Faustus* is unique in so specifically dramatizing the importance of the written word to moral conflict.

If You Know Not Me is unusual, too, though the prologue of the 1637 edition, which followed a revival at the Cock-pit, indicates that *If You Know Not Me* received a warm reception from its original audience: it was "receiv'd, as well perform'd at first, / Grac't and frequented, for the cradle age, / Did throng the Seates, the Boxes, and the Stage."[39] Despite its broad appeal, this play is exceptional on the late Elizabethan and early Jacobean stage in so squarely placing the kind of theological contention familiar to Erasmus and Luther at the center of the dramatic action. In making the play an instrument of propaganda, the playwright—probably Thomas Heywood—draws his inspiration from an earlier era of English drama when dramatists enlisted on one side or the other in the wars of truth.

When *If You Know Not Me* was first staged, the drama had long since ceased to focus principally on controversial issues of a theological nature. In fact, Heywood's play might have seemed old-fashioned a generation earlier. "By the 1570s," Paul Whitfield White suggests, "the Word dramatized, as opposed to the Word preached, came under serious attack."[40] During the second half of Elizabeth's reign, "the growing reverence for the Bible as the literal word of God, and the concern that nothing be added or omitted in modern expositions or renditions of original biblical texts"[41] made the stage seem a less appropriate venue for religious indoctrination. By the time Marlowe and Shakespeare began writing for the stage, the nature of the drama had changed: the moral interludes gave way to more secular plays wherein personified abstractions of the kind that appear in *Doctor Faustus* appeared less frequently and wherein worldly concerns increasingly displaced the explicitly religious. Playwrights were also insulated from controversy by the stability of Elizabeth's reign, by the Elizabethan settlement, and by the power that authorities, religious and civic, exercised over the London theaters. The censorship imposed by church and state deflected dramatists from too overtly aligning themselves with one faction or another.[42] Playwrights could and did find ways of commenting on the issues and institutions of their time. My point is simply that such comment was made at their own discretion—and at their own risk. Audiences, for their part, were less interested in polemic than in entertainment, even if their taste was notably didactic by our standards. Freed of an overriding ideological imperative, playwrights could respond variously to the requirements of the stage, employing attitudes toward the written word that had developed over many decades and creating new theatrical uses for books, letters, and documents.

If You Know Not Me and *Doctor Faustus* are also atypical in that most reading on the Elizabethan and Jacobean stage does not involve the scrutiny of words in Scripture or in competing texts. In fact, most reading involves not printed books or handwritten pages, but rather the figurative perusal of other forms of inscription, those manifest in the body and face, the mind and heart. In *Troilus and Cressida,* for instance, when Ulysses watches Cressida kissing the Greeks, we witness figurative rather than literal reading: "There's language in her eye, her cheek, her lip, / Nay, her foot speaks; her wanton spirits look out / At every joint and motive of her body" (4.5.55–57). Ulysses' remark recalls Thomas Wilson's observation that "The gesture of a man, is the speache of his bodie."[43] Later in the same scene of Shakespeare's play, Hector remarks on the language that Achilles sees in him: "O, like a book of sport thou'lt read me o'er; / But there's more in me than thou understand'st. / Why dost thou so oppress me with thine eye?" (ll. 239–41). And in *Titus Andronicus* Marcus beholds the mutilated Lavinia and says, "Thou shalt not sigh, nor hold thy stumps to heaven, / Nor wink, nor nod, nor kneel, nor make a sign, / But I, of these, will wrest an alphabet, / And by still practice learn to know thy meaning" (3.2.42–45). To understand more fully the significance of characters "reading" one another, we must consider more closely figurative language involving writing and print on the stage.

4
Writing and Print as Figurative Language

1

ALTHOUGH such hand properties as books and letters are the most tangible expression of interest in the written word, Renaissance playwrights also use other sorts of writing that do not require conventional ink and paper. Of these none is stranger than the writing that mysteriously appears when Doctor Faustus cuts his arm and tries to sign in blood a contract with the devil. At first the blood congeals, and when Mephistopheles brings a chafer of fire to melt it, the blood configures itself into words. Faustus reacts with consternation: "what is this inscription on mine arm? / '*Homo, fuge!*' Whither should I fly?" (2.1.76–77).[1] Although this may be the most extravagant instance of unusual writing on the stage—blood becomes ink; skin, a surface for writing—Renaissance plays are filled with language likening the body, mind, and soul to written materials.

What is literal in the case of Doctor Faustus becomes figurative elsewhere. Characters talk about themselves and others as though they were tablets, title pages, or books. And characters define their relationship to one another through metaphors of the written word.[2] Although this metaphoric language may seem to promise a direct, immediate form of communication, the reading that ensues becomes problematic, for interpreting a face, body, or mind can prove as uncertain and perilous as interpreting Scripture.

2

Some reading is fairly straightforward: for example, those descriptions of the human face that take the form of comparisons with books. In *King John* Philip of France bids John of England:

> Look here upon thy brother Geffrey's face:
> These eyes, these brows, were moulded out of his;
> This little abstract doth contain that large
> Which died in Geffrey; and the hand of time
> Shall draw this brief into as huge a volume.
>
> (2.1.99–103)

The combination of the words "abstract," "brief," and "volume" suggests that King Philip refers to shorter versions of a large book, for those three words have in common an application to actual letters written on paper or parchment.[3] Since a face is like a book, a change in the flesh represents a changed inscription. The book of the face alters with age, as the Prince of Cyprus suggests in *Soliman and Perseda:* "unmaske thyselfe, that we may see / What warlike wrinckles time has charactered / With ages print upon thy warlike face" (1.4.5–7).[4] "Characters" can, of course, be letters,[5] and "print" has as a principal meaning "to commit (anything) to writing; to express in written words; to inscribe" (*OED*). The conjunction of the words "character" and "print" in *Soliman,* then, suggests the kind of inscription we identify with the written word. Egeon, in *The Comedy of Errors,* speaks of similar writing in the countenance, the consequence of time's passage: "O! grief hath chang'd me since you saw me last, / And careful hours with time's deformed hand / Have written strange defeatures in my face" (5.1.298–300). In *The Honest Whore, Part 2,* however, Hippolito raises the possibility of a disjunction between such inscription and actual reality when he expresses surprise at Orlando's unusually youthful face: "Scarce can I read the Stories on your brow, / Which age hath writ there, you looke youthfull still" (1.2.44–45).[6]

If something is charactered, impressed, or imprinted in the face, then another person may see and interpret what has been marked there. In *The Wounds of Civil War* Granius tells Scilla, "I see imprinted in thy brows / A fortunate, but froward, governance" (2.1.86–87).[7] This remark indicates that qualities of personality and disposition manifest themselves in the face, especially in the brows or forehead. The opponents of Marlowe's Tamburlaine, for instance, see either menace or friendship in his face, depending on his mood: "His lofty brows in folds do figure death, / And in their smoothness amity and life" (2.1.21–22).[8] In *The Two Noble Kinsmen* Emilia says that "Palamon / Has a most menacing aspect, his brow / Is grav'd, and seems to bury what it frowns on" (5.3.44–46). In *Edward II* the king can, simply by looking at another's countenance, recognize the unmistakable harbinger of his own fate: "These looks of thine can harbour nought but death. / I see my tragedy written in thy brows" (5.5.72–73).[9] And in Brome's *A Jovial Crew* Clack, the Justice, boasts, "I have taken a hundred examinations i' my days of felons, and other offenders, out of their very countenances; and wrote 'em down verbatim to what they would have said" (5.1.51–54).[10]

What is written externally expresses what has been written internally, for the mind or heart is itself conceived as a page, tablet, or book. In Chapman's *All Fools* the Notary remarks of certain offenders, "you may set capital letters on their foreheads," a reference to the practice of forcing criminals to wear hats with initials or words specifying the nature of their crimes; Cornelio replies, "What's that to the capital letter that's written in mind?" (4.1.250–51).[11] Hamlet speaks of "the book and volume of my brain" (1.5.103); communication with another person involves disclosing the contents of that internal book. Sometimes the inner book finds instant expression in the outer book without the individual realizing it: Lady Macbeth reproves her husband, "Your face, my thane, is as a book, where men / May read strange matters" (1.5.62–63). And Brutus in *Julius Caesar*, acknowledging the cares betrayed by his face, promises to disclose them fully to Portia: "All my engagements I will construe to thee, / All the charactery of my sad brows" (2.1.307–8).

To acquire knowledge of another person entails making a new inscription within one's own internal book; and that inscription, in turn, may be perused by other people. In *Coriolanus* Menenius explains that Coriolanus's benevolence towards him is recorded in his heart, which others may read:

> I tell thee, fellow,
> Thy general is my lover. I have been
> The book of his good acts, whence men have read
> His fame unparallel'd, happily amplified.
>
> (5.2.13–16)

The Volscian sentries to whom Menenius speaks, however, adopt a skeptical, even hostile, attitude toward his claim, for they cannot easily read his "book." In *Chabot, Admiral of France* the king professes the sincerity of his respect for the admiral by this description of the royal body following death:

> dissect me then,
> And in my heart, the world shall read thee living,
> And by the vertue of thy name writ there,
> That part of me shall never putrifie,
> When I am lost in all my other dust.
>
> (5.3.101–5)[12]

The extraordinary nature of this self-description is intended to reassure Chabot, who has reason to doubt the king's good will toward him. In

Dekker's *The Virgin Martyr* Theophilus pesters Macrinus for information about a friend, information that remains hidden to the speaker: "thou art the Manuscript / Where *Antoninus* writes downe all his secrets" (2.2.14–15).[13] What these speakers have in common is the notion that self-disclosure takes the form of figurative writing in the confidant's book, a writing that may remain obscure to other observers. Of course, even when such writing occurs, it does not always signify a communion of spirit. Thus in *Richard III* Richard, Duke of Gloucester, professes shock at the execution of Lord Hastings, a man to whom Richard claims to have confided his innermost thoughts: "I took him for the plainest harmless creature / That breath'd upon the earth a Christian; / Made him my book, wherein my soul recorded / The history of all her secret thoughts" (3.5.25–28).

In *Twelfth Night* Duke Orsino, revealing his deepest feelings, adopts the image of clasps, used to protect a book by keeping the pages pressed together (and sometimes locked): "Cesario, / Thou know'st no less but all. I have unclasp'd / To thee the book even of my secret soul" (1.4.12–14). Orsino's remark suggests that what may be revealed may also be withheld. Hence the frustration of the heroine in *Soliman and Perseda:* "If heavens were just, men should have open brests, / That we therein might read their guilefull thoughts" (2.1.124–25).[14] In *The Honest Whore, Part 2* Orlando expresses surprise by asking, "Is't possible the Lord *Hipollito*, whose face is as civill as the outside of a Dedicatory Booke, should be a Mutton-munger?" (2.1.254–56). And in Jonson's *Catiline* Cicero feels the anxiety of one forced to guess what others think: "let it be writ in each man's forehead / What thoughts he bears the public" (4.2.375–76).[15] By their remarks all of these characters register the difficulty of seeing clearly that which in inscribed in the observed but which remains somehow inaccessible to the observer.

Some people are considerably more successful at such reading than others. For instance, in *The Conspiracy of Charles, Duke of Byron,* Savoy compliments King Henry for interpreting the true nature of an impious nobleman: "those strange characters writ in his face, / Which at first sight were hard for me to read, / The doctrine of your speech hath made so plain / That I run through them like my natural language" (1.1.170–73).[16] In Webster's *Appius and Virginia,* what is written within another functions as the means whereby Icilius comes to understand himself: "You give me (noble Lord) that character / Which I cood never yet read in my selfe" (1.2.7–8).[17] To discern another's intentions—to read face, mind, heart—may require particular application, as Lady Frampul indicates in Jonson's *The New Inn:* "One woman reads another's character / Without the tedious trouble of deciphering / If she but give her mind to't"

(4.4.301–3).[18] The task of discernment, however, can prove daunting. In Dekker's *The Noble Spanish Soldier,* Medina tells the king:

> Mine eyes have lost th'acquaintance of your face
> So long, and I so (little) late read o're
> That Index of the royall booke your mind,
> That scarce (without your Comment) can I tell
> When in those leaves you turne o're smiles or frownes.
>
> (5.4.4–8)[19]

In *The Honest Whore, Part 2*, the language of printing is used to express a combination of frustration and foreboding when Hippolito tells his wife:

> I read
> Strange Comments in those margines of your lookes:
> Your cheekes of late are (like bad printed Bookes)
> So dimly charactred, I scarce can spell,
> One line of love in them. Sure all's not well.
>
> (3.1.127–31)

At times appearance simply defeats the enterprise of discernment; as a character in R. A.'s *The Valiant Welshman* observes, "Tis true, that heathen Sages have affirmed, / That Natures tablet fixt within our looke, / Gives scope to reade our hearts, as in a booke. / Yet this affirmative not alwayes holds" (2.1.14–17).[20]

If the mind is a book inscribed with thoughts, then a perspicacious individual may, at least in theory, bypass the face and directly discern the psyche, ensuring the accuracy of one's knowledge: this constitutes mind reading. In *Westward Ho,* the Earl suggests that the mind is a truer book than the countenance when he tells a woman he has misjudged: "henceforth the booke / Ile read shall be thy mind, and not thy looke" (4.2.165–66).[21] Such reading, however, can prove difficult. Othello claims that an Egyptian, who gave his mother a certain handkerchief, "could almost read / The thoughts of people" (3.4.57–58), but his phraseology implies that even this mysterious Egyptian was not fully successful. In *The Wounds of Civil War,* a disgruntled Scilla, eager to be named Dictator for life but offered a term of unspecified duration, tells the people of Rome that they have misjudged his intention: "No, citizens, who readeth Scilla's mind / Must form my titles in another kind" (5.5.41–42).

Just as the faculty of understanding may be described in terms of a book, so too may the faculty of memory, which consists of reading what has been written in the mind or heart. Erasmus observes, "we have true knowlage & perfecte intelligence, onely of suche thynges as we have suerly enprinted & engraven in our memorie."[22] The reading of such writing may prove vexing, however, precisely because it is so accessible: Pausanias, in *The Wounds of Civil War*, explains his melancholy by saying, "age hath printed in my thoughts / A memory of many troubles past" (2.2.79–80). Similarly, the Old Man in *Macbeth* contemplates the past as though it were a book recording unfortunate occurrences: "Threescore and ten I can remember well, / Within the volume of which time I have seen / Hours dreadful and things strange" (2.4.1–3). Of course, that which is remembered need not be unpleasant, for in the same play Macbeth assures his comrades, "Kind gentlemen, your pains / Are regist'red where every day I turn / The leaf to read them" (1.3.150–52). But memory has its perils, for deeds once inscribed in the mind persist; they may be difficult, if not impossible, to expunge. Macbeth's words to the Doctor suggest the capacity of memory to afflict the present: "Canst thou not minister to a mind diseas'd, / Pluck from the memory a rooted sorrow, / Raze out the written troubles of the brain?" (5.3.40–42). The very act of remembering can harbor a threat to other people as well: Richard Plantagenet in *1 Henry VI* warns Somerset, "I'll note you in my book of memory, / To scourge you for this apprehension" (2.4.101–2).

As an internal activity, memory duplicates ordinary practice. That is, people, motivated by a desire to remember the prized action of another, customarily write things down. Such writing may be figurative rather than literal, though when in *The Conspiracy of Charles Duke of Byron* the protagonist pledges loyalty to the king by predicting his own future as set down in a history book, he perhaps blurs the distinction between the two kinds of writing: "I will see / That all your chronicles be filled with me" (5.1.137–38). In *The Virgin Martyr* the saintly Dorothea expresses her gratitude to the angelic Angelo by referring to writing that is presumably figurative: "In golden letters downe ile set that day / Which gave thee to me" (2.1.191–92). Whether literal or figurative, written records may express not only an individual's opinion but also a society's collective judgment. And that judgment, rendered in words and publicly displayed, has the power to shape conduct. In *2 Tamburlaine* Callapine imagines the prospect of defeating his Scythian adversary and thereby redeeming his family's reputation. In the event of victory, he says, "all the world should blot our dignities / Out of the book of base-born infamies" (3.1.19–20).

The history recorded in words, however, may intimidate as well as exalt. So powerful is the prospect of recording virtue or villainy that future writing, merely imagined in the present, may determine a person's behavior. Hence Volumnia's appeal to Coriolanus:

> Thou know'st, great son,
> The end of war's uncertain; but this certain,

> That, if thou conquer Rome, the benefit
> Which thou shalt thereby reap is such a name
> Whose repetition will be dogg'd with curses;
> Whose chronicle thus writ: "The man was noble,
> But with his last attempt he wip'd it out,
> Destroy'd his country, and his name remains
> To th' ensuing age abhorr'd."
>
> (5.3.140–48)

Moved by this appeal, Coriolanus relents, preserving Rome but sacrificing his own spirit as well as his new allies. The Duke in *The Revenger's Tragedy* frets about the damage wrought by the Duchess's youngest son, who has "Thrown ink upon the forehead of our state, / Which envious spirits will dip their pens into / After our death, and blot us in our tombs" (1.2.4–6).[23] So concerned is the Duke by the possibility of some unfavorable chronicle being writ in the future that he requires the young man to submit to the rigor of the law. Nothing less than the son's death can forestall that anticipated writing and subsequent reading.

Figurative writing, preserving noble deeds in the memory, can provide a model for others' behavior. Lady Hotspur says of her dead husband: "He was the mark and glass, copy and book, / That fashion'd others" (*2 Henry IV*, 2.3.31–32). Here the speaker envisions Hotspur's military prowess. Similarly, in *The Noble Spanish Soldier,* Medina reports of a warrior, "I have seene this man / Write in the field such stories with his sword, / That our best Chieftaines swore there was in him / As 'twere a new Philosophy of fighting" (4.1.47–50). In *Antony and Cleopatra*, Decretas says of Antony's death, "that self hand / Which writ his honor in the acts it did / Hath, with the courage which the heart did lend it, / Splitted the heart" (5.1.21–24). Reading such writing, however, can be a formidable task, especially when that writing describes private behavior rather than public deeds. When a puzzled Desdemona asks, "what ignorant sin have I committed?" Othello answers, "Was this fair paper, this most goodly book, / Made to write 'whore' upon?" (4.2.70–72). The irony here, of course, is that Desdemona is just as innocent as she claims to be; Othello completely misreads the writing in front of him. Another kind of misreading is the subject of Hal's pledge to the chief justice in *2 Henry IV*—that he will "rase out / Rotten opinion, who hath writ me down / After my seeming" (5.2.127–29). Earlier in this play Hal concedes his still unsavory reputation to Poins: "thou thinkest me as far in the devil's book as thou and Falstaff" (2.2.45–46). The audience knows what Hal knows but what Poins and others apparently do not—that the disparaging judgments of the Prince represent misreading on a massive scale.

To the extent that they are about reading and writing, the plays cited above dramatize the difficulty of interpreting figurative inscriptions accurately: present intentions and past actions are routinely misread and misunderstood; characters experience a discrepancy between, on the one hand, what they believe to be actuality, and, on the other, what seems to be recorded in mind or flesh.

3

All the language of writing and reading we have examined may be termed metaphoric in that it conjoins apparently unrelated elements. According to Aristotle's *Poetics,* "Metaphor is the application of the name of a thing to something else."[24] Renaissance discussions of metaphor are often predicated on the meaning of the word in Greek—to carry over.[25] George Puttenham, in *The Arte of English Poesie,* asks, "what els is your *Metaphor* but an inversion of sence by transport."[26] Or, as Erasmus remarks of metaphor, "the Latin term is *translatio* 'transference,' so called because a word is transferred away from its real and proper signification to one which lies outside its proper sphere" (*CWE* 24:333).[27] Terence Hawkes provides the modern counterpart when he defines metaphor: "It refers to a particular set of linguistic processes whereby aspects of one object are 'carried over' or transferred to another object, so that the second object is spoken of as if it were the first."[28] What modern understandings have in common is the conviction that metaphor is fundamental to the way that language and the human mind work. Recent studies suggest that metaphor participates in the instability and variability of language itself and that a simple definition of metaphor is virtually impossible to achieve.

Renaissance formulations of metaphor, while perhaps not so subtle as the modern, nevertheless have much to tell us about metaphor, especially those metaphors involving the written word in sixteenth-century culture. Among these a painting known as "The Librarian" (ca. 1566) seems to provide a graphic counterpart of the metaphors that we have been considering in Renaissance plays. The painting was made by Giuseppe Arcimboldo (1527–93), who worked for Rudolf II in Prague and for Ferdinand I and Maximilian II in Vienna, the same Maximilian whom Sir Philip Sidney salutes at the beginning of *An Apology for Poetry.* Arcimboldo's painting depicts the torso and head of a man, and it does so entirely by means of books and their accouterments: the upper body, shoulder, and arm by large folios, bound in leather and stamped with gold, piled one atop another; the fingers of a hand by bookmarks; the face by additional books; the hair by the pages of a book lying open; the ear by a ribbon

A painting known as "The Librarian" (ca. 1566) by Giuseppe Arcimboldo (1527–93). The torso and head of the subject are depicted entirely by means of books and their accouterments. By permission of Statens Konstmuseer, Stockholm.

used for tying the covers of a book closed; the moustache and beard by marten-tails, used for dusting books; the eyes by lenses.

Arcimboldo is celebrated for such composite heads, constructed, in other paintings, of flowers, fruits, vegetables, animals, and creatures of the sea. For Roland Barthes such paintings display "The triumphant reign of metaphor: all is metaphor in Arcimboldo. Nothing is ever *denoted*, since the features (lines, forms, whorls) that go to make up a head *already* have a meaning, and this meaning is diverted toward another meaning, in some way thrown beyond itself."[29] Although Arcimboldo's designs are commonly regarded as playful, fanciful, even fantastic, they are based upon a profound understanding of the created world: that the various levels of existence correspond to one another, that analogies exist between the macrocosm of the world and the microcosm of man, that the affinities constitute an essential unity underlying multiplicity, and that, as Montaigne observes, "There is a wonderful relation and correspondence in this universal government of the works of nature, which well shows that it is neither accidental nor conducted by divers masters."[30] Arcimboldo's constructions are, Roland Barthes observes, "not simple observations of affinities," for the paintings "undo familiar objects to produce strange, new ones."[31] Still, Arcimboldo's portraits imply connections between seemingly different things. Specifically, "The Librarian" seems predicated on the notion that writing appears not only on the printed page but also in the lineaments of the face, the operations of the mind, and, by extension perhaps, the very frame of the cosmos.

Such ideas have long been a part of European culture. They can be traced back at least as far as Greek civilization. Plato's account of creation in his *Timaeus,* for instance, contains this discussion of words and things:

> the world is the fairest of all things that have come into being and he [the maker] is the best of causes. That being so, it must have been constructed on the pattern of what is apprehensible by reason and understanding and eternally unchanging; from which again it follows that the world is a likeness of something else. Now it is always most important to begin at the proper place; and therefore we must lay it down that the words in which likeness and pattern are described will be of the same order as that which they describe.[32]

Judaism, too, came to accept the relationship of words and natural objects, affirming the concept of a deity who shapes creation by his very words (Genesis 1). As Godfrey Goodman observes, "God speaking the Word, all things were made: God speaks to nothing, and by vertue of his words, behold a Creation."[33] And for Christians the incarnation of God translates word into flesh: "And the Worde was made flesh, and dwelt among us" (John 1:14). Since God's word takes natural form, that word preserves something of its original essence as word. The relationship of words and things is not arbitrary; words are not what they may be for a modern semiotician—culturally constructed signs. In the Renaissance this notion led Paracelsus to say that "The art of signs teaches us to give each man his true name in accordance with his innate nature. A wolf must not be called a sheep, a dove must not be called a fox; each being should be given the name that belongs to its essence."[34] Similarly, Francis Bacon observes that a true understanding of nature is impeded when words and things fail to correspond: "The idols imposed by words on the understanding are of two kinds. They are either names of things which do not exist . . . or they are names of things which exist, but yet confused and ill-defined, and hastily and irregularly derived from realities."[35]

Sir Thomas Browne more explicitly describes the writing immanent in the created world: "The finger of God hath left an inscription upon all his workes, not graphicall or composed of Letters, but of their severall formes, constitutions, parts, and operations, which aptly joyned together doe make one word that doth express their natures. By these Letters God cals the Starres by their names, and by this Alphabet *Adam* assigned to every creature a name peculiar to its Nature."[36] Browne continues, applying writing to human flesh, "there are besides these Characters in our faces, certaine mysticall figures in our hands." This conviction led to the science of chiromancy, which posits the existence of signs in the human hand, especially the palm; from the study of such signs, it was believed that one could determine not only a person's inclination but also his or her future. Thus in *A Warning for Fair Women,* Mistress Drury examines the hand of a fretful Anne Sanders, saying, "I see disciphered, / Within this palme of yours . . ., / Faire signes of better fortune to ensue" (ll. 675–77).[37] Signs capable of interpretation are also found in the face and head; hence the science of physiognomy, which reveals, according to Paracelsus, "in what relation his heart stands to God and his neighbour, what eyes are those of a rogue and what eyes are not, which tongue is cunning and which is not, which ears are open to evil and which to good."[38] This notion finds frequent expression on the stage. In Jonson's *Every Man in His Humour,* for example, Edward Knowell tells Stephen, "Come, wrong not the quality of your desert with looking downward, cos; but hold up your head, so; and let the Idea of what you are be portray'd i' your face, that men may reade i' your physnomy, 'Here, within this place, is to be seen the true, rare, and accomplished monster—or miracle—of nature' (which is all one)" (1.3.104–9).[39] In addition to hands and faces, the shape of the body and the gestures of an individual were also the subject of scrutiny. Collectively, all of these were thought to provide a reasonably complete knowledge of a person's interior life.

Given a belief in a world of signs that could be rendered in words, it was inevitable that writers should be concerned with the particular meanings inherent in objects, whether animals, plants, body parts, or other natural materials. To ascertain those meanings aright, it was important to assign the proper word to the object. In the beginning, Louis LeRoy suggests, people more successfully applied names to things: "the first which imposed names on things, having no other of whom they might learne them, did miraculously learne them in that tongue, wherein the nature, and trueth of things agreed with their originals, and Etimologies: which men even to this present have endeavoured to seeke in all tongues, in the significations of words."[40] In time, though, languages drift from the things signified; as a result an attempt to decipher the inscriptions produced by earlier cultures may be met with defeat. Leon Battista Alberti, contrasting Egyptian writing in the form of hieroglyphs with the more recent language spoken and written by the forebears of the Romans, laments: "we have seen sepulchers uncovered in city ruins and cemeteries throughout Etruria inscribed with an alaphabet universally acknowledged to be Etruscan; their letters look not unlike Greek, or even Latin, yet no one understands what they mean. The same, the Egyptians claimed, would happen to all other alphabets, whereas the method of writing they used could be understood easily by expert men all over the world."[41]

Ideally, to study words is to learn about things, and to study the things represented by words is to learn about their maker-author, for those things which preserve their origin in words may be read and interpreted. An incident in *Cymbeline* suggests that divinity actually invites such reading. Jupiter places a tablet on the chest of Posthumus, who awakes in consternation to discover this writing on it: "When as a lion's whelp shall, to himself unknown, without seeking find, and be embrace'd by a piece of tender air; and when from a stately cedar shall be lopp'd branches, which, being dead many years, shall after revive, be jointed to the old stock, and freshly grow; then shall Posthumus end his miseries, Britain be fortunate and flourish in peace and plenty" (5.5.435–42). Although Posthumus is unable to decipher the meaning, he has the good sense to summon a soothsayer, who interprets the oracle successfully by paying close attention to those things that the words stand for:

> Thou, Leonatus, art the lion's whelp;
> The fit and apt construction of thy name,
> Being *Leo-natus,* doth import so much.
> [*To Cymbeline.*] The piece of tender air, thy
>   virtuous daughter,
> Which we call *mollis aer,* and *mollis aer*
> We term it *mulier;* [*to Postumus*] which *mulier* I

> divine
> Is this most constant wife, who, even now,
> Answering the letter of the oracle,
> Unknown to you, unsought, were clipt about
> With this most tender air.
>
> (5.5.443–52)

Jane Donawerth comments: "the soothsayer in *Cymbeline* interprets the oracle—and unravels the confusions of the fable—by explaining the connection between words and reality, between the 'lion's whelp' and Leonatus, between the metaphorical 'cedar' and Cymbeline, and between the Latin word '*mulier*' and Imogen's tender loyalty. . . . Words that to others appeared nonsense are, to the soothsayer, connected to the workings of the world by a certain and profound link."[42]

That profound link implies not only a parallel between writing in the world at large and in the little world of man but also an influence of the one upon the other, as Tamburlaine indicates when he looks at his adversary Theridimas and asks:

> Art thou but captain of a thousand horse,
> That by characters graven in thy brows,
> And by thy martial face and stout aspect,
> Deservest to have the leading of an host?
>
> (1.2.167–70)

Tamburlaine's speech suggests that writing in the face is owing to the writing in the heavens, that the Persian warrior is the beneficiary of celestial influence, for the word "aspect" can mean "favourable astrological conjunction"[43] as well as "expression of countenance" (*OED*); and "character" can denote "the astrological symbol of a planet" as well as a person's "face or features" (*OED*). Tamburlaine's description, then, unites earthly flesh with heavenly firmament, a correlation that constitutes the very basis of astrology.

If celestial writing exerts an effect on the mundane world, the ambitious individual may seek access to that writing. In *Doctor Faustus* Wagner, speaking as chorus at the beginning of act 3, reports that "Learnèd Faustus, / To know the secrets of astronomy / Graven in the book of Jove's high firmament" (ll. 1–3), rides off to the heavens for a firsthand look. What motivates Faustus is not merely intellectual curiosity but also the prospect of exercising power. Writing—of whatever kind—presents a field of opportunity to those who know how to read and who have the boldness to capitalize on what they learn. The illiterate person, accordingly, easily imagines that a literate individual has access to a world of extraordinary possibilities. In Marlowe's play, when Robin filches "one of Doctor Faustus' conjuring books" (2.2.1–2), he lords it over Dick; in the B-text he says, "Keep further from me, O thou illiterate and unlearned ostler" (2.2.9–10). In this comic episode Robin manages to summon Mephistopheles (3.2.25–28), thereby demonstrating the capacity of words to effect momentous change, no matter how humble the reader or speaker. The tragic counterpart of Robin's conjuring is that of Faustus himself, when he uses words signifying the deity and saints, thereby tapping into the power immanent in those words:

> Within this circle is Jehovah's name,
> Forward and backward anagrammatised,
> The breviated names of holy saints,
> Figures of every adjunct to the heavens,
> And characters of signs and erring stars,
> By which the spirits are enforced to rise.
>
> (1.3.8–13)

The title page of the second quarto (1616), along with subsequent reprints, depicts Faustus just after he utters these words: in the woodcut he stands within a magic circle "inscribed with anagrams of Jehovah's name, figures of the heavens, characters of signs and planets."[44] He has a conjurer's wand in one hand and an open book in the other; behind him on the wall is an armillary sphere and a shelf holding three volumes; in front of Faustus is the devil he has summoned. By placing a book in Faustus's hands, Marlowe signals that although this magician is a daring iconoclast, his power is based upon a world of correspondences and influences, upon writing throughout the cosmos, so widely understood that its workings have been collected, recorded, and disseminated through books.

That realm of correspondences, so tantalizing in the power it seems to offer, can also prove a source of frustration when efforts at decipherment are stymied by hearts and minds that guard their secrets, by a natural world that proves opaque to the observer, and by heavenly forces that remain stubbornly inscrutable. Unsuccessful efforts to read the world can even lead an individual to question the very assumptions underlying the metaphoric language we have examined.

Suppose the recourse to that language represents not so much confidence in the capacity to understand as merely the desire to locate some meaning. Suppose the desire to find coherence in a world of discrete and disparate things cannot be satisfied. Suppose that assumptions about the connection between words and things are seen as resting upon a dubious foundation. And, further, suppose that the ability of language to represent reality were itself questioned. We might then in the Renaissance confront the skepticism expressed in our own time by Jacques Derrida:

If, for Aristotle, . . . "spoken words . . . are the symbols of mental experience . . . and written words are the symbols of spoken words" (*De interpretatione,* 1, 16a 3) it is because the voice, producer of *the first symbols,* has a relationship of essential and immediate proximity with the mind. Producer of the first signifier, it is not just a simple signifier among others. It signifies "mental experiences" which themselves reflect or mirror things by natural resemblance. Between being and mind, things and feelings, there would be a relationship of translation or natural signification: between mind and logos, a relationship of conventional symbolization. And the *first* convention, which would relate immediately to the order of natural and universal signification, would be produced as spoken language. Written language would establish the conventions, interlinking other conventions with them.[45]

For Derrida and many others today, no necessary connection exists between language and what it purports to represent. Summarizing Derrida's argument, S. K. Heninger observes, "There is no objective reality, no *logos,* to act as a signified motivating signifiers. There is no transcendental signified."[46]

Although the contemporaries of Erasmus and Luther, of Marlowe and Shakespeare, may not voice the counterpart of modern agnosticism, Renaissance writers sometimes express doubt about the relationship of words and things. For instance, Richard Mulcaster, reflecting on the development of a written language in antiquity, says: "The letters being thus found out, to serve a nedefull turn took the force of expressing everie distinct *sound* in voice, not by them selves or anie vertew in their form (for what likenesse or what affinitie hath the form of anie letter in his own natur, to answer the force or sound in mans voice?) but onelie by consent of those men, which first invented them, and the pretie use therof perceaved by those, which first did receive them."[47] Similarly, Montaigne writes: "There is the name and the thing. The name is a sound which designates and signifies the thing; the name is not a part of the thing or of the substance, it is an extraneous piece attached to the thing, and outside of it."[48]

What Mulcaster and Montaigne assert of literal words may usefully be extended to figurative words as well: the language of Renaissance drama may apply to either literal or figurative experience. For example, the word "read," which at least hints at, if it does not denote, the perusal of actual written words, may refer to almost any kind of discernment, depending on the context.[49] If literal writing cannot offer the certainty attendant on a correspondence immanent in things and the words that represent those things, then why should figurative writing be any less problematic? No wonder so much of the figurative reading that we have examined in Renaissance plays is fraught with difficulty. The connection between the figurative inscription of a face and the disposition of a mind or heart may be no more secure than the connection between a written word and the phenomenon it means to represent.

4

Whether it culminates in enlightenment or bewilderment, the impulse that animates the metaphoric language of writing and printing in Renaissance drama manifests itself particularly when actual written materials appear onstage. Consider their conjunction in Marlowe's *Edward II*, when the barons and clergy, intent on banishing the royal favorite, confront the king. They demand that Edward "subscribe" the document exiling Gaveston; and, having no choice, the king accedes. But as he does so, he says, "Instead of ink, I'll write it with my tears" (1.4.86). Presumably, Edward does not mean this literally even though he is temperamentally histrionic; rather, his language is meant to convey his grief. In itself, the conceit is both explicable and appropriate. It gains additional force, however, because of the theatrical context: he has a paper before him and, probably, a quill pen. So smooth is the transition from literal to figurative writing that it feels almost inevitable. There is nothing contrived or jarring about the idea of Edward writing with tears. The character's language combines with the physical object—the paper—to give an ordinary action (the signing of a document) an extraordinary charge.

The figurative language that accompanies a theatrical property sometimes takes the form of a metaphoric book. A scene in George Peele's *King Edward I* is illustrative. There a character brings "letters" (probably a single letter) to Lluellen, who learns that his beloved Elinor has been taken captive and who resolves to free her at any cost: "To armes true *Britaines* sprong of *Trojans* seede. / And with your swordes write in the booke of Time, / Your *Brittish* names in Characters of bloud" (ll. 657–59).[50] The relationship between the hand property (the letter brought to Lluellen) and the figurative book (the book of time) is not arbitrary. That is, the use of the one fosters use of the other; the presence of an actual letter seems to engender thinking about a metaphoric book. Here, as elsewhere in drama, characters tend to invoke metaphoric books when they are confronted by ink and paper. In this instance one sort of writing (the metaphoric) is intended to take the place of or compensate for the other (the writing in the letter). Lluellen's military exploits will, in effect, create the metaphoric writing that he envisions.

Another such conjunction of theatrical property and metaphoric book occurs in Shakespeare's *2 Henry IV* when the crown confronts the rebels near Gaultree Forest. In this emotionally charged scene Westmoreland, the king's representative, berates the archbishop of York for choosing the tented field over his customary life of study and preaching:

> Wherefore do you so ill translate yourself
> Out of the speech of peace that bears such grace,
> Into the harsh and boist'rous tongue of war?
> Turning your books to graves, your ink to blood,
> Your pens to lances, and your tongue divine
> To a loud trumpet and a point of war?
>
> (4.1.47–52)

As Westmoreland sees it, York exchanges a world of words for one of deeds. Instead of explicating the book of God's word, this clergyman now prepares for combat. In reply York represents himself as occupying a point at the fulcrum of contemplation and action. Having turned from one to the other, he is now prepared to change back: the rebels have prepared "the summary of all our griefs / (When time shall serve) to show in articles" (ll. 73–74). He is willing to allow a battalion of words to take the place of soldiers. And, in any event, York explains, his call to arms is anything but arbitrary. It is a prudent response to "The dangers of the days but newly gone, / Whose memory is written on the earth / With yet appearing blood" (ll. 80–82). What he seeks now is to rectify past injustices and ensure his own future. In answer Westmoreland preserves the metaphor of writing but changes the figure so that it reflects his contempt for the archbishop's action:

> What peer hath been suborn'd to grate on you?
> That you should seal this lawless bloody book
> Of forg'd rebellion with a seal divine.
>
> (ll. 90–92)

This language—the book of rebellion—not only captures the calculation and threatened violence of the archbishop's campaign but also complements the list of grievances which York has just spoken of and which is formally handed over only moments later ("take, my Lord of Westmerland, this schedule" [l. 166]).

Metaphoric books of the kind invoked by Westmoreland and Lluellen may be envisioned as possessing the characteristics of actual books—pages, cover, margins—without being subject to their material limitations. These metaphoric books are imaginative artifacts, emulating the format of conventional books but without their tactile three-dimensionality. They are, paradoxically, both easily recognizable and highly individualized. They are recognizable as conceptual formulations that appear with some frequency in literature and, presumably, in everyday conversation. They are individualized in that a particular metaphoric book varies from one person to another; in each instance that book exists as a unique composite, constructed out of the individual's reading and experience. What Michel Foucault has said of actual books is relevant here: "The frontiers of a book are never clear-cut: beyond the title, the first lines, and the last full stop, beyond its internal configuration and its autonomous form, it is caught up in a system of references to other books, other texts, other sentences: it is a node within a network."[51] If this is true of books printed with ink on paper, it is even more true of metaphoric books, which exist in the mind.

Metaphoric books, while long a feature of European culture, enjoyed an extraordinary efflorescence in the Renaissance, and for reasons that are not difficult to conjecture. The intense preoccupation with the written word, proceeding from the work of Lorenzo Valla, Erasmus, and their successors, enhanced the status of books as guides to salvation, sources of knowledge, and models of aesthetic excellence. The Reformation, moreover, gave reading an urgency that it had not previously possessed: people were encouraged not merely to read but also to apply what they read to their lives. The invention of the printing press made books available in such vast quantities that even people of modest means could own and peruse them at home. The experience of personal private reading (as opposed to participating in the written word as an auditor in a group) intensified the impact of books, which could now more easily be read and re-read, discussed and debated. As people turned increasingly to the written and printed word for instruction and inspiration, conduct books became popular; and early in the seventeenth century people read "characters" to learn the essence of various walks of life, which were to be either emulated or avoided, depending upon their moral content. It was natural that such a culture would increasingly conceive of experience in terms of books, that people would speak about their lives in language inspired by the print shop, library, or study. In this conflation of experience and technology, metaphors of reading and writing gained prominence.

The more people read, the more they require ways of accommodating their reading. Every encounter with the written word, after all, invites an adjustment with words already read. As Robert Scholes observes, "Reading consists of bringing texts together. It is a constructive activity, a kind of writing."[52] That "writing," on a conceptual level, may take the form of metaphors, which provide a means of putting reading in a context conducive to assimilation. George Lakoff and Mark Turner point out that "Metaphorical understanding is not a matter of mere word play; it is endemically conceptual in nature. It is indispensable to comprehending and reasoning about concepts like life, death, and time."[53] The more profound the concept, the more urgently it demands metaphoric expression. And the bookishness of Renaissance culture provided a ready language for that expression.

Metaphoric books allow people to accommodate even experience not directly dependent on the written or printed word. Suzanne Langer notes that "Metaphor is our most striking evidence of *abstractive seeing,* of the power of human minds to use presentational symbols. Every new experience, or new idea about things, evokes first of all some metaphorical expression. As the idea becomes familiar, this expression 'fades' to a new literal use of the once metaphorical predicate, a more general use than it had before."[54] Metaphors in general, then, and metaphoric books in particular allow people to organize conceptually the diversity and unruliness of everyday life, accommodating it within the form of a familiar artifact. Metaphors help make comprehensible the welter of sensory information that bombards the mind. In the words of John Middleton Murry, "metaphor appears as the instinctive and necessary act of the mind exploring reality and ordering experience. It is the means by which the less familiar is assimilated to the more familiar, the unknown to the known."[55]

Not every hand property or verbal image involving writing is necessarily related to a metaphoric book. Some books, letters, documents may have a function limited to the mechanical demands of a plot. Nevertheless, theatrical properties and figurative language involving writing frequently have a significance that transcends the immediate requirements of the action. That is, properties and verbal images are akin to those characters and incidents in Renaissance plays that point beyond themselves to some other meaning. An Elizabethan audience would easily recognize the symbolism of the unnamed Old Man who proffers good advice to Doctor Faustus or of the Mower who looms behind the dejected king in *Edward II.* Similarly, a Jacobean audience would recognize, as a modern audience may not, the symbolism of consigning Kent to the stocks in *King Lear* or of the dancing madmen in *The Duchess of Malfi.* Inanimate objects involving writing convey no less meaning to an audience accustomed to seeing a symbolic application in the written word. Through their evocation of metaphoric books, playwrights endow actual books, letters, and documents with an extra dimension. By understanding the significance of metaphoric books, we can better appreciate the handling of particular properties. Activities onstage that may seem improbable or inexplicable take on additional meaning; apparently casual details of staging are revealed as symbolic. Language that may seem ordinary gains added force as we recognize the metaphoric book that lies behind the image. If metaphoric books do not assume palpable form, they enjoy an existence in the minds of theatrical characters and audiences alike.

Part Three

5
The Book of Conscience

1

ALTHOUGH the penchant for likening spiritual life to a book reached its apogee in English theology of the seventeenth century, writing and morality had been allied for millennia. In ancient cultures laws were typically inscribed on clay, stone, or bronze: Hammurabi's code in Mesopotamia, Solon's laws in Greece, the Twelve Tables in Rome. The Ten Commandments that Moses brought down from Mount Sinai were presumably written in stone and displayed to the Israelites. Scripture, in the form of the Old Testament, presented a history of God's people with their experience of divine judgment. Christians, while insisting on the primacy of spirit over word, nevertheless committed their experience of Christ to the written form of the Gospels. And St. Paul addressed Christian communities of the Mediterranean by writing letters as well as by preaching. Whether civic or spiritual, all such records and guidelines for behavior in antiquity had a social character: that is, the precepts were intended to be read by or to individuals, who were answerable to their fellow citizens or believers as well as to their deity. As Christianity evolved in the Middle Ages, this corporate dimension persisted, especially in the sacrament of penance: sins were confessed to a priest who, in keeping with the precedent of church teaching, assigned a penalty.

With the Reformation, however, a change with far-reaching implications occurred. Theologians increasingly conceived of moral law as something private rather than public, as the province of the individual rather than of society at large. A single incident illustrates the shift: Martin Luther's appearance at the imperial Diet of Worms, where he was ordered to defend or renounce his opinions. Luther adamantly refused to recant. Both he and his interrogator acknowledged Scripture, but Luther was unwilling to submit his interpretation of Scripture to the approval of other men. He told Johann Eck, chancellor of the archbishop of Trier, "Unless I am convinced by the testimony of the Scriptures or by clear reason . . . I am bound by the Scriptures I have quoted and my conscience is captive to the Word of God. I cannot and I will not retract anything, since it is neither safe nor right to go against conscience" (*LW* 32:112).¹ For Luther the path to salvation did not lie in adherence to the published laws of the church or in obedience to clerical authority. Instead, salvation was to be found in fidelity to his own conscience. A design by Peter Visscher the Younger, dated 1524, illustrates the primacy of conscience for the German reformer: Luther grasps the arm of personified Conscience, from whose wrist a manacle hangs; and he leads Conscience, together with Juventus and Plebes, toward Christ, visible in the distance.²

For Luther and the other reformers, conscience represents the site where law is recorded, understood, and applied—in short, where moral judgments are made. According to Luther, "conscience is not the power to do works, but to judge them. The proper work of conscience (as Paul says in Romans 2 [:15]), is to accuse or excuse, to make guilty or guiltless, uncertain or certain. Its purpose is not to do, but to pass judgment on what has been done and what should be done . . ." (*LW* 44:298). Similarly, John Calvin defines conscience in a way that specifies both its judicial character and its operation within: "just as when through the mind and understanding men grasp a knowledge of things, and from this are said 'to know,' this is the source of the word 'knowledge,' so also when they have a sense of divine judgment, as a witness joined to them, which does not allow them to hide their sins from being accused before the Judge's tribunal, this sense is called 'conscience.'"³ The words "accused," "tribunal," and "judgment" suggest a judicial setting; the conscience is, in effect, a psychic courtroom. Similarly, Sir Thomas Browne says that "Conscience only, that can see without Light, sits in the *Areopagy* and dark Tribunal of our Hearts, surveying our Thoughts and condemning their obliquities."⁴ Such a concept presupposes that divine law is accessible, that it may be understood by the individual who, through reason, is capable of applying that law to specific cases, that the individual need not look outside for guidance—to a confessor, for instance. Conscience, then, is much more than a momentary twinge over misdeeds. "To the Renaissance mind," observes Camille Wells Slights, "the conscience was less the still, small voice that disturbs the sleep of the sinful than the intellectual and practical activity of judging past actions and legislating future ones."⁵

To describe the workings of conscience, Reformation theologians envisioned a metaphoric book which combines the functions of judging and recording. This chapter explores the theological representation of that book and the reasons for its popularity during the Reformation. Chapter 6 explores the significance of the book of conscience for Thomas Heywood's *Woman Killed with Kindness* and George Chapman's *Bussy D'Am-*

bois and offers a speculation about the appeal of this metaphoric book to playwrights of the early seventeenth century.

2

Reformation thinkers typically identify the operation of conscience with the activity of writing. For Richard Carpenter conscience is "a noble and divine power and faculty, planted of God in the substance of mans soule, working upon it selfe by reflection, and taking exact notice, as a Scribe or Register, and determining Gods Viceroy and deputy, Judge of all that is in the mind, will, affections, actions, and whole life of man."[6] In short, the conscience compiles a spiritual biography, an account of transgressions, though virtuous deeds are recorded too. As Carpenter explains, "conscience, as a Scribe or Notary, sitting in the closet of mans heart, with pen in hand, records and keepes a Catalogue, or Diary of all our doings, of the time when, place where, the manner how they were performed, and that so cleere and evident, that goe where we will, doe what we can, the characters of them cannot be cancelled or razed."[7] Robert Burton actually uses language befitting an account book: "Our conscience . . . is a great Ledgier booke wherein are written all our offences."[8] Burton, Carpenter, and their contemporaries were attracted to this figure because it so aptly expresses the intersection of individual accountability and divine judgment. The book of conscience entails personal responsibility, for that book remains in one's keeping for a lifetime. As a book, however, the conscience is destined to be scrutinized by another: God will be the ultimate reader. Thus John Downame, reflecting on the uncertainty of the hour of death, urges that the book of conscience be always ready for auditing: "we know not how soone our Lord and master will call us to a reckoninge and therefore it behoveth us to have our accompts alwayes perfect and the bookes of our consciences made up in readinesse."[9] Knowing that the book of conscience will fulfill its purpose at the Last Judgment, the prudent individual must act now. George Gascoigne warns of Doomsday: "Then the bookes of conscience shall be opened. Then shall the dead be judged by those thinges which are written in the booke: for theyr works do folow them."[10]

Reformation thinkers, balancing this emphasis on accountability with a parallel emphasis on subjection to the divine will, find biblical sanction for a second book, which is in God's keeping, the book of life: "And I sawe the dead, bothe great & smal stand before God: and the bokes were opened, & another boke was opened, which is the boke of life, and the dead were judged of those things, which were written in the bokes, according to their workes" (Revelation 20:12). This passage contains two kinds of books: one consists of the books opened while the dead stand before God awaiting their judgment—the books of conscience. The other is the book of life, which contains the names of the faithful, destined to achieve salvation. Those names are written in redemptive blood, according to John Donne: "in that first Scripture of his, which is as old as himself, in the book of life he wrote thy name in the blood of that Lamb which was slain for thee, not only from the beginning of this world, but from the writing of that eternal Decree of thy Salvation."[11] The book of life, then, is an indispensable part of the Last Judgment, as important as the books of conscience. Patrick Forbes explains: "the ground and cause of the judgement, is the booke of life: according as in it mens names are written, or are passed by."[12] The book of life and the book of conscience are not independent of one another; the one may usefully be considered the counterpart of the other. What is recorded in God's book has implications for the individual's book and vice versa. Forbes makes the connection explicit: "Now, then in the judgement, so are workes lookt on, as collation alwaies must bee of the bookes, to see if our names be written in the booke of life, as assurance of life and joyfull peace are written in our consciences."[13]

This comment by Forbes appears in his exegesis of the Book of Revelation, a work closely studied by those Reformation thinkers who conceived of conscience as a book. It was Revelation apparently that encouraged them to posit a correspondence between the books of life and conscience. Thus John Napier, commenting on Revelation 20:12, specifies the double examination to take place on judgment day: "the register bookes of all mens consciences [shall] bee opened up, and laide abroad, and the great register of God his predestination, & booke of life shall be opened, and made patent, and the dead shal bee judged according to their workes, written and registred in their consciences."[14] As this explication indicates, the book of life suggests to at least some theologians the notion that God had, from all eternity, determined the destiny of individual souls.

John Calvin in particular embraced this idea, as his commentary on Paul's Epistle to the Philippians makes clear: "The booke of life is the catalogue of the just which are predestinate unto life. . . . This catalogue the Lorde keepeth with himselfe. Therefore the booke is nothing els but his eternall counsell determined in his brest."[15] Calvin found support for this view in *The City of God,* where Augustine cites Revelation 20:15— "And whosoever was not founde written in the boke of life, was cast into the lake of fyre"—and goes on to say: "This book is not intended to refresh God's memory and to save him from forgetfulness; rather it signifies the predestination of those to whom eternal life is to be given."[16] Not every theologian affirms that people are "predestinate" to heaven or hell as rigidly as do Augustine and Calvin. Immanuel Bourne, for example, distinguishes between the book of life, *Liber vitae,* and what he calls the *Liber praescientiae,* "the Booke of Gods eternall prescience or foreknowledge."[17] Bourne is concerned to differentiate between foreknowledge and determinism. Nevertheless, in whatever way it is envisioned, the book of life implies permanence. In the words of Robert Bolton, "his name is written in the booke of life; which no malice of men, or policie of hell is ever able to blot out."[18]

The book of conscience presupposes a standard against which deeds are to be judged, a standard having its origin in divine law. Conscience, then, represents an amalgam of divine injunction and human recognition of action as either conforming to or diverging from God's will. Moralists express this twofold dimension variously. George Hakewill envisions a book of law as present at the Last Judgment; the sinner will have no recourse, no means to conceal misdeeds: "deny them hee cannot, being convinced by two evidences against which there can bee no exception, the booke of the Law, & the booke of his owne Conscience, the one shall shew him what he should have done, & the other what hee hath done."[19] For Hakewill the miscreant is doubly damned: "against the booke of the Law, hee shal be able to speake nothing, his Conscience telling him that the commaundements of the Lord are pure and righteous altogether: and for the booke of Conscience, against that he cannot possibly except, it being alway in his owne keeping."[20] Most thinkers envision not separate books of law and conscience but rather the book of conscience as itself containing the law. In John Donne's description, the conscience incorporates law that applies to all and dooms the sinner: "it is not Conscience it selfe that bindes us, but that law which the Conscience takes knowledge of, and presents to our understanding."[21] Similarly, William Ames imagines the conscience as the faculty that internalizes divine law, with concomitant judicial application: "The Conscience of man . . . Is a mans judgement of himselfe, according to the judgement of God of him."[22] John Hughes formulates the relationship of conscience and law by positing the book of conscience as itself containing not one but two books: "This booke consisteth of two parts, or volumes; The one is a law-booke, wherein are set downe the grounds and principles of truth, and equity. . . . The other part is a *Chronicle,* or a *Registrie,* wherein all our workes are written."[23] However many books are envisioned, introspection becomes a preeminent value for all of these moralists, for divine law is applied by the individual. The act of judgment is synonymous with self-knowledge.

When divine law is internalized, it is said to be inscribed in the conscience, or the heart, words that in practice are used interchangeably. William Tyndale, for example, speaks of "the herte and consciences of men."[24] William Ames, in a reference to Romans 2:15, observes, "the onely rule of our conscience, is the Law of God written in our hearts."[25] John Downame speaks of "the heart and conscience of a man."[26] Robert Bolton, describing a hypocrite, refers to "the slumber of his conscience, the deadnesse of his heart."[27] John Favour speaks of "the hearts and consciences of men."[28] And John Donne makes the same conflation when discussing a reprobate so depraved that he would expunge every written law in an effort to evade judgment: "if this obdurate sinner could be such a *Goth* and *Vandal,* as to destroy all Records, all written Laws; if he could evacuate and exterminate the whole Bible, yet he would finde this Law in his own heart, this Sentence pronounced by his own Conscience, *Stipendium peccati Mors est,* Treason is Death, and sin is Treason."[29]

Reformation moralists find in Scripture a basis for this identification of heart with conscience. Immanuel Bourne, for instance, notices both when he traces the etymology of "conscience":

> *Conscientia dicitur cum alio scientia* (saith *Aquinas*) Conscience is said to bee knowledge with another: and well it may, because God and conscience beare witnesse together. Or, Conscience is *Cordis scientia,* the science or knowledg of the *heart,* because the heart knoweth both it selfe and other things. When it knoweth other things, it is called *science;* and when it knoweth it selfe, it is called *conscience,* (as *Hugo, de anima* observes). Therefore the Scripture calleth Conscience the Heart, 1 Joh[n] 3.20 and rightly it may in this respect, because *Conscience* reflects upon the *Heart,* being enlightened by the understanding.[30]

The identification of "conscience" with "heart" has a basis in Greek linguistic practice, for when the Vulgate Bible was made, the Latin *conscientia* replaced the Greek *syneidesis,* and, "For the Greeks, *syneidesis* referred to a human reaction of shame and fear produced by the knowledge that one's personal actions in the past, or at least begun in the past, are wrong or evil."[31] Conscience, then, has not only a rational aspect (the faculty that understands and applies the law to one's actions) but also an emotional one, as the very word "heart" implies: conscience makes a person feel guilty. Martin Luther's understanding of conscience embraces this twofold quality. As Michael G. Baylor observes, "he frequently equated the conscience with the 'heart' (*cor*), a term he used to describe the emotional or affectional center of man."[32]

The concept of writing in the heart, or conscience, as an expression of internalized divine law did not originate in the Reformation, even though it flourished in that era; it had precedent in the work of the church fathers. Jeremy Taylor cites this commentary of St. Bernard: "According to the words of S. Bernard, . . . 'we shall be judged by that which is written in our own books,' (the books of conscience), 'and therefore they ought to be written according to the copy of the book of life; and if they be not so written, yet they ought to be so corrected.' "[33] Even earlier, St. Augustine, describing his youthful theft of some pears, spoke of inscribing the law: "Surely thy law, O Lord, punishes thievery; yea, and this law is so written in our hearts [*lex scripta in cordibus hominum*], that iniquity itself cannot blot it out."[34] Christian theologians found a basis for this idea in the New Testament. In fact, Jeremy Taylor sees the Christian concern with conscience as distinguishing the new dispensation from the old: "Our mind being thus furnished with a holy rule, and conducted by a divine guide, is called conscience; and is the same thing which in scripture is sometimes called, 'the heart,' there being in the Hebrew tongue no proper word for conscience, but instead of it they use the word . . . [meaning] 'the heart.' "[35] Taylor is essentially correct. As Timothy C. Potts observes, "One would expect to find that the motivation for raising questions about conscience was theological and that it came into European thought from Hebrew sources; yet both the term and the topic (except at a superficial level) are Hellenistic in origin."[36] It was largely owing to a Hellenistic rather than a Judaic heritage, then, that conscience became central to Christianity.

There exists in the Old Testament, however, a prefiguration of conscience, and Jeremy Taylor identifies it when he cites God's covenant with the houses of Israel and Judah: "I wil put my Law in their inwarde partes, & write it in their hearts, & wil be their God, and thei shalbe my people" (Jeremiah 31:33). To this verse may be addded Ezekiel 36:26— "A new heart also wil I give you, and a new spirit wil I put within you, and I wil take away the stonie heart out of your bodye, & I wil give you an heart of flesh." St. Paul seems to recall both of these passages when, in his Second Epistle to the Corinthians, he defines the new covenant in terms of writing:

> Ye are our epistle, written in our hearts, which is understand and red of all men,
> In that ye are manifest, to be the epistle of Christ, ministred by us, and written, not with yncke, but with the Spirit of the living God, not in tables of stone, but in fleshlie tables of the heart. (3:2–3)

Theologians discussing the book of conscience frequently cite these verses and with good reason, for St. Paul, more than any other person, made conscience central to Christian thought: "The term is not found in the Synoptic gospels and among the New Testament authors; it is only Paul, or authors influenced by him, who employ the term with any regularity or significance."[37] John Calvin, for instance, finds the book of conscience implicit in Paul's words quoted above: "The commendations of other men flye about in the sight of men: but our commendation hath hys seate and place in mens consciences. It may also partly be referred to the Corinthians, in this sense, They which get commendations, have not that in conscience which they carry about in writing: and they which commend others, doo so commend oftentymes rather of favour than of judgement: but we have the testimonie of our Apostleship written in mens hartes."[38]

To the extent that divine law is inscribed in every individual's heart, or conscience, that law may be called "natural" in the sense that it is universal and uniform. Reformation theologians had at hand, moreover, biblical support for what has come to be called natural law:

> For when the Gentiles, which have not the Law, do by nature the things conteined in the Law, they having not the Law, are a Law unto them selves.
> Which shewe the effect of the Law written in their hearts, their conscience also bearing witnes, & their thoghts accusing one another, or excusing.
> (Romans 2:14–15)

Calvin comments: "If the Gentiles by nature have law righteousness engraved upon their minds, we surely cannot say they are utterly blind as to the conduct of life. There is nothing more common than for a man to be sufficiently instructed in a right standard of conduct by natural law (of which the apostle is here speaking)."[39] Meditating on the same verses in Romans, William Ames concludes that there reside within every person certain rules beyond dispute: "There are some principles so cleare, and written in the hearts of all men, that they cannot erre to obey and practise them."[40] Elsewhere Ames explicitly speaks of "the Law of Nature, or . . . the Law of God, which is naturally written in the hearts of al men."[41] William Perkins voices similar confidence: "There is a ground or principle written in every mans heart in the world, none excepted, that there is a God."[42] The congruence of natural and written law is clear to Pierre de la Primaudaye too: "The law is a singular reason imprinted in nature, commanding those things that are to be done, and forbidding the contrarie. We have both the law of nature, and the law written. The law of nature is a sence and feeling, which everie one hath in himself, and in his conscience, wherby he discerneth between good and evil, as much as sufficeth to take from him the cloke of ignorance, in that he is reprooved even by his owne witnes."[43]

If the figurative reading of the divine law within is the work of conscience, the literal reading of Scripture may enhance an understanding of God's will and thereby strengthen the recognition of natural law inherent in the conscience. In a treatise on conscience Richard Greenham cites a verse in Proverbs (18:14) and comments: "This Scripture is not only worthie to be graven in steele with the pen of an Adamant, and to be written in letters of gold: but also to bee laid up and registred by the finger of Gods spirit in the tables of our hearts."[44] Other kinds of writing also contribute to the formation of conscience, though the literal words that one reads are less important than the spirit animating those words. As Pierre Charron cautions, "a man [must] gather from bookes the marrow and spirit (never enthrawling himselfe so much as to retaine the words by heart, as many use to do, much lesse the place, the booke, the chapter; that is a sottish and vaine superstition and vanitie, and makes him lose the principall) and having sucked and drawne the good, feed his mind therewith, informe his judgement, instruct and direct his conscience and his opinions, rectifie his will."[45] Owen Felltham, similarly, acknowledges the importance of reading for the formation of conscience at the same time that he warns against a mindless literalism: "The best *guide* that I would chuse, is the *reason of an honest man:* which I take to be a *right-informed Conscience:* and as for *Bookes,* which many rely on, they shall be to me, as *discourses* but of *private men,* that must bee judged by *Religion,* and *Reason;* so not to tie me, unlesse *these* and my *conscience* joyne, in the *consent* with them."[46]

As the foregoing survey suggests, the concept of conscience in the late sixteenth and early seventeenth centuries is inextricably connected with the activities of reading and writing. In treatises we learn about the inscription of divine law on the conscience by God; the strengthening of conscience by reading Scripture as well as other religious writing; the inscription of one's deeds in the conscience, a permanent record of virtue and vice; the individual's scrutinizing of those written records to ensure that whatever is recorded there conforms to divine law; God's reading of books of conscience at the Last Judgment, together with his reading of the book of life and, in Patrick Forbes' expression, the "collation" of the two.

So insistent was the language of reading and writing that artists began to depict the workings of conscience in terms of literal reading and writing. Maarten van Heemskerck, for instance, relates conscience to the divine mandate as set forth in the decalogue: he depicts Moses holding a skull in his right hand while tables of stone, representing the Ten Commandments, are propped up next to his leg and supported by his left hand; on the ground by his feet lie two books. The caption reads, "Lex conscientiam arguens mortem peccati generat" (The law which convinces the conscience of guilt brings about the death of sin).[47] Heemskerck's print seems a visualization of what Calvin says about conscience and the decalogue: "that inward law, which we have . . . described as written, even engraved, upon the hearts of all, in a sense asserts the very same things that are to be learned from the two Tables."⁴⁸ Emblematists, too, represented conscience pictorially. Daniel Cramer's *Emblemata Sacra* (1624) contains a design illustrating an inscription upon the heart, or conscience: the emblem shows a heart resting on a book while God's hand, stretching out of a cloud, writes with a pen the name of Jesus upon that heart. Emphasizing divine will over human accountability, this emblem has for its motto "Praedestinor" (I am predestined), and beneath the picture is this explanatory poem: "Annumeror Christo, cui sum de nomine notus. / Rubrica is vitae est penna liberque meae" (I am numbered with Christ to whom I am known by name. He is the rubric, the pen, and the book of my life).⁴⁹

So common is the representation, artistic and written, of conscience as a book that one is encouraged to imagine the book of conscience in quite literal terms. Richard Carpenter even speaks of conscience as though he were thinking of a conventional book, the subject of scholarly commentary: "he spake best, that cald it a booke, *ad quem emendandum omnes scripti sunt libri,* for whose sake all other bookes are written: all other are but glosses upon this Text."⁵⁰ Immanuel Bourne, however, in his explication of Revelation 20:12, reminds us that the reading and writing applied to conscience are in fact figurative: "Almighty God in Scripture is said to have Books, not properly, but . . . by that usuall metaphor in which the Scripture speakes to mens capacity, that men might understand the will of God: so in the former, and so in this part of the Vision; for God needs not bookes to register mens names or actions, hee is infinite in knowledge, and of endlesse memory."⁵¹ John Calvin, in his explication of Corinthians 3:2, explains why the Apostle Paul and, by implication, later theologians, were drawn to the metaphor of the book when discussing conscience: "The comparisons of, *Ynke, and of the spirit: of stones, and of the hart,* are of great force. For he expresseth more when he compareth ynke with the spirit of God, and stones with the harte, than if he had named the spirit and the harte without comparison."⁵²

The appeal of the metaphor helps to explain why we find it immanent in so many descriptions of spiritual experience, as in this simile by Pierre de la Primaudaye: "The minde is as a white paper, wherein as a man groweth in age and judgement, he writeth his cogitations and thoughts, which the studie of letters and learning do affoord him."⁵³ Evoking a commonplace book, La Primaudaye's trope connects actual reading with figurative writing. Pierre Charron more explicitly links the image of paper with moral action, drawing on the symbolism of whiteness as innocence: an "evill and hinderance to wisdome . . . is the confusion and captivitie of his passions, and turbulent affections, whereof he must disfurnish and free himselfe, to the end he may be emptie and neate, like a white paper,

DECAS III.

EMBLEMA XXIII.

Ille vocabit in nomine Iacob, & hic scribet manu sua Domino.

Esa. 44. 5.

Jener wird genennet werden mit dem Namen Jacob. Und dieser wird sich mit seiner Hand dem HErren zuschreiben.

Annumeror Christo, cui sum de nomine notus,
Rubrica is vitæ est penna liberque meæ.

An emblem from Daniel Cramer's *Emblemata Sacra* (Frankfurt, 1624). Beneath the picture are the explanatory verses: "I am numbered with Christ to whom I am known by name. He is the rubric, the pen, and the book of my life." By permission of The British Library (95.a.22).

and be made a subject more fit to receive the tincture and impressions of wisdome, against which the passions do formallie oppose themselves."[54] Implicit here are a series of related similitudes: innocence is like emptiness, which in this context means plain white paper; passion represents figurative writing on that paper; and such writing contrasts with the very different inscription identified with virtue. John Donne also construes sin in terms of assembling letters into words and writing those words on paper: "as a man can remember when he began to *spell,* but not when he began to *reade perfectly,* when he began to joyne his letters, but not when he began to write perfectly, so thou remembrest when thou wentest timorously and bashfully about sinne, at first, and now perchance art ashamed of that shamefastnesse, and sorry thou beganst no sooner."[55]

Such characteristics of writing as syntax and punctuation also lent themselves to the description of spiritual experience. Owen Felltham adopts an ancient motif—life as journey—but makes it new by defining the journey in terms of writing: "A *Christians* voyage to *Heaven* is a *Sentence* of three *Stops; Comma, Colon, Periodus.* He that *repents,* is come to the *Comma.* . . . 'Tis *he that confesseth and forsakes his sinne, that shall find mercy:* 'tis his leaving his *wickednesse,* that is as his *Colon:* and carries him halfe way to *heaven.* Yet heere also is the *Clause* unperfect, unless he goes on to the *practice of righteousnesse,* which as a *Period* knits up all, and makes the *Sentence* full."[56] Richard Hooker also envisions the soul's journey through life, though he imagines an entire book of pages, gradually filled up with writing: "The soule of man being therefore at the first as a booke, wherein nothing is, and yet all thinges may be imprinted; we are to search by what steppes and degrees it ryseth unto perfection of knowledge."[57] And John Donne likens the appearance of a physical book in the eyes of one's sovereign to the condition of one's soul in the eyes of God. No one, he says, would present a mutilated book to the king; therefore, "when thy book (the history of thy life,) is torn, 1000. sins of thine own torn out of thy memory, wilt thou then present thy self thus defac'd and mangled to almighty God?"[58]

Donne's similitude of a subject presenting a book to his sovereign seems particularly apt, for the sermonist's king was James I, the recipient of countless printed books, a man with strong opinions about other people's books, and a prolific author himself. Disdaining those who thought it beneath his dignity to write for a popular readership, James not only wrote extensively on religion and monarchy but also published his collected works in a handsome folio. He recognized, however, that a metaphoric book of his making was destined to be more important than his *Works* of 1616, for in *Basilicon Doron,* ostensibly written for Prince Henry, the king describes the activity of conscience, asking, "have wee not a great advantage, that have within our selves while wee live here, a

Count-booke and Inventarie of all the crimes that wee shall be accused of, either at the houre of our death, or at the Great day of Judgement."[59] For all his hauteur, King James was able to imagine himself presenting a metaphoric book of conscience to his deity.

6
Conscience on the Stage

1

WRITERS of imaginative literature were drawn to the book of conscience for much the same reason as theologians: it helped make an abstract concept immediate and vivid. Dramatists even made a character of conscience, who appears in such plays as *The World and the Child, Impatient Poverty, Apius and Virginia,* and *The Conflict of Conscience.* We don't know how this personification was costumed, but it is not unlikely that a book served as a hand prop. Samuel Daniel, in his *Civil Wars,* presents the personification of conscience with just such a book: Henry IV, in his last illness, is confronted by an apparition. Conscience stands before the king, "holding out a Booke, wherein he read / In bloudy lines the deedes of his owne hand."[1] And in *The Three Ladies of London,* a moral interlude printed in 1584 and in 1592, personified Conscience is closely identified with writing. The first action that Conscience performs onstage is "setting her hand" to a letter written by another character. Later, quoting wise sayings to the villainous Lucre, Conscience is criticized as "bookish." At the end of the drama, a corrupted Conscience is asked by the Judge, "What letter is that in thy bosom, Conscience?" Inspected by the Judge, this letter proves the undoing of Lady Lucre.[2]

Conscience also appears in major Elizabethan and Jacobean plays, though as a concept rather than as a character. Camille Wells Slights examines *Richard III, Julius Caesar, Hamlet,* and *Macbeth* to show "how contemporary ideas about conscience inform and illuminate the central themes and dramatic actions of these plays,"[3] while John S. Wilks studies *Doctor Faustus, Richard III, Hamlet, Macbeth, The Atheist's Tragedy, The Duchess of Malfi* and *'Tis Pity She's a Whore,* exploring "plays where the theme of moral choice is compounded with an internal recognition, by the protagonist, of the moral quality of motive and action."[4] Although both of these studies are valuable, neither treats conscience as a book in any detail.[5] Consequently, they do not relate, for example, the strange activity of a guilt-ridden Lady Macbeth to their subject. A waiting-gentlewoman tells the doctor of physic:

Since his Majesty went into the field, I have seen her rise from her bed, throw her night-gown upon her, unlock her closet, take forth paper, fold it, write upon't, read it, afterwards seal it, and again return to bed; yet all this while in a most fast sleep.

(5.1.4–8)

This action not only dramatizes how circumscribed Lady Macbeth's world has become but also makes literal the figurative writing that occurs within the conscience, a writing destined to be read by no one else except God. The doctor attending Lady Macbeth alludes to the moral nature of her affliction after he hears about her writing and witnesses the effort to scrub the metaphoric blood from her hands: "More needs she the divine than the physician" (5.1.74).

Neither Slights nor Wilks examines the two plays that are the chief subject of this chapter: Heywood's *Woman Killed with Kindness* and Chapman's *Bussy D'Ambois*. Slights limits her consideration of the drama to Shakespeare, and Wilks believes that conscience does not figure importantly in Heywood or Chapman. Explaining why he excludes Heywood's tragedy, Wilks argues that conscience "is merely implied rather than overtly stated, and the dramatic action invites critical discourse in terms rather of remorse or penitence than of conscience as a linguistically specific concept."[6] Although the word may not appear as frequently in Heywood's play (or Chapman's) as in certain of Shakespeare's, nevertheless conscience as an idea becomes a principal concern of the two plays. It figures in the characters' thinking when they contemplate future action and when they ponder past mistakes. Conscience informs speech and action even when the term itself is not specifically used. Especially in its formulation as a book, conscience helps to account for both the figurative language of Heywood's play and the theatrical properties of Chapman's.

2

A Woman Killed with Kindness is perhaps the least esteemed of great Renaissance tragedies, its disfavor owing to a protagonist, in the main plot, whose abasement offends the sensibilities of a modern audience; and to a subplot that, for such an audience, ranks somewhere between puzzling and irrelevant.[7] That subplot dramatizes the killing of two men by Sir Charles Mountford during a hawking contest; his apprehension and imprisonment for the crime; his extrication from a legal predicament by waging a financially ruinous defense; his unwise borrowing of money from the unscrupulous Shafton, who later has Sir Charles arrested; Charles' release from jail a second time when the conniving Sir Francis

Acton puts up the money; Charles' scheme to repay his debt by offering his sister to his enemy; and the sudden conversion of Sir Francis from hatred of Charles to love of Susan. Although deemed improbable, bizarre, and even offensive today, this material is valuable for what it reveals of the play's overall design.[8] In the triangular relationship of Charles, Susan, and Francis, Heywood dramatizes moral choice, vengefulness, and redemption.[9] Precisely because the subplot is schematic and unsubtle, it throws into sharp relief the contours of the larger dramatic action.

Very early in the play we recognize that Heywood's dramatic world is defined by the characters' moral sensitivity. Immediately after an enraged Sir Charles kills the two hawkers, he regrets the act: "My God! what have I done? what have I done? / My rage hath plung'd into a sea of blood, / In which my soul lies drown'd" (3.42–44).[10] His plight in the eyes of the law is only part of his predicament; more vexing is his guilt in his own eyes. When he tells Susan that he is "wounded at the heart" (3.61), she at first thinks he is bleeding and would seek medical help, but he bids her, "Call me a surgeon, sister, for my soul" (l. 66). When a worried Susan points out that "Sir Francis hath great friends, and will pursue you / Unto the utmost danger of the law" (ll. 70–71), her brother replies that he is more concerned with the judicial proceeding enacted within: "My conscience is become my enemy, / And will pursue me more than Acton can" (ll. 72–73).

Of course, Sir Charles must face the penalties of criminal law, too. Only moments after he invokes his conscience, he is confronted by the Sheriff: *Enter Sheriff with Officers* (3.92.s.d.). Later, having been released from jail, Sir Charles again faces arrest: *Enter Shafton with a Sergeant* (7.8.s.d.). These two arrests dramatize Charles' vulnerability to society's strictures, but they may also, for Heywood's audience, have suggested the claims of a moral law within. Jeremiah Dyke observes of a person *in extremis,* suffering a guilty conscience: "A man that hath an ill Conscience, if his eyes be opened, and his Conscience awakened, he sees death in all the terrible shapes that may be. Sometimes he sees death comming like a merciles Officer, and a cruell Sergeant, to arrest, and to drag him by the throat to the prison, and place of Torment."[11] Although Sir Charles, in his suffering, may not speak explicitly of death's specter, Susan does: "My heart's so hard'ned with the frost of grief / Death cannot pierce it through" (7.72–73). Later Charles confides to his sister, "Had I remain'd / In prison still, there doubtless I had died" (14.65–66).

It may seem odd that Sir Charles, so preoccupied with responsibility for the deaths of two men, should conceive a plan whereby he will discharge a debt by offering his sister to his enemy. It is no less odd that Susan, who expresses extreme distaste at the prospect of becoming a sexual gift, should accede to the plan, citing her brother's "extremity of need" (14.78); decked out as a bride, she is presented as a bedmate to Sir Francis. The modern audience does not know whether to be more appalled by the apparent caddishness of Sir Charles or by the self-abnegation of Susan.[12] But the psychological probability expected by that audience seems not to be a part of Heywood's dramaturgy, at least in the subplot. We may perhaps best appreciate the playwright's purpose by recalling that the composition of *A Woman Killed with Kindness* is much closer in time to that of *The Canterbury Tales* or *Everyman* than to our own day. Just as those late medieval works subordinate psychological probability to moral didacticism, so, too, does Heywood's tragedy. Sir Charles behaves as he does not only because Susan is so spiritually strong that she is prepared to take her own life but also because he knows that Susan is not really at risk; that is why he says in an aside, "Her honour she will hazard though not lose" (14.89). She will preserve her honor because, as Charles knows, the recipient of the gift will be transfixed: "I'll bear him such a present, / Such an acquittance for the knight to seal, / As will amaze his senses and surprise / With admiration all his phantasies" (ll. 94–97).

As Charles accurately foresees, Francis is so powerfully affected by the stunning act of generosity that he transcends his baser impulses:

> Stern heart relent;
> Thy former cruelty at length repent.
> Was ever known in any former age
> Such honourable wrested courtesy?
>
> (14.118–21)

Surely no reader or spectator of Heywood's tragedy imagines that either Sir Charles or Sir Francis behaves in a way that would be thought credible today, and I suspect that an audience in 1603 would have felt much the same. For what Heywood dramatizes is the counterpart of Chaucer's *Franklin's Tale,* wherein Arveragus sends his wife Dorigen to Aurelius in order to satisfy a pledge that she had unwisely made; and Aurelius, moved by this "gentil dede," sends Dorigen back to her husband. Heywood's dramatic world, though hardly that of a Breton lay, is in its own way just as remote from our experience. His characters, after all, display traits that while recognizable are curiously intensified: Heywood's men and women have the capacity to distinguish clearly between a course of action that is right and one that is wrong, the insight to recognize when they have gone astray, and (usually) the strength to act upon that knowledge. Theirs is a world where the afflictions of one's own psyche are more to be feared than the chastisements of the law.

The qualities displayed by Charles, Susan, and Francis are manifest in the principal plot as well. That is, the chief characters—Anne Frankford, her husband John, and his friend Wendoll—display an extraordinary degree of self-awareness, the capacity to anticipate the pragmatic consequences of their actions, and a penchant for seeing their deeds within a moral framework. Here, as in the subplot, the sudden eruption of passion disturbs the triangular relationship of two men and a woman. Wendoll's seduction of Anne precipitates catastrophic changes within the Frankford household and endangers the souls of wife, lover, and husband. These three are, of course, accountable to other people (no less than is Sir Charles), but Heywood, while treating the social cost of wrongdoing, stresses the price exacted by each individual conscience. Indeed, the characters most fully come to life when they enter the courtroom within.

The scene of Anne Frankford's seduction darkens the tone and redirects the action of the main plot. Although it turns on Anne's decision to betray her husband, this crucial scene is dominated by Wendoll. He speaks the greater number of lines by a proportion of three to one. He opens with a soliloquy in which he meditates "on her divine perfections" (6.11). He speaks lengthy asides while importuning Anne, and his words convey, straightforwardly and affectingly, his passion: "Beggary, shame, death, scandal, and reproach— / For you I'll hazard all" (ll. 137–38). Like Anne in the play, we are made to feel the force of this man's personality.

Despite his powerful feelings, Wendoll, at least in this scene, is self-conscious and reflective. What he ponders is not just Anne's beauty but John Frankford's generosity towards him. Looking back on that largesse, Wendoll rebukes himself in an aside:

> Hast thou the power straight with thy gory hands
> To rip thy image from his bleeding heart?
> To scratch thy name from out the holy book
> Of his remembrance, and to wound his name
> That holds thy name so dear, or rend his heart
> To whom thy heart was join'd and knit together?
>
> (6.45–50)

When Wendoll thinks of his benefactor, he calls to mind a book, an image suggestive of Frankford's civilized qualities—his reason, learning, and thoughtfulness. Wendoll's own nature could scarcely be more different; he is passionate, willful, selfish. Equipped with these traits, he will emotionally vandalize Frankford's household.

The violence of Wendoll's language—"rip," "scratch," "wound"—suggests his destructiveness. What he destroys by the seduction of Anne is not only another man's marriage but also his own identity as a trustworthy, loyal friend. The word "name," used three times in the speech quoted above, points to Wendoll's awareness of the change he is undergoing. By seducing Anne, he becomes something he was not, though precisely what he becomes is not clear to him at first. As if trying to locate his new identity, he says in an aside, "Give me a name, you whose infectious tongues / Are tipp'd with gall and poison" (6.81–82). A name, of course, is a verbal sign by which someone is known and recognized. Wendoll's plea for a new name thus underscores his concern with other people's judgment. Indeed, we cannot speak of a character's identity in this play without also taking into account his relationship to the larger community. Anxiously Wendoll anticipates the opprobrium in which he will be held: "Print in my face / The most stigmatic title of a villain / For hatching treason to so true a friend" (ll. 85–87). This image, so different from the "holy book" associated with Frankford, points to the wider implications of Wendoll's deed: not only will his relationship to Frankford be irrevocably changed but so too his relationship to everyone else. For what is "printed" in his face will eventually be seen by all. The public consequences of a private deed are also suggested when Wendoll imagines his coat of arms altered, new words in the motto substituted for old: "shall I purchase to my father's crest / The motto of a villain?" (ll. 95–96). This rhetorical question, implying that other people will come to recognize his treachery and scorn him, prefigures his future isolation.

Wendoll has good reason to be apprehensive. In a society with a keen sense of right and wrong, his behavior defies the moral norms. If the community honors relationships that have a religious sanction, as in the marriage celebration of the play's opening scene, it abhors the betrayal of such relationships. This principle applies to the friendship between John and Wendoll no less than to the marriage of Frankford and Anne. In fact, friendship has an almost sacramental quality in this play. Earlier, when Frankford welcomed Wendoll into the Frankford home, Wendoll made a solemn pledge, inviting God to witness the forging of their friendship: "when your last remembrance I forget, / Heaven at my soul exact that weighty debt" (4.76–77). In the opening soliloquy of the seduction scene, moreover, Wendoll speaks of the claims of friendship in specifically religious terms:

> Thou God of thunder,
> Stay in Thy thoughts of vengeance and of wrath
> Thy great almighty and all-judging hand
> From speedy execution on a villain,
> A villain and a traitor to his friend.
>
> (6.21–25)

Such utterances place the formation or dissolution of a human bond within a theological framework.[13]

As Wendoll beseeches Anne, his words signal an awareness of his deteriorating moral state. He answers Anne's initial reproach by saying, "O speak no more, / For more than this I know and have recorded / Within the red-leav'd table of my heart" (6.125–27). The metaphor of the heart as a "table" or notebook would have been familiar to Heywood's audience, as would have been the interchangeability of the words "heart" and "conscience." If Wendoll's remark is specifically meant to recall what St. Paul writes in 2 Corinthians 3:2 ("Ye are our epistle, written in our hearts, which is understand and red of all men"), then Heywood suggests that the miscreant's own selfish interests, conceived imaginatively in verbal terms, displace the words of divine injunction. Instead of being Christ's instrument, Wendoll is the tool of another power, identified in this remark by Frankford's servant: "The Devil and he are all one in my eye" (4.88).

So profound is Wendoll's change of identity that it cannot be concealed indefinitely. In time his affair with Anne becomes known, first by the household servants, then by Frankford, still later by the larger community. Faced with this ever widening discovery, Wendoll is forced to pay an ever greater social penalty. He is driven out of Anne's bed, out of Frankford's house, and finally out of the country. Near the end of the play he speaks of the pressure created by public censure:

> And I must now go wander like a Cain
> In foreign countries and remoted climes,
> Where the report of my ingratitude
> Cannot be heard.
>
> (16.126–29)

Wendoll must also, of course, face God's judgment, as the biblical allusion suggests, for he transgresses divine as well as human law. We are, then, invited to judge him accordingly; that is, we do not indulge his penchant for self-pity. Precisely because Wendoll recognizes at every step this sinfulness, he forfeits a claim on our sympathies. Through the biblical frame of reference, the playwright insists that we regard Wendoll as a reprobate, not a helpless victim of passion.

By acknowledging the unabashed moralism of *A Woman Killed with Kindness,* we may better come to terms with a feature of the play that has bewildered and displeased Heywood's modern audience: the seemingly inadequate motivation for Anne Frankford's fall. August Wilhelm von Schlegel was among the first to complain that "A due gradation is not observed in the seduction."[14] Similarly, Arthur Melville Clark finds the seduction too sudden to be credible: "According to modern standards of stage credibility Heywood has failed to convince us in one essential."[15] And Kathleen McLuskie speaks of the play's "complete failure to explore the motivation or the process of the relationship between Wendoll and Anne. Their adultery is presented as given, an unaccountable deformation of the conjugal happiness with which the play begins."[16] Such charges are not entirely without merit, for we never see what leads to Anne's fateful decision. All we know is that years have passed since the wedding, and, as we learn later, Anne is now the mother of two children. Before the seduction we hear nothing from Anne about domestic discontent nor, for that matter, anything from other characters to indicate that her marriage is less than happy.

However explicable the criticisms of the seduction scene, they spring from a failure to appreciate Heywood's purpose. The scene represents no sudden flagging of the playwright's imagination: had he wished to provide Anne with some easily grasped motivation, this prolific and accomplished dramatist surely had the skill to do so. Instead, he recognized that to give Anne a credible motive—any motive—for adultery would compromise his intent: to dramatize the grievous consequence of wrongdoing within the individual's soul and in society. To have supplied a motive would have meant explaining and thus, implicitly, condoning Anne's transgression, something Heywood would not do. For him some things are clearly right and others just as clearly wrong: even for his time he seems a little old-fashioned. He does not share the taste for the ambiguous and ambivalent indulged in by some of his contemporaries. He means us to judge Anne and Wendoll in unequivocal terms, and so he defines their liaison as unequivocally sinful. In language of salvation and damnation, for example, Wendoll ponders the significance of seduction: "to attempt the deed— / Slave, thou art damn'd without redemption" (6.2–3). For her part, the faltering Anne confesses, "This maze I am in / I fear will prove the labyrinth of sin" (6.160–61). By such statements Heywood places the lovers against a moral gridwork just as carefully as perspective painters of the Renaissance place their human subjects in a precisely rendered architectural setting.

Anne's speeches, like those of Wendoll, suggest her consciousness of the moral norms that she transgresses. Thus even as she accedes to Wendoll's importuning, she fears the revelation of her sin:

> I ne'er offended yet;
> My fault, I fear, will in my brow be writ:
> Women that fall not quite bereft of grace
> Have their offences noted in their face.
>
> (6.154–57)

The image of writing may well be a biblical allusion, a reference to the mark of Cain, which, according to one tradition, was imposed by God after the slaying of Abel as an outward sign of the malefactor's evil.[17] Jeremiah Dyke interprets it differently; he identifies the mark of Cain with a bodily tremor, itself the product of guilty conscience: "*Cain* had a marke of God upon him, *Gen* 4.15. And what might that marke be? *Chrysostom* thinks it was a continuall shaking and trembling of his body. If that were his mark, why might not that trembling come from the horror of his guilty Conscience, following him with a continuall hue and cry for murther, and reproaching him for a bloody murtherer."[18] Whether or not Anne has in mind specifically the mark of Cain, her words signify an unmistakable recognition of culpability: they arise from a guilty conscience. John Downame comments on the persistence of guilt even when one's face manages to conceal it: "what will it profit us though time weare our offences out of mans remembrance, if God keepe a faithfull register of them, and ingrave our reckoning with a penne of yron? what will it helpe us if by our cunning conveyances, we can hide our sinnes and avoyde shame, or with an impudent forehead can face them out without blushing, if our nakednesse be discovered, and our shame proclamed in the presence of God and all his Saints and Angels?"[19]

Anne's remark about her face betraying guilt also combines an acknowledgment of wrongdoing with an understanding of the social consequences. Earlier, at the wedding, she displayed her concern for what other people say and think. In that scene she conveyed her sensitivity by reference to facial expression. The demure bride deflected Sir Charles' praise, turning the conversation to her husband: "His sweet content is like a flattering glass, / To make my face seem fairer to mine eye: / But the least wrinkle from his stormy brow / Will blast the roses in my cheeks that grow" (1.33–36). In the seduction scene, Anne seems scarcely less concerned over her husband's judgment. When she expresses, initially, shock at Wendoll's advances, she is thinking not so much of herself as an individual but of her identity as the wife of another man. She responds to Wendoll's profession of love, exclaiming, "The host of Heaven forbid / Wendoll should hatch such a disloyal thought" (6.110–11). Making the assumption that one's inner disposition is necessarily reflected outwardly, she asks him: "O with what face of brass, what brow of steel, / Can you unblushing speak this to the face / Of the espous'd wife of so dear a friend?" (ll. 119–21). Her question points to the social implications of adultery: Wendoll's intended deed represents not the seduction of a maid but of a wife, and a friend's wife at that.

Even if the adultery remained secret, it would, in Heywood's view, be heinous; the playwright represents the illicit relationship as having the most dire spiritual consequences. With the continuation of the affair and its revelation to other people, a social dimension is introduced. To the self-reproach of the lovers is added public opprobrium. Once the affair is begun, Anne, like Wendoll, finds that her identity undergoes a profound alteration. Later, when Frankford discovers her in bed with Wendoll, Anne's first thought is of her lost identity. So traumatic is the change that she cannot think how to address Frankford: "O by what word, what title, or what name / Shall I entreat your pardon?" (13.78–79). Abjectly she confesses her metamorphosis: "I have lost that name; / I am no more your wife" (ll. 82–83). Like Wendoll desperately searching for a name in the seduction scene, Anne here recognizes that her social identity is contingent upon her moral status. To lose one is to lose the other.

That Anne should express greater concern over the revelation of her adultery than over its significance, more concern over the social than the moral, is indicative of her skewed values. Not even the shock of discovery by Frankford jolts her into a more thoughtful assessment. When he says, "'tis more hard / For me to look upon thy guilty face / Than on the sun's clear brow" (13.87–89), Anne's reply betrays a latent narcissism: "mark not my face / Nor hack me with your sword, but let me go / Perfect and undeformed to my tomb" (ll. 98–100). Her self-description recalls Sir Charles' praise of Anne at the wedding as "perfection's eldest daughter" (1.23) and Frankford's judgment of his wife as "Perfection all" (4.12). In retrospect these laudatory words seem highly ironic, for her perfection now is of a merely outward sort. She would preserve that appearance even though her inner beauty is lost.

Once the shock of discovery is past and Anne has the opportunity to ponder what she has done, she once again uses imagery of writing. This time, however, it carries a significance different from that which it had in the seduction scene. Now the language expresses a new concern for her spiritual state. Her resolve never to eat or drink again, spoken to Frankford's servant, becomes a sign of repentance: "This to your master you may say and swear, / For it is writ in Heaven and decreed here" (16.64–65). She means that her determination has the force of a solemn vow to God; and since her resolve is "writ in Heaven," it promises permanent reformation. True to her word, Anne rebuffs Wendoll when he reappears late in the play to tempt her once again: "This sin that with an angel's face / Courted my honour till he sought my wrack, / In my repentant eyes seems ugly black" (16.109–11).

As Anne repents, she repairs the relationships that had been shattered by her adultery. On her deathbed she is, as she was in the play's opening scene, surrounded by family and friends. Their physical presence now, as on her wedding day, expresses their emotional closeness. Repentance has salvaged Anne's identities as wife, mother, and friend. Less easily mended, at least in her own eyes, is her moral standing. Although forgiven by Frankford, she is still afflicted by her conscience. She asks, "Can you not read my fault writ in my cheek? / Is not my crime there?" (17.56–57).

Despite her contrition she fears that sin has permanently marked her spiritual identity, and that spiritual corruption finds physical expression on her countenance. In this concern she recalls the experience of the character Conscience in *The Three Ladies of London:* when Conscience is compromised, Lady Lucre directs Usury to "bring me the box of all abhomination, that stands in the window," and he returns *with a painted box of ink in his hand.* The dramatic action that follows makes visible the change in Conscience's moral condition: *Here let Lucre open the box, and dip her finger in it, and spot Conscience' face;* Lady Lucre, applying the ink, speaks explicitly of the victim's face, including "her temples high, and forehead white as snow."[20] Nothing so literal happens in Heywood's play, but Anne Frankford speaks as though her face were indeed marked. Significantly, Frankford wishes, following his discovery of the guilty Anne, that he could "take her / As *spotless* as an angel in my arms" (13.61–62). He tells her, "'tis more hard / For me to look upon thy guilty face / Than on the sun's clear brow" (ll. 87–89).

Like Anne and Wendoll, John Frankford uses imagery related to writing, but his use of it differs from theirs, and that difference suggests the distinctive qualities of his character. Nowhere are these qualities more evident than when he surprises Anne and Wendoll. Addressing the friend who has betrayed him, Frankford says:

> Go, villain, and my wrongs sit on thy soul
> As heavy as this grief doth upon mine.
> When thou record'st my many courtesies
> And shalt compare them with thy treacherous heart,
> Lay them together, weigh them equally,
> 'Twill be revenge enough.
>
> (13.70–75)

For John Frankford this moment is utterly devastating. Yet he adopts a curiously formal, almost impersonal, tone. His speech is that of a revenger, but a revenger as moralist, a tabulator of right and wrong. His language—"record'st," "compare," "weigh"—expresses a deliberative temperament. He seems almost incapable of action, even when provoked. True, he draws his sword in anger and seems momentarily poised to slay Wendoll. One wonders, though, whether the villain is ever in real danger, for Frankford is a man who can be dissuaded by a servant's intercession: "I thank thee, maid; thou like the angel's hand / Hast stay'd me from a bloody sacrifice" (13.68–69). As this likening of himself to Abraham suggests, Frankford is concerned with obeying the divine will. His evocations of the New Testament, moreover, suggest that he is mindful of the injunction against requiting evil with evil; Frankford could have read in Romans

12:19: "Dearly beloved, avenge not your selves, but give place unto wrath: for it is written, Vengeance is mine: I will repaye, saith the Lord." His alertness to biblical precept inhibits the impulse to bloody vengeance. At the same time, however, something in his very nature seems to lead him from violence to verbal condemnation. In fact, it is difficult to know whether Frankford's decision to spare Wendoll owes more to his moral code or to his personality.

Much the same question applies to his treatment of Anne, who is forced to wait while her husband deliberates her fate. When Frankford states his decision, moral concerns are uppermost in his mind:

> My words are regist'red in Heaven already;
> With patience hear me: I'll not martyr thee
> Nor mark thee for a strumpet, but with usage
> Of more humility torment thy soul
> And kill thee even with kindness.
>
> (13.152–56)

Frankford's banishment of Anne to a manor house some miles away must have seemed generous to Heywood's audience. Robert Ornstein observes, "For centuries the unwritten law had allowed a husband the right of private vengeance on his faithless wife."[21] What concerns Frankford, however, is not the unwritten but the written law, as expressed in the New Testament and registered in his mind. His language—"Heaven," "martyr," "soul"—has a religious denotation, and his attitude toward revenge is recognizably Christian. Waldo F. McNeir remarks, "If he can rise above the feudal tradition of blood revenge and the Italianate code of honor that prescribed it, he may become spokesman and advocate of a higher code, that which stems directly from Christ's treatment of the woman taken in adultery."[22] In that episode Christ tells the Scribes and Pharisees, "Let him that is among you without sinne, cast the first stone at her"; and to the accused woman, he says, "go, and sinne no more" (John 8:7, 11). Frankford does not reveal whether he ponders this particular incident when he disappears into his study to decide Anne's future. But, significantly, in this same scene he compares himself to Christ: before confronting Anne, he tells Wendoll, "Go, to thy friend / A Judas" (13.75–76). Moreover, just as Christ wrote on the ground while listening to the indictment of the adulterous woman, so Frankford uses imagery of writing when addressing his adulterous wife. In a biblical allusion—probably to Philippians 4:3 or to Revelation 20:12—he begins his edict with these words: "as thou hop'st for Heaven, as thou believ'st / Thy name's recorded in the Book of Life, / I charge thee . . ." (ll. 172–74). As we have seen, the book of life contains a list of those who will gain salvation; it is the heavenly counterpart of the individual's book of conscience. By speaking of the book of life, Frankford signals his desire to align himself with Christ's will.[23] Suppressing any impulse to violent retribution, he metes out a sentence that preserves the possibility of Anne's redemption and preserves his own spiritual condition as well. He will not send Anne and Wendoll "laden / With all their scarlet sins upon their backs / Unto a fearful Judgement" (ll. 45–47).

Although Frankford's policy of mercy toward an adulterous wife is in keeping with Christian precept, he withdraws into a forbidding and embittered silence. Frankford exhibits his enveloping isolation by the device that he invents to catch Anne and Wendoll *in flagrante delicto*. He writes a fake letter that Nicholas will deliver to him, calling him away on business: "there it is. / And when thou seest me in my pleasant'st vein / Ready to sit to supper, bring it me" (11.6–8). That Frankford should choose to base his ruse on the written word seems in keeping with what we know of his nature, especially his deliberate quality, his thoughtful, introspective temperament. He turns to the written word almost instinctively, so much is it a part of the way he lives. The letter also anticipates the extraordinary reference to writing and recording that will characterize Frankford later when, communing only with his God, he ponders his wife's fate. That a man should write a letter of which he will be the recipient suggests how circumscribed his world is becoming, socially and psychologically.

Frankford's isolation is conveyed further by the extraordinary order issued to Anne following the discovery:

> I charge thee never after this sad day
> To see me, or to meet me, or to send
> By word, or writing, gift or otherwise
> To move me, by thyself or by thy friends,
> Nor challenge any part in my two children.
>
> (13.174–78)

She must, moreover, take to her new residence every one of her belongings. When we hear Frankford's terms, we are made uneasy, for there seems something inhuman about what is asked. No matter how sympathetic we may be to Frankford's plight, we cannot help being disturbed by a treatment of Anne that verges on the sadistic. We may question Frankford's judgment for another reason, too: on a purely practical level his charge to Anne is characterized by a certain naiveté. He seems to believe that human ties can be obliterated readily. Otto Rauchbauer notes that when Frankford tells Anne, "Take with thee everything that hath thy mark" (13.164), and when he searches for relics of their life together, he seeks "to make *tabula rasa* of his wife's memory."[24] What Frankford would do is, of course, impossible: human relationships cannot be terminated as easily as one banishes artifacts from a house. They are too complicated, reaching out and affecting too many people to be so neatly ended, and they involve too much of a person's being. Frankford himself may be conceding as much when he tells Anne that her sin is "character'd" in their children (13.121); she has, he adds, "stain'd their names with stripe of bastardy" (l. 125). No matter how hard he tries, he will never rid himself of Anne's memory; the faces of their children will be an ever present reminder.

In place of his relationship with Anne, Frankford substitutes words. His response upon finding Anne and Wendoll together is to withdraw and formulate an edict: "I will retire awhile into my study, / And thou shalt hear thy sentence presently" (13.130–31). He seems to think that his words can define their emotional bond out of existence. What a contrast with Anne who, in the discovery scene, proclaims the insufficiency of words to convey what she feels: "How full my heart is in my eyes appears; / What wants in words, I will supply in tears" (13.181–82).[25] And later, as she approaches death, she again affirms the supremacy of feelings over written or spoken expression:

> You have beheld the woefullest wretch on earth,
> A woman made of tears. Would you had words
> To express but what you see; my inward grief
> No tongue can utter.
>
> (16.77–80)

Unlike his wife, Frankford never really surrenders his faith in words. He continues to manipulate words as though they somehow held the solution to his problems. Thus, having decided at last to forgive Anne, he restores her lost identity with a verbal flourish:

> My wife, the mother to my pretty babes,
> Both those lost names I do restore thee back,
> And with this kiss I wed thee once again.
>
> (17.115–17)

Although Frankford's effort to end his self-imposed isolation is undoubtedly salutary, the gesture is marred by its lateness; Anne is already dying. Moreover, even as she lies on her deathbed, Frankford still behaves as a judge, weighing and evaluating—and writing. Only moments after her death he devises an inscription for her tomb:

> on her grave
> I will bestow this funeral epitaph,
> Which on her marble tomb shall be engrav'd.
> In golden letters shall these words be fill'd:
> "Here lies she whom her husband's kindness kill'd."
>
> (17.136–40)

Inhibited by his rigidity and his judgmental bent from coming to terms with Anne's transgression, Frankford never regains his relationship to Anne. Despite his noble effort to imitate Christ, Frankford has been unable to bring himself to forgive her fully until it is too late. Forever looking within, retreating to his study, writing to himself, discovering what his morality dictates, John Frankford dooms himself to a desperate loneliness.

3

Few plays would seem to have less affinity with domestic tragedy than George Chapman's *Bussy D'Ambois,* which takes for its setting the court of Henry III, king of France.[26] Instead of receptions, dinner parties, and card games in rural England, Chapman presents a continental milieu of duels and chess-playing, friars and spirits. Instead of mischief within a middle-class household, Chapman dramatizes political intrigue, aristocratic rivalry, royal power. And in the midst of the dramatic action Chapman locates a character whose energy, bravado, and eloquence match the splendor of setting. Exuding not only a self-confidence verging on arrogance but also a disdain for the niceties of social decorum, Bussy D'Ambois could never realize his ambitions in an English village or manor house; even the French court can scarcely accommodate his belligerent egotism. The acknowledgment of no code but his own suggests a resemblance to the characters of Marlowe, Marston, and Jonson rather than those of Heywood or the author of *Arden of Faversham*. In Bussy, individualism attains heroic, if lawless, status.

In one respect, however, *Bussy D'Ambois* displays a kinship with domestic tragedy, for the play dramatizes a story of infidelity leading to catastrophe, as Bussy undertakes an illicit sexual relationship with Tamyra, the Countess of Montsurry. Despite the social standing of the characters, the dramatization of their affair shares with *A Woman Killed with Kindness* a common pattern: the onset of sudden passion, followed by guilty second thoughts, followed by a sensational demise.[27] Like practitioners of domestic tragedy, moreover, Chapman is concerned not only with the lovers themselves but also with the triangular relationship of husband, wife, and lover. Although initially Montsurry seems more of a bystander than a participant, his role as cuckold draws him inexorably toward the vortex of action. Learning of his wife's infidelity, he is consumed by jealousy. He may not alone be responsible for the paroxysm of violence that engulfs the lovers, but it is essentially his fury that leads to the murder of Bussy and to the torture of Tamyra. Thomas D'Urfey, adapting the play in 1691, signaled Montsurry's importance by providing the apt subtitle, *The Husband's Revenge*.

Chapman may have little taste for the moralizing endemic in domestic tragedy, but he presents, in Tamyra, a character with a well-defined sense of propriety and an alertness to social expectations. Hence her disquietude when she contemplates the death of her suitor Barrisor, killed in a duel. Tamyra fears that she may unwittingly have contributed to his demise, as the friar explains when advising Bussy:

> You must say thus then, That you heard from me
> How much herself was touch'd in conscience
> With a report (which is in truth dispers'd)
> That your main quarrel grew about her love.
>
> (2.2.202–5)[28]

Seizing on the very word supplied by the friar—*conscience*—Bussy makes it the basis of his appeal to her: "I only heard / By this my honour'd Father, that your conscience / Was something troubled with a false report / That Barrisor's blood should something touch your hand, / Since he imagin'd I was courting you . . ." (2.2.268–72).[29] If Tamyra requires little importuning, and if her affair with Bussy follows rather closely her dalliance with Barrisor, she is nonetheless a woman whose peace of mind is disturbed by the thought of having harmed another, or so she says. Even if her concern over Barrisor is to some degree exaggerated, she nevertheless chooses to represent herself as possessing a personal code capable of engendering remorseful self-doubt.

Although Tamyra may strike us as more than a little disingenuous at times, she is undeniably anxious by temperament and her anxiety springs, at least in part, from a sense of the moral norms she transgresses. Even after the consummation of her affair with Bussy, she continues to fret, presumably because her relationship is adulterous. Recognizing that uneasiness, Bussy seeks to assuage her concern by accusing her (in the 1641 quarto) of being morally fastidious: "Sweet Mistresse cease, your conscience is too nice, / And bites too hotly of the Puritan spice."[30] Although Bussy fails to share her moral scruple—"Sin is a coward Madam" (3.1.18)—Tamyra is sincere when she laments, "O my dear servant, in thy close embraces, / I have set open all the doors of danger /

To my encompass'd honour, and my life" (3.1.1-3). In a speech that might almost have been lifted from *A Woman Killed with Kindness,* Tamyra goes on to explain the source of her anguish:

> Before, I was secure against death and hell;
> But now am subject to the heartless fear
> Of every shadow, and of every breath,
> And would change firmness with an aspen leaf:
> So confident a spotless conscience is;
> So weak a guilty.
>
> (ll. 4-9)

These lines evoke the sentiments of a rueful Anne Frankford: the contrast between past tranquillity and present agitation; the language of religion—"hell," "spotless," "guilty"; the sense of vulnerability to public exposure; and, above all, the conviction that she is morally accountable for her deeds. For Tamyra, as for Anne Frankford, serenity of mind depends upon a clear conscience.

If she proves a more complicated character than Anne, it is because Tamyra's "Puritan spice" coexists with a sexual impulse worthy of Bussy himself. In soliloquy she concedes, "my licentious fancy / Riots within me" (2.2.42-43), and she pursues her desires resourcefully; she has little compunction, for instance, about enlisting the aid of Friar Comolet, "that holy man" (2.2.47), in fostering her affair.[31] Such exploitation of circumstance allows her to satisfy her longings while she continues to worry about the consequence of her deeds. The tension between passion and conviction flares most intensely when she confides to Bussy her feelings of sinfulness. In the very speech wherein she acknowledges the claims of conscience, she also speaks fatalistically of her sexuality: "It is not I, but urgent destiny, / That . . . Enforceth my offence to make it just" (3.1.43-46). In these lines we hear rationalization of the kind voiced by Wendoll in *A Woman Killed with Conscience:* "The swift Fates drag me at their chariot wheel / And hurry me to mischief" (6.101-2). No less self-serving is Tamyra's plaintive question: "What shall weak Dames do, when th'whole work of Nature / Hath a strong finger in each one of us?" (ll. 47-48). Quick to announce her frailty, this clever and tough-minded woman would here disclaim and thus evade the responsibility that her conscience only moments earlier forced her to acknowledge.

Despite her capacity for temporizing, we do not judge Tamyra unreservedly. If she succumbs to Bussy, she does manage to resist the blandishments of another suitor (Monsieur). If she deceives her husband, he is singularly lacking in traits that might prove endearing. It is he, after all, who urges her to bed Monsieur, and who, after learning of her rela-

The personification of Truth in Henry Peacham's *Minerva Britanna* (London, 1612). Department of Printing and Graphic Arts, The Houghton Library, Harvard University.

tionship to Bussy, turns abruptly from complacency to fury. Jealous and spiteful, this injured husband has none of John Frankford's decency, only his rage. Montsurry's brutal treatment of Tamyra reveals a cold-bloodedness that, in retrospect, makes explicable her rejection of him for another man. By contrast with her husband, Tamyra is lively and engaging; her sensual appetite imbues her with a vitality that blunts, if it does not forestall, our disapproval. Insofar as the play identifies the life of the senses with the power of nature, the lovers' pursuit of that life has a logic of its own. Enacting their affair against the background of Henry's court, Tamyra and her Tamburlaine of the boudoir exude a certain glamour; their appeal to an audience is undeniable.

The ambiguity that informs Tamyra's character is implicit in a theatrical property she carries when she and Bussy have their first tryst. Awaiting the arrival of Bussy and Friar Comolet, she is accompanied by a single object: *Enter Tamyra with a book* (2.2.237.s.d.). The sight of Tamyra

The personification of Philosophy in Cesare Ripa's *Iconologia* (Rome, 1603). Department of Printing and Graphic Arts, The Houghton Library, Harvard University.

carrying a book may suggest to a beholder a range of virtues. Henry Peacham's *Minerva Britanna* depicts the personifications of Faith, Learning, and Truth with open books; "Salomonis prudentia" is also represented by an open book; and Virtue holds a scroll with writing on it.[32] In Cesare Ripa's *Iconologia* the personifications who possess books include Authority or Power, Knowledge, Doctrine, Philosophy, Merit, Reform, Wisdom, and Truth.[33]

Tamyra explains to her visitors that solitude has left her restless; her husband is away and "since I cannot sleep / When he is absent, I sit up

The personification of Hypocrisy in Cesare Ripa's *Iconologia* (Rome, 1603). Department of Printing and Graphic Arts, The Houghton Library, Harvard University.

to-night" (ll. 258–59). The book is tangible evidence of her anxiety, precisely what the two men might expect to see in the hands of a thoughtful, concerned wife. The impression she creates on them, however, is not without an element of calculation; the sleepless Tamyra, after all, has not simply plucked the volume from her bookshelf while pacing in her chamber. Earlier, we heard her ask Pero for this very book: "Go maid, to bed, lend me your book I pray: / Not like yourself, for form; I'll this night trouble / None of your services" (ll. 152–54). The request arises from a desire for something other than intellectual diversion: Tamyra does not intend to spend the night alone. Even Pero suspects a hidden purpose:

"I will watch to know why you watch" (l. 156). The manner of Tamyra's request, especially her denial that she seeks the book "for form," hints at a sexual motive. By her remark, Tamyra means that, earlier, while she was propositioned by Monsieur, Pero only pretended to be occupied with the book—"come on Dame, you are at your book / When men are at your mistress" (2.2.108–9)—a comic situation used by Chapman in *All Fools* and *Monsieur D'Olive*.[34] Although Tamyra specifically denies that her own request involves any such contrivance, the audience recognizes that Tamyra seeks and uses the book for a pragmatic purpose: she does not want to appear unduly eager when her suitor arrives. As she concedes while the secret door to her chamber opens, "he I love, will loathe me, when he sees / I fly my sex, my virtue, my renown, / To run so madly on a man unknown" (2.2.173–75). Iconographically, then, the book in Tamyra's hands may signify something other than virtue: in Ripa's *Iconologia* Hypocrisy seems to be reading an open volume.[35]

A second hand property in the same scene creates a similarly ambiguous impression in the mind of the audience. Tamyra, professing uneasiness over Barrisor's death, presents for Bussy's inspection a letter that had been sent by that unfortunate suitor:

> because
> You shall not think I feign it for my glory
> That he importun'd me for his Court service,
> I'll shew you his own hand, set down in blood
> To that vain purpose. . . .
>
> (2.2.284–88)

Written in blood, this letter has a theatrical lineage reaching back to Belimperia's bloody letter in *The Spanish Tragedy*. The letter here, however, is not used chiefly to urge someone to action. Rather it functions as an expression of Tamyra's moral qualms. As we have seen, she frets over the possibility that she may have been indirectly responsible for Barrisor's death. By offering the letter, she seeks to assuage her own conscience as she supplants one suitor with another.[36] At the same time, she also means to impress Bussy with her moral sensitivity. The letter, then, objectifies her solicitude. As with the book, however, Tamyra's calculation compromises her moral earnestness, for in presenting the letter she hopes to make herself appear the more attractive in Bussy's eyes. And that, of course, leads directly to adultery.

Chapman's use of the book and letter to dramatize Tamyra's moral sensitivity makes an instructive contrast with Heywood's practice in *A Woman Killed with Kindness*. Anne Frankford's scruple is suggested largely through figurative language: her face, like a tablet, records her guilt, or so she imagines. Chapman occasionally uses imagery identifying the human face with writing (2.1.50–52), but for the most part his reliance upon the written word takes a more tangible form. He prefers to employ theatrical properties rather than metaphor alone, and he feels that if one is good, two are better. Whereas Heywood, in his main plot, uses a single property involving the written word (the letter that Frankford writes to himself), Chapman favors several: not only Barrisor's bloody letter and Tamyra's book but also another property that takes on greater importance than either of these.

From the outset an air of mystery surrounds this third property, which involves virtually all the principal characters and helps to shape the subsequent development of the plot. Mentioned for the first time when Monsieur reveals to Montsurry the infidelity of Tamyra, a certain "paper," Monsieur claims, contains evidence of her transgression. But before yielding it to the astonished husband, Monsieur attaches a condition: "you must pawn / Your honour having read it to return it" (4.1.125–26).[37] Almost immediately Tamyra enters and, after an acrimonious exchange, Montsurry blurts out what he has just heard from Monsieur:

> he would have resolv'd me,
> Had you not come; not by his word, but writing,
> Would I have sworn to give it him again,
> And pawn'd mine honour to him for a paper.
>
> (ll. 191–94)

If the accusation discomfits Tamyra, she does not concede as much. Unlike Anne Frankford, who collapses into guilty admission when confronted by her husband, Tamyra radiates self-possession. This results partly from circumstance (she has not been caught *in flagrante delicto*, like Anne), and partly from temperament; adversity evokes boldness in Tamyra, not the self-abnegation that exposure engenders in Anne. Betraying none of the misgivings about adultery that she earlier confided to Bussy, Tamyra aggressively denies the accusation, virtually daring her husband to obtain the proffered paper:

> good my Lord make haste
> To see the dangerous paper: be not nice
> For any trifle, jewell'd with your honour,
> To pawn your honour.
>
> (ll. 196–99)

In a bravura display of pluck, Tamyra actually invites her husband, once he acquires the paper, to ascertain its accuracy by questioning Pero: "and with it confer / My nearest woman here, in all she knows" (ll. 199–200).

The prominence that Chapman gives Monsieur's paper yields obvious theatrical advantage, for the audience's curiosity is piqued: Will Montsurry ever see the paper? If so, how will it affect his marriage? Whatever does Tamyra hope to accomplish by urging her husband on? And what does Monsieur's paper contain? In addition to creating suspense, the paper is the occasion of conflict as one group of characters works to discover its contents while another, just as assiduously, seeks to preserve the secret. Both adopt extraordinary measures—they enlist the aid of supernatural forces—thereby providing an opportunity for stunning spectacle. This lively excursion into the occult holds little interest for modern students of Chapman, especially for those who regard him chiefly as a playwright of ideas.[38] In fact, the latter part of the play has been deemed the playwright's concession to a benighted audience. Whatever the expectations of that audience, however, the pursuit of the paper has a significance transcending visual effect. That paper contributes to the revelation of Tamyra's character—not so much by what it contains but rather by the very desperation of her pursuit. The urging on of Montsurry is a corollary of Tamyra's insistence on her innocence. What the audience recognizes, even as she brazenly taunts her husband, is that Tamyra is not as blameless as she claims to be: we have already witnessed her secret liaison with Bussy and heard her misgivings. Her preoccupation with the paper thus accentuates the disparity between her private situation and her public stance. The greater the effort to retrieve the paper, the more closely are we led to identify Tamyra with culpability.

Monsieur's revelation to Montsurry is the pivot on which the play turns. Once Monsieur makes his disclosure, the momentum of events changes decisively: Tamyra's anxiety intensifies; Bussy loses his air of invincibility; the lovers are thrown on the defensive, their lives and love at risk. From this point onward, their energy is consumed by the effort to discover the nature of Monsieur's paper and to fend off their enemies.

The importance that the written word will have in the remainder of the play is foreshadowed by Tamyra's initial reaction to the news—she drafts a letter to Monsieur: "I will write (for I shall never more / Speak with the fugitive), where I will defy him, / Were he ten times the brother of my King" (4.1.223–25). Her action is consonant with that of someone who has already wielded a book and bloody letter to considerable effect. But she herself must recognize that this new letter is a cry of pain rather than a realistic effort to defuse a threat since, following the stage direction, *Tamyra enters with her Maid, bearing a letter,* she expostulates, "O may my lines / (Fill'd with the poison of a woman's hate / When he shall open them) shrink up his eyes / With torturous darkness . . ." (4.2.1–4). The effort to oppose one letter with another is doomed to fail, for something more than hate-filled lines is required to defeat so dangerous an adversary as Monsieur. It must seem fortuitous to Tamyra that extraordinary measures are at hand in the person of Friar Comolet, who promises her,

> we will know
> What now the Monsieur and your husband do;
> What is contain'd within the secret paper
> Offer'd by Monsieur, and your love's events.
> (4.2.19–22)

His confidence that he can solve the mystery derives from his access to the supernatural: "by my power of learned holiness / Vouchsaf'd me from above, I will command / Our resolution of a raised spirit" (ll. 25–27). With this assurance the consternation of Tamyra and Bussy is replaced by the hope that their fortunes may be salvaged from "shame and infamy" (4.2.9).

When Comolet recites a Latin incantation summoning Behemoth, the play veers away from the precincts of political tragedy and toward the realm of grand guignol. By precipitating this change, Chapman achieves some brilliant theatrical effects. His purpose, however, is not confined to particular *frissons,* for by dramatizing the supernatural, Chapman invests the plot with an ethical significance. Through the interaction of the lovers with Behemoth, the playwright creates a moral context for the characters' deeds. The dogged pursuit of Monsieur's "paper"—in particular the willingness to utilize magical means to further their ends—indicates that Tamyra and Bussy, for all their romantic appeal, belong to a tainted enterprise.

This point can perhaps best be illustrated by considering the playwright's dependence on another drama, the popular comedy by Robert Greene, *Friar Bacon and Friar Bungay* (ca. 1589). Outwardly disparate, the two plays share a common interest in magic and a common attitude toward those who wield its power. The plays also bear an uncanny resemblance in certain details of plot and staging. Consider, for instance, the use of magic to procure the written word in one form or another. Just as Friar Comolet endeavors to learn the contents of a mysterious document, so, too, Friar Bacon uses magic in order to obtain a book. The incident, which constitutes the first demonstration of Bacon's powers, arises when an Oxford doctor charges the Friar with claiming "more than magic can perform" (2.77).[39] In defense, Bacon reveals that his accuser spent the previous night in secret study at a tavern; and when the man denies this, Bacon conjures a spirit (Belcephon), who magically brings into their presence the mistress of the tavern where the doctor pursued his investigation, along with the (alchemical) book itself.[40] In *Bussy D'Ambois* a "paper" rather than a book is at issue, but the similarities point beyond coincidence. Both plays dramatize the use of magic to achieve an otherwise impossible task. In both, a friar plies the magic, calling upon a spirit by means of a Latin incantation; and a task to be performed involves the acquisition of written (or printed) materials.

The parallel between *Bussy D'Ambois* and *Friar Bacon* extends even further, for the plays dramatize a conflict between rival magicians, one that concerns the written word. In *Bussy* Friar Comolet sets the struggle in motion when he bids Behemoth, "send one then / Out of thine own command, to fetch the paper / That Monsieur hath to shew to Count Montsurry" (4.2.60–62). Behemoth, in turn, entrusts the mission to another spirit whose special province is the written word:

> Cartophylax, thou that properly
> Hast in thy power all papers so inscrib'd,
> Glide through all bars to it and fetch that paper.
>
> (ll. 63–65)

With the dispatching of this spirit, it seems that Tamyra may at last know the nature of the danger she faces. But the very complexity of the action—a distraught Tamyra turns to Bussy, who turns to the friar, who turns to Behemoth, who turns to Cartophylax—gives the mission a precarious quality. So it may not entirely surprise us when Cartophylax, whose name is glossed as "a post-classical Greek term for 'guardian of papers,'"[41] returns empty-handed, explaining that his effort has been thwarted:

> He hath prevented me, and got a spirit
> Rais'd by another, great in our command,
> To take the guard of it before I came.
>
> (ll. 73–75)

Precisely who or what "prevents" Cartophylax is never specified, but presumably Monsieur and Montsurry use their own magic to foil that of Friar Comolet. Such a conflict of magical forces has a precedent in *Friar Bacon,* when Bacon contends with the German conjuror Vandermast to determine whose power is the greater. A less formal but no less dramatic contest occurs in the same play when Bacon uses his magic to strike dumb a rival magician, Friar Bungay, as he prepares to officiate at the wedding of Margaret and Lacy. Bacon's superiority is epitomized by the book that lies useless in Bungay's hands, a book that Lacy refers to when he promises to overcome the obstacles blocking his marriage: "Peggy, what he cannot with his book, / We'll 'twixt us both unite it up in heart" (6.158–59).

Even details of staging in *Bussy D'Ambois* recall those of *Friar Bacon*, making it likely that when Chapman dramatized the Friar's magic, he had Greene's example in mind. The similarity is apparent when Behemoth, subsequent to the failed mission, offers a consolation of sorts. Comolet and the lovers may not be able to see for themselves what the paper contains, but they can at least, through magic, observe the paper in the hands of its possessors: "Yet shall you see it, and themselves: behold / They come here and the Earl now holds the paper" (4.2.78–79). The stage direction, *Enter Monsieur, Guise, Montsurry with a paper,* indicates that the audience in the theater witnesses what Tamyra and Bussy witness. This peculiar dramaturgy—two groups of characters in different settings but together on the same stage—closely resembles that of *Friar Bacon*.[42] In one scene Bacon uses his magic glass to show King Edward "what's done in merry Fressingfield / 'Twixt lovely Peggy and the Lincoln earl" (6.6–7); this, of course, is the scene wherein Bacon stops the wedding. (And just as Tamyra and Bussy are unable to hear what Montsurry, Monsieur, and the Guise are saying even though the audience can, so, too, King Edward and Bacon cannot hear what happens in Fressingfield, even though the audience can.) At another point in Greene's play, two scholars, by means of the same "glass prospective," watch as their distant fathers fight and kill one another (onstage), whereupon the young men fall to arms and re-enact the violence they have just witnessed, slaying one another (scene 13).

Those deaths prompt a crisis in Friar Bacon, illustrating something implicit throughout Greene's play: the moral peril that practitioners of magic risk. Bacon concedes to Bungay, "it repents me sore / That ever Bacon meddled in this art" (13.85–86). Daniel Seltzer comments on the reason for regret: "there could be no sorcery which was not to some degree suspect. Any power which could call up spirits—be they neoplatonic 'daemons' or necromantic 'demons'—could not claim the assistance of God, and must, therefore, receive the aid of the devil."[43] If the magic itself is suspect, then so must be the written materials on which it depends. Thus in the same speech wherein he repents dabbling "in this art," Bacon also laments "The hours I have spent in pyromantic spells, / The fearful tossing in the latest night / Of papers full of nigromantic charms . . ." (ll. 87–89). The title page of Greene's play demonstrates the magician's reliance on such "papers" by depicting Bacon, in the Brazen Head scene, asleep at a table, a book lying open before him, and, above, a shelf full of other books. The open book is presumably that wherein he finds access to the world of spirits, for at the beginning of this scene (11) Bacon enters with *a book in his hand* and with the white wand of a conjuror. Other stage magicians display a similar dependence on written materials. The title page of *Doctor Faustus*, for instance, depicts the

The title page of Robert Greene's *Friar Bacon and Friar Bungay*, written ca. 1589–90 and first printed in 1594. The woodcut illustrates the scene in which Friar Bacon, having formed "a monstrous head of brass," seeks to surround England with a wall of brass but misses his opportunity when he falls asleep. By permission of the Houghton Library, Harvard University.

protagonist with a book in his hand, standing within a magic circle. Like Friar Bacon, Marlowe's magician achieves his power with the help of magical books—in Faustus' case, "necromantic books" (1.1.52)—which later he offers to burn in an effort to ward off his imminent demise.[44] In much the same fashion Shakespeare's Prospero, having determined to renounce his "art"—"this rough magic / I here abjure" (5.1.50–51)—resolves to destroy the source of his magic: "I'll drown my book" (l. 57). What these magicians come to recognize is that the penalty for failing to renounce books of magic and thus magic itself may be nothing less than damnation.

Guided by Greene's example, Chapman takes over not only particular details of plot and staging but also something of the jaundiced attitude toward magic that one finds in *Friar Bacon, Doctor Faustus,* and other Renaissance plays. Admittedly, there is no overt renunciation of magic in *Bussy D'Ambois*. One editor, Maurice Evans, contends that Chapman, influenced by Giordano Bruno, was drawn to Hermetic philosophy, which held that "the truly virtuous magician could invoke all spirits with impunity"; but even Evans concedes that the magic of the Hermetic philosophers was "of a nobler kind than the necromancy of the middle ages or of Faust or Bussy's Friar."[45] Comolet's magic has, in fact, a distinctly sinister quality, manifest in the scene where the friar (who would likely have a book in his hand) recites a long incantation summoning the spirit.[46] Behemoth, upon his first entry, announces that he is emperor of "that inscrutable darkness, where are hid / All deepest truths, and secrets never seen" (4.2.49–50).[47] This self-description may not in itself have had an untoward connotation for the author of *The Shadow of Night,* a poem positing darkness as a source of knowledge.[48] But the onstage spectacle is less ambiguous. Spirits encircle Behemoth in "blue fires" (l. 54), evoking the flames of hell. Comolet addresses the spirit as "great Prince of darkness" (l. 66), an epithet commonly applied to Satan. Even if Bussy, Tamyra, and the friar evince no sign of regret in their dealings with Behemoth, their dependence on such a creature to secure Monsieur's paper diminishes their stature. Although they may see themselves as embattled victims, their traffic with the prince of darkness imbues them with guilt by association. Consorting with spirits, the would-be beneficiaries of magic risk a fate worse than the public opprobrium they fear.

The paper sought with such ingenuity is itself not without a moral dimension, though, curiously, Chapman fails to identify the exact nature of the document that lies at the center of the struggle between Friar Comolet and Monsieur. Scholars debate whether the paper has been written by Monsieur himself or by someone else, and whether it is a forgery or a genuine communication that somehow falls into the hands of Monsieur.[49] Reviewing the evidence, Nicholas Brooke comments: "I am not sure Chapman had a very clear notion what this paper exactly was."[50] Brooke may well be correct; certainly the audience shares the ignorance of the friar about the nature of the paper. But if Chapman fails to make the issue wholly clear, it probably does not greatly matter. More important than the words written on Monsieur's paper is the theatrical effect which the pursuit of the paper engenders, an effect in keeping with the prevailing attitude toward magic on the Renaissance stage. In the theater the audience must assume what Tamyra assumes: that the paper is incriminating.[51] Were it not, the lovers would scarcely need to resort to such desperate measures to retrieve it. In performance, then, the effect of the paper is to underscore Tamyra's moral frailty. The paper so much sought after is the objective correlative of her guilt, an externalization of the guilty conscience that all along has troubled her.

The 1641 quarto of *Bussy D'Ambois* contains a passage that makes explicit what remains largely implicit in the 1607 quarto: namely, the symbolic significance of the letter in Montsurry's possession. When Montsurry reveals what he has just learned from Monsieur, Tamyra replies:

> good my Lord make haste
> To see the dangerous paper: Papers hold
> Oft-times the formes, and copies of our soules,
> And (though the world despise them) are the prizes
> Of all our honors. . . .
>
> (4.1.196 ff.)

The written word, she means, is the outward exemplification of inner character. As Frederick S. Boas notes, "written documents often contain the revelation of our true selves, and, though of no material value, put the crown to our reputations."[52] Musing aloud, Tamyra speaks more truly than she knows, for in her case the "dangerous paper" is indeed the form and copy of her soul: that paper reveals her moral ruin.[53]

Given the importance of the written word for Tamyra, it is a cruel irony that when her husband finally calls her to account, he has a servant place a portable writing desk beside her (5.1.s.d.). We know what he wants because in the previous scene we heard the Guise suggest that she be forced "to write / Such loving stuff to D'Ambois as she us'd / When she desir'd his presence" (4.2.101–3). Montsurry's effort to compel such a letter takes the form of relentless badgering, his questions alternating with commands: "Sing (that is, write)" (5.1.68); "Why write you not?" (l. 87); "Write: for it must be" (l. 96); "Speak: will you write?" (l. 102). With each verbal assault—and each refusal—the emotional temperature of the scene rises, making more likely the eventual fusion of writing and violence. These coalesce in extraordinary fashion when Montsurry, frustrated by the unsuccessful exhortations, stabs his wife and envisions the violence as a form of writing:

> Till thou writ'st
> I'll write in wounds (my wrongs' fit characters)
> Thy right of sufferance. Write.
>
> (ll. 124–26)

Still Tamyra resists. Only when Montsurry subjects her to the rack does she finally capitulate, and even then she manages to wrest from her desperate situation some advantage. She accomplishes this by capitalizing on the convergence of writing and violence: "I'll write, but in my blood that he may see, / These lines come from my wounds and not from me" (ll. 168–69). What inspires such ingenuity is unclear, but we recall that earlier Tamyra was herself the recipient of a bloody letter (from Barrisor). So the letter that she now writes to Bussy evokes the memory of another such letter, which helped lead to her affair with him in the first place.

For Montsurry, Tamyra's attempt to protect Bussy must seem a final reproach. In his mind her intransigence has little to do with rectitude and everything to do with passion: to him Tamyra's fierce resistance betokens a continued attachment to her lover. But even if love for Bussy guides her behavior now, Tamyra's action arises out of complicated motives which are not by any means contemptible. To betray Bussy offends her sense of right and wrong: penitence is one thing, cooperation in the ambush of her lover quite another. So throughout this long scene she tries to frustrate her husband's purposes. Her strategy is eminently straightforward: she frankly acknowledges her transgressions and she appeals to Montsurry's better nature. However disingenuous she may have been in the past, there is little reason to doubt the sincerity of her guilty admissions, couched in religious language: "Sweet Lord enjoin my sin / Some other penance than what makes it worse" (5.1.102–3); "Heaven, I ask thee remission of my sins, / Not of my pains" (ll. 145–46).

Despite the homiletic quality of her diction in the final scenes, the heroine of *Bussy D'Ambois* stops short of unqualified contrition. Tamyra is too much the Countess of Montsurry to find a psychological resting place in humiliation, à la Anne Frankford. Looking back wistfully over her *liaison dangereuse* with Bussy, she allows herself to imagine what might have been:

> O had I never marry'd but for form,
> Never vow'd faith but purpos'd to deceive:
> Never made conscience of any sin,
> But cloak'd it privately and made it common.
>
> (5.3.219–22)

Wishing that she had never acknowledged a moral framework for her deeds, never subjected them to the scrutiny of her conscience, she wishes instead that her conduct had been altogether more expedient. By her thinking she exposes the element of self-deception that has all along marked her character. Imagining that an action may be arbitrarily assigned either to the purview of society's expectations or to that of individual conscience, Tamyra suggests that her mistake lay in choosing the wrong rubric for her behavior. But for someone of her temperament and sensitivity, that was never an option. She possesses neither the supreme self-confidence nor the indifference to others' suffering that would have allowed her to emulate Bussy's moral insouciance. She herself seems to recognize as much when, at the end of her speech, she cries: "O my conscience!" (5.3.230). If she has not always had the strength to follow the dictates of her conscience, she at least has had sufficient awareness to recognize its claims.

Were *Bussy D'Ambois* a domestic tragedy, Tamyra's struggle with her conscience would seem more urgent than it does. As it is, the play is so crowded with incident, especially near the end, that moral issues may seem submerged beneath the savagery and visual shock: the stabbing and torture of Tamyra, the delivery of her letter by a hooded Montsurry (in disguise as the friar); the collapse and death of Comolet, and the subsequent appearance of his ghost; the stabbing of Pero and the shooting of Bussy. Tamyra's speeches, moreover, compete for our attention with those of other characters, as Chapman finds fit matter for his grandiloquence: the colloquy of Monsieur and the Guise on nature and fortune (5.3.1–56); Bussy's declamation on death and destiny (ll. 123–70); and his vision of himself in Herculean terms (ll. 178–93). In contrast with such splendor of language and spectacle, Tamyra's moral crisis may seem pallid, but it is remarkable nonetheless, since we do not expect to find it in a play that takes the French court for its setting, a play based upon a historical account of aristocratic derring-do.[54] That Chapman should have given such prominence to Tamyra's story is in keeping with the didacticism that informs his definition of tragedy. In the dedicatory preface to *The Revenge of Bussy D'Ambois,* Chapman lists the constituent parts of "authentical" tragedy as "materiall instruction, elegant and sententious excitation to Vertue, and deflection from her contrary."[55] However inadequate this may be as a description of *Bussy D'Ambois* and its sequel, Chapman's formulation reveals a moralistic bent worthy of an author of domestic tragedy.

4

As we have already seen, the Gospel of St. John describes Christ as writing on the ground when he confronts the accusers of the woman taken in adultery. In his *Paraphrases* of the New Testament, Erasmus explains the meaning of this incident: "Jesus wrote upon the grounde, even to geve us warnyng that God shall judge everye man after the lawe of the gospel: The lawe written in tables, made them by an untrue righteousnes proude and arrogant. The law written upon the grounde, maketh every man through a conscience and knowlage of his owne infirmitie, meke and mercifull unto his neighbour" (fol. lix).[56] This story had already found expression in the Chester mystery play based on John's account (8:6). In the words of the Doctor, Jesus "wrote in claye—leeve yee mee— / their owne synnes that they might see, / that ichone fayne was to flee, / and they lefte hir alonne" (ll. 301–4).[57] Such writing, is of course, the outward counterpart of the writing that has already taken place internally, in the conscience. Authors of morality plays, like their predecessors, continued to imagine guilt or innocence in terms of writing. Thus in *Everyman* the protagonist is told by Death: "On the thou must take a longe journey. / Therfore thy boke of counte with the thou brynge, / For tourne agayne thou can not by no waye" (ll. 103–5).[58] Everyman acknowledges the obligation but worries that his book is not prepared for scrutiny: "all unredy is my boke of rekenynge. / But xii. yere and I myght have a bydynge, / My countynge boke I wolde make so clere, / That my rekenynge I sholde not nede to fere" (ll. 134–37). Such a book, notes Philippe Ariès, was a feature of judgment scenes in late medieval art: "This book, the *liber vitae,* must first have been conceived of as a cosmic book, the formidable census of the universe. But at the end of the Middle Ages it became an individual account book. At Albi, in the vast fresco of the Last Judgment dating from the end of the fifteenth or the beginning of the sixteenth century, the risen wear this book about their necks, like a passport, or rather like a bank book to be presented at the gates of eternity."[59] The fresco shows the books open, their pages full of writing (even with decorated capital letters!), as though affixed to the chest—the heart—of each person.

This iconographic and dramatic tradition, however important, does not alone account for the significance that conscience, especially as a book, assumes in the drama of the early seventeenth century. For the impetus we must look to the ecclesiastical and political circumstances of Elizabethan England, when people were forced to confront the claims of conscience in an immediate and sometimes painful way. What a person owes his or her conscience had particular urgency then, for a concerted effort was made to enforce uniformity of religious observance and to squelch dissent.

Early in her reign Queen Elizabeth sought to confront Catholics who refused to surrender their traditional allegiance and to support the English church. In 1559 the faithful were asked to subscribe to the Act of

Uniformity, which provided for "one uniform order of common service and prayer and of the administration of sacraments, rites and ceremonies in the church of England."[60] Penalties were assigned for any minister violating this regulation. The laity, for their part, "shall diligently and faithfully, having no lawful or reasonable excuse to be absent, endeavour themselves to resort to their parish church or chapel accustomed, or upon reasonable let thereof to some usual place where common prayer and such service of God shall be used in such time of let, upon every Sunday and other days ordained and used to be kept as holy days."[61] Most people acceded to these regulations; some did not. Edmund Plowden, for example, a Catholic lawyer and landowner, could not square the Act of Uniformity with his conscience: "he saide he could not subscribe, butt beleiff must precede his subscription. And therefor he saide grete impietie should be in hym if he should subscribe in full approvance or beleiff of those things in which he was scrupulous in beleiff."[62] Like Thomas More and William Tyndale before him, whose contests with authority have been so memorably described by Stephen Greenblatt,[63] Plowden found that expediency was not an option for him.

The requirement of obedience to ecclesiastical authority must have caused at least some qualms among the enforcers since Protestants ostensibly prized the individual conscience and, in an earlier era, had looked to conscience as a justification for defying the church of Rome. On 15 June 1570 William Cecil somewhat defensively addressed this issue in the Star Chamber: "Where certen rumors are caried and spredd amonst sundry hir Ma^{tes} subjectes, that hir Ma^{ty} hath caused or will herafter cause inquisition and examination to be had of mens consciences in matters of Relligion: Hir Ma^{ty} wold have it knowen that such reportes are utterly untrue and grounded ether of malice or of some feare more than there is cause"; Cecil added, "Hir Ma^{tes} meaning is not to have any of them molested by any Inquisition or examination of their consciences in causes of Relligion."[64] This assurance was cold comfort to Catholics, who saw that the English church was not reluctant to compel obedience to the corporate will, regardless of individual conscience.[65] In an effort to deal with the state-sanctioned assault on liberty of conscience, Catholics devised strategies for coping with interrogators. Paradoxically, they sought escape from jeopardy in the law itself, an effort known as casuistry. Proffering advice on how to behave and what to say when questioned, Catholic thinkers urged an appeal to scruple, not arrogant defiance of authority: "The note struck was rather a deprecatory one: 'Look, I'm sorry, but my silly old conscience is acting up again. You wouldn't want to bring on those terrible guilt feelings I get, would you?' What was claimed for conscience was not that it was right but that a man couldn't act against it without great mental suffering."[66]

Specific strategies designed to cope with the machinery of Elizabeth's church took the form of equivocation and mental reservation. Equivocation meant deliberate ambiguity on the part of the person being interrogated: "the speaker's words if closely examined will prove to be capable of being taken in two senses: the sense in which they are true, and the sense in which he hopes his hearer will take them."[67] Mental reservation denotes a somewhat different technique: "the words audibly and expressly spoken amount to one statement, which is untrue, and they cannot be twisted into a true statement, but the speaker 'mentally' adds an understood condition, which would turn it into another, true, statement if it was said aloud."[68] Together these stratagems allowed at least some people to satisfy the demands of their interrogators without fatally compromising their own consciences.

These strategies were of no avail, however, to Edmund Campion and his associates, who, returning to England from the continent, were arrested in 1581 and charged with high treason. Campion, who denied the charge, was forced to listen as John Hart offered evidence against him: "Yea, saith Campion, never shall you proove this, that we came over either for this intent or purpose: but onelie for the saving of soules, which meere love and conscience compelled us to doo, for that we did pittie the miserable estate of our countrie."[69] Holinshed's account of this episode makes it clear that the accused based his defense largely on an appeal to conscience: he said that "the jurie were not men learned, and therfore causes of conscience ought not to be committed to them, neither was that barre appointed to define on causes of conscience: wherfore all that you doo (saith he) is but to bring us in *odium* with the jurie. After this order he deluded the people, appealing still to the devoutnesse of his conscience . . ." (1324). The prosecution sought to discredit this defense by producing a book written in Latin and ostensibly brought by Campion and his friends into England. The book specified how, in the event of their arrest, they were to answer questions: "If they be examined as concerning their allegiance to hir majestie, they will make their answer after this maner; She is our lawfull sovereigne ladie & queene, and we obeie hir. But then object unto them; Will you obeie hir excommunication, or anie thing that he commandeth to the contrarie? Then will they answer: We desire you not to charge our conscience, and that you would not enter so deepe into our consciences, we trust the pope will not command us anie thing aginst hir: & a hundred such like sleevelesse ansers they make, never agreeing to anie certeintie, but holding the pope in more reverence than they doo hir majestie" (1325). Even if we suppose that the "evidence" of the book were genuine, Campion's accusers were clearly reluctant to concede that conscience may represent a legitimate reason for defying the ecclesiastical policies of the government. Despite the changes wrought by the Reformation, many people continued to see conscience not so much as individual scruple but rather as the common conscience of Christendom, defined by a commonalty of belief.

If the church of England had targeted Catholics only, the issue of conscience might never have become so prominent or controversial during the later years of Elizabeth's reign. But the clergy, enthusiastically supported by the crown, also set out to enforce conformity among English Protestants, some of whom were offended by the persistence of vestments, ceremonies, holy days, and prayer books that resembled those of the repudiated Roman church; they also questioned the autocratic form of ecclesiastical administration that bore a close resemblance to Rome's. Although patriotic by modern standards, these dissenting Christians seemed seditious at a time when there existed no dividing line between church and state. Because they were perceived as a threat, they were subject to detention, interrogation, and even worse. This pressure led some Protestants to develop an intellectual justification for supporting a liturgy and a form of church government markedly different from those sanctioned by the state, and they found a rationale in allegiance to conscience.[70] As John Bartlett asserts, "Neither the prince nor any prelate hath any authority by the word of God to make any ecclesiastical law or rite, to bind men's consciences in pain of deadly sin to keep them."[71]

Among the Protestants most offended by the intractability of Elizabeth's clergy were the Puritans, and among their most eloquent spokesmen was Thomas Cartwright. He became Lady Margaret professor of divinity at Cambridge in 1570 and in that year gave a series of lectures arguing that the primitive church was very different from the English church as then constituted. Cartwright, for instance, wanted the elimination of archbishops; bishops should exercise spiritual authority only; ministers should be elected by their congregations. John Whitgift, who became vice-chancellor at Cambridge in 1570, saw Cartwright's ideas as dangerous. Not only did Whitgift oppose Cartwright intellectually but he also contrived to deprive Cartwright of his professorship. In September 1583 when this no-nonsense prelate became Archbishop of Canterbury, his power to root out dissent was greatly enhanced, and he quickly put it to work. He set about enforcing subscription to some twenty-four articles as a requisite for ministers to exercise ecclesiastical functions; in particular these articles demanded recognition of the queen as ecclesiastical and temporal ruler; the adoption of the Book of Common Prayer for use in public prayer and in the administration of sacraments; and acceptance of the Articles of Religion as they had been set forth in 1562. The demand was particularly vexing to Puritans. In their eyes, agreement implied moral complacency: "To subscribe to the Prayer Book and the Articles was to acknowledge that the Church of England had no fundamental faults which could justify the pursuit of a divergent policy by any of its members, or the organization of a sectarian faction within the Church."[72] For Puritan preachers, moreover, Whitgift's campaign caused a grave dilemma by forcing a choice between their livelihoods and consciences. To capitulate to the subscription meant surrendering their integrity; to refuse meant losing their livings and also abandoning their pastoral role as preachers.

The parallel between what was now being done to fellow Protestants and what Catholics had formerly done to Protestants was so obvious that even William Cecil was moved to complain. On 1 July 1584 Cecil wrote to Archbishop Whitgift about the harsh treatment of ministers: "according to my simple judgement this kind of proceeding is too much savouring of the Romish inquisition, and is rather a device to seek for offenders than to reform any. This is not the charitable instruction that I thought was intended."[73] On 3 July Whitgift wrote in reply: "Touching the 24 Articles which your lordship seemeth so much to mislike, as written in a Romish style, smelling of the Romish inquisition etc. I cannot but greatly marvel at your lordship's vehement speeches against them (I hope without cause), seeing it is the ordinary course in other courts likewise, as in the Star Chamber, the Court of the Marches, and other places."[74] Whitgift's intractability was not, as Cecil surely knew, the result of mere pique, for Protestants had long asserted the need to obey religious and civic authority. John Calvin, for example, said of magistrates: "it has not come about by human perversity that the authority over all things on earth is in the hands of kings and other rulers, but by divine providence and holy ordinance. For God was pleased so to rule the affairs of men, inasmuch as he is present with them and also presides over the making of laws and the exercising of equity in courts of justice."[75] Such sweeping judgments gave legitimacy to Whitgift and his ilk. As C. S. L. Davies notes, "We should not forget the extent to which most sixteenth-century thought was deeply corporate. . . . There was little room for private conscience; or rather private conscience could be 'discharged' and responsibility assumed by higher authority."[76]

In response to Elizabeth's magistrates, Puritan thinkers, like their Catholic counterparts, developed a theology explicitly assigning to individuals the right and the duty to exercise conscience in all matters.[77] The most influential of these theologians was William Perkins who in 1596 wrote *A Discourse of Conscience*. Perkins examines the proposition that "Gods authority binds conscience: magistrates authority is Gods authority: therefore magistrates authority binds conscience properly." To this syllogism Perkins answers:

> Gods authority may be taken two waies: first for that soveraigne and absolute power which he useth over all his creatures: secondly, for that finite & limited

power which he hath ordained that men shall exercise over men. If the *minor,* namely that Magistrates authority is Gods authority, be taken in the first sense, it is false: for the soveraigne power of god is incommunicable. If it be taken in the second sense, the *proposition* is false. For there be sundry authorities ordained of God, as the authority of the father over the childe, of the master over the servant, the authority of the master over his scholer, which doe not properly and simply bind in conscience as the authority of gods lawes doth.[78]

Perkins does not deny a person's duty to authority; but he affirms another responsibility, too: "necessary obedience is to be performed both to civil and ecclesiasticall jurisdiction: but that they have a constraining power to bind conscience as properly as gods laws do, it is not to be prooved, neither can it be."[79]

Puritans expected no amelioration in their condition as long as the queen lived. Under a successor, however, they saw the possibility of gaining some independence from the established church. With the accession of James they anxiously anticipated an improvement in their fortunes. Initially, James seemed to sustain their hopes: he "deliberately led the puritans—as he did both the other major religious parties—to expect some benefit from his accession."[80] Those hopes were focused at the Hampton Court Conference, which began on 14 January 1604.[81] There John Whitgift on his knees implored James not to change either the liturgy or governance of the church. On 16 January the Puritans made their case, arguing, among other things, that the power of the bishops be limited. When John Reynolds of Corpus Christi College, Oxford, suggested that "Presbyteri" assist bishops in resolving disputed points, James shot back: "then Jack and Tom, and Will and Dick, shall meet, and at their pleasure censure me and my Council and all our proceedings. Then Will shall stand up, and say, 'It must be thus'; then Dick shall reply, and say, 'Nay, marry, but we will have it thus.'"[82] What seems to have concerned the king the most was not the prospect of change in the liturgy but rather in church governance, for such change had the capacity to undermine the authority of this autocratic monarch. If the Puritans had hoped for improvement in their situation, they were now deeply disappointed: "Far from achieving what was hoped of it, the conference did the puritan cause positive harm. It was now clear, if it had not been so before, that James was as hostile to the very principles of dissent and nonconformity as ever Elizabeth had been. A lifetime's acquaintance with the pertinacity of the puritan conscience in Scotland had taught him to make no concessions whatsoever to this spirit."[83]

Confident of their rightness, Puritans continued to find justification for their cause in a profound sense of responsibility to themselves and to their God. Embattled, they asserted the supremacy of the conscience ever more forcefully. In daily life they turned to the written word to record their examination of conscience and their experience of divine grace. Of the Puritans Paul S. Seaver has observed, "Their culture was the product not only of deliberate learning but of literacy, and books gave them both a vocabulary and a set of conventions."[84] One such Puritan, Nehemiah Wallington, a London artisan of the early seventeenth century, who filled no fewer than fifty notebooks between 1618 and 1654 with reflections on his life, adopts the conventional metaphor of an account book: "he wrote that he would begin the examination of his 'soul's estate' by looking 'over some books, even the book of my conscience [to] see what increase of grace my book of conscience will show me.'"[85] Four pages of analysis follow, explaining "what his conscience would say."

In the years following the Hampton Court Conference Puritan theologians redoubled their efforts; that era became the golden age of Puritan writing, as John Downame, Robert Bolton, William Ames, Richard Greenham, Jeremiah Dyke, William Perkins, and many others saw their work printed and read by an ever-wider audience. It was also around the time of the Hampton Court Conference that conscience assumed increasing prominence on the stage. Shakespeare's *Measure for Measure* and *Macbeth* both explore the claims of conscience. And, significantly, the two plays examined in this chapter specifically identify conscience with Puritan values. In *A Woman Killed with Kindness,* Heywood's villain upbraids a guilty and increasingly reluctant Anne Frankford: "Fie, fie, you talk too like a Puritan" (11.109). In *Bussy D'Ambois,* as we have seen, the protagonist chides an apparently diffident Tamyra: "Sweet Mistresse cease, your conscience is too nice, / And bites too hotly of the Puritan spice."[86]

Although Thomas Heywood's religious views have been the subject of debate, a persuasive case has been made that *A Woman Killed with Kindness,* especially in its dramatization of Anne Frankford's demise, is "a play in which both Puritan ideology and politics intersect to create what seems to be a paradigm of puritan resistance."[87] Although Chapman almost certainly belonged to no religious sect, the emblematic design he chose for the title page of *Ovid's Banquet of Sense* (1595) has a motto suggesting an almost Puritan-like conviction of personal rectitude: "Sibi conscia recti" (the mind, conscious of its own righteousness).[88] A similar emblem, appearing in Henry Peacham's *Minerva Britanna* (1612), concludes its explanatory poem with these verses: "if thou know'st, thy conscience cleere within, / What others say, it matters not a pinne."[89] Among the contemporaries of Chapman and Heywood who also were drawn to the metaphoric book of conscience was Thomas Middleton, whose "early work strongly suggests that he came from a moderate Puritan background."[90] Middleton uses the concept of conscience as book in

The Changeling. There De Flores turns on Beatrice-Joanna, who is vainly trying to disassociate herself from the murder he has committed for her, and he says:

> Look but into your conscience, read me there.
> 'Tis a true book, you'll find me there your equal.
>
> (3.4.132–33)[91]

The book of conscience thus becomes the turning point in the crucial scene of this Calvinist tragedy—but it is used for no moral purpose. By compelling Beatrice-Joanna to look within and discover what is already written there, De Flores ensures his hegemony over her. He invokes the book of conscience not to align himself with divine design or to reform conduct but to achieve surprise and disarm his prey.

Playwrights did not need to have any specific religious allegiance, of course, to envision conscience as a book, for the trope came to enjoy extraordinary popularity in the early seventeenth century. In *The Duchess of Malfi,* for example, Bosola adopts it when he reflects on his part in the death of the Duchess: "a guilty conscience / Is a black register, wherein is writ / All our good deeds and bad, a perspective / That shows us hell!" (4.2.356–59).[92] A similar conceptualization appears in *The Virgin Martyr,* when Angelo turns on the hypocrites who surround him, saying, "Your hearts to me lie open like blacke bookes, / And there I reade your doings" (2.1.111–12).[93] It was John Ford, however, who ingeniously brought the metaphor to a culmination of sorts. In *'Tis Pity She's a Whore* Annabella evokes the writing in her conscience when she reflects: "My conscience now stands up against my lust / With depositions charactered in guilt, / And tells me I am lost" (5.1.9–11).[94] Ford conflates metaphoric book and dramatic action when Annabella writes a letter to her brother, declaring her repentance and urging his as well. Receiving the letter from the friar, Giovanni asks whence the letter comes, and the friar answers, "Thy conscience, youth, is seared, / Else thou wouldst stoop to warning" (5.3.30–31). The moral significance of that letter is implicit in its very ink, for the letter has been written in Annabella's own blood, blood that originates in her *heart,* the site of conscience.

7
The Book of Nature

1

WHEN in *Paradise Lost* Milton describes what his blindness has cost him, he chooses a metaphor familiar to every seventeenth-century reader:

> ever-during dark
> Surrounds me, from the cheerful ways of men
> Cut off, and for the Book of knowledge fair
> Presented with a Universal blanc
> Of Nature's works to me expung'd and ras'd,
> And wisdom at one entrance quite shut out.

Appearing in the prologue to book 3,[1] these lines adopt an ancient formulation, the concept of nature as a book. Because of his blindness, Milton is denied access to that book, commonly imagined as a form of revelation parallel to the sacred book of Scripture; hence the reference to "wisdom" in the last line above. For the poet, it is as though God's figurative writing has been "expung'd and ras'd." As a result, he lacks a source not only of knowledge but also of inspiration which earlier he enjoyed. The deprivation must have been acute, for in *Paradise Lost* Milton lavishes considerable attention on visual appearances, especially to the way things look from a distance, whether it be Satan's vista of the world as he stares into space or the narrator's comparison of Satan's shield to the moon as seen through Galileo's telescope.

For Milton's contemporaries, nature's book offered a plethora of benefits. Owen Felltham looks back to a time when conventional books were few but compensation was everywhere: "He was a *Monke* of an honester *age,* that being asked how he could indure that *life,* without the *pleasure* of *bookes,* answered: The *Nature* of the *Creatures* was his *Library:* wherein, when he pleased, he could muse upon *Gods deepe Oracles.*"[2] The word "oracles" suggests the divine voice speaking to humankind, but those words take material shape: they become the book of creatures, or the book of nature. Hence for the unnamed monk, written words of the customary sort are unnecessary; the figurative word suffices. The book of nature contains the constituent parts of the created world, and these, in turn, express divine design. Nature, therefore, provides a fruitful source of meditation. To read and ponder that book is to experience illumination no less surely than by reading Scripture.

This chapter treats the book of nature as a metaphor with particular appeal in the sixteenth and seventeenth centuries, and also the ways in which the concept of nature's book changed during the Renaissance. Chapter 8 explores the significance of that book for two Shakespearean plays, *As You Like It* and *Pericles,* and offers evidence that the book of nature, a subject of investigation by some Elizabethan courtiers, was evolving in a direction that leads toward the modern understanding of nature.[3]

2

Like John Milton and Owen Felltham, other Renaissance authors envision the book of nature when discussing the past, especially the culture of pre-Christian antiquity. They argue that God's decision to reveal himself through nature provided humankind with a means of knowing divinity even before Scripture came into existence. The utility of nature's book, moreover, did not cease with the writing of Scripture: anyone, whether ancient or modern, literate or not, may profit from the study of God's creation. Sir Thomas Browne makes the point in *Religio Medici:* "there are two bookes from whence I collect my Divinity; besides that written one of God, another of his servant Nature, that universall and publik Manuscript, that lies expans'd unto the eyes of all; those that never saw him in the one, have discovered him in the other: This was the Scripture and Theology of the Heathens; the naturall motion of the Sun made them more admire him, than its supernaturall station did the Children of Israel; the ordinary effects of nature wrought more admiration in them, than in the other all his miracles."[4] Scripture does not supplant nature, for the latter continues to offer what it always did: graphic evidence of the creator's attributes. Those are defined by Pierre de la Primaudaye when he invokes "God his great booke of nature": "I meane the admirable frame of this Univers, or whole world. Wherein the infinite varieties and sorts of creatures, like so many visible wordes, doe proclaime and publish unto man the eternitie, infinitie, omnipotency, wisedome, justice, bountie, and other essentiall attributes of his dread and soveraigne creatour."[5] Nature, animate and inanimate alike, has the capacity to inspire admiration of the deity. In the words of John Donne, "Outward and visible means of knowing God, God hath given to all Nations in the book of Creatures, from the first leaf of that book, the firmament above, to the last leaf, the Mines under our feet."⁶ Humankind, therefore, has both an opportunity and an obligation to study nature's book: "There they have a book which they read; and they have a sentence of condemnation if they doe not."

Perusal of nature's book affords not only intellectual comprehension but also emotional reassurance, for the knowledge gained instills a spirit of abiding contentment. Richard Baxter speaks in joyful, almost ecstatic, terms of the effect engendered by reading that book: "the World is Gods book, which he set man at first to read; and every Creature is a Letter, or Syllable, or Word, or Sentence, more or less, declaring the name and will of God. There you may behold his wonderful Almightiness, his unsearchable Wisdom, his unmeasurable Goodness, mercy and compassions; and his singular regard of the sons of men! . . . Those that with holy and illuminated minds come thither to behold the footsteps of the Great and Wise and bountiful Creator, may find not only matter to *employ,* but to *profit* and *delight* their *thoughts.*"⁷ By following God's footsteps along the path of enlightenment, the reader achieves "delight," which in this context means the solace arising from a sense of God's solicitude.

To the extent that salvation depends upon knowledge of the divine will, this life requires assiduous attention to both books of God. In the next life, however, all such searching and study will become irrelevant. Since knowledge then will be instant and complete, the book of God's created world and the book of Scripture alike will hold no secrets. John Donne, tracing the soul's journey after death, emphasizes the totality of the enlightenment that accompanies salvation:

> We shall not pass from Author, to Author, as in a Grammar School, nor from Art to Art, as in an University; but, as that General which Knighted his whole Army, God shall Create us all Doctors in a minute. That great Library, those infinite Volumes of the Books of Creatures, shall be taken away, quite away, no more Nature; those reverend Manuscripts, written with Gods own hand, the Scriptures themselves, shall be taken away, quite away; no more preaching, no more reading of Scriptures, and that great School-Mistress, Experience, and Observation shall be remov'd, no new thing to be done, and in an instant, I shall know more, then they all could reveal unto me. I shall know, not only as I know already, that a Bee-hive, that an Ant-hill is the same Book in *Decimo sexto,* as a Kingdom is in *Folio.*⁸

Although Donne and Baxter, Browne and Felltham all view the book of nature as part of the Christian God's revelation, the metaphor antedates Christianity by centuries. Greek writers used the figure: Plotinus, for instance, describes the diviner's art as "a reading of letters written in nature, declaring an order and never deviating into disorder."⁹ Roman writers, too, identified nature with the written word. Claudian envisions nature personified, guarding a cavern where the laws of nature are recorded: "Before the entrance sits Nature, guardian of the threshold, of age immense yet ever lovely, around whom throng and flit spirits on every side. A venerable old man writes down immutable laws."[10] Christian authors also adopted the metaphor, identifying nature's book with Scripture. In his *Confessions* St. Augustine asks, "who, except thou, O our God, made that firmament of the authority of thy divine Scripture to be over us? As 'tis said: For the heaven shall be folded up like a book; and is even now stretched over us like a skin," and he continues, "Wherefore hast thou like a Skin stretched out the Firmament of thy book, that is to say those words of thine so well agreeing together; which by the ministry of mortal men thou spreadedst over us."[11] In the Middle Ages the metaphor continued to flourish. Hugh of St. Victor uses it to express evidence of the divine hand in creation: "this whole visible world is as a book written by the finger of God, that is, created by divine power; and individual creatures are as figures therein not devised by human will but instituted by divine authority to show forth the wisdom of the invisible things of God. But just as some illiterate man who sees an open book looks at the figures but does not recognize the letters: just so the foolish natural man who does not perceive the things of God sees outwardly in these visible creatures the appearances but does not inwardly understand the reason."[12] Alain de Lille envisions personified Nature recounting her gift of a writing implement to Venus: "I had also bestowed on her an unusually powerful writing-pen for her work so that she might trace the classes of things, according to the rules of my orthography, on suitable pages which called for writing by this same pen and which through my kind gift she had in her possession, so that she might not suffer the same pen to wander in the smallest degree from the path of proper delineation into the byways of pseudography."[13] And Dante the wayfarer, in the *Paradiso,* calls the primum mobile a *volume,* and, later, uses the same word to describe the eternal light: "Within its depths I saw ingathered, bound by love in one volume, the scattered leaves of all the universe."[14]

Although nature-as-book enjoyed popularity in both antiquity and the Middle Ages, it gained even greater appeal in the sixteenth and seventeenth centuries. This development was owing to the confluence of several factors, and among these none is plainer than the increased interest in the things of this world. The magnificence of Renaissance courts, with their palaces, paintings, apparel, and jewelry, is the most extravagant evidence of this looking outward and prizing what the senses behold. The minutely detailed objects in northern European painting reflect an interest in materiality, as do the exquisitely rendered furs, fabrics, and furnishings of Italian art. The trompe l'oeil wall paintings in the palaces of Sabbioneta and Mantua, along with the frescoes by Veronese in Palladio's

Villa Barbaro and the frescoes by the same painter in the church of San Sebastiano, Venice, signal a fascination with the way that people, plants, animals, and buildings look to the eye. None of this would have been possible without an understanding of the ways in which things are related to one another in space, the representation of which was made possible by linear perspective. This system, in turn, would scarcely have been invented unless the things of this world were thought important in themselves and worthy of artistic delineation.

As artists expressed their fascination with physical objects, so, too, philosophers increasingly directed their attention to the tangible. They urged that nature be looked at closely and carefully, that preconceptions be set aside, that the observer be attentive to what was actually seen, that such observation was intrinsically valuable. To advance their arguments, they deployed rhetorically the book of nature. Nicholas of Cusa (1401–1464), for example, frames a colloquy between a learned man and a layman to suggest the enlightenment available from experience of the natural world. When the Orator asks, "Where is the food of wisdom, if not in the books of wise men?" the Layman replies, "I do not say that it is not there, but that it is not there naturally. Those men who first applied themselves to writing about wisdom did not receive an increase of wisdom from the food of books that did not yet exist. They attained perfect manhood by natural nourishment. And they by far exceed others who think that they have advanced by books."[15] The Layman goes on to explain that the knowledge he possesses comes from God's books, "The ones that He has written with His own finger"[16]—an unmistakable allusion to the book of nature.

A century after Nicholas of Cusa affirmed the value of creation as a source of knowledge, Bernardino Telesio (1509–1586) developed a philosophy distinguished by "an emphatic denunciation of the arbitrary superimposition of abstractly rational schemata on to concrete physical processes which should instead be investigated *iuxta propria principia* (according to their own principles)."[17] Telesio, whom Francis Bacon called "the first of the moderns,"[18] believed that the knowledge achieved by the senses was indispensable. "Not by reason," he declared, "but by sense," and his pragmatism became an informing presence in such works as *The City of the Sun* by Tommaso Campanella. Similarly, Giordano Bruno (1548–1600), who admired Telesio, argued that the material world is capable of furnishing a pathway to the highest and most noble knowledge. In his *Heroic Frenzies* he uses the image of the soul journeying through "the forest of natural phenomena" to discover the truths hidden in caverns and thickets: "To that forest Pythagoras proceeded, seeking the truth by following its traces and vestiges in nature, that is, in the numbers which in a certain way make the progress, considerations, modes and operations of the truth apparent; for it is in number insofar as it applies to the many, to measurements, to time and to weight that the truth and essence of all things is found."[19] Here Bruno seems to be offering a methodology for exploring the very principles that animate nature, and in so doing he sounds more like a scientist than the author whose love poems fill *The Heroic Frenzies.*

Attention to the physical facts of nature was, of course, a precondition for advances in science and medicine. Those who pursued such research in the sixteenth century had come to feel that conventional learning was no longer a satisfactory guide to the natural world. A more direct approach was needed, one dependent not on the resources of great libraries but rather upon the ears and eyes of the individual investigator. As proponents pressed this argument, they enlisted the metaphor of nature as book. Perhaps no one articulated the new concern with practical research more forcefully than Philippus Aureolus Theophrastus Bombastus von Hohenheim, known as Paracelsus (1493–1541). Inveighing against the prevailing prestige of book knowledge, this contemporary of Erasmus and Luther envisioned himself as leading a one-man campaign against ignorance. As a pragmatist, especially in the treatment of disease, Paracelsus had little use for the medical authorities of his day: "In order . . . that truth may not give place to a lie, and that the obscurities of Galen, with his accomplices, may not quench and suppress the light of Nature in medicine, it is necessary that I, Theophrastus, in this book, should speak, not as a quack, but as a scientist who is not ashamed of his achievements in medicine."[20] He goes on to ask his rivals and detractors, "Have you ever cured the gout? Have you dared to attack leprosy?" His concern with results was incompatible with the deference customarily paid the ancients, whose medical treatises mixed observation with legend: "What Pliny and Dioscorides wrote about herbs they did not prove by experience, but gathered from the famous authors who knew many such matters, and then they filled many books with their feminine chatter. Dare to make the experiment for yourselves whether what they hand down is true."[21] During his brief tenure as physician to the city of Basel, Paracelsus expressed contempt for bygone authorities by throwing Avicenna's work on medicine into a bonfire. "Book knowledge," said Paracelsus on another occasion, "has never made a single physician."[22]

Although he successfully treated such well-known figures as Johann Froben, the printer of *Novum Instrumentum,* and although he corresponded with Erasmus, who suffered from the array of ailments recounted in his letters, Paracelsus alienated most contemporaries by his arrogance: "I am Theophrastus, and in addition I am *monarcha medicorum,* monarch of physicians, and I can prove to you what you cannot prove. I will let Luther defend his cause, and I will defend my cause, and I will defeat those of my colleagues who turn against me."²³ Eccentric and impolitic, Paracelsus possessed a supreme self-confidence that led him to challenge conventional wisdom. For him nature was truly a form of revelation; and there was nothing irreligious in scorning obtuse authority, particularly those who looked exclusively to Scripture for truth, rather than to the material world: "Nor do we care much for the vain talk of those who say more about God than He has revealed to them, and pretend to understand Him so thoroughly as if they had been in his counsels; in the meantime abusing us and depreciating the mysteries of Nature and of philosophy, about all of which they are utterly ignorant."²⁴ To experience nature directly is entirely compatible with acknowledging divinity: "This is to walk in the ways of the Lord, to be occupied in admiring His works, and to carry out His will, so far as is in us, or as it should and can be in us. This has been my Academia, not Athens, Paris, or Toulouse. After I had read many deceitful books of wise men I betook myself to this one alone, from which I learnt all that I write, which also I know to be true."²⁵ By "this one alone," Paracelsus means, of course, the book of nature, his chief source of knowledge: "From the light of Nature must enlightenment come, that the text *libri naturae* be understood, without which enlightenment no philosopher nor natural scientist may be."²⁶ If nature is a book, then that book should actually be scrutinized, not treated as though it were merely a poetic figure. To peruse nature's book entails, in practice, experimentation and observation; it is the business of the laboratory as well as the study.

For Francis Bacon (1561–1626), too, there was no substitute for firsthand observation of the natural world, and he expressed his conviction in language remarkably similar to that of Paracelsus. In *The Advancement of Learning* Bacon chastises those who are so wrapped up in their own mental processes that they fail to appreciate the world around them: "[an] Error hath proceeded from too great a reverence, and a kinde of adoration of the minde and understanding of man: by meanes whereof, men have withdrawne themselves too much from the contemplation of Nature, and the observations of experience: and have tumbled up and downe in their owne reason and conceits.²⁷ For Bacon such withdrawal represents not only foolish self-absorption but also a denial of the value of divine revelation: "they disdaine to spell, and so by degrees to read in the volume of Gods works."²⁸ Here he aligns himself with those who stress the continuing significance of creation, each expression of which has a legitimate claim on our attention: God, he says, places before us "two Bookes or volumes to studie, if we will be secured from errour: first the scriptures, revealing the will of God; and then the creatures expressing his power; whereof the later is a key unto the former; not onely opening our understanding to conceive the true sence of the scriptures, by the generall notions of reason and rules of speech; but chiefely opening our beleefe, in drawing us into a due meditation of the omnipotencie of God, which is chiefely signed and ingraven uppon his workes."[29] In an argument reminiscent of Paracelsus, Bacon justifies an examination of the natural world in the name of learning more fully God's design: "let no man upon a weake conceite of sobrietie, or an ill applyed moderation thinke or maintaine, that a man can search too farre, or bee too well studied in the Booke of Gods word, or in the Booke of Gods workes; Divinitie or Philosophie; but rather let men endeavour an endlesse progresse or proficience in both."[30] What Bacon urges is pragmatic investigation, and in so doing he implicitly modifies the traditional understanding of nature's book. That book had always been considered useful at least for the purpose of contemplation, but now it was being subjected to telescopes and, not long afterward, to microscopes as well; inferences about nature's book were being arrived at in a new way and they were beginning to point in a new direction.[31]

Like Bacon and Paracelsus, Galileo (1564–1642), too, saw the need to investigate the created world with alertness and without preconception. This scientist, who helped to discredit the notion of a geocentric universe by perfecting the telescope and who won John Milton's admiration by his lonely stand against ignorant orthodoxy, also chose to identify his research with the book of nature.[32] In the dedication of his *Dialogue Concerning the Two Chief World Systems—Ptolemaic and Copernican,* Galileo writes:

> He who looks the higher is the more highly distinguished, and turning over the great book of nature (which is the proper object of philosophy) is the way to elevate one's gaze. And though whatever we read in that book is the creation of the omnipotent Craftsman, and is accordingly excellently proportioned, nevertheless that part is most suitable and most worthy which makes His work and His craftsmanship most evident to our view.[33]

For the reader of Paracelsus and Bacon, these sentences have a familiar sound: nature is a book; that book is the creation of God; and by reading that book humankind gains knowledge of the deity. Galileo's decision to cast his apologia in such language may well reflect his confidence that a close examination of nature reveals design rather than chaos, that nature is an artifact. Galileo's language, however, may also be inspired by another consideration, one that becomes clearer as we recognize that he tends to use the trope not when he is enthusiastically advancing the frontiers of knowledge but rather when he feels most embattled.

What especially irritated Galileo about his countrymen was their penchant for relying so exclusively on what they learned in books, especially those of antiquity. For such people, he has only scorn:

> So far as I can see, their education consisted in being nourished from infancy on the opinion that philosophizing is and can be nothing but to make a comprehensive survey of the texts of Aristotle, that from divers passages they may quickly collect and throw together a great number of solutions to any proposed problem. They wish never to raise their eyes from those pages—as if this great book of the universe had been written to be read by nobody but Aristotle, and his eyes had been destined to see for all posterity.[34]

Galileo's words, written in 1612 and published the following year, evince the frustration of someone who looks around him and sees everywhere contentment with the status quo. His adoption of nature as book may represent, in part, an effort to challenge complacency by appealing to people who assume that everything worth knowing about the world is already contained in conventional books. If you are willing to read the works of Aristotle, Galileo argues, then why be reluctant to read this other book whose characters reveal no less? The metaphor, in Galileo's hands, seems designed to engage those accustomed to finding their most prized knowledge in books.

The use of the metaphor need not imply, incidentally, an absolute hostility to books of the conventional kind. Like Paracelsus and Bacon, Galileo was himself a prolific writer, and the printing press enabled him to disseminate his views and influence public opinion. In fact, the shift from a culture of script to one of print helped to advance the growth of scientific knowledge. As Elizabeth L. Eisenstein remarks, "Manuscript margins show skillful renderings of species of recognizable insects and birds. But the chance to discard inherited schemes, collect fresh data, and build improved models on them came only after print."[35] As for Sir Thomas Browne's characterization of nature as "that universall and publik Manuscript," Eisenstein comments: "there is no way of making fresh observations 'universal' and 'public' as long as they can be recorded only in manuscript form."[36]

Like Paracelsus, Galileo recognized that the greatest obstacle to scientific progress was not mere complacency but the active hostility of the clergy, who feared that a close study of secondary causation—what we call natural processes—may tend to obscure the providential hand of the creator.[37] The investigative study of nature's book was also disturbing to religious orthodoxy, for it requires each researcher to become his own interpreter; and such a prospect was unpalatable to those clerics who already fretted over the faithful reaching their own conclusions about Scripture. Protestant thinkers were more flexible than their Catholic counterparts. Galileo's contemporary, John Donne, actually seems to give primacy to the book of nature: "There is an elder booke in the World then the Scriptures; It is not well said, in the World, for it is the World it selfe, the whole booke of Creatures; And indeed the Scriptures are but a paraphrase, but a comment, but an illustration of that booke of Creatures."[38] And Calvin extolls the value of nature as a source of knowledge: "The reason why the author of The Letter to the Hebrews elegantly calls the universe the appearance of things invisible [Heb. 11:3] is that this skillful ordering of the universe is for us a sort of mirror in which we can contemplate God, who is otherwise invisible."[39] Calvin, however, makes the proviso that Scripture must provide the "spectacles" with which one contemplates creation: "Just as old or bleary-eyed men and those with weak vision, if you thrust before them a most beautiful volume, even if they recognize it to be some sort of writing, yet can scarcely construe two words, but with the aid of spectacles will begin to read distinctly; so Scripture, gathering up the otherwise confused knowledge of God in our minds, having dispersed our dullness, clearly shows us the true God."[40] It follows that the various sources of knowledge must be subordinated to Scripture: "we ought to hold to one rule of modesty and sobriety: not to speak, or guess, or even to seek to know, concerning obscure matters anything except what has been imparted to us by God's Word."[41] This conviction, which springs from a fear that original sin has significantly weakened humankind's intellect, presented a formidable problem for anyone extolling the evidence of the senses and insisting that all useful knowledge had yet to be discovered.

In his 1615 letter to the Grand Duchess Christina, Galileo addresses the value of first-hand observation and its relationship to Holy Writ:

> in discussions of physical problems we ought to begin not from the authority of scriptural passages, but from sense-experiences and necessary demonstrations; for the holy Bible and the phenomena of nature proceed alike from the divine Word, the former as the dictate of the Holy Ghost and the latter as the observant executrix of God's commands. It is necessary for the Bible, in order to be accommodated to the understanding of every man, to speak many things which appear to differ from the absolute truth so far as the bare meaning of the words is concerned. But Nature, on the other hand, is inexorable and immutable; she never transgresses the laws imposed upon her, or cares a whit whether her abstruse reasons and methods of operation are understandable to men. For that reason it appears that nothing physical which sense-experience sets before our eyes, or which necessary demonstrations prove to us, ought to be called in question (much less condemned) upon the testimony of biblical passages which may have some different meaning beneath their words.[42]

Galileo here ponders the respective claims of Scripture and the material world, maintaining that the latter is as important as the former. In defense of this position, Galileo adopts a twofold argument. First, he points out that the words of Scripture, while divinely inspired, cannot always be taken literally. As a successor to Erasmus and Luther, Galileo knew well that words in the Bible may be altered by translators and copyists. Some readers, at least, will be foiled by the biblical authors' or the translators' need to accommodate the ordinary believer. Galileo knew as well that commentators frequently disagree over the meaning of biblical texts. An exclusive focus on the words of Scripture, therefore, may fail to advance knowledge as fully as we would wish. Second, Galileo maintains that the facts of creation and the words of Scripture are simply different expressions of the same divine will. Because God is the author-maker of both, each has validity.[43] Logically, one form of divine expression cannot be set against the other; it makes no sense to claim, for instance, that observations of physical phenomena, along with resulting inferences, must be erroneous because the Bible appears to contradict them. Indeed, if one posits both God's creation of the world and his inspiration of Scripture, then there can be no such contradiction. The book of nature, if studied closely, will be found congruent with the truth of Scripture.

Whether Galileo's metaphor of the book represents confidence in nature or a concession to familiar ways of thinking about nature, his description of that book's language is unusual. He suggests that one does not read nature's book in conventional fashion, for its characters are not the letters of the alphabet but the mathematical expression of measurements:

> Philosophy is written in this grand book, the universe, which stands continually open to our gaze. But the book cannot be understood unless one first learns to comprehend the language and read the letters in which it is composed. It is written in the language of mathematics, and its characters are triangles, circles, and other geometric figures without which it is humanly impossible to understand a single word of it; without these, one wanders about in a dark labyrinth.[44]

Gerald Bruns relates Galileo's preference for mathematical language to apprehension about human speech, with its capacity for concealment: "To understand anything is necessarily to enter into a secret, or anyhow into the special reserve of natural languages. Scientists and philosophers prefer mathematics—Pythagoras, Galileo, and Descartes, for example, believed mathematics to be the language of God."[45] Whatever Galileo's reservations about language, "It is significant," writes Edwin Jones, "that, for the expression of this most critical aspect of his underlying conception, Galileo relied on a poetic device—metaphor. In light of modern analysis of language, it becomes clear that this was not merely a stylistic flourish."[46] That a scientist, concerned with mathematics, should adopt this particular metaphor testifies to its continuing force and its rhetorical appeal. What Galileo must have recognized was that his research would seem less threatening if it were couched in the form of so familiar a metaphor.

3

Perhaps only a few of Galileo's contemporaries considered the language of nature's book to be mathematical, but many felt that specialized knowledge was necessary if nature's book were to be read with comprehension. Increasingly in the sixteenth and seventeenth centuries, people believed that although the surfaces of nature were available to every sighted person, the meaning contained therein was not. Intelligence, learning, and the ability to decipher were required to understand nature's book. Sir Thomas Browne, who affirms the importance of both God's books, suggests that nature's signs may remain inscrutable to the uninitiated: "I have often admired the mysticall way of *Pythagoras,* and the secret Magicke of numbers; Beware of Philosophy, is a precept not to be received in too large a sense; for in this masse of nature there is a set of things that carry in their front, though not in capitall letters, yet in stenography, and short Characters, something of Divinitie, which to wiser reasons serve as Luminaries in the abysse of knowledge, and to judicious beliefes, as scales and roundles to mount the pinnacles and highest pieces of Divinity."[47] It is significant that Browne should name a pagan philosopher, Pythagoras, rather than a Christian; he sees the ancients as possessing keys to unlocking the information inherent in nature: "surely the Heathens knew better how to joyne and reade these mysticall letters, than wee Christians, who cast a more carelesse eye on these common Hieroglyphicks, and disdain to suck Divinity from the flowers of nature."[48] To some extent the revelation represented by nature, Browne suggests, has become inaccessible, for we have lost the language of signs and so look without comprehension upon what he calls "Hieroglyphicks," a word that came into wide use during the Renaissance.[49] Sir Walter Ralegh uses the same term when he speaks of studying the created world: "by his owne word, and by this visible world, is God perceived of men, which is also the understood language of the Almightie, vouchsafed to all his creatures, whose Hieroglyphical Characters are the unnumbred Starres, the Sunne, and Moone, written on these large volumes of the firmament: written also on the earth and the seas, by the letters of all those living creatures, and plants, which inhabit and reside therein."[50]

Interest in hieroglyphics was triggered by the discovery in 1419 of the *Hieroglyphics* of Horapollo Niliacus (Horus Apollo). A Florentine priest named Cristoforo Buondelmonti found a Greek manuscript of the book on the island of Andros in the Aegean and brought it back to Italy; it was subsequently printed by Aldus Manutius in 1505 and, in Latin translation, in 1515. Whether the author was himself an Egyptian is uncertain, but his work, perhaps dating from the fourth century, displays knowledge of Egyptian culture, especially writing. Europeans were already disposed to see writing as one of the special achievements of Egyptian civilization: Plato's *Phaedrus* attributes its very invention to the Egyptian god Theuth,[51] sometimes identified with the Greek Hermes and the Roman Mercury. To European eyes Egyptian writing was altogether different from their own; obelisks brought to Rome from Egypt in ancient times, along with other sculpture, displayed a writing by picture rather than letters. For Lodowick Bryskett, this form of writing represented an appropriate effort to deny a knowledge of profound truths to ordinary folk: "the Philosophers of old [did] write their mysteries under similitudes, to the end they might not be straight comprehended by every dul wit, and lose their reputation, by being common in the hands and mouth of every simple fellow. This manner first began among the wiser Aegiptians, and was afterwards followed by *Pythagoras* and *Plato*."[52] Renaissance readers of Horapollo thought that hieroglyphs were pictures symbolizing ideas exclusively, rather than representations of sounds. This mistake led them to believe that the key to reading hieroglyphs was an understanding of the connection between a visual symbol and a transcendent concept. Horapollo's work, which consists chiefly of symbolic pictures together with interpretations, seemed to promise access to a lost language and to the wisdom it contained.

Florentine Neoplatonists, convinced that the outward appearance of physical objects could be studied to discover some underlying idea, were attracted to Horapollo's work, which appeared to confirm their assumption about the relationship of things and ideas. Marsilio Ficino, for instance, wrote the following gloss on a passage in Plotinus, who identified hieroglyphs with Platonic ideas in visual form:

> The Egyptian priests, when they wished to signify divine things, did not use letters, but whole figures of plants, trees, and animals; for God doubtless has a knowledge of things which is not complex discursive thought about its subject, but is, as it were, the simple and steadfast form of it. Your thought of time, for instance, is manifold and mobile, maintaining that time is speedy and by a sort of revolution joins the beginning to the end. It teaches prudence, produces much, and destroys it again. The Egyptians comprehend this whole discourse in one stable image, painting a winged serpent, holding its tail in its mouth. Other things are represented in similar images, as Horus describes.[53]

Ficino, who refers to the author of the *Hieroglyphics* in that last sentence, was fascinated by Egyptian symbols because they seemed to offer immediate initiation into a nonmaterial reality. In this he followed Plotinus. As Liselotte Dieckmann observes, "What impressed Plotinus in the hieroglyphics as he saw them was the idea, so dear to his thinking, that they do not analyze wisdom discursively, but rather put it before the human eye to be understood intuitively in that flash of insight he treasured above all other ways of understanding."[54]

Even those thinkers who were not Neoplatonists in the manner of Ficino came to share his fascination with a language of visual symbols. Erasmus, in his *Adages,* tells how Aldus Manutius one day showed him an ancient coin: on one side was the image of Titus Vespasianus, accompanied by an inscription; on the other side was the picture of an anchor with a dolphin wrapped around it. Erasmus was quite taken with this image, which became the printing mark of the Aldine press: "This means nothing else than the saying of Augustus Caesar, 'hasten slowly,' or so the books on hieroglyphics tell us. That is the word for the enigmatic carvings which were so much used in early times, especially among the Egyptian soothsayers and priests, who thought it wrong to exhibit the mysteries of wisdom to the vulgar in open writing, as we do; but they expressed what they thought worthy to be known by various symbols, things or animals, so that not everyone could readily interpret them. But if anyone deeply studied the qualities of each object, and the special nature and power of each creature, he would at length, by comparing and guessing what they symbolised, understand the meaning of the riddle."[55] As this passage in Erasmus's *Adages* suggests, sixteenth-century thinkers came to see virtually any sort of pictorial symbol as "hieroglyphic" and to identify it specifically with Egyptian culture.[56] Moreover, the hieroglyphic came to be regarded as particularly important because, for Erasmus and others, it constitutes what Thomas M. Greene calls "the absolute signifier": "Hieroglyphics represent semiotic perfection; they present the ultimate code, and thus they dramatize the imperfection, the vulnerability of language."[57]

In a sense the belief that symbols drawn from the material world are signs of a nonmaterial reality was familiar to anyone who conceived of nature as a book. But implicit in much of the thinking about hieroglyphs was a modification of the view that nature's book lies open to all, that anyone, simply by gazing upon that book, may draw conclusions about the creator and his providence. Nature might be a book, but one written by an author given to communicating through arcane symbols: nature withholds meaning from the casual observer. To be sure, those truths might still be accessible. Paracelsus even argues that God intends humankind to progress to a world of ideas by studying natural phenomena: "It is not God's will that all He has created for the benefit of man and has given him as his own should remain hidden. . . . And even if He did conceal some things, He left nothing unmarked, but provided all things with outward, visible marks, with special traits—just as a man who has buried a treasure marks the spot in order that he may find it again."[58] This optimism about decoding nature's signs, however, was not shared universally. Instruction was necessary if the signs were to be read aright, and so authors, inspired by Horapollo, began to compile and systematize known symbols so as to provide the basis for interpretation. The most prodigious of these scholars was Giovanni Pierio Valeriano Bolzani, who began writing a commentary on Horapollo and who gradually increased the scope of his work until it became an encyclopedia of animal and plant, pagan and Christian symbols. His *Hieroglyphica sive de Sacris Aegyptiorum Literis Commentarii* (1556) includes many hundreds of signs without precedent in Horapollo: "A list containing the names of no less than about 200 authors used as references follows the introduction, and no less than about 1400 hieroglyphical categories, each with a variety of subdivisions, are mentioned in the index."[59] Valeriano ransacked the ancient world for clues to the language of symbols which, as recorded in stone, was vanishing even as he wrote: "In his dedication to Cosimo de'Medici, Valeriano describes his joyous labors in collecting and discovering these mysterious, lost meanings from the writings of Egyptians, Greeks, Romans, and barbarians. He remembers his dinner conversations with Cardinal Bembo about the obelisks at Rome and the current movement among Roman leaders to rescue from the lime-burners' kilns ancient monuments no more worthy to be destroyed than the statues of Michelangelo Buonarroti in St. Lorenzo."[60]

The popularity of hieroglyphs helped to inspire a revolution in book publishing, for symbolic illustrations began to accompany literary texts. Francesco Colonna's *Hypnerotomachia Poliphili,* published by Aldus Manutius in 1499, led the way. Colonna's book "employs as an adjunct to its text highly suggestive figures which go well beyond mere decoration, for by inserting them and their symbolism the reading of the text is modified. The combination indicates an awareness of the ambiguity of language and that extraction of the meaning of the book is a complex, arduous and not an obvious business."[61] This combination of the verbal and the pictorial became the essence of emblem books, which consist of visual images and written words: the image takes the form of a picture wherein animals, plants, people, topography, and mythological figures have symbolic meaning; the written words take the form of a brief motto, adjoining the picture, and an explanatory poem wherein the symbolism is made explicit. Andrea Alciato, the Milanesi jurist and author of the first emblem book, *Emblematum Liber* (1531), specifically aligns his constructions with hieroglyphics: "Words signify. Things are signified. Nevertheless things may also sometimes signify, such as Horapollo's and Chaeremon's hieroglyphics, and to prove it, we too have composed in verse a book entitled *Emblems*."[62] Designers of emblems may have believed that there existed a necessary connection between natural objects and the ideas they represented, but presumably that connection was not clear to every reader. Significantly, Claude Mignault wrote a commentary on Alciato's *Emblematum Liber*, and the huge size of Mignault's work, published in 1573, suggests that considerable learning was required to comprehend the meaning of symbolic signs. What Mignault, Valeriano, and other commentators did was to search humankind's store of knowledge in both its principal forms—as recorded in writing and in the world's materiality. If the pursuit of resemblances seems esoteric to us, the reader of emblem books finds that his eyes oscillate constantly between words (the motto and accompanying poem) and things (the symbolic picture). The more that things seem to contain meaning, the more words seem immanent in things. Language and signs, Michel Foucault observes, are not discrete categories: "The great metaphor of the book that one opens, that one pores over and reads in order to know nature, is merely the reverse and visible side of another transference, and a much deeper one, which forces language to reside in the world, among the plants, the herbs, the stones, and the animals."[63]

Implicit in the metaphor of nature's book, as evoked by emblematists, philosophers, scientists, and theologians, is a cluster of related assumptions: that the deity has created nature, that nature is therefore imbued with the creator's design, that the design contains truths about the creator, that those truths are conveyed by the shape of the natural world, that the natural world consists of signs, that those signs have a counterpart in the realm of ideas, that those ideas are capable of being expressed in words. Not everyone who conceived of nature as a book necessarily embraced all of these assumptions. Nor did everyone attribute the same significance to each. Nevertheless, the preponderance of thinking, especially in the late sixteenth and early seventeenth centuries, suggests a growing conviction that, if indeed nature is a book, much is required of anyone who would read that book with comprehension. Such readers must be equipped with knowledge. They have to be capable of deciphering signs. In his *Dialogue Concerning the Two Chief World Systems*, one of Galileo's speakers asserts that "nature first made things in her own way, and then made human reason skillful enough to be able to understand, but only by hard work, some part of her secrets."[64] Significantly, when the soothsayer in *Antony and Cleopatra* speaks of nature's book, he imagines that book as containing secrets, and he speaks with diffidence of his own ability to read it: "In nature's infinite book of secrecy / A little I can read" (1.2.10–11). By the time Shakespeare wrote these lines, reading nature's book had become analogous to reading conventional books in that both activities depended upon skill at interpretation. In fact, reading the book of nature could be as problematic as reading Scripture.

8
Nature on the Stage

1

ON the stage nature's book typically appears within the context of the art-nature topos.[1] Depending on the genre of a play, the representation of the topos may vary and, with it, the significance of nature's book. When, for example, that topos appears in a pastoral, nature's book is identified with the design informing the pastoral world, exerting a benign, restorative effect on those within it. For the inhabitants of pastoral, especially lovers, the book of nature constitutes a source of pleasure and an inspiration for their own writing. When the art-nature topos appears in a tragicomic romance, however, the book of nature is more problematic, even seemingly implicated in the experience of corrupt courts and dangerous seas; only in time is the providential design responsible for aligning art and nature made manifest. For the inhabitants of such a world, nature's book proves less scrutable and more mysterious than in pastoral; similarly, the characters' own writing may conceal and mislead as often as it reveals. To the extent that it expresses the relationship between art and nature, the book of nature represents a touchstone of value and a clue to the written word's significance in a play. On the stage nature's book affects what people write and how they write, the way they read and how they interpret what they read. The implications of nature's book for both theatrical properties and dramatic language may be usefully explored in two plays that dramatize the art-nature topos: a pastoral comedy, *As You Like It,* and a romance, or tragicomedy, *Pericles.*

2

Like lovers in other settings, lovers in pastoral have an impulse to express their joy or frustration in writing. But whereas those in courts and cities record their feelings with ink and paper, the implement of choice in pastoral is often a knife, and the medium, bark. Thus Shakespeare's Orlando, newly ensconced in the forest of Arden, expresses his love for Rosalind by writing poems which he carves on trees: "these trees shall be my books, / And in their barks my thoughts I'll character" (3.2.5–6).[2] This declaration in *As You Like It* signals the pastoral lover's closeness to nature, which fosters not only the experience of love but also the expression of that love in verse: nature exerts this effect by furnishing inspiration to the sensitive soul, a multitude of images out of which to construct his poetry, and the very material on which he writes. Within the precincts of pastoral, Orlando's writing on trees is identified with the writing of nature, for through the lover's inscription the book of nature becomes "a series of blank leaves which, inscribed with the thoughts of lovers, is not only symbolically but almost literally a book on whose pages a lover can record the amatory effusions of his heart and the names of his girl."[3] Rensselaer W. Lee calls Orlando's poetry a "variation on the grand and serious theme of nature as a book."[4] Shakespeare's dependence upon that book of nature extends beyond Orlando's poems, and may best be understood by examining his adaptation of the pastoral romance that furnished the basis of *As You Like It*.[5]

Paradoxically, although it celebrates a nature encompassing animal and plant, air and water, forest and field, the pastoral as an aesthetic form is highly artificial, a sophisticated author's entertainment for a sophisticated audience.[6] The world of pastoral is unlike any encountered in life, for the streams are clearer, the fountains purer, the grass greener; the trees are more stately, the atmosphere more serene, the shepherds more accomplished. Whatever shadows may fall across the pastoral, it offers inhabitants both the opportunity to fall in love and the leisure to write about that love. The shepherd-lover's daily round, which outside of pastoral might appear humdrum, becomes a source of satisfaction, for he is nourished by the rhythms of that life. Ordinarily, no outward catastrophe distracts him from a preoccupation with his own feelings: although nominally a shepherd, his real business is the contemplation of nature without and his heart within. So idealized is the world of pastoral that it can exist only in artistic form—on a stage, for instance, or in the pages of a book. Were a real breeze to blow through it, the pastoral landscape would shrivel and vanish like a blossom in the chilly wind of autumn.

Epitomizing the convergence of the natural and the artificial is a metaphor implicit in much pastoral literature—the book of nature. When Shakespeare's Orlando says, "these trees shall be my books," he means that the trees are like blank pages in which he will write. His remark presupposes a similarity between trees and books. If books are like trees in that both receive the impression of letters and thus contain words that may be read and understood, so trees are like books in possessing the quality of an artifact, even before they become a medium for poetry. Like other natural objects, trees are the product of intelligence and so manifest a principle of design. That design, in turn, affords both aesthetic pleasure and moral enlightenment to the receptive beholder. As Duke Senior observes, "this our life, exempt from public haunt, / Finds tongues in trees, books in the running brooks, / Sermons in stones, and good in every thing" (2.1.15–17). What the pastoral life offers the exiled duke and others who sojourn in Arden is enhanced sensitivity to the meaning and artistry of nature.

When a character within the pastoral writes, he takes his cue from the book of nature. Eschewing the overly clever and the neoteric, he prizes what he finds at hand: rusticity and simplicity. Such qualities are the source of his poetry's attractiveness. As Jacopo Sannazaro explains in the prologue to his *Arcadia,* "woodland songs carved on the rugged barks of beeches no less delight the one who reads them than do learned verses written on the smooth pages of gilded books."[7] Similarly, a character in Gil Polo's *Enamoured Diana* observes, "these pastorall and country songs, being full of simplicitie and plainnes, please me more, then the delicate voices set togither with curious skill, and full of newe inventions and conceits in the brave pallaces of Kings and Princes."[8] A certain disingenousness characterizes such claims, for pastoral literature is scarcely the creation of country bumpkins. Indeed, it finds a readership in those "brave palaces" disparaged in *Enamoured Diana.* Nevertheless, Sannazaro and Gil Polo indicate the appeal of pastoral poetry: a reliance upon an artful simplicity which has its origins in nature.

The confluence of the artistic and the natural underlies Thomas Lodge's *Rosalynde,* a pastoral romance first published in 1590 (the same year as Sidney's *Arcadia*) and, later in the decade, the inspiration for *As You Like It.* According to Lodge, the forest of Arden serves an aesthetic principle: it decorates and celebrates. The narrator describes the foliage with figurative language befitting a work of art. For instance, of the place where two shepherds meet, Lodge writes, "The ground where they sat was diapred with *Floras* riches, as if she ment to wrap *Tellus* in the glorie of her vestments."[9] Montanus and Coridon have chosen this spot, intuiting its suitability for their conversation. They are attracted by a landscape that seems not the result of happenstance but of purposeful arrangement: "round about in the forme of an Amphitheater were most curiouslie planted Pine trees, interseamed with Limons and Citrons, which with the thicknesse of their boughes so shadowed the place, that *Phoebus* could not prie into the secret of that Arbour" (183). The secret preserved by the configuration of the trees is one with direct relevance for the young Montanus: "so united were the tops with so thicke a closure, that *Venus* might there in her jollitie have dallied unseene with her deerest paramour" (183). The natural world, then, conspires to provide an aesthetically pleasing milieu that is conducive to love; although Venus herself may not make an appearance, Montanus experiences her beneficent influence.

Susceptibility to love in Lodge's Arden presupposes sensitivity to nature. Montanus, for example, recognizes what he owes to the nature that has bestowed on him a temperament amenable to passion: he describes himself as one "whom nature makes of tender molde, / And youth most pliant yeeldes to fancies fire" (185). Falling in love, Montanus discovers, entails not only his response to a particular woman named Phoebe but also to the nature that has created her. As he gazes upon her, late in Lodge's romance, the shepherdess seems almost the embodiment of nature: she wears "a peticoate of scarlet, covered with a greene mantle; and to shrowde her from the Sunne, a chaplet of roses: from under which appeared a face full of Natures excellence" (228). By falling in love with such a woman, Montanus expresses his own innate affinity with nature and, in effect, pays tribute to the nature that has endowed Phoebe with such beauty.

In the everyday world, especially the realm of shepherds, sensitivity to nature and to love rarely issues in verse. Even Montanus acknowledges that those who live in the country seldom command the resources of art: "The ploughman little wots to turne the pen, / Or bookeman skills to guide the ploughmans cart, / Nor can the cobler count the tearmes of Art" (185). And, he continues, the impulse to express his feelings takes a form appropriate to his station: "My sheephooke is my pen, mine oaten reede / My paper, where my manie woes are written" (186). This comment is not without some sly humor on Lodge's part, for Montanus does possess the capacity to write in a more orthodox fashion; like other pastoral figures, he turns out poems in considerable number. But his remark about sheephook and oaten reed indicates something important about his approach to poetic composition: his writing is not the result of laborious practice, much less the conscious imitation of another's poetic invention. Rather, Montanus's poetry derives its characteristic features from his immediate surroundings. He constructs his poems out of natural images, for he sees natural phenomena as the counterpart of his own activity. In weeping, for instance, he emulates rain and rivulets of water: "So streame my teares as showers from Alpine hills" (184). Even his inner experience finds a material parallel. His very thoughts and feelings correspond to the topography and animal life of a shepherd's bailiwick:

> My sheepe are turnd to thoughts, whom froward will
> Guides in the restlesse Laborynth of love,
> Feare lends them pasture wheresoere they move,
> And by their death their life renueth still.
>
> (186)

A reciprocal relationship exists between nature and humankind, allowing the one to be identified with the other. Thus Montanus's insistent imagery of trees, flowers, and seasons of the year suggests that his passion belongs to elemental forces in the world at large, that his love for Phoebe has a precedent elsewhere in nature.

When the visitors to Arden—Rosalynde in the guise of Ganimede, Alinda under the name Aliena—eavesdrop on the shepherds, it is difficult to know whether the women are more affected by Montanus's passion, itself a manifestation of sensitivity to nature, or by his artistry, which allows him to express that passion in verse. In the spirit of good will that suffuses Arden, the women reveal their presence, Alinda saying, "Shepheards all haile, (for such wee deeme you by your flockes) and Lovers, good lucke; (for such you seeme by your passions) our eyes being witnesse of the one, and our eares of the other" (187). Rosalynde, of course, is herself in love and so understands the yearning that Montanus expresses. What disposes her favorably, however, is not just the subject of his eclogue with Coridon but also his style. The women, who have discovered the shepherds by following a trail of madrigals and roundelays, are so agreeably moved that they ask Montanus to recite yet more of his verse: "You shall goe, quoth *Aliena,* but first I will intreate *Montanus* to sing some amorous Sonnet, that hee made when he hath been deeply passionate" (189–90). The sonnet they hear conflates nature and art, for the poem consists of natural images in profusion, images articulated through meter, rhyme, and stanzaic form that bespeak the shepherd's craftsmanship; the design of his verse complements the design of nature.

If Lodge's women discover that writing is as much a part of Arden as the trees themselves, Shakespeare's women find something quite different, for the shepherds in *As You Like It* do not enjoy the same relationship to nature as those in *Rosalynde*.[10] In fact, they seem rather indifferent to their setting. The character corresponding to Montanus is called Silvius, and although his name is conventional in pastoral[11] (and perhaps even links him to his habitat since *silva* means forest in Latin), he no longer belongs to the fields and bowers of Arden in the way Lodge's shepherd does. Shakespeare preserves the incident of the women finding the shepherds in conversation, but he declines to identify those shepherds with their locale. Silvius's speeches lack the natural imagery that pervades those of Montanus, and there is no equivalent in the play of Lodge's detailed description of the place where the shepherds converse. Instead of the affinity between humankind and nature described by Lodge, Shakespeare dramatizes a disjunction. The shepherds in *As You Like It* could just as easily belong to another realm entirely; neither their language nor demeanor suggests that they are necessarily part of a pastoral landscape.[12]

The women, meanwhile, are largely unmoved by the shepherds' speech. Although Rosalind may say to herself, "Alas, poor shepherd, searching of thy wound, / I have by hard adventure found mine own" (2.4.44–45), she maintains a certain distance, physical and psychological, from him. Eavesdropping, she conceals her presence, thereby precluding the kind of interchange that Lodge presents. More circumspect than their counterparts in *Rosalynde,* Rosalind and Celia remain detached, as though wary of being drawn into an awkward meeting with the shepherds.[13]

Shakespeare's heroines take no delight in Silvius's verse, for there is none to enjoy. The playwright strips the shepherd of his role as writer. Although Silvius's speeches are stylistically elaborate, he merely talks like a poet. His discussion with Corin is not called an eclogue, as it is in Lodge; the shepherds' lines seem to represent a rarefied kind of conversation. With his verbal parallelism and repetition, Silvius sounds like a man who has just stepped out of a sonnet. When, in a later scene, he speaks directly to his beloved, his language, similarly, belongs to Renaissance love lyrics. He calls Phebe an "executioner" and envisions himself as her victim (3.5.3); he complains of suffering "wounds visible" made by love's arrows. This shepherd has become, in Shakespeare's hands, a highfalutin Petrarchan lover, transported to the green world. No wonder the women initially decline to engage him in conversation. They cannot take this self-absorbed, earnest figure as seriously as he takes himself, and they find no aesthetic delectation in his stilted language.

In Silvius the balance which the pastoral usually maintains between the natural and the artificial is tipped in the direction of the latter. Unlike the character of William, whose manner and speech are redolent of a humble habitat, Silvius seems curiously disconnected from his setting. Despite being immersed in nature, this shepherd evidently spends little time communing with the meadows or creatures of Arden. His language lacks, for the most part, images drawn from experience of the natural world. He sounds as though he finds inspiration not in the book of nature but in the books of poets.

That Silvius or, for that matter, anyone else in pastoral should emulate the language of another, especially a well-known author, is hardly surprising, for as Thomas G. Rosenmeyer observes, authors of pastoral are acutely conscious of their predecessors.[14] Nevertheless, Shakespeare's Silvius, considered in the context of other pastoral figures, seems unusually affected; and he creates this impression because, paradoxically, he is *not* presented as a poet. Were Silvius a writer, like the shepherd-lovers of Sannazaro or Gil Polo or Lodge, we should expect his language to be artful in ways dictated by generic tradition. But since his speeches are not designated as eclogues or sonnets or madrigals, they must be considered spoken—rather than written—language. As such they seem mannered and overwrought, the sort of thing one might hear in those "brave palaces" disparaged by Gil Polo.

To underscore the deficiencies of the shepherd's language, Shakespeare subjects it to a form of criticism highly unusual in pastoral, and he does this through the character of Rosalind. Viewing the shepherds more with impatience than indulgence, she chides them for affecting stereotyped roles—Silvius, the unrequited lover; Phebe, the disdainful mistress. Although Rosalind is herself a visitor in Arden, she possesses a sensitivity to both the place and its inherent values which the natives lack. Adopting an image befitting the nature which is her touchstone, she asks Silvius: "You foolish shepherd, wherefore do you follow her, / Like foggy south, puffing with wind and rain?" (3.5.49–50). And she lambastes Phebe for being too attentive to the surfaces of life—specifically, for becoming enamored of "Ganymede": "'Tis not your inky brows, your black silk hair, / Your bugle eyeballs, nor your cheek of cream / That can entame my spirits to your worship" (ll. 46–48). As this catalogue of Petrarchisms suggests, the shepherds make the mistake of allowing literary patterns to guide their conduct and speech; the term "inky" evokes those women who exist in books as the consequence of black ink imprinted on white paper. Rosalind affirms the value of another model when she tells Phebe: "I see no more in you than in the ordinary / Of nature's sale-work" (ll. 42–43). Phebe, then, is not the woman whom Silvius's language describes; she is, rather, the woman whom nature has created.

If the native inhabitants of Arden are not immune to affectation, neither are those who sojourn in the forest. Of no one is this more true than Orlando, who shares with Silvius the experience of youth, love, and frustration. Both men, moreover, seem to be made foolish rather than ennobled by the way they deal with the formidable women in their lives. Awkward in Arden, Silvius and Orlando prove comic to others even if they themselves are in earnest. For their behavior they earn a reproof from the same woman, who sees in them both the telltale marks of imposture. In Rosalind's view the men are insufficiently straightforward and excessively studied, and she sees it as her task to reform their action and speech.

Although he differs from Silvius in being a poet, Orlando writes the way Silvius would, were the shepherd to express himself in written form. Orlando appears in 3.2 with poem in hand,[15] looking for a tree to which he might attach it:

> Hang there, my verse, in witness of my love,
> And thou, thrice-crowned queen of night, survey
> With thy chaste eye, from thy pale sphere above,
> Thy huntress' name that my full life doth sway.

> O Rosalind, these trees shall be my books,
> And in their barks my thoughts I'll character,
> That every eye which in this forest looks
> Shall see thy virtue witness'd every where.
> Run, run, Orlando, carve on every tree
> The fair, the chaste, and unexpressive she.
>
> (3.2.1–10)

We do not immediately hear the text of Orlando's lyric, but so hyperbolic is his praise that, one imagines, the poem will prove more extravagant than affecting. That assumption is borne out moments later when Rosalind appears, paper in hand, and recites a poem, presumably the very one that Orlando affixed to a tree:

> "From the east to western Inde,
> No jewel is like Rosalind.
> Her worth, being mounted on the wind,
> Through all the world bears Rosalind.
> All the pictures fairest lin'd
> Are but black to Rosalind.
> Let no face be kept in mind
> But the fair of Rosalind."
>
> (3.2.88–95)

The combination of trite imagery and banal content makes us grateful that the poem is no longer than eight lines. Devoid of subtlety or elegance, the verse, with its relentless rhyme, assaults the ear. The poem's deficiencies are magnified by the way Rosalind reads it aloud—presumably with something less than complete approbation; although she is in love with Orlando, she consistently finds his expression of affection wanting. Orlando's poetry is undercut still further when Touchstone provides an impromptu parody, as for instance: "If a hart do lack a hind, / Let him seek out Rosalind" (ll. 101–2). Through clever mimicry of Orlando's rhyme scheme, the clown, who has no precedent in Lodge's romance, subjects Orlando's love poetry to a withering critique.

Touchstone's criticism of the jejune Orlando illumines the challenge that Shakespeare confronts in seeking to adopt a pastoral romance to the theater: how to preserve pastoral attitudes and behavior without so encasing the play in artificiality that it fails to engage an audience. Shakespeare's solution is not to tone down the activity we might expect of a pastoral lover, but to accentuate it, pushing the characterization of Orlando toward the saccharine and even the ludicrous. When, for example, Orlando bursts upon the stage with poem in hand, he throws himself into the role of pastoral lover so intensely that he seems a caricature. Rosalind scoffs at his attitudinizing when she complains, later in the scene, "There is a man haunts the forest, that abuses our young plants with carving 'Rosalind' on their barks; hangs odes upon hawthorns, and elegies on brambles; all, forsooth, deifying the name of Rosalind" (3.2.359–63). With this speech Shakespeare pokes fun not only at Orlando but also at the very tradition of pastoral romance in which such behavior represents the norm. This reflects the playwright's shrewd assessment that what works in a prose narrative will not necessarily succeed onstage: transforming a narrative into drama alters the effect of certain pastoral conventions. Although a writer of prose fiction may be able to treat them straightforwardly, a dramatist knows that they may appear precious in the theater. Accordingly, instead of surrounding Orlando with other characters who are as trapped in conventional roles as he—and thus risking derisive laughter from the audience—Shakespeare contrasts him with Rosalind, Touchstone, and others, inviting the audience to share in the laughter of those who find Orlando a trial.

By turning Orlando into a caricature, Shakespeare applies pastoral convention to advantage, for in addition to achieving comic effect, Shakespeare also allows for a deepening of the characterization. Orlando is most silly when most closely observing conventional behavior, but those conventions represent merely a starting point for the character; they exist to be repudiated, and it is precisely in such repudiation that Orlando comes to life onstage. The further he distances himself from self-conscious poses, the more compelling he becomes as a character. In short, Shakespeare makes a virtue of necessity when he portrays Orlando by means of such pastoral conventions as carving names and poems on trees: the playwright creates the basis for the character's growth and maturation.[16]

Shakespeare's readiness to satirize its trappings does not betoken any contempt for the pastoral ideal. Indeed, his dramatization of Arden demonstrates an allegiance to the essence of pastoral: the representation of a nature whose design ensures a benign influence on humankind. In *As You Like It,* as in *Rosalynde,* the forest exerts a salubrious effect, offering refuge to those who flee civilization, solace to those saddened by loss, redemption to those besmirched by ambition.[17] The forest may not be entirely idyllic, but neither was the pastoral world of Theocritus or Virgil, Mantuan or Boccaccio. If a cool wind is not unknown in Arden, and if mercantile concerns occasionally intrude, Shakespeare's pastoral world proves more hospitable to love, romantic and brotherly, than does the corrupt court. It also supplies the conditions for expressing that love in verse.

Orlando is the exemplar of the forest's beneficent influence. At first he is estranged from the ways of Arden: sword in hand, he blunders into

Duke Senior's camp, full of unnecessary threats and bluster, only to be greeted by kindness and hospitality. Almost immediately Orlando falls under the spell of Arden, abandoning inappropriate attitudes as readily as he changes costume to that of a forester, and begins to appreciate nature in a new way. This development is reflected in his second effort at verse. Although recited in the same scene as his first, this poem represents artistic accomplishment of a very different order:

> " . . . upon the fairest boughs,
>   Or at every sentence end,
> Will I 'Rosalinda' write,
>   Teaching all that read to know
> The quintessence of every sprite
>   Heaven would in little show.
> Therefore heaven Nature charg'd
>   That one body should be fill'd
> With all graces wide-enlarg'd."
>
> (3.2.135–43)

This expression of love, while conventional, is superior to the poem found by Rosalind and read aloud only moments earlier. Here the rhyme scheme is not so insistent nor are the ideas quite so simple-minded. Orlando achieves this result because he is inspired by nature or, more precisely, by the nature immanent in Rosalind: "Nature presently distill'd / Helen's cheek, but not her heart, / Cleopatra's majesty, / Atalanta's better part, / Sad Lucretia's modesty" (ll. 144–48). He envisions his beloved as the creation of heaven, and heaven as directing nature to fashion this woman. Nature, the poem asserts, has in Rosalind assembled the most attractive features of the world's fairest women.[18]

In portraying Orlando as a man capable of appreciating nature and of expressing that appreciation through the written word, Shakespeare depends closely upon Lodge's characterization of Rosader, Orlando's counterpart. When Rosader celebrates Rosalynde's beauty, he does so in language that betokens the inspiration of nature: "Of all sweete flowers the Rose doth sweetest smell, / Of all faire maides my *Rosalynde* is fairest"; and "Of all high trees the Pine hath hightest crest, / Of all soft sweetes I like my Mistres brest" (199). Rosader turns to poetry out of feeling of oneness with nature: "One day among the rest, finding a fit oportunitie and place convenient, desirous to discover his woes to the woodes, hee engraved with his knife on the barke of a Myrtle tree, this pretie estimate of his Mistres perfection" (199). Putting knife to bark, Rosader extolls not only his beloved but also the world of nature which she epitomizes. Although we do not see Orlando actually incise words on trees—an actor could not do so without bringing the dramatic action to an abrupt stop—his second poem demonstrates his affinity with nature no less effectively than does Rosader's carving.

As a paean to nature, Orlando's second poem deserves a more sympathetic rendering than his earlier poem received at the hands of Rosalind. Accordingly, Shakespeare has Celia find and read it aloud. Presumably she gives the poem a more impartial recitation than it would receive from Rosalind; after all, Celia is, throughout the play, less dismissive of Orlando than is her companion. To have allowed either Rosalind or Orlando himself to recite the poem would have compromised its theatrical effect by, in the one instance, sarcasm, or, in the other, by enthusiasm. Celia is able to strike the right balance, complementing the content of the poem by her modulated delivery.

Were he endeavoring to preserve the spirit of Lodge's romance unalloyed, Shakespeare would have sustained this moment, perhaps by having Celia reflect on the substance of Orlando's poem. Characteristically, however, Shakespeare breaks the spell cast by Celia's recitation and moves the scene toward comic effect. Rosalind, who has been eavesdropping, reveals her presence and immediately begins criticizing the lines: "some of them had in them more feet than the verses would bear" (3.2.165–66). Celia protests, "That's no matter; the feet might bear the verses," but Rosalind is not assuaged so easily: "Ay, but the feet were lame, and could not bear themselves without the verse, and therefore stood lamely in the verse" (ll. 169–71). Rosalind's scorn may arise out of embarrassment at being the subject of extravagant compliment: by talking about metrical deficiencies in the verse, she deflects her companion's attention away from the content of the poem. Of course, it is also possible that Rosalind finds the poem as deficient as she claims. After all, characters in *As You Like It* are connoisseurs of style, seemingly more interested in the manner of expression than in the matter; Shakespeare's heroine certainly takes as much notice of these concerns as does her counterpart in *Rosalynde*.

Lodge's heroine, to be sure, is not insensitive to the niceties of poetic expression. At one point she even wonders aloud whether Rosader's poetry accurately conveys what she feels: "I can smile (quoth *Ganimede*) at the Sonettoes, Canzones, Madrigales, rounds and roundelayes, that these pensive patients powre out, when their eyes are more ful of wantonnesse, than their hearts of passions" (207–8); and she goes on to make this indictment of poet-lovers: "they onely have their humours in their inckpot." Her remark is specifically aimed at Rosader who, she observes, does not necessarily foster his relationship to the woman he loves by spending time roaming through Arden, composing tributes: "Such gentle Forrester we may deeme you to bee, that rather passe away the time heere in these Woods with writing amorets, than to bee deeply enamoured (as you saye) of your *Rosalynde*" (208). If Lodge is willing, momentarily, to call into question one of the most conventional of pastoral activities, he is not prepared to allow the charge to be sustained. Immediately Rosader affirms the validity of his verse, explaining that his poetry is a testament to his passion, the outward manifestation of the deep change he has experienced within: "Trust me Swayne (quoth *Rosader*) but my Canzon was written in no such humour: for mine eye & my heart are relatives, the one drawing fancie by sight, the other entertaining her by sorrowe" (208). His poetry, moreover, is not simply a tribute to his beloved (though it is that). The poetry also celebrates the nature that has created Rosalynde: "If thou sawest my *Rosalynde,* with what beauties Nature hath favoured her, with what perfection the heavens hath graced her, with what qualities the Gods have endued her; then wouldst thou say, there is none so fickle that could be fleeting unto her" (208). By this affirmation of his poetry's purpose, Rosader invests his writing with a dignity and value that Rosalynde does not again challenge.

Lodge's hero is an accomplished poet from the beginning: even before he enters Arden, Rosader writes, as for instance when he receives a gift from Rosalynde, following the wrestling match: "he stept into a tent, and taking pen and paper writ this fancie" (172). Orlando has no similar history. He can scarcely articulate his thanks when Rosalind gives him a chain following his victory: "What passion hangs these weights upon my tongue? / I cannot speak to her, yet she urg'd conference" (1.2.257-58). Nor does he write to her; Orlando becomes a poet only after he visits Arden. Although the forest may liberate his creative energies, what he writes evokes only Rosalind's disdain. By contrast, Lodge's hero composes verse that his beloved enjoys. For example, when Rosalynde asks Rosader what perfection the woman he loves possesses, "he pulde a paper forth his bosome, wherein he read this" (202). Far from irritating her, the verses delight Rosalynde. In fact, she would hear still more: "hast thou not, said she, (having so melancholie opportunities as this Forrest affoordeth thee) written more Sonnets in commendations of thy Mistres?" (203). Rosalynde relishes the poems not only because she enjoys his attentions but also because she finds his poetry aesthetically pleasing.

By making Orlando a less accomplished poet than Rosader, Shakespeare establishes the basis for a more complicated character. Less mature than Rosader, Orlando has more to learn from his beloved; indeed, he must change to be worthy of her. Rosalind's "cure" of her man, which is more central to the plot of *As You Like It* than to that of *Rosalynde,* involves the reformation of Orlando's style.[19] For her, style reflects character, and if one's manner of expression is deficient, then so, in a sense, is he. She would rid Orlando of his propensity for prolix, extravagant speech. In the best pastoral tradition, Shakespeare's character prefers simplicity to complication.

Despite her concern with style, writing occupies a comparatively small role in Rosalind's tutelage of Orlando; she would much rather hear an expression of love than read one. This points to a major difference between the prose romance and the play: Shakespeare's characters write a good deal less than do Lodge's. The play contains only two poems by Orlando, whereas in Lodge we find Rosader's sonnet, engraved on a myrtle tree (199–200); "Rosalyndes Description," recited to Ganimede (202–3); Rosader's sonnet, recited under a fig tree (207); Rosader's "Second Sonetto" (209–10); and his "Third Sonnet" (210). Moreover, as we have seen, Shakespeare's shepherd is not a writer at all, whereas Lodge's Montanus composes his "passion," carved in a pine tree (180–81); a second poem, carved on a beech tree (181–82); the eclogue between Montanus and Coridon (183–87); Montanus's sonnet, recited at the request of Aliena (190); a sonnet spoken directly to Phoebe (228–29); Montanus's sonnet read by the king (249); and a second sonnet read by the king (250). The reader of *Rosalynde* also finds Rosalynde's madrigal (175–76); the wooing eclogue between Rosalynde and Rosader (211–13); Phoebe's sonnet (229–30); Saladyne's sonnet (234–35); Phoebe's sonnet to Ganimede (240–41); and Coridon's song (254–55).

The difference between *Rosalynde* and *As You Like It* involves much more than the number of poems included in each work, as we can see by comparing an incident common to both Lodge and Shakespeare: the shepherd's delivery of a message from the shepherdess he loves to the "man" with whom she is smitten. Here is Lodge's account of the recipient's response: "[Ganimede] taking the letters unript the seales, and read over the discourse of *Phoebes* fancies. When shee had read and overread them, *Ganimede* began to smile, & looking on *Montanus* fell into a great laughter: and with that called *Aliena,* to whom she shewed the writings" (241). Ganimede then gives the "letters"—actually a letter in prose and a sonnet—to Montanus so that he may read and thereby realize the folly of his passion for Phoebe. While preserving the essentials of this episode, Shakespeare makes a series of alterations that enhance its theatricality. He creates tension between messenger and recipient by having Rosalind accuse Silvius of being the author; by having Rosalind read the letter aloud (instead of merely handing it to the shepherd); and by having Rosalind criticize the letter's meaning and style while Silvius questions her interpretation. Thus, for example, when Rosalind reads, "'Art thou god to shepherd turn'd, / That a maiden's heart hath burn'd?'" and says to Silvius, "Can a woman rail thus?" he replies, "Call you this railing?" (4.3.40–43).

Even more important, Shakespeare's handling of the incident alters our attitude toward both the shepherd and the poem he delivers. First, Silvius seems more silly than does Montanus; because the missive is read aloud, there is something more public about Silvius's humiliation, even if there are only three characters onstage. Second, any feeling of compassion for Silvius is blunted by Rosalind's treatment of him; she squelches Celia's instinctive sympathy for Silvius, saying, "Do you pity him? No, he deserves no pity" (l. 66). Third, Silvius is shown to be on a fool's errand because the poem itself is absurd. That poem, directed to a woman disguised as a man, suggests a certain shallowness and imperception on the part of the writer; the language of the poem reflects the writer's self-absorption. Significantly, the shepherdess' poem contains not a single image drawn from nature. Her diction—prayers, mind, offers, study—bespeaks cerebration, a psyche divorced from the vital world around her. It would be bad enough if Silvius delivered a well-written expression of love, but for him to deliver this particular love letter makes him appear all the more deficient—and all the more comic.

Shakespeare's treatment of the episode also contains a significant omission, one that has the effect of depriving Silvius of the dignity that his counterpart in *Rosalynde* enjoys. In Lodge's account Montanus says to Ganimede, who has just perused Phoebe's letter: "those characters which true Love hath stamped, neither the envie of Time nor Fortune can wipe awaye" (242). By this remark Lodge's shepherd affirms the value and permanence of a metaphoric writing that Silvius never mentions. At the same time Montanus affirms his devotion, lending a significance to writing that it never achieves in the play. As a writer himself, moreover, Montanus can go on, as Silvius cannot, to proffer poetry of his own, as tangible testimony of his love for Phoebe. Thus following the delivery of Phoebe's letter, Montanus presents his own poems for King Gerismond's inspection. The king praises Montanus both for the depth of his passion and for its expression in verse: "When the King had read this Sonnet, hee highly commended the device of the Shepheard, that could so wittely wrap his passions in a shadow, and so covertly conceale that which bred his chiefest discontent" (249). Both Lodge's shepherd and Shakespeare's may feel aggrieved, but Montanus possesses, on account of his own poetry, a stature that Silvius is denied.

Despite his skill as a poet, even Lodge's shepherd knows when to put aside the written word. On the day appointed for the wedding of Aliena and Saladyne, Montanus arrives, looking melancholy: "on his head he wore a garland of willowe, his bottle hanged by his side wheron was painted despaire, and on his sheephooke hung two sonnets as labels of his loves & fortunes" (248).[20] But when "Ganimede" is revealed to be a woman in disguise, and when Phoebe finally agrees to accept Montanus, the shepherd has the good sense to throw "away his garland of willow, his bottle, where was painted dispaire, and cast his sonnets in the fire, shewing himselfe as frolicke as *Paris* when he hanseled his love with

Helena" (253). Since his days as a suitor are over, he no longer needs the accouterments of the would-be lover. The only writing he requires now is the writing in his heart, which he has borne all along.

Shakespeare's "variation" (to use Rensselaer Lee's term) on nature as book in *As You Like It* involves diminishing the prominence that writing achieves in Lodge's *Rosalynde*. Although Shakespeare preserves the convention of nature's book as accessible in the pastoral realm and of a lover's poetry as consonant with that book, he has chosen to limit both the number of writers in Arden and the number of poems written. The playwright's decision undoubtedly owes much to the exigencies of the stage, which is less hospitable to the recitation of written materials than are the pages of a prose romance. Such recitations must be kept fairly brief onstage lest they try the patience of the audience. An impromptu parody of a poem, such as Touchstone's, is one thing; the straightforward reading aloud of a thirty-six-line poem is quite another. Shakespeare must have been mindful of how different was his theatrical audience from Lodge's readership. In his title Lodge specifically alludes to John Lyly, the Elizabethan progenitor of the elegant, euphuistic romance. Following *Rosalynde* in Lodge's title are these words: *Euphues golden legacie: found after his death in his Cell at Silexedra. Bequeathed to Philautus sonnes noursed up with their father in England. Fetcht from the Canaries.* The Londoner who purchased a copy of *Rosalynde* was presumably literate, sophisticated, and possessed of a taste for leisurely narrative. For that reader the poems that appear with such frequency throughout the work would not be regarded as unduly slowing the story but rather as furnishing a pleasing amplitude to the action.

A theatrical audience containing a significant number of illiterate people, however, would be less likely to find interesting the attention to written style that characterizes *Rosalynde*. That audience would more readily enjoy discussion of the spoken word, and this, of course, is what Shakespeare dramatizes. Significantly, when Celia describes Orlando, she expounds at greater length about his speech than his writing: "O, that's a brave man! he writes brave verses, speaks brave words, swears brave oaths, and breaks them bravely, quite traverse, athwart the heart of his lover . . ." (3.4.40–43). This emphasis represents the playwright's understanding of what will work best on the stage. So, too, does his send up of such pastoral conventions as the lover's effusive poetry. This implies no particular hostility to the pastoral but simply an acknowledgment of how the convention needs to be accommodated in the theater. What Shakespeare discovered was that he could gently mock the world that Lodge had created in such a way as to provide amusement for a theatrical audience while at the same time retaining the idealization that marks that world. In a sense he has his pastoral cake and eats it, too.

Shakespeare's concern with theatrical effect expresses itself in what he enlarges upon as well as what he reduces. This is particularly clear at the end of the play, where no fewer than four marriages are sanctioned. Lodge recounts the weddings with extraordinary (for him) simplicity: "*Gerismond* led the way [to the church], and the rest followed, where to the admiration of all the countrey swaines in *Arden* their mariages were solemnely solemnised" (253). By contrast, Shakespeare treats the moment with considerable elaboration, creating a ceremony of formality and dignity, with a resulting mood of joyous solemnity. Presiding over the action is Hymen, who has no precedent in *Rosalynde*. An embodiment of fertility and generative power, he represents a primal human drive toward sexual union. Bedecked with flowers, the god of marriage represents a nature powerful and universal. At the same time Hymen embodies artifice, too, for this personification exists only in a work of art—in the pages of a book or, as here, on a stage: he is "truly at home in Arden and the remote world of pastoral."[21] His distinction from all the other characters onstage is at once apparent through speech. Instead of blank verse, Hymen expresses himself in short (seven-syllable) lines that are metrically regular and rhymed. In its formality, the style of his remarks to courtiers and citizens of Arden alike has a quality that evokes conventions of writing rather than of conversation. In fact, his lines bear a resemblance to the poems of Orlando, written in short lines that are also metrically regular and rhymed.

The content of Hymen's speeches, moreover, specifically recalls Orlando's poem in praise of Rosalind, read aloud by Celia. Both speak of a benevolent heaven (3.2.140 and 5.4.108), which smiles on beauty and love; of a person's "heart" (3.2.145 and 5.4.115), the seat of affection leading to marriage; and of "peopling" the world—Orlando compensates for an "unpeopled" forest by hanging his poems on trees (3.2.126); in his final speech the god of marriage says that he "peoples every town" (5.4.143). Even Hymen's physical appearance may recall something written and enacted by Rosalind's beloved: Orlando speaks of the "fairest boughs" on which he writes his beloved's name (3.2.135), while Hymen may have a torch made out of a pine tree bough in his hand.[22] By his presence in the play's concluding scene, Hymen conflates art and nature. He accomplishes this through his role as ordainer of marriage, an institution subsuming both nature and art. Marriage, after all, represents a negotiation between natural impulse and artful ceremony; contrived by society, marriage accommodates the most primitive and instinctive of desires. In *As You Like It* the god of marriage appears within "that most artificial of forms, a masque," and at the same time he helps "to celebrate a series of natural truths."[23] "Like Spenser's 'Aprill,'" writes Eamon

Grennan, "the masque stands in relation to the entire work as the perfect pastoral epiphany."[24]

3

As a metaphor the book of nature elucidates the realms of art and nature in Shakespeare's late plays, too, especially *Pericles*. Although the metaphor may not explicitly appear in this play, the written word does, and it takes a variety of forms, including a riddle, an impresa, a message in a coffin, an inscription on a tomb. Each of these artful constructions describes or applies to one or another young woman who, by her appearance, evokes the personification of nature herself. Nature, then, is evoked both as a person and as an artifact evincing aesthetic design. Together, these two formulations reveal more than either alone. The juxtaposition of written material and nubile woman achieves what the debate over flowers in *The Winter's Tale* or the argument over painting and poetry in *Timon of Athens* achieves: it clarifies the subtle relationship between art and nature, suggesting that, here at least, cooperation rather than strife prevails.

If the courtly world that Pericles discovers at Antioch seems artificial in the extreme, it is because everyone present has agreed to participate in a ritual whose bizarre nature is accentuated by its longstanding practice. In seeking marriage to the daughter of King Antiochus, Pericles enacts a ceremony performed many times before. The skulls of other prospective suitors stare down at him, and he will join their number if he fails a test administered by the king—the solving of a riddle. Despite the high stakes and the simmering sexual tension, the characters behave in studied fashion; passions are sublimated, proprieties observed.

The use of a riddle contributes to the stylization of the action.[25] By presenting a truth enigmatically, a riddle usually defies immediate comprehension; it requires the challenger to pause and ponder—in this instance the relationship between the "I" of the riddle and someone else.[26] The playwright specifically indicates such a lull by the fifteen-line aside of Pericles, following his recitation of the riddle, as he realizes the meaning and expresses it to himself. The theatrical effect of the riddle, then, is to slow down the action almost as soon as it has begun. The characters seem frozen for a moment and, as a result, the sense of strangeness is prolonged.

Even when the action resumes, it has an oddly formal quality, for, however shocked Pericles may be by his recognition of incest, he is as indirect in dealing with Antiochus as the king has been with him. Pericles' strategy takes advantage of the protocol dictating an elaborate politesse.

If he publicly discloses what he knows, he risks death at the hands of a man who sees him not as a future son-in-law but rather as a sexual rival. Hence Pericles preserves a bland exterior despite a seemingly desperate situation and manages to extricate himself, ironically, by capitalizing on the manner of the king's challenge. That is, Antiochus has presented the riddle in written form to Pericles.[27] Now, taking his cue from what the king has just given him, Pericles utilizes a metaphor involving the written word: "Who has a book of all that monarchs do, / He's more secure to keep it shut than shown" (1.1.94–95).

This metaphoric book not only signals the king that Pericles has deduced the riddle's meaning but also complements the literal words of that riddle by subtly implicating the king's daughter in wrongdoing. Presumably she is part of the "book of all that monarchs do" since her relationship to her father is the (largely) unspoken issue of the scene. The metaphor is doubly apt because she has already been likened to a book earlier when Pericles admired her beauty: "Her face the book of praises, where is read / Nothing but curious pleasures" (ll. 16–17). The fact that both father and daughter are compared to books in the same scene and by the same character suggests an underlying similitude.

That a riddle should be required to explain the nature of a tie binding father and daughter illustrates something important about this play: that some familial relationships may be discerned only with difficulty. Ordinarily we think of kinship as being readily apparent to the observer; a child, for instance, resembles its parents, while husband and wife indicate their relationship by their demeanor. In *Pericles* a character may perceive the obvious and natural bond, as Pericles does when he beholds the king and his daughter. But ascertaining the other bond between father and child, unusual and secret, is more problematic. Elsewhere in the play, discovering even the most basic relationship may require what is needed here: the explanation of the written word.

Appropriately, the written word is present in yet another form in the opening scene, though one not so easily read: the book of nature. It is implicit in the figure of the king's daughter, whose dramatic presentation seems almost to evoke a tableau vivant. Following her entry, she stands still; nothing in the script, at least, requires her to move. Moreover, she has neither soliloquy nor aside with which to reveal her feelings; she speaks only two lines in the entire scene, a mere expression, dictated by circumstance, of good will toward her suitor. Although at the center of the action, she is curiously remote. More the outline of a character than a character, she lacks even the individualizing feature of a name. Her identity is established not by what she herself says but rather by what others say about her, and through their remarks she comes to bear a double association. First, she resembles nature in that she embodies (apparently) vitality and sensuality. Introducing her, Antiochus cites her most salient feature, her physical beauty: "Nature this dowry gave" (l. 9). In keeping with her appearance, she seems to promise fertility, too. Pericles likens her to the season of the year heralding fruitfulness: "See where she comes, apparelled like the spring" (l. 12). Her beauty is such that it leads to the formulation of a second comparison. Using a metaphor belonging as much to the realm of art as of nature, Pericles calls her face "the book of praises" (l. 15). That the same woman should evoke both nature herself and an artifact containing the written word is consistent with a culture that can personify nature as a woman and also imagine nature as a book. It is consistent, too, with the world of a play that defines a woman's identity by means of the written word (the riddle).

Although the personality and disposition of the king's daughter are shrouded by her nearly complete silence and by a public behavior of inflexible decorum, she nevertheless creates a vivid image, one that lingers in the mind's eye. Indeed, the image will, with variations, recur in the subsequent dramatic action, at divers times and places. As here the audience will behold a young woman who appears in the company of her father, who embodies simultaneously the natural and the artificial, and whose identity is revealed through the written word.

When Pericles flees Antioch, he takes with him his memory of the woman he so recently sought in marriage. Arriving in Pentapolis, he must experience a sense of déjà vu, for he discovers a situation eerily reminiscent of that which he left behind. He finds another young woman, also a king's daughter, and again she seems an embodiment of nature. Just as Antiochus personified nature when he spoke of his daughter, saying, "Nature this dowry gave" (1.1.9), so Simonides personifies nature when he says that his daughter Thaisa "Sits here like beauty's child, whom nature gat / For men to see, and seeing wonder at" (2.2.6–7). The king speaks these words on an occasion that pays tribute to nature's fruitfulness—a "triumph," or tournament, celebrating the anniversary of Thaisa's birth. Her role at the subsequent banquet underscores her association with nature as generative force: she presents to the victorious Pericles a wreath made, presumably, of green leaves (2.3.9–11).

While not herself an artist, Thaisa becomes an interpreter of art through the action she performs at the tournament, one which, incidentally, has no precedent in either of the play's chief narrative sources, John Gower's *Confessio Amantis* and Lawrence Twine's *The Patterne of Painfull Adventures*[28]: Thaisa assumes the task of describing designs which decorate the knights' shields at the tournament. Those shields are painted with imprese, Renaissance formulations combining picture with written word; typically these served as coats of arms, symbolizing a family's identity. Thaisa gives an account of each in turn, receiving shields from the knights' pages, inspecting them, and finally returning them to the pages. Five times Thaisa performs this ritual, enumerating the designs and reading aloud the Latin of the accompanying mottoes.

The sixth (and last) of the designs, unlike the others, is presented directly by the hand of the knight. Thaisa tells her father:

> He seems to be a stranger; but his present is
> A withered branch, that's only green at top;
> The motto: "*In hac spe vivo.*"
>
> (2.2.42–44)

In the motto which means "In this hope I live," Simonides perceives a particular relevance for his daughter: "A pretty moral: / From the dejected state wherein he is, / He hopes by you his fortunes yet may flourish" (ll. 45–47). The impresa may have a still more profound application than even the king realizes, for as Douglas L. Peterson observes, "The hope in which Pericles 'lives,' and which leads to eventual victory, is in the living though seemingly dead branch that represents the family of whom he is the only survivor."[29] Interpreted in these terms, the green branch betokens nature as life and fertility, hence the issue of the future marriage between Thaisa and Pericles—their child Marina. The branch thus evokes a genealogical tree, a symbol long used to represent a family's lineage.[30]

In her own desire to marry, Thaisa identifies herself with vitality and fruitfulness, qualities that signal her allegiance to nature. Her intention of taking Pericles as her husband, however, is expressed in unusual form: she writes a letter to her father. In another play this might strike us as improbable, but not here. As F. David Hoeniger comments, "The unlikelihood of a daughter who lives in the same palace as her father communicating with him that way is consistent with the nature and spirit of the story."[31] Hoeniger does not go on to explain specifically how Thaisa's action is "consistent," but his judgment seems correct. For one thing her writing is in keeping with what the audience witnessed earlier at Antioch: the use of a written message to set forth the bond existing between a man and a woman. We do not know for certain that Antiochus' daughter is the author of the riddle, but the personal pronouns of the riddle refer to her, and the incestuous relationship described is unquestionably hers.[32] Now at Pentapolis, as earlier at Antioch, a character turns to the written word when seeking to express a sexual relationship.

Thaisa's action is consistent in another sense as well—in the theatrical effect that it achieves. Just as Antiochus' riddle presented Pericles with a *fait accompli,* so, too, does Thaisa's letter; it reflects the unyielding quality of her decision. Had she expressed in conversation her desire to marry Pericles, she might have been subject to importuning or imprecation. By casting her decision in written form, she forecloses any effort to change her mind. Her readers within the play confront a page which hears no plea, observes no body language, feels no emotion. Consequently, the dramatic emphasis falls where it did in the play's opening scene: on the reader, as first Simonides peruses the letter and then as Pericles does the same. Along with the king, we watch and listen as Pericles studies, comprehends, and reacts. Through the use of soliloquy and aside, the playwright focuses on Pericles' emotional response and mental processes. Here, as at Antioch when he read the riddle, we are made to feel Pericles' sense of peril, which leads him to blurt out, "O, seek not to entrap me, gracious lord" (2.5.45).

Thaisa's letter is also in keeping with the figurative language at her father's court. Following the tournament, Simonides addressed his knights, praising their accomplishment:

> Knights,
> To say you're welcome were superfluous.
> To place upon the volume of your deeds,
> As in a title-page, your worth in arms,
> Were more than you expect, or more than's fit,
> Since every worth in show commends itself.
>
> (2.3.1–6)

Thaisa, of course, hears these words, for she is present as "queen of the feast," and, following Simonides' speech, she turns to Pericles, bestowing on him the victor's wreath. The letter that she subsequently writes complements the metaphor and simile applied to Pericles and the other competitors. Her letter befits a dramatic world wherein a person witnesses public feats and imagines the title page of a volume,[33] infers private conduct and imagines "a book" of deeds (1.1.94). For Thaisa and her father, as for Pericles, action and the written word, whether literal or figurative, are one.

Thaisa's letter is consistent with the dramatic action in still another way as well, for additional instances of silent reading on Pericles' part both precede and follow his perusal of the letter. At the beginning of act 2, Gower's speech breaks off for this dumb show:

> Enter at one door Pericles talking with Cleon; all the train with them. Enter at another door a Gentleman with a letter to Pericles; Pericles shows the letter to Cleon; Pericles gives the Messenger a reward and knights him. Exit Pericles at one door and Cleon at another.

The letter that passes from hand to hand has been written by Helicanus to warn Pericles, now at Tharsus, of danger from emissaries of King Antiochus. Later, at the beginning of act 3, Gower reappears and we watch a dumb show curiously similar to the first:

> Enter Pericles and Simonides, at one door, with attendants. A messenger meets them, kneels, and gives Pericles a letter. Pericles shows it Simonides; the Lords kneel to him. Then enter Thaisa with child, with Lychorida, a nurse. The King shows her the letter; she rejoices. She and Pericles take leave of her father, and depart.

This dumb show duplicates, in essential respects, the previous one.[34] Again Pericles enters with another man, receives a letter, shows it to his companion, and departs with the purpose of immediately undertaking a voyage. In both instances the travel has implications for Thaisa. Shipwrecked, in act 2, Pericles meets and marries her; buffeted by a violent storm, in act 3, Pericles suffers her loss. The dumb shows dramatize the moment when these developments are set in motion by delivery of the letters, and these deliveries visually bracket Pericles' experience at Pentapolis.

The similarity between the dumb shows points to an important feature of the play's dramaturgy: although the action of *Pericles* may be episodic and the changes in locale abrupt, the play contains an extraordinary number of parallels and correspondences, many of them visual. For example, when Pericles arrives in Pentapolis, he finds himself in a world resembling Antioch. Again a widowed king presides over a court. Again a nubile daughter attends the king. Again Pericles beholds the woman on a ceremonial occasion. And again that woman seems the embodiment of nature. These resemblances not only lend coherence to the disparate materials of the story but also suggest that we are witnessing something archetypal.[35] Despite evident incongruities in the textually ragged script of *Pericles,* perhaps the result of collaboration or of the playwright adapting the work of another writer, the play is coherent in performance. The audience sees that behind and beyond the particular incidents of Pericles' adventures is a pattern, transcending time and place, of the relationship between father and daughter: Antiochus and his daughter; Simonides and his; Pericles and his.[36] In the persistence of this pattern we behold nothing less than an expression of nature herself. Even where there is a departure from the norm, as when Pericles confronts an instance of incest, we are made to feel the fundamental strength of the nature that has been violated, and we share the characters' sense of relief when nature reasserts herself through the destruction of those who betray her purposes, especially the impulse to be fruitful.

So powerful is the nature that animates humanity that she is capable of affirming herself under even the most dire of circumstances, indeed, even in the face of death. Thus amid the storm which threatens to destroy Pericles' ship, the nurse brings word that Thaisa has succumbed during childbirth. In the arms of that nurse, however, is the continuation of life and the potential for future fertility: "Here's all that is left living of your queen: / A little daughter" (3.1.20–21). Like the other daughters who have appeared in previous episodes, this one is aligned with nature, for when Pericles looks upon the infant girl, he says, "Poore inch of Nature." At least this is what he says in George Wilkins' *The Painfull Adventures of Pericles Prince of Tyre* (1608), a narrative probably based on the play about Pericles that was performed by Shakespeare's company.[37] For more than a century, scholars have recognized these words as almost certainly Shakespearean.

The promise of a resurgent nature is here, as elsewhere, closely identified with the written word. When the sailors insist that the body of Thaisa be consigned to the waves, Pericles resolves to write a message that will be enclosed in his wife's coffin: "Bid Nestor bring me spices, ink and paper" (3.1.65).[38] With the subsequent discovery of the coffin, Pericles' words are read aloud:

> "Here I give to understand,
> If e'er this coffin drives a-land,
> I, King Pericles, have lost
> This queen, worth all our mundane cost.
> Who finds her, give her burying,
> She was the daughter of a king.
> Besides this treasure for a fee,
> The gods requite his charity!"
>
> (3.2.68–75)

The message proves crucial to both Pericles and his daughter, for it justifies the extraordinary efforts of the physician Cerimon to revive this woman. Without it, the discoverers of the coffin would not know that the body belongs to the wife and daughter of kings. Her restoration, then, and her eventual reunion with husband and daughter depend upon the identity which the written word discloses.

In its revelation of a woman's identity, the message in the coffin recalls another communication—the riddle read aloud by Pericles in the play's opening scene:

> I am no viper, yet I feed
> On mother's flesh which did me breed.
> I sought a husband, in which labor

> I found that kindness in a father.
> He's father, son, and husband mild;
> I mother, wife—and yet his child.
> How they may be, and yet in two,
> As you will live, resolve it you.
>
> (1.1.64–71)

The content of the riddle and of Pericles' message is similar in that both describe a sexual relationship, and the woman in each instance is the daughter of a king. In addition, the riddle and message consist, stylistically, of similar verse—eight lines in four couplets—and the high proportion of monosyllables in both gives to each the same staccato rhythm. Thus although Pericles' message in the coffin may strike us as singular and strange, it has about it a familiar quality.

Why should the message in Thaisa's coffin recall, by its form and content, certain features of the riddle? Through this resemblance the playwright contributes to the air of stylization, of patterned action, of recollection and anticipation that characterizes the play. One message takes the place of another just as one woman takes the place of another just as one relationship takes the place of another. With this substitution nature's continuity is reasserted. Thaisa's return to life, thanks to the efforts of the physician, represents not just an individual's triumph over death but also a larger restoration. When she revives, Cerimon says not that Thaisa awakes but rather that *nature* awakes: "Gentlemen, this queen will live. Nature awakes, / A warmth breathes out of her" (3.2.92–94).

Not only is the power of nature reasserted but so, too, the efficacy of art. For Cerimon identifies his physician's skill with what he calls "secret art":

> 'Tis known, I ever
> Have studied physic; through which secret art,
> By turning o'er authorities, I have,
> Together with my practice, made familiar
> To me and to my aid the blest infusions
> That dwells in vegetives, in metals, stones;
> And can speak of the disturbances
> That nature works, and of her cures. . . .
>
> (3.2.31–38)

His art, then, depends upon his study: "I heard of an Egyptian / That had nine hours lien dead, / Who was by good appliance recovered" (ll. 84–86). Or, as George Wilkins writes, perhaps in words that more closely approximate the original words of the playwright, "I have read of some Egyptians, who after foure houres death, (if man may call it so) have raised impoverished bodies, like to this, unto their former health."[39] In the revival of Thaisa, we witness the exercise of art as well as the resilience of nature. What allows nature to realize fully the potential for continued life and future growth is the written word—in the form of Pericles' message, a carefully constructed artifact that justifies the application of Cerimon's art; and in the form of Cerimon's reading, which provides the technique of his life-saving art.

The significance of the written word to the relationship of art and nature underlying this episode is elucidated by a passage in George Puttenham's *Arte of English Poesie* (1589):

> In some cases we say arte is an ayde and coadjutor to nature, and a furtherer of her actions to good effect, or peradventure a meane to supply her wants, by renforcing the causes wherein shee is impotent and defective, as doth the arte of phisicke, by helping the naturall concoction, retention, distribution, expulsion, and other vertues, in a weake and unhealthie bodie.[40]

That the author of a treatise on poetry should enlist the analogy of a physician mending a body may seem odd until we reflect on the way that the written word mediates between art and nature.[41] For a culture that conceived of nature as a book and thus of nature as possessing inherent artistry, the analogy would seem less strange. If nature is a book, then art may cooperate with and reinforce the excellence of that book. Art can minister to nature because there is in nature something amenable to art. In the written word, which constitutes the contents of a book, art and nature converge. Peter Paul Rubens gives pictorial form to this convergence in a design used for the title page of *De Symbolis Heroicis* (Antwerp, 1634) by Sylvester Pietrasanta (or Petrasancta). It depicts nature as a multibreasted woman with flowers in her hair, and holding a laurel wreath. Opposite her stands Mercury, caduceus in one hand, representing art. He hands a pen and brushes to the personification of talent, standing between himself and nature, so that the heroic devices contained in the volume may be recorded. (Mercury's representation, incidentally, recalls his ancient association with the invention of the alphabet.[42]) Between art and nature is a stone altar, inscribed with the author's name and with the title of the book. The written word thus quite literally occupies the space where art and nature are conjoined.

The cooperation of art and nature informs the climactic meeting of Pericles and the young woman who is his daughter. Even before that point, Marina is identified with nature. As an adult, she makes her first appearance carrying a basket of flowers (4.1.12). In the brothel, moreover, she is specifically associated with nature's bounty; the Bawd tells Boult, "When nature fram'd this piece, she meant thee a good turn" (4.2.139–40).

The title page designed by Peter Paul Rubens for *De Symbolis Heroicis* (Antwerp, 1634) by Sylvester Pietrasanta. Mercury, representing art, hands a pen and brushes to the personification of talent. At the right is Nature personified. By permission of the Houghton Library, Harvard University.

Boult evokes Marina's initial appearance with flowers when he advertises her beauty to Lysimachus: "For flesh and blood, sir, white and red, you shall see a rose, and she were a rose indeed . . ." (4.6.34–35). By aligning Marina with nature, the playwright identifies her with the other young women who have preceded her onstage. We recall that Pericles, seeing Antiochus' daughter, spoke of tasting "the fruit of yon celestial tree" (1.1.21). We recall, too, that Pericles' device at the tournament—a branch green at top—was presented to Thaisa. Now at Mytilene, Marina applies to herself a vegetative metaphor evocative of a family tree: "My derivation was from ancestors / Who stood equivalent with mighty kings. / But time hath rooted out my parentage" (5.1.90–92).

Although Marina's natural beauty is her most salient characteristic, she is also herself an artist. Gower says that she successfully limns the natural world:

> Deep clerks she dumbs, and with her neele composes
> Nature's own shape of bud, bird, branch, or berry,
> That even her art sisters the natural roses.
>
> (act 5 chorus, ll. 5–7)

When Pericles describes Marina, he does so in terms that specifically connote artistic creation:

> My dearest wife was like this maid, and such a one
> My daughter might have been. My queen's square
>   brows,
> Her stature to an inch, as wand-like straight,
> As silver-voic'd, her eyes as jewel-like
> And cas'd as richly. . . .
>
> (5.1.107–11)

The language, particularly "silver-voic'd," "jewel-like," and "cas'd," befits a work of art, something made of natural materials for aesthetic delight; a jewel, after all, is typically fashioned of a precious metal which provides the setting, and of a gem shaped by the cutter's skill. The appellation "jewel-like" also identifies Marina with the woman who gave birth to her. We recall that Pericles encloses jewels in Thaisa's coffin; and when Thaisa revives, Cerimon speaks of her as though she were herself a jewel: "behold / Her eyelids, cases to those heavenly jewels / Which Pericles hath lost, begin to part / Their fringes of bright gold" (3.2.97–100).[43] When Pericles, at Mytilene, calls Marina "jewel-like," he is not, of course, suggesting that her appearance is the result of Boult's contrivance; she has not been gussied up with precious stones or make-up. Rather, her natural beauty is such that it evokes in the beholder the language of art.

It is precisely because she conflates the natural and the artistic that Marina can minister successfully to Pericles, who is described as her "kingly patient" (5.1.71). Lysimachus, governor of Mytilene, addresses her as though she were a physician, when he urges her to help the ailing Pericles:

> If that thy prosperous and artificial feat
> Can draw him but to answer thee in aught,
> Thy sacred physic shall receive such pay
> As thy desires can wish.
>
> (5.1.72–75)

"Physic" epitomizes her participation in both nature and art, for that term, deriving from a Greek word meaning "knowledge of nature," can signify "natural science, the knowledge of the phenomenal world," according to the *OED*, and also "the art of practice of healing, the healing art." Insofar as Marina possesses knowledge of nature, she is capable of acting as physician, performing what Lysimachus calls an "artificial feat." Unlike Cerimon, she relies not on learning but rather upon an intuitive sympathy with nature, which Lysimachus alludes to when he calls her "of a gentle kind and noble stock" (5.1.68). Hers is, then, not a power *over* nature so much as it is a power achieved *through* nature.

Although Marina is not a professional physician, she goes about her task in much the same way that Cerimon did when he sought to revive Thaisa. Confronting an inert and seemingly dead body, isolated from its surroundings by a coffin, Cerimon instructed his servant, "The rough and woeful music that we have, / Cause it to sound, beseech you" (3.2.88–89). The music has the effect of evoking Thaisa's latent vitality, reestablishing her link with the phenomenal world.[44] Now in Mytilene, Marina confronts a man whose self-absorbed silence is death-like and whose isolation is expressed by the curtain behind which, apparently, he lies or sits.[45] Lysimachus hopes that Marina, "with her sweet harmony" (5.1.45), may restore Pericles; and Marina, "train'd / In music's letters" (act 4 chorus, ll. 7–8), sings to him, hoping to accomplish what Queen Katherine's song in *Henry VIII* achieves: "In sweet music is such art, / Killing care and grief of heart . . ." (3.1.12–13). Here in *Pericles* music may not immediately succeed in banishing the patient's "grief of heart," but that music begins the process of reestablishing his relationship to his surroundings, a relationship that attains its most sublime form when he hears the music of the spheres (5.1.229). As a maker of music Marina imitates the creator himself, who brings order and proportion out of his multifarious creation. In the words of Godfrey Goodman, praising God: "O excellent Artist, that could so sweetly tune nature to make such a melody, where there is such a concent and agreement on every side; the parts to the whole, the whole to the parts, each to it selfe, all to the Maker! O excellent melody! here is neither sound, nor voice to the eare, yet a most sweet and delectable harmony, a musicke of nature."[46]

As physician Marina balances graceful solicitude with a certain detachment; she is characterized by extraordinary poise. Even though her effort initially seems ineffectual, as Pericles pushes her away following her song, she remains serene. When Pericles says, "thou dost look / Like Patience gazing on kings' graves, and smiling / Extremity out of act" (5.1.137–39), he describes the courteous though reserved demeanor that compels admiration. Like Antiochus' daughter and Simonides' daughter earlier, this daughter of Pericles has the composure and restraint befitting someone of noble ancestry.

In the comparison of Marina to a statue on a tomb, Pericles implicitly likens her to a work of art. Missing from the comparison, though, is any reference to what one usually sees on such a monument—an inscription. This absence points to something that earlier scenes may lead us to expect: the representation of the written word in some literal form, shaped by the writer's art and used to define the identity of a woman whose beauty evokes the personification of nature. The written word, however, has already been used to describe Marina. Earlier, when Pericles, supposing his daughter dead, visits her tomb, he reads an inscription that has been written "In glitt'ring golden characters" (4.3.44). Gower presents the text:

> "The fairest, sweetest, and best lies here,
> Who withered in her spring of year.
> She was of Tyrus the King's daughter,
> On whom foul death hath made this slaughter.
> Marina was she call'd, and at her birth,
> Thetis, being proud, swallowed some part a' th'
>   earth.
> Therefore the earth, fearing to be o'erflowed,
> Hath Thetis' birth-child on the heavens bestowed;
> Wherefore she does, and swears she'll never stint,
> Make raging battery upon shores of flint."
>
> (4.4.34–43)

Reading this epitaph and seeing the tomb are what trigger Pericles' passion, which is presented in a dumb show:

> Enter Pericles at one door with all his train; Cleon and
> Dionyza at the other. Cleon shows Pericles the tomb; whereat

> Pericles makes lamentation, puts on sackcloth, and in a mighty passion departs.
>
> (4.4.22)

This pantomimic action has the effect of fixing the moment powerfully in our minds. And coming near the conclusion of act 4, the dumb show precedes, with the intervention of the brothel scene, the meeting of Marina and Pericles in the first scene of act 5.

As Pericles and Marina confront one another, they evoke, by sight, sound, and speech, a much earlier meeting—that in the play's opening scene when Pericles gazes upon Antiochus' daughter. Again Pericles beholds a young woman who is as beautiful as she is poised. Again music accompanies their meeting: instrumental music earlier, at Antiochus' direction; song here, followed by the music of the spheres. Again there is talk of physic: earlier "Sharp physic," in the words of Pericles, referring to the last lines of the riddle; now, "sacred physic," in the words of Lysimachus, referring to Marina's power. And again there is a riddling quality to the conversation, in Marina's replies.[47] When Pericles asks her, "What country-woman? / Here of these shores?" (5.1.102–3), she answers, "No, nor of any shores, / Yet I was mortally brought forth, and am / No other than I appear" (ll. 103–5). Similarly, when Pericles asks where she lives, she replies elliptically, "Where I am but a stranger. From the deck / You may discern the place" (ll. 114–15). Throughout this conversation Pericles seeks to discover who the woman really is. This time no literal message is available to help him. But he has a clue in the very features of her face. Scrutinizing her, Pericles figuratively reads her countenance and moves toward the answer: "thou lookest / Like one I lov'd indeed" (5.1.124–25).

The recognition of Marina leads within moments to Pericles' vision of the goddess Diana. Like many previous incidents, the theophany may seem sudden—no deities have appeared in any earlier scene. Yet, as elsewhere, the action is not entirely without precedent. In fact, from the opening lines of the play Diana has been present in the characters' minds.[48] Under her name Lucina,[49] Diana is invoked by Antiochus when he speaks of his daughter's birth; by Simonides when he tells Thaisa's suitors that she will continue to "wear Diana's livery" (2.5.10); by Pericles (again under the name Lucina) when his wife gives birth to their daughter; by Thaisa herself when she is revived by the physician and cries, "O dear Diana" (3.2.104); by Pericles, who swears "By bright Diana" (3.3.28) when he leaves his daughter at Tharsus; and by Marina who, in the brothel, says, "Diana aid my purpose!" (4.2.148). Since so much of the dramatic action has occurred under the aegis of the goddess, there is a logic to her appearance and to her instructions that Pericles journey to her shrine at Ephesus and recapitulate his story there. After all, she has been involved, in some way, with virtually every turn of his fortunes.

Pericles' journey to Ephesus is consistent, too, with the very meaning of the goddess whose temple he visits. Although she is the goddess of chastity, Diana is also frequently depicted amid the world of external nature, hunting in a forest. Hence her customary implement is the bow, along with quiver and arrows. Diana's other principal symbol, the crescent moon, points to a still more profound association with nature.[50] She is identified with cyclicity, with natural rhythms, whether of the moon, tide, or human body. Thus she is a deity associated with childbirth and nurturing and with nature herself. In some Renaissance representations, Diana's identity with nature is unmistakable. Her statue at Villa d'Este in Tivoli, created about 1565–72, presents her as a multibreasted herm,[51] as do Renaissance books of mythography. Vincenzo Cartari's chapter on Diana includes a picture of a multibreasted figure and, beneath, a caption that begins, "Imagine della Dea Natura."[52] Giordano Bruno, moreover, in his *Heroic Frenzies* identifies Diana with "the world, the universe, the nature which is in things."[53] As a symbol of nature, Diana rightly presides over the reunion of Pericles, Marina, and Thaisa at Ephesus. For at the moment that husband and wife, mother and daughter, and father and daughter are reunited after so many years, we feel nature's essential stability, permanence, and capacity for renewal. It is this that Pericles celebrates when, in his joy, he says, "Pure Dian, / I bless thee for thy vision, and will offer / Night-oblations to thee" (5.3.68–70).

Diana's shrine, legendary for its splendor, provides the appropriate site for the culmination of Pericles' story in another way as well, for the goddess was traditionally identified with the written word[54] and she is the recipient of the written word in accounts of Pericles. In Lawrence Twine's *Patterne of Painefull Adventures,* the narrator reports that, following the hero's reunion with his family,

> he applied his vacant time to his booke, and hee wrote the whole storie and discourse of his owne life and adventures at large, the which he caused to be written foorth in two large volumes, whereof he sent one to the Temple of Diana at Ephesus, and placed the other in his owne library. Of which historie this is but a small abstract.[55]

The history befits a narrative in which the written word, in its various forms, has proved so important. Like Lawrence Twine, the author of the play, too, associates divinity with the written word.[56] When Cerimon opens Thaisa's coffin and finds a message, he calls upon the twin brother of Diana: "A passport too! / Apollo, perfect me in the characters!" (3.2.66–67). Later, in the reunion scene, this same physician appears at

Diana's shrine bearing "letters of good credit," with news of Thaisa's father. Gower makes explicit the connection between Diana and the artistry of the written word when he relates that in childhood Marina "would with rich and constant pen / Vail to her mistress Dian" (act 4 chorus, ll. 28–29).[57]

Although the Pericles of the play neither records the story of his adventures with pen and ink nor sends an account to Diana's shrine, the presenter of the dramatic action, Gower, possesses Pericles' story in written (or printed) form. We know this because the title page of George Wilkins' *Painfull Adventures of Pericles Prince of Tyre* is adorned with a woodcut showing "what Gower probably looked like on stage during the play's first performance."[58] In the illustration Gower stands beside a lectern on which is set an open book, presumably a book containing Pericles' story. It seems likely that in performance the actor playing Gower would lift that book from the lectern and refer to it during his summary of Pericles' experience. (This seems especially likely when Gower reads aloud the inscription on Marina's monument.) That book would, along with Gower's presence, serve a theatrical purpose, emphasizing the antiquity of the events dramatized, the psychic distance separating past and present, the remoteness of the actual events from the lives of the spectators. The book would also suggest that Pericles' wondrous adventures have a discernible shape and purpose. Turbulent and disorderly as individual episodes of tempest and passion may seem, they manifest coherence when viewed collectively in the written words of a book. To stand back from the immediacy of events, as Gower does and as he invites us to do, is to recognize the pattern that Lawrence Twine names in the very title of his book about Pericles, a pattern that finds its genesis in an artful nature.

4

In the year that *Pericles* was entered in the Stationers' Register, 1608, an English experimenter, astrologer, and mathematician died at his home outside London. His name was John Dee, and in his more prosperous days he had enjoyed the friendship of Queen Elizabeth and of courtiers who sought his advice and visited his estate, Mortlake, near the River Thames in Surrey. Early in his career Dee tutored the Duke of Northumberland's children, among whom was Robert Dudley, the future Earl of Leicester. Dee also instructed Sir Philip Sidney in chemistry.[59] And he entertained Sir Francis Walsingham and Sir Edward Dyer at Mortlake. Dee's activity as scientist and teacher has led a modern biographer to conclude: "After Robert Recorde's death in 1558, Dee became the most influential teacher and adviser on scientific subjects in England, and he

THE
Painfull Aduentures
of *Pericles* Prince of Tyre.

Being

The true History of the Play of *Pericles*, as it was lately presented by the worthy and ancient Poet *Iohn Gower*.

AT LONDON
Printed by T.P. *for* Nat: Butter,
1608.

The title page of George Wilkins's *Painfull Adventures of Pericles Prince of Tyre* (London, 1608). The woodcut depicts the character of Gower as he probably looked during the first performances of *Pericles*. By permission of The British Library (C.34.l.8).

retained this position for at least twenty-five years."[60] What animated the manifold activities of John Dee, at least in part, was his conviction that nature is a book to be read, interpreted, and exploited. His work, moreover, suggests the evolution that was taking place in the very concept of that book.

Although his father was a minor official at the court of Henry VIII, Dee owed his social connections chiefly to his intellectual precocity. He received his B.A. from St. John's College, Cambridge, in 1544–45 and subsequently was named one of the original fellows at the newly founded Trinity College. From 1548 to 1550 he studied in Louvain, where he befriended Gerard Mercator, the cartographer. Upon returning to England, he was introduced to Sir William Cecil by Sir John Cheke, and then to Edward VI. At court he was called upon for astrological advice: he cast horoscopes for King Edward and Queen Mary, among others. This activity, however, rendered him vulnerable to accusations that he trafficked with the supernatural. Accused of having designs on the life of Queen Mary, he was arrested at Hampton Court in the early summer of 1555. Although Dee was eventually cleared of the charges, John Foxe branded him a conjurer in the *Acts and Monuments* of 1563,[61] and Dee never entirely overcame a reputation for dabbling in the occult. When in the 1580s he employed Edward Kelley as a "scryer," or medium, and began to commune with invisible spirits, dark suspicions were revived. These were held not only by certain critics like John Foxe but also by Dee's own neighbors. When he left Mortlake in September 1583 to accompany Albert Laski, palatine of Sirodz in Bohemia, to the continent, a mob descended on his home, destroying his laboratories and vandalizing his books. This incident foreshadowed future troubles. After adventures in Europe, where he sought the financial reward that eluded him in England, Dee returned home in December 1589 and met the queen at Richmond. No longer, however, did he enjoy the same celebrity; his powerful friends Leicester and Sidney were dead, and time had not expunged his notoriety for conjuring: even though he was named Warden of Manchester College in 1596, his reputation continued to plague him. In fact, he actually petitioned King James in June 1604 to have him tried on charges of sorcery so that he might at last clear his name. James, a believer in witchcraft, must have recoiled from the prospect of helping someone associated with seances and spirits; the king never granted Dee his wish.

If his last years were difficult, there is no reason to doubt that John Dee was on amicable terms with Queen Elizabeth from the earliest days of her reign. He was introduced to her by William Herbert, Earl of Pembroke, and by Robert Dudley; and Dee was consulted about the most auspicious date for her coronation. Elizabeth came to his defense in 1564 when he published, in Antwerp, his most controversial and enigmatic work, *Monas Hieroglyphica*. Years later, in 1592, Dee reflected on the queen's willingness to support him when he came under attack:

> I must highly esteme her Majesties, most gratious Defending of my Credit (in my absence beyond the seas) as concerning my boke, titled *Monas Hieroglyphica* . . . against such Universitie graduates of high degree, & other Gentlemen, who, therefore, dispraysed it, because they understode it not: Whereuppon her most excellent [Majestie (after my coming home from beyond the seas; when also I brought the Lady Marquiss of Northampton from Antwerp to Greenwich) did vouchsafe to read that book *obiter* with me at Greenwich].[62]

Returning from Antwerp, Dee met Elizabeth, who "in most heroicall & princely wise did comfort me & encourage me in my studyes philosophicall and Mathematicall &c."[63] The queen proved no less generous in subsequent years. In 1571 when he fell ill, Elizabeth sent two of her physicians from Hampton Court to treat him. The following year he was consulted for his opinion of the new star, a supernova. In 1575 Elizabeth went in person to Mortlake so that she might see his library, now thought to have been "the largest library of the English renaissance."[64] There the queen saw his magic glass through which he claimed to have access to the spirit world. The queen also asked Dee to visit her at Windsor in 1577 and explain the significance of a new comet, and the following year he was consulted about the various ailments from which Elizabeth suffered. In the early 1580s Dee was asked his opinion about adopting the Gregorian calendar. Assessing Dee's importance to Queen Elizabeth, Richard Harvey in 1583 wrote, "hir majestie vouchsafeth [him] the name of hyr Philosopher."[65]

Dee's close association with Queen Elizabeth helps explain why his scientific research was fused with nationalism. He was anxious to apply the results of his investigations to practical ends so that his monarch and his nation would grow in eminence. His interest in mathematics, for instance, led to a study of navigation, which Dee saw as indispensable to expanding trade routes and gaining for England hegemony over newly discovered lands. In particular he encouraged the search for a northern passage to China, advising the Muscovy Company and Martin Frobisher on the most promising routes. Dee also probably had some connection with Sir Francis Drake, whose voyages were supported by Dee's friends, Walsingham, Dyer, and the Earl of Leicester. A proponent of English empire, Dee in 1577 published his *General and Rare Memorials pertayning to the Perfect Arte of Navigation*. The title page, by its symbolism, encourages Elizabeth to develop the navy and seize the opportunity to seek new territories. A farsighted man, Dee did not live to witness England's success in the Americas; the colony at Jamestown was not founded until 1607, the year before his death.

Dee's varied interests, from astronomy to navigation, were united by a common grounding in mathematics. Convinced that mathematical investigation could reveal what was latent in nature, Dee wrote that "All thinges (which from the very first originall being of thinges, have bene framed and made) do appeare to be Formed by the reason of Numbers. For this was the principall example or patterne in the minde of the Creator."[66] Dee's definitions of the various arts, set forth in his introduction to Euclid's *Elements of Geometry* (translated by Henry Billingsley), emphasize their common basis in mathematics. For instance, he writes that "Astronomie, is an Arte Mathematicall, which demonstrateth the distance, magnitudes, and all naturall motions, apparences, and passions propre to the Planets and fixed Sterres: for any time past, present and to come."[67] Similarly, "Of Astrologie, here I make an Arte, severall from *Astronomie:* not by new devise, but by good reason and authoritie: for, Astrologie, is an Arte Mathematicall, which reasonably demonstrateth the operations and effectes, of the naturall beames, of light, and secrete influence: of the Sterres and Planets: in every element and elementall body."[68] Mathematical computation, then, is essential to any investigation of nature, an idea that Galileo would later embrace.

Dee's ideas have perhaps their most important expression in his early work *Monas Hieroglyphica,* which Queen Elizabeth defended against detractors. On its title page appears a design, composed of planetary and zodiacal symbols, intended to depict the underlying unity of the natural world. Describing the design, with its prominent symbol of Mercury (also used by astronomers and alchemists), Dee envisions his formulation as a kind of writing: "Mercury may rightly be styled by us the rebuilder and restorer of all astronomy [and] an astronomical messenger [who was sent to us] by our IEOVA so that we might either establish this sacred art of writing as the first founders of a new discipline, or by his counsel renew one that was entirely extinct and had been wholly wiped out from the memory of men."[69] What Dee sought to restore was nothing less than the lost language of Adam. Knowledge of nature, he believed, must be based on knowledge of language. Dee, however, conceived of that language less in terms of sound than of writing: "the first and mystical letters of the Hebrews, the Greeks, and the Latins, issued from God alone and were [by Him] entrusted to the mortals; [also] . . . (whatever it may be the custom of human arrogance to vaunt) the shapes of all those [letters] (which are disposed by a wonderful and most wise artifice) are derived from points, straight lines and the circumferences of circles."[70] The language of the ancients, then, must be imagined in terms of geometry and mathematics. Dee shared with those adherents of Renaissance cabala the

The title page of John Dee's *Monas Hieroglyphica* with planetary and zodiacal symbols. Queen Elizabeth defended this book (printed in Antwerp in 1564) against its detractors. By permission of the British Library (G.7505).

notion that letters are capable of being expressed numerically; significantly, two years before the publication of *Monas Hieroglyphica* Dee wrote a work, now lost, called *Cabalae Hebraicae Compendiosa Tabella*. Martin Elsky comments on the practice of relating letters to numbers:

> As letters acquired the status of things in the Renaissance, they also took on a property commonly attributed to natural objects: they were understood to possess symbolic significance. In this chirographic tradition, which made an impact both in England and on the continent, letters came to signify more than just sounds. They became the foundation of a system of alphabetical symbolism in which they assumed the symbolic properties ordinarily associated with hieroglyphs. Renaissance Neoplatonists, for instance, saw in the physical configurations of letters, particularly Roman letters, ideal mathematical proportions that were believed to have symbolic, almost Pythagorean, meaning, much like the mathematical proportions humanist architects used in designing buildings.[71]

Significantly, the symbol that Dee devised for the title page of *Monas Hieroglyphica,* he wrote, "teaches without words."[72] Like many of his contemporaries, Dee saw hieroglyphics when he looked upon nature; his library, incidentally, contained a copy of Pierio Valeriano's *Hieroglyphica*. Dee's hieroglyphics, however, lent themselves to specifically mathematical expression: "Though I call it hieroglyphic, he who has examined its inner structure will grant that all the same there is [in it] an underlying clarity and strength almost mathematical, such as is rarely applied in [writings on] matters so rare."[73] This notion Dee superimposed on the concept of nature's book. According to Nicholas H. Clulee, "Dee's new language is an alphabet of nature and a 'writing of things' because it corresponds to the 'written memorial . . . which from the Creation has been inscribed by God's own fingers on all Creatures' and speaks of 'all things visible and invisible, manifest and most occult, emanating by nature or art from God himself.'"[74]

We do not know the extent to which John Dee may have discussed these ideas with Queen Elizabeth when he met her at Greenwich and talked about the recently published *Monas Hieroglyphica*. Nor do we know the extent to which the ideas expressed in that work informed his instruction of Sir Philip Sidney or his conversations with Walsingham, Dyer, and others. We do know that Dee was sufficiently famous for Ben Jonson to mention him by name in *The Alchemist* (2.6.20). Frances Yates has even suggested that Shakespeare's Prospero may be indebted to John Dee.[75] Whatever his relationship to the Renaissance stage, his articulation of a newly conceived book of nature is clear. Although his alchemical interests and his communication with spirits may point backward to the Middle Ages, his concept of nature's book looks to the future. As Nicholas H. Clulee observes, "Dee invested the idea with significant ramifications. He seems to have considered it not merely a parallel revelation to supplement scripture but a self-sufficient and adequate alternative to biblical theology with the advantage of greater certainty than scripture which was prone to varieties of human interpretation."[76] Such a development was precisely what Galileo's antagonists intuited and rightly feared—that nature would supplant Scripture as a source of knowledge. As John Dee recognized, nature had the considerable advantage of being exempt from the drawbacks associated with Scripture since the time of Erasmus and Luther: corrupt texts, diverse translations, a plurality of meanings. Nature's book seemed to offer an incontestability and reliability which the written word of Scripture could no longer provide. Nature's book, after all, was filled not with words or inscrutable hieroglyphs but with numbers. The divine artisan was metamorphosing into the divine mathematician.

9
The Book of Fate

1

IN an entertainment devised for King James I and his wife, 22 May 1607, Ben Jonson presents the Fates as they had commonly been depicted since antiquity: three women, equipped with distaff, spindle, and shears, proceed to spin, weave, and cut the thread of life.[1] In front of Clotho, Lachesis, and Atropos, Jonson adds something else as well—a book of adamant that lies open. This representation was not entirely original with Jonson: an illustration in Vincenzo Cartari's *Imagini de i dei de gli antichi* depicts the Fates as seated and handling the thread of life while immediately in front of them are a pot of ink and sheets of paper.[2] As antiquarians, Cartari and Jonson knew that there was ample precedent for identifying the Fates with writing. In the text of his coronation entertainment for King James, Jonson appends this note to a line about "Clotho's booke": "The *Parcae,* or *Fates, Martianus* calls them *scribas ac librarias superum.*"[3] Jonson refers to a passage in *The Marriage of Philology and Mercury* by Martianus Capella: "Clotho, Lachesis, and Atropos, who by their study of true and correct writing recorded the decisions of Jove—being the librarians of the gods and the keepers of their archives—when they saw that the senate and council was being summoned and that the Thunderer himself was donning his magisterial robes, sharpened their styluses and collected their tablets to record the decisions of the president and the deliberations of the gods."[4] Even before Martianus Capella, the Romans customarily linked fatality with writing. For instance in Virgil's *Aeneid* Jove says to Venus, "I will speak and, further unrolling the scroll of fate, will disclose its secrets."[5] Ovid uses similar language, too, as Abraham Fraunce observes: "*Ovid* in the last book of his transformations, bringeth in *Jupiter* talking with *Venus* concerning the immutable decrees of these inexorable Ladies, written in Iron, brasse, and Adamant."[6] So closely identified were writing and fatality in the ancient world that Hyginus could attribute the very invention of certain Greek letters to the Fates.[7]

The Fates depicted in *Imagini de i dei de gli antichi* (Venice, 1571) by Vincenzo Cartari. In front of the three Fates, who handle the thread of life, are a pot of ink and sheets of paper. By permission of the Houghton Library, Harvard University.

Writing had become virtually synonymous with destiny long before the ascendancy of Greek and Roman culture. Jean Bottéro explains that this confluence originated in ancient Mesopotamia, especially in Sumer and Babylonia, societies which saw the development of writing: "According to the opinion of their devotees, the gods had to determine and to decide first of all the *destinies* of all things, in order to produce and govern the world and the people from day to day. Their orders had to be *written down* in order to give them substantiality, publicity, and force. Utilizing as pictograms and ideograms the *things* to come, which they created as needed, they impressed in them the 'individual words' of their decrees by anomalies and surprises in their presentation or their evolution."[8] Such writing offered humankind an extraordinary opportunity to learn the divine will: "Whoever understood the code used by the gods (a real transposition of the code of cuneiform writing), in other words, the significant value of their 'ideographic signs' materialized in the objects of the universe, could decipher the signs and read in them the irrevocable will of their authors." The conviction that the gods expressed their will in writing, however, would also introduce a new anxiety in western culture, especially among those whose effort to read divine signs met with only partial success and who came to feel, consequently, that they could neither anticipate nor comprehend a future that was already ordained.

This chapter examines the connection between writing and fatality in classical culture and its survival in the Christian era as well as the persistent relationship between writing and astrology from antiquity to the Renaissance. Chapter 10 explores the significance of the book of fate for two exemplary plays, *The Spanish Tragedy* and *The Duchess of Malfi*, and looks briefly at attitudes toward fatality in Elizabethan England, as revealed in the dispute that pitted Nashe and Greene against the brothers Harvey.

2

What contributed to the alliance of fate with the written word for Ben Jonson and his contemporaries was not just pagan precedent but also Christian tradition, which had accommodated the Sibyls of antiquity, giving them a new home. The Sibyls, apparently a creation of Greek culture, probably made their first appearance in Asia Minor. At various sites the women received petitions and questions about the future, and they responded in verse. The Sibylline oracles were subsequently collected and eventually took the form of books. The most famous story about them was recounted in Terentius Varro's lost *Antiquitates Rerum Humanarum et Divinarum*, partly preserved by Lactantius in his *Divinae Institutiones*.

Varro related the meeting of King Tarquin with the Cumaean Sibyl.[9] It seems that an old woman offered Tarquin nine books (scrolls) for a huge sum. He declined to pay, and so she promptly burned three of them, offering the remainder at the original price. Again Tarquin spurned the proposal, whereupon she burned another three, offering the rest for the same sum. Finally realizing that the contents must be too momentous to forgo, Tarquin acceded to the asking price, receiving only three of the original nine books. These were subsequently deposited in Rome, first at the temple of Jupiter Optimus Maximus, then later, in the time of Augustus, at the temple of Apollo.[10]

The spoken and written words of the Sibyls were closely identified in antiquity, as Virgil's account of the Cumaean Sibyl illustrates. In the *Aeneid* the hero finds a Sibyl at Cumae, originally a Greek colony on the west coast of Italy. This Sibyl, who dwells in a cave, communicates through speech: "The huge side of the Euboean rock is hewn into a cavern, whither lead a hundred wide mouths, a hundred gateways, whence rush as many voices, the answers of the Sibyl."[11] Virgil also records, however, another tradition—that the inspired prophetess "deep in a rocky cave sings the Fates and entrusts to leaves signs and symbols. Whatever verses the maid has traced on leaves she arranges in order and stores away in the cave."[12] This twofold manner of expression—speech and writing—is in keeping with the ancient understanding of fate: "The Latins did not draw a distinction between a god's spoken prophecy and destiny itself. By derivation *fatum* could be the word foretelling the future or the decree which determined it. The Sibylline oracles were regularly called the *Libri Fatales*. There is even some indication that the Sibyls and the Fates could be confused."[13]

For early Christians the Sibyls and their prophecies presented a quandary, as did the concept of destiny itself. To credit the Sibyls might obscure the uniqueness of Christ's life and work; to renounce Sibylline prophecy might risk alienating those people who saw the Sibyls as a link to divinity. Christianity managed to accommodate the Sibyls by much the same strategy used to accommodate fate: appropriation and subordination. The notion of fate was accepted, but it was subordinated to a providential scheme which, in turn, was identified with the Christian deity. Boethius sets forth the essentials of this solution in *The Consolation of Philosophy:* he interprets fate as the appearance of events from a human perspective, while providence represents the same events from the perspective of God. Christians also managed to assimilate the pagan Sibyls, identifying them with a divine design that was understood imperfectly in this world. In their role as prophesiers of the future, the Sibyls were akin to the Jewish prophets, intermediaries through whom God communicated with humankind.

Some early Christians were close adherents of the Sibyls, who retained their popularity throughout the Mediterranean world. A detractor of Christianity about 160 A.D. "tried to discredit the faith by calling attention to heresies and aberrations in it. One of these sects was the Sibyllistae, who apparently gave much credit to the authority of the prophetess."[14] Not all Christians were so comfortable with this survival of pagan culture. Tertullian in his *Apology,* an open letter to Roman magistrates, declares: "You have, I know, a Sibyl, inasmuch as this name for a true prophetess of the true God has been everywhere appropriated for all who appeared to have the gift of prophecy; and just as your Sibyls have been deceitful regarding the truth in the matter of their name, so also have your gods."[15] But Lactantius, who describes ten Sibyls, quotes from the Sibylline books and states that they all "proclaim one God"; he also says that the Erythraean Sibyl "declares that there is a son of god," that the Sibyl foretold Christ's miracles of the loaves and fishes, and that the Sibyl even predicted the resurrection of the dead and the Last Judgment.[16] St. Augustine expresses a similarly approving attitude, maintaining that the "Erythraean Sibyl certainly wrote some passages that openly refer to Christ"; Augustine is careful, however, to distinguish this Sibyl from pagan deities: "she even inveighs so strongly against them and against their worshippers that she is clearly to be assigned to the number of those who belong to the City of God."[17] This view of the Sibyls gained wide acceptance in the Middle Ages. John of Salisbury, for instance, asserts that they foretold many details of Christ's life: "there is written evidence that a revelation was made to many Roman citizens concerning the mystery of the Incarnation, as a result, some believe, of a prophecy of the Sibyl. She indeed, instructed by the Holy Spirit, disclosed the mysteries not only of the Incarnation but of the passion, ascension after resurrection, and of the second coming, as you may discover for yourself in the Sibylline prophecies."[18]

By accommodating the Sibyls and crediting their role as prophets, Christians also embraced the conflation of Sibylline prophecy with the written word. This is particularly apparent in the sculpture and art of the late Middle Ages and Renaissance, when Sibyls and their books appeared with surprising frequency. In the German cathedral of Ulm, carved wooden Sibyls, each holding a book, decorate the choir. In the cathedral of Siena, ten Sibyls appear in the pavement, five in each of the aisles flanking the nave.[19] These designs depict the Sibyls as carrying books or tablets. The Cumaean Sibyl, for instance, bears in her hands the three volumes she sold to Tarquin; the other six lie at her feet. In the Tempio Malatestiano of Rimini, which Leon Battista Alberti converted from a Gothic to a Renaissance structure, Agostino di Duccio carved in relief the images of the Sibyls, each of whom is accompanied by a banderole.[20]

Artists as well as sculptors presented the Sibyls in a Christian context, illustrating their association with the written word. Woodcuts designed by Lucas van Leyden and Jacob Cornelisz. van Oostsanen depict scenes from the life of Christ, while below each appears the Sibyl who foresaw that incident.[21] Frescoes depicting the Sibyls appear with some frequency in Italian churches. Pinturicchio painted four Sibyls in the Baglioni Chapel of S. Maria Maggiore, Spello. Of these the Erythraean is the best preserved: she is seated and writes upon the book in her lap; other books lie on the step near her chair.[22] Pinturicchio also painted four Sibyls on the ceiling of the choir in S. Maria del Popolo, Rome. The Delphic Sibyl holds a book while she leans upon two other books; the Erythraean leans against an altar decorated with an inscription; the Cimmerian Sibyl leans upon three clasped books; and the Persian writes in a book with a quill pen.[23] The Borgia room of the Sibyls at the Vatican also contains frescoes of several Sibyls: in lunettes these Sibyls are paired with Old Testament prophets. Daniel, for instance, appears facing the Erythraean Sibyl, and the two figures hold banderoles containing their names and prophecies.[24]

In the best known depiction of Sibyls in Christendom, Michaelangelo painted five Sibyls alongside prophets on the ceiling of the Sistine Chapel. The Sibyls alternate with the prophets on the lower part of the vault, beneath the panels illustrating biblical history.[25] Thus at one end is Zechariah paging through a book; on the adjoining wall are Jeremiah deep in thought, the Persian Sibyl reading a book, Ezekiel holding a scroll, the Erythraean Sibyl turning pages in a book, Joel reading a scroll, and then, on the end wall opposite Zechariah, is Jonah. On the adjoining long wall appear the Libyan Sibyl holding open a huge book with two hands, Daniel with an open book on his lap, the Cumaean Sibyl reading a book, Isaiah with his fingers holding his place in a closed book, and the Delphic Sibyl holding a scroll while she stares into the distance. This pattern of alternation in one of Christianity's holiest places demonstrates the extent to which the Sibyls had become identified with providential design and, simultaneously, the extent to which that design was manifested in the written word.

In the late sixteenth century some theologians, while not so enthusiastic as their medieval and early Renaissance forbears, were nevertheless inclined to see the Sibyls as part of God's providence. John Napier, for example, in a book explicating Revelation, explains his decision to append a treatment of the Sibyls: "Here Followeth Certaine Notable Prophecies agreable to our purpose, extract out of the books of Sibylla, whose authorities neither being so authentik, that hitherto we could cite any of them in matters of scriptures, neither so prophane that altogether we could omit them: We have therefore thought very meet, severally and apart to insert the same here, after the end of this worke of holy scripture, because of the famous antiquitie, approved veritie, and harmonicall consentment thereof with the scriptures of God, and specially with the 18. Chapter of this holy Revelation."[26] As late as the early eighteenth century, Sir John Floyer could quote sibylline verses for the purpose of demonstrating their congruence with Scripture.[27]

In the Renaissance Sibyls appear in quasidramatic displays, and their prophetic power is noted on the stage. For example, Sibyls welcomed King James I on a visit to Oxford on 27 August 1605. In a pageant designed by Matthew Gwinn, the *Sibyllae* greet the king in Latin, addressing him as the descendant of Banquo. Three in number, they refer to themselves as *fata*.[28] Shakespeare may have known of this pageant when he created the three weird sisters of *Macbeth,* though his principal inspiration was, of course, Holinshed's account. Shakespeare explicitly evokes the prophetic function of Sibyls in *Othello,* when the Moor tells Desdemona the identity of the person who made the handkerchief he gave her: "A sibyl, that had numb'red in the world / The sun to course two hundred compasses, / In her prophetic fury sew'd the work" (3.4.70–72).[29] Similarly, in *1 Henry VI* the Bastard of Orleance alludes to the power of the Sibyls when he characterizes Joan de Pucelle: "The spirit of deep prophecy she hath, / Exceeding the nine sibyls of old Rome" (1.2.55–56).

3

The identification of fatality with writing, fostered by the Christian acceptance of Sibylline prophecy, was powerfully reinforced by another creation of the ancient world, astrology. Believing that the heavens constitute a book, the ancients imagined that they could therein discern cosmic design. As Plotinus suggests, "Let us suppose that the stars are like characters always being written on the heavens, or written once for all and moving as they perform their task."[30] The stars, then, are signs in a universe wherein all things are joined one to another in a purposeful arrangement which may be "read." This notion persisted in the Middle Ages when it was adopted by Bernardus Silvestris, who identifies the stars with writing, and that writing with human destiny: "the firmament is inscribed with stars, and prefigures all that may come to pass through decree of fate."[31] Later in this same work the deity confers upon nature the Table of Destiny, which "is nothing else but the sequence of those things which come to pass by the decrees of fate."[32] The force of classical tradition, together with the penchant of Christian thinkers to trace all events back to a single deity, led John of Salisbury, among others, to credit the notion of astral influence, while adopting a wary attitude toward those astrologers who would obscure the power of God or annihilate free will. He cites Psalms 19:1 ("The heavens declare the glorie of God, and the firmament sheweth the worke of his hands") and says: "If . . . there are celestial indications of things which are undeniably to come to pass, since immutable destiny has so ordained, what is there to prevent that those things which are foretold by the testimony of the heavenly bodies be known by man and in turn transmitted by him to man? Signs have indeed been given to man for his edification and not to those who, being acquainted with the celestial bodies, are not in need of them."[33]

Astrology did not fade in the Renaissance. In fact, it flourished. Nor was astrological belief confined to the common folk or the superstitious: it enjoyed considerable popularity among intellectuals and in the very citadel of Christianity. D. C. Allen, who notes that astrologers were a common feature of Renaissance courts, cites the career of Luca Gaurico: "Gaurico was born in 1476 and had a long and distinguished career as an astrologer. He predicted the fall of Giovanni Bentivoglio, tyrant of Bologna, and was punished for his prediction although it eventually was fulfilled. He predicted that Alessandro Farnese would become pope; and when Farnese was Paul III, he summoned Gaurico to Rome, knighted him, and eventually made him Bishop of Giffoni."[34] Italian palaces of both princes and clergy were decorated with zodiacal symbols. For example, frescoes by Francesco del Cossa and Ercole de'Roberti decorate the Room of the Months (completed ca. 1470) in the Palazzo Schifanoia, Ferrara.[35] Each month is represented by a panel with three compartments arranged vertically. At the top is an ancient deity, then below a sign of the zodiac, and finally a scene depicting activities at the Este court proper to that sign. Somewhat smaller but equally impressive is the Zodiac Room in the Palazzo d'Arco, Mantua. The walls are covered with frescoes by Giovanni Maria Falconetto (1468–1535); these depict the zodiacal signs and, below, legends associated with those signs.[36] And the glory of the richly decorated Palazzo Farnese, Caprarola, is the Sala del Mappomondo, with a stunning ceiling fresco of the constellations painted in 1575.[37] What underlies each of these room designs is the assumption that the stars exercise a powerful influence on the sublunary world and that such influence may be traced and understood.[38]

Not even the development of astronomy, made possible by refinements in the telescope and by a rigorous method of observing and recording the movements of the stars, inhibited the popularity of astrology, as the case of Johannes Kepler illustrates. Early in his career this greatest of Renaissance astronomers supplemented his income by devising calendars containing astrological predictions. Later he would serve as court astrologer to the Duke of Wallenstein. His attitude toward this activity seems to have been ambivalent. At one point he scorned astrology in harsh terms: "A mind accustomed to mathematical deduction, when confronted with the faulty foundations [of astrology] resists a long, long time, like an obstinate mule, until compelled by beating and curses to put its foot into that dirty puddle."[39] His treatises, however, indicate that he never entirely discounted astral influence: "That the sky does something to man is obvious enough; but what it does specifically remains hidden."[40] Kepler believed that the development of astronomy had the capacity to refine astrology, giving it greater credibility by making it more accurate.

Astrology had detractors, to be sure, and perhaps none was more uncompromising than Pico della Mirandola. Other thinkers, while sometimes looking askance on divinatory astrology, were less rigid in their thinking. The case of Marsilio Ficino, examined by Eugenio Garin, is illustrative:

> Side by side with the defence of divine providence and human liberty is an insistent and detailed scrutiny of the various astrological theories. This examination unites the attempt at a rigorous scientific analysis with the objections of practice and the banal criticisms of the time. On the other hand it is also true that Ficino never carried his anti-astrological censure to its conclusion; that he left aside the most bitter and often conventional objections in his published works; that he did not hide uncertainties and ambiguities; that, above all, he showed that he wanted to fight the materialistic and atheist issues in astrology more than astral determinism.[41]

Erasmus, too, displays something of the same divided opinion. On the one hand, he can be quite skeptical: "Such, I perceive, are the convictions of the majority of men, that they look for the sources of their happiness or unhappiness among the heavenly bodies. For my part, I know no luminary whose propitious radiance surpasses a sincere and congenial friend, and none on the contrary more fatal and sinister than the company of one who is counterfeit and insincere. Let others then watch the stars, if they will; in my view we should seek on earth what can make us happy or unhappy" (*CWE* 7:43).[42] On the other hand, Erasmus sent to Giovanni Battista Boerio, physician to Henry VII and Henry VIII of England, a treatise on astrology by Lucian: "The very title delighted me, and I began eagerly to hope that it might be something which would seem worthy . . . of a man who has so distinguished himself in this most excellent science of astrology . . ." (*CWE* 2:238). The most interesting inconsistency, however, is that of Martin Luther, who said, "astrology is not a science because it has no principles and proofs. On the contrary, astrologers judge everything by the outcome and by individual cases and say, 'This happened once and twice, and therefore it will always happen so.' They base their judgment on the results that suit them and prudently don't talk about those that don't suit" (*LW* 54:173).[43] Yet, like Kepler, Ficino, and Erasmus, Luther, too, could adopt a more indulgent attitude: this reformer, so vehement in denouncing astral determinism, had a profound sense of fatality, at least in spiritual matters. As J. D. North points out, "It is amusing to observe that the most implacable opponents of astrology, with its often tacit fatalism, were precisely those who themselves preached predestination, albeit predestination of a different sort."[44] North's observation is borne out by Luther's own words, when he concedes a parallel between his sense of the human will constrained by God and the ancient sense of freedom constrained by fate. In *De Servo Arbitrio* Luther cites several passages about fate in the *Aeneid* and concludes of Virgil: "he makes even their immortal gods subject to Fate, to which even Jupiter himself and Juno must necessarily yield. Hence the current conception of the three Parcae, immutable, implacable, irrevocable" (*LW* 33:41). Luther goes on to assess the significance of that ancient belief in destiny: "we can see that the knowledge of God's predestination and foreknowledge remained with the common people no less than the awareness of his existence itself." Luther aligns his notion of predestination with pagan fatality, seeing the one as the dimly perceived reality of the other.

Not every adherent of astrology envisioned the stars as a book, but most did both in the Middle Ages and the Renaissance. In the *Cosmographia* of Bernardus Silvestris, Providence invites Nature to contemplate the sky: "I would have you survey the heavens, inscribed with their manifold array of symbols, which I have set forth for learned eyes, like a book with its pages spread open, containing things to come in secret characters."[45] For Marsilio Ficino, "The celestial configurations are like the letters in a book which explain the divine concepts ('the notions of divine beings are made clear by the disposition of the heavens, as if through letters'); the decrees of the intelligences are shown through the stars, 'through signs rather than causes' (*per signa potius quam per causas*). And astrologers can sometimes read these signs."[46] Paracelsus in his *Labyrinthus Medicorum Errantium* enumerates the books out of which the physician must learn, and among these is "the firmament, of which book the stars are the alphabet."[47] Robert Burton in his *Anatomy of Melancholy* envisions the stars collectively as a book: "the Heaven is Gods Instrument, by mediation of which, he governes & disposeth these elementary bodies, or a great booke, as one cals it, wherein are written many strange things, for such as can reade."[48]

Burton's words point to a pronounced tendency in Renaissance thought: to find such reading of the stars difficult, if not impossible. Owen Felltham, arguing that "Wee are govern'd by a *Power,* that wee cannot but *obey,*" claims not to know "Whether this be *Nature* order'd and relinquisht; or whether it bee *accidentall;* or the operating *power* of the *Starres*; or the *eternall connexion* of *causes;* or the *execution* of the *will of God;* whether it takes away all *freedome* of *will* from *Man;* or by what meanes we are thus wrought upon."⁴⁹ Felltham goes on to acknowledge his inability to arrive at a definitive answer: "I see, there are both *Arguments* and *objections* on every side. I hold it a kinde of *Mundane predestination,* writ in such *Characters,* as it is not in the wit of *man* to reade them."⁵⁰ In another essay Felltham ponders the inscrutability of the stars: "suppose there were a *Fate* transferr'd from the *Starres* to *Man;* who can reade their *significations?*"⁵¹

Like those who sought to scrutinize the book of nature, those who read the book of fate found that much knowledge was required, that the book withholds its secrets from the uninitiated, and that even among the learned what may formerly have seemed accessible may actually prove mysterious. On the Renaissance stage characters betray uncertainty when they speak of reading the book of fate, especially as it is expressed in the stars. For instance, in Chapman's *Conspiracy of Charles Duke of Byron* a character says that the stars "are divine books to us, and are read / By understanders only" (4.1.217–18).⁵² When Imogen in *Cymbeline* recognizes the handwriting of a newly arrived letter, she compares her knowledge with that of an accomplished astronomer: "O learn'd indeed were that astronomer / That knew the stars as I his characters; / He'd lay the future open" (3.2.27–29); Imogen implies that such an astronomer is rare. Finally, in Middleton's *No Wit, No Help Like a Woman's,* Mistress Low-water implies the inaccessibility of the book of fate when she directs another character: "Turn o'er the leaves, and where you left, go forward; / To me, it shall be like the book of fate, / Ever clasp'd up" (5.1.175–77).⁵³

On the stage a feeling of fatality may be generated by explicit reference to the stars or to other forces that are perceived to impinge on the characters, often in destructive fashion. The chorus to *Romeo and Juliet* announces: "From forth the fatal loins of these two foes / A pair of star-cross'd lovers take their life" (ll. 5–6), and the characters enact the meaning of these lines: they come to recognize their subjection to fate and, in opposing it, they commit suicide. Thus Romeo, hearing a report that Juliet is dead, cries, "Then I defy you, stars" (5.1.24). At Juliet's tomb he says, "O, here / Will I set up my everlasting rest, / And shake the yoke of inauspicious stars / From this world-wearied flesh" (5.3.109–12). Such invocations of astral power are sometimes accompanied by reference to written materials. In this same speech, for example, Romeo uses a metaphor involving writing to express his sense of victimization at having been forced by circumstance to fight and kill Paris: "O, give me thy hand, / One writ with me in sour misfortune's book!" (ll. 81–82). Although Fortune and fate are usually discriminated in the Renaissance (the one suggesting contingency, the other determinism),⁵⁴ and although fate was more commonly identified with writing, nevertheless Fortune, who is personified in *Romeo and Juliet* and who may be implicitly evoked by the expression "misfortune's book," could be identified with the written word. In *2 Henry IV* when King Henry receives letters reporting the news from Gaultree Forest, he imagines the writer in symbolic terms: "Will Fortune never come with both hands full, / But write her fair words still in foulest terms?" (4.4.103–4).[55] The written word may even be used to distinguish between Fortune and fate. Abraham Fraunce explains the distinction with this tableau: "At the feete of *Tyme,* stoode *Desteny,* with a booke before her: which *Fortune* and *Chaunce* did tosse & turne incessantly, sometimes overskipping five leaves, sometimes ten, sometimes an hundred, sometimes a thousand, as they thought good."[56]

Onstage a feeling of fatality may be generated not only by language but also by the actual use of written materials. Theatrical properties contribute to a sense that the characters are subject to external powers. The undelivered letter from Friar Lawrence to Romeo is one such instance; another is the "schedule" that Artemidorus presses Julius Caesar to read (3.1.3).[57] These unread messages contain news having the capacity to avert disaster; unread and unheeded, they suggest by their very existence that the intended readers are doomed. In *Titus Andronicus* the written word functions somewhat differently to convey fatality: the mutilated Lavinia "tosseth a book," which proves to be Ovid's *Metamorphoses.* Her purpose is to explain her plight by pointing to a literary parallel. Because the crime that has befallen her has a precedent in the "tragic tale" of Philomel and Tereus, and because that tale has been written down and widely read, Lavinia by her experience reenacts an ancient narrative. To the extent that she does so, her violation seems part of an already determined scheme.

The convergence of language and property is apparent in *2 Henry IV* when the dispirited king enters with letters in his hands and, having directed his men to read them, says:

> O God, that one might read the book of fate,
> And see the revolution of the times
> Make mountains level, and the continent,
> Weary of solid firmness, melt itself
> Into the sea. . . .
>
> (3.1.45–49)

The confidence that earlier allowed Henry to challenge King Richard has been undercut by illness, guilt, and disappointment. His mood now verges on despair:

> O, if this were seen,
> The happiest youth, viewing his progress through,

THE BOOK OF FATE 231

>What perils past, what crosses to ensue,
>Would shut the book, and sit him down and die.
>
>(ll. 53–56)

Henry's pessimism finds expression in language of reading, and what he reads admits of no amelioration: nothing he does can alter the book of fate, which is as real to him as the letters he has received.[58] Although that book does not, of course, take concrete form onstage, nevertheless the verbal image (of a book) and the hand props (the letters) work in tandem: the king's reading of those letters seems to prompt his meditation on the book of fate.

10
Fate on the Stage

1

SOME plays achieve much of their effect onstage by virtue of their ability to sustain a feeling that the characters are fated, as modern productions of Renaissance plays enable us to understand. Performances of *The Spanish Tragedy* and the *Duchess of Malfi* at the National Theatre in London in the 1980s depended to a considerable extent for their power on the creation of claustrophobic worlds, wherein the protagonists in particular found themselves buffeted by forces they could neither see nor comprehend. This chapter, exploring the handling of both properties and language, examines in detail the ways in which these two plays, using a variety of written materials, create a sense of fatality.

2

Unlike most other plays of its time, Thomas Kyd's *Spanish Tragedy* generates an aura of inexorability not by verbal evocations of destiny but by the working out of an extraordinarily intricate plot. Likened to a detective story by T. S. Eliot,[1] that plot is full of twists and turns, all the more theatrically effective for their apparent originality with Kyd and thus their surprise to the audience. Although the induction announces an action culminating in revenge, the audience has no idea how convoluted the path to that end will be. There is, in fact, not a single revenge but a series: Kyd "chose to set layer within layer, wheels within wheels, revenge within revenge."[2] The sequence of interlocked revenges, together with insistent dramatic irony, evokes a world where actions have manifold unforeseen consequences and where characters emerge as agents of manipulative powers.

In a plot justly renowned for its sensationalism, the written word proves decisive. The protagonist finds in writing of various kinds the information that motivates him to action, the justification for his vengefulness, and even the vehicle of revenge.³ Written materials have, in the aggregate, a force greater than the sum of their parts. Any single one may not necessarily lead to another in a tight chain of cause and effect, but each, seemingly independent of the others, contributes to the revenge promised in the induction. These materials prove to be not mere pieces of paper that find their way into the revenger's hands by happenstance, but determinants of his action, orchestrated from without.

The induction reveals that writing is common to the next world as well as this, and its function is much the same in both. Thus when the Ghost of Andrea relates his approach to the judges of the underworld, "To crave a passport for my wand'ring ghost" (1.1.35),⁴ he indicates that in death the passport functions much as does such a document in life: it is a written authorization to go from one place to another (across a significant boundary). The request reflects Andrea's present powerlessness and his as yet unsettled status following death in battle. He reports that, in an effort to determine his proper resting place, Minos "in graven leaves of lottery, / Drew forth the manner of my life and death" (1.1.36–37). Even more clearly than the passport, this leaf, drawn from an urn, suggests the significance that writing has in the play: it is a source of guidance, direction, control. Brooke and Paradise gloss "leaves of lottery" as "books of fate,"⁵ which is metaphorically accurate, for the course of Andrea's life, from birth to death, has all along been fated.

Because the leaf drawn from the urn records that Andrea was in life both a lover and a soldier, his future poses a problem for the judges of the underworld: Aeacus believes that Andrea should "walk with lovers in our fields of love," while Rhadamanth thinks that he belongs in "martial fields" (1.1.42, 47). Resolution of this disagreement entails further use of the written word, for Minos decides to send the Ghost to "our infernal king," and, says Andrea, "To this effect my passport straight was drawn" (l. 54). Through the underworld he moves until at last he reaches the monarch of the realm: "Here finding Pluto with his Proserpine, / I show'd my passport humbled on my knee" (ll. 76–77). The passport, mentioned here for the third time, is an outward sign of Andrea's vulnerability, his complete subjection to the will of the nether powers.⁶ Fortunately for him, Proserpine asks to render judgment; his plight, especially his truncated love affair, evokes her tenderness. It is decided that Andrea be permitted to return to the realm of the living where he will watch his former lover dispatch the man who killed him. As Revenge tells him at the close of the induction,

> Then know, Andrea, that thou art arriv'd
> Where thou shalt see the author of thy death,

> Don Balthazar the prince of Portingale,
> Depriv'd of life by Bel-imperia.
>
> (1.1.86–89)

Such knowledge of the future implies an already determined course of events. And the presence of Revenge (along with Andrea) onstage thoughout the play is for the audience in the theater a harbinger of the fate that will eventually overtake Don Balthazar.

As the induction concludes and the story of Hieronimo and his son comes to prominence, Andrea's long expository speech recedes in our memory. But that speech, together with the spectacle of the restless Ghost, anticipates much of the subsequent action: Andrea creates in our mind's eye the image of a man wandering, perplexed and vulnerable, seeking guidance from supernatural powers, and finding it through the written word. The induction, then, prefigures the plight of Hieronimo, whose quest and whose coming to terms with destiny become the chief subject of the play. Both Andrea and Hieronimo feel victimized; each loses a person he loves on account of death. And what leads to requital for that death in both instances is writing in one form or another. For Andrea the leaf in Minos's urn sets in motion a sequence of events resulting in his witnessing the slayer's demise. For Hieronimo a panoply of letters, documents, and books culminate in his retribution.

Despite its importance the written word functions obliquely to bring about the end foreseen by Revenge: the process will not be nearly so direct as Andrea supposes. Consider Balthazar, whose death Revenge predicts. The Portuguese Prince, having been captured by the Spaniards, seeks to woo Bel-imperia by letter but to no avail: "My words are rude and work her no delight. / The lines I send her are but harsh and ill, / Such as do drop from Pan and Marsyas' quill" (2.1.14–16). The "quill" is apparently not a pen but a reed (instrument) played by these mythological figures in contests with Apollo. Since Pan and Marsyas were defeated by the deity, Balthazar's allusion represents a confession of inadequate rhetoric, the corollary of his affected, self-conscious speech.[7] Where his letters fail, those of Horatio succeed. Just returned from the war, Horatio benefits from Bel-imperia's desire to spite Balthazar for having caused her lover's death. She encourages Horatio to write to her so that she may allay his misgivings about their clandestine relationship: "Write loving lines, I'll answer loving lines" (2.2.36). Unbeknownst to them, those very love letters provide the means whereby knowledge of their affair is betrayed to others. Bel-imperia's brother Lorenzo, through intimidation and bribery, prompts her servant Pedringano to reveal the identity of her new lover Horatio: "She sent him letters which myself perus'd, / Full fraught with lines and arguments of love, / Preferring him before Prince Balthazar" (2.1.84–86). Enraged, the Prince and Lorenzo determine to eliminate this rival for Bel-imperia's affections. Their plot culminates in the arbor, where an aroused Bel-imperia bids Horatio, "O let me go, for in my troubled eyes / Now may'st thou read that life in passion dies" (2.4.46–47). But before the reading can proceed very far, Balthazar and Lorenzo, accompanied by two servants, emerge from the darkness and stab to death and hang the defenseless Horatio.

If an exchange of letters contributes to Horatio's demise, another sort of letter aids in unmasking the killers. This one falls at Hieronimo's feet while he bewails his son's death and cries aloud for guidance:

> Eyes, life, world, heavens, hell, night, and day,
> See, search, shew, send, some man, some mean, that
>   may—
>   *A letter falleth.*
> What's here? a letter? tush, it is not so!
> A letter written to Hieronimo!
> "For want of ink, receive this bloody writ.
> Me hath my hapless brother hid from thee:
> Revenge thyself on Balthazar and him,
> For these were they that murdered thy son.
> Hieronimo, revenge Horatio's death,
> And better fare than Bel-imperia doth."
>   (3.2.22–31)

In keeping with the violent world of the play, the letter is written in blood, prefiguring a gruesome retribution. (The stage direction specifies *Red ink*.) Despite its explicitness, however, and the appeal to "revenge Horatio's death," the letter does not in itself lead directly to the punishment or even the apprehension of the malefactors, since the allegations contained in the letter seem so improbable to Hieronimo that he suspects a trap. As befits this Knight Marshal, a judicial officer of the crown, Hieronimo resolves to act prudently. Before he levels any charges at the men named in the letter, he will ascertain its accuracy: "I . . . will by circumstances try / What I can gather to confirm this writ" (ll. 48–49). If the letter does not itself effect retribution, it nonetheless provides a hypothesis for Hieronimo to test.

The confirmation Hieronimo seeks arrives in the form of another letter, writen by Pedringano, imprisoned for killing Serberine, a fellow accomplice in Horatio's murder.[8] The way in which this second letter finds its way into Hieronimo's hands is extraordinarily intricate, even for the world of revenge tragedy. It seems that Lorenzo, wanting both servants dispatched, has inveigled Pedringano into shooting Serberine and has arranged for the killer's arrest. Apprehended, Pedringano naturally expects Lorenzo to intercede for him; the prisoner writes to Lorenzo, who instructs a servant, "Tell him his pardon is already sign'd" (3.4.67). The page then carries to prison a box ostensibly containing the promised pardon. Its arrival obviates—or so Pedringano thinks—the need to send another letter (already written) to Lorenzo. As the relieved prisoner tells the page,

> Gramercy boy, but it was time to come,
> For I had written to my lord anew
> A nearer matter that concerneth him,
> For fear his lordship had forgotten me;
> But sith he hath remember'd me so well—
>
> (3.6.18–22)

His thought is never completed: not knowing what the page knows—that the box contains nothing—the confident Pedringano begins to banter with Hieronimo and the hangman; within moments the condemned man goes jesting to his death. Lorenzo's scheme would appear to have worked brilliantly. But so swiftly has execution followed the arrival of the empty box that the second letter to Lorenzo is never destroyed; it survives to be discovered on Pedringano's body and brought to Hieronimo by the hangman.[9] In wonderment Hieronimo reads aloud the letter addressed to Lorenzo:

> "My lord, I writ as mine extremes requir'd,
> That you would labour my delivery:
> If you neglect, my life is desperate,
> And in my death I shall reveal the troth.
> You know, my lord, I slew him for your sake,
> And as confederate with the prince and you,
> Won by rewards and hopeful promises,
> I holp to murder Don Horatio, too."
>
> (3.7.32–39)

Thanks to Pedringano's industry as a writer, Hieronimo now has confirmation of Bel-imperia's accusations. He knows with certainty that she is the author of the letter written in blood and that the charges she made are true: "Now see I what I durst not then suspect, / That Bel-imperia's letter was not feign'd, / Nor feigned she" (ll. 49–51). With Pedringano's letter in hand, Hieronimo can assemble his evidence and petition the king for redress.

In Hieronimo's mind the letters have not come to him by accident: "now I feelingly perceive, / They did what heaven unpunish'd would not leave" (3.7.55–56). His reference to "heaven" expresses the conviction that the letters represent supernatural soliciting. When the scene began, he spoke of his sighs and passions beating "at the windows of the brightest heavens" for justice and revenge (3.7.13). His entreaties, it seems, have been answered. Hieronimo's interpretation is consistent with his experience. After all, the first letter falls into his hands at precisely the moment he seeks guidance; so quickly and helpfully does the second turn up that its arrival must be more than coincidence. As a theatrical stratagem, the use of two letters may seem contrived. But that effect is calculated, not inadvertent. The playwright wants the audience to feel what Hieronimo feels—that the letters are part of a larger pattern, that design rather than chance is at work, that human events are directed by supernatural forces. The very improbability of the action and its convoluted nature are, in the world of the play, testimony of divine control.

Although Hieronimo presumably has in his hands the two letters and can therefore prove the murderers' identities, he fails to present his evidence effectively before the king and thus fails to achieve his goal: the evidence seems to count for nothing. Actually, those letters, though unread by the king, serve the cause of retribution, for, having failed to gain the king's attention, Hieronimo concludes that he cannot find satisfaction through judicial means. Consequently, he must consider afresh how to apply the knowledge gained from the letters. He meditates upon the avenues open to him in a speech that is pivotal: the "*Vindicta mihi*" soliloquy. Before the speech we feel that he may or may not have the inclination and capacity to exact retribution; afterward we feel that his requital of Horatio's murderers is only a matter of time. The soliloquy, then, marks the turning point of the play, and crucial to its development are the words that he reads while pondering his plight. The stage direction is explicit: *Enter Hieronimo with a book in his hand.*

His opening words, "*Vindicta mihi!*" are usually interpreted as biblical since the subsequent lines—"Ay, heaven will be reveng'd of every ill, / Nor will they suffer murder unrepaid" (3.13.2-3)—are an apparent reference to the injunction against personal vengeance in Romans 12:19: "Vengeance is mine: I will repaye, saith the Lord"; Hieronimo's Latin words are part of this sentence in the Vulgate—"Mihi vindicta, ego retribuam, dicit Dominus." His resolution, "Then stay, Hieronimo, attend their will, / For mortal men may not appoint their time" (ll. 4-5), is, of course, in keeping with the New Testament precept. Hence it seems logical to assume that he has in his hands a Bible.[10] His very next words, however, are from a different source altogether, Seneca's *Agamemnon;* they are spoken by Clytemnestra as she resolves to anticipate the deadly fury of her husband: "*Per scelus semper tutum est sceleribus iter*" (The safe way for crime is always through crime). Following several lines in English, Hieronimo again quotes Seneca, this time *Troades* (a speech by

Andromache to her son Astyanax). Still later in the soliloquy Hieronimo quotes a few words from Seneca's *Oedipus*. The quotations suggest that the book he carries is a collection of the Roman dramatist's tragedies. But if so, why does the speech begin with a biblical quotation?

Fredson Bowers long ago proposed a solution to this question, now widely accepted: that Hieronimo enters carrying an edition of Seneca but that at the outset of the soliloquy he is thinking about the passage in Romans.[11] This hypothesis accounts for the disparate sources of the Latin quotations; and it obviates the need to find a Senecan precedent for the words "*Vindicta mihi*," which their putative origin in *Octavia* cannot readily support.[12] Whatever the identity of the book, this theatrical property diminishes the sense that Hieronimo behaves irresponsibly. Even if he no longer has full control of his rational faculty, he is still sufficiently prudent to seek guidance in the written word. He remains Knight Marshal, and when he reads from the book he defers, in a sense, to precedent, something we should expect of a judicial officer.[13] The book, then, has the theatrical effect of enhancing our impression that Hieronimo is embarking on a course sanctioned by external agency. When he says of Horatio, "I will revenge his death!" (3.13.20), he follows, or so he believes, a principle enunciated by an acknowledged authority. What he reads has the prestige conferred by the printed word.

Congruent with Hieronimo's commitment to revenge is a growing fatalism, manifest in the same soliloquy. As he considers the prospect of taking revenge, he reflects on the risk entailed. Mindful of his possible death, he quotes these lines of Andromache from *Troades:* "*Fata si miseros juvant, habes salutem; / Fata si vitam negant, habes sepulchrum*" (ll. 12–13). Rendering the Latin *fata* with the English "destiny," Hieronimo proceeds to translate the lines and draw a personal inference:

> If destiny thy miseries do ease,
> Then hast thou health, and happy shalt thou be:
> If destiny deny thee life, Hieronimo,
> Yet shalt thou be assured of a tomb:
> If neither, yet let this thy comfort be,
> Heaven covereth him that hath no burial.
>
> (ll. 14–19)

Hieronimo's fatalism, though profound, engenders neither fear nor lasting despair. For him acceptance of the inevitable is liberating; no matter what the future holds, destiny, he feels, will compensate for the peril of the enterprise.[14]

Whatever we may think of Hieronimo's logic, there is no question of how he sees his endeavor: by resolving to act upon the precepts which he has just read in Seneca, Hieronimo aligns himself with destiny. Nor is this a delusion on his part. The play encourages us to credit Hieronimo's view, for not long after the "*Vindicta mihi*" speech, Revenge tells the increasingly impatient Andrea:

> Behold, Andrea, for an instance how
> Revenge hath slept, and then imagine thou
> What 'tis to be subject to destiny.
>
> (3.15.26–28)

As if to demonstrate the point, a dumb show is enacted wherein Hymen quenches with blood the torches of a nuptial couple. The presentation vividly adumbrates the demise of Balthazar and Bel-imperia, whose wedding is being planned. In powerfully visual fashion the dumb show reminds both Andrea and the audience that destiny encompasses everyone, Bel-imperia as well as Balthazar, and, by implication, Hieronimo as well as Lorenzo. All are part of a design whose shape they perceive dimly if at all. As G. K. Hunter observes, the characters "are not to be taken by the audience as the independent and self-willed individuals they suppose themselves to be, but in fact only as the puppets of a predetermined and omnicompetent justice that they . . . cannot see and never really understand."[15]

It seems fitting that Hieronimo's decision to take matters into his own hands should be shaped by the written word, for writing and revenge are frequently conjoined in the Renaissance. An emblem in Geoffrey Whitney's *A Choice of Emblemes* is illustrative. It depicts a man carving words on a stone tablet with mallet and chisel. The writing symbolizes the pain of the man who has been wronged and the preservation of that pain in the memory. The motto, which reads "*Scribit in marmore laesus*" (Wronged, he writes on marble), is elaborated in the accompanying poem:

> In marble harde our harmes wee alwayes grave,
> Bicause, wee still will beare the same in minde:
> In duste wee write the benifittes wee have,
> Where they are soone defaced with the winde.
> So, wronges wee houlde, and never will forgive,
> And soone forget, that still with us shoulde live.[16]

So long as a person vividly remembers an injury, the emotions of pain, grief, and rage have the capacity to generate retribution.

A theatrical counterpart of this emblem appears in *Titus Andronicus*. There Titus, having suffered the rape and mutilation of his daughter, the deaths of his sons, and the loss of his hand, makes a pledge to his brother:

An emblem from Geoffrey Whitney's *A Choice of Emblemes* (Leiden, 1586). The motto, *Scribit in marmore laesus*, may be translated as "Wronged, he writes on marble." By permission of the Houghton Library, Harvard University.

> You are a young huntsman, Marcus, let alone;
> And come, I will go get a leaf of brass,
> And with a gad of steel will write these words,
> And lay it by. The angry northen wind
> Will blow these sands like Sibyl's leaves abroad,
> And where's our lesson then?
>
> (4.1.101–6)

Shakespeare also aligns writing with revenge in a play shaped, in part, by *The Spanish Tragedy* and by Kyd's lost *Hamlet*.[17] When Hamlet meets his father's ghost and hears the command to take revenge, the Prince makes a vow that combines pain and memory, writing and revenge:

>   Remember thee!
> Yea, from the table of my memory
> I'll wipe away all triveal fond records,
> All saws of books, all forms, all pressures past
> That youth and observation copied there,
> And thy commandement all alone shall live
> Within the book and volume of my brain,
> Unmix'd with baser matter.
>
> (1.5.97–104)

FATE ON THE STAGE

A design from Henry Peacham's *Minerva Britanna* (London, 1612), a book of emblems. Depicted is a winged book symbolic of divine justice. By permission of the Houghton Library, Harvard University.

One form of writing (the new command) supplants an earlier form (the religious precepts, including the Ten Commandments, inculcated in the young Hamlet).[18] Later in the same play, writing is aligned with still another revenger when Claudius asks an enraged Laertes, "is't writ in your revenge / That, swoopstake, you will draw both friend and foe, / Winner and loser?" (4.5.142–44). The conjunction of writing and retribution has a pictorial counterpart in Henry Peacham's *Minerva Britanna*. One of the emblems, whose motto reads "Vindicta Divina," depicts an open book borne aloft by wings; the accompanying poem includes this admonition: "ere many yeares be past, / A plague will come, with winged speede at last."[19] Claudius and Laertes hardly seek to enact divine retribution; theirs is a personal motivation, of course. But Hamlet, who beseeches the Ghost to reveal all—"Haste me to know't, that I with wings as swift / As meditation, or the thoughts of love, / May sweep to my revenge" (1.5.29–31)—ultimately enacts his revenge under the aegis of providence (5.2.220). Hamlet's revenge is made possible by his discovery of Claudius's letter, which condemns him to death in England, and by his authorship of a substitute letter, condemning Rosencrantz and Guildenstern. Like Hamlet's, Hieronimo's retribution, however bloody, conflates the human and the divine: the revenge that satisfies his own quest for justice enjoys the sanction of the gods.

Hieronimo's revenge depends specifically upon the written word. As he considers how to go about avenging his son's death, Balthazar unwittingly provides an opportunity by inviting the Knight Marshal to present an entertainment for the visiting Portuguese Viceroy. Hieronimo immediately hits upon the idea of using a play written years earlier:

> When in Toledo there I studied,
> It was my chance to write a tragedy,
> See here my lords,   *He shows them a book.*
> Which long forgot, I found this other day.
>
> (4.1.77–80)

He then bids Balthazar and Lorenzo, along with Bel-imperia, to participate in a performance that will enact their demise. If Hieronimo has been guided by the written word—in the form of letters and book—he will now seek to guide others by much the same means—through the playbook. So he distributes the players' parts: "here, my lords, are several abstracts drawn, / For each of you to note your parts, / And act it as occasion's offer'd you" (4.1.141–43). This parceling out of the written materials exemplifies his mastery of the situation: as author (and stage manager), he controls his unsuspecting prey. At the same time, however, Hieronimo is himself, in a sense, controlled. After all, the story on which his play is based is not one of his own invention. He informs his actors that "The chronicles of Spain / Record this written of a knight of Rhodes" (ll. 108–9). Evidently he came across the narrative of Soliman and Perseda in his student days and adapted it to the stage. Therefore when he now pursues his revenge by means of that same play, he accommodates himself to the requirements of a historical account and to the requirements of a script written long ago, before the thought of vengeance for a murdered son ever entered his mind. To the extent that his actions are shaped by already extant writing, Hieronimo has something in common with his performers: the script that guides them guides him.

Not only do his actors receive their parts but so, too, does the courtly audience receive a copy of the script. Thus Hieronimo provides one to the king's brother: "let me entreat your grace / To give the king the copy of the play: / This is the argument of what we show" (4.3.5–7). Castile carries out the request, for in the following scene the king enters with the script in his hands. Nor is this the last time that it changes hands;

just before "Soliman and Perseda" begins, the king returns the script to Castile:

> Here brother, you shall be the book-keeper:
> This is the argument of that they show.
> *He giveth him a book.*
>
> (4.4.9–10)

Castile then looks from page to playing area, and from playing area back to the page. Such insistent attention to the playbook before performance has an important theatrical effect: it emphasizes the extent to which the courtly actors are creatures of their script.

The courtly audience has, of course, practical need of the playbook, for the actors speak their assigned lines in "unknown languages"—Latin, Greek, Italian, and French (4.1.173).[20] The significance of this odd requirement becomes apparent when Hieronimo says to himself, "Now shall I see the fall of Babylon, / Wrought by the heavens in this confusion" (ll. 195–96). Since the name of this ancient city is given as Babel in the Geneva Bible, it is likely, S. F. Johnson observes, that Kyd intends an analogy: "'The fall of Babylon' is Hieronimo's description of the catastrophe that Kyd has had him devise, and the device that he has wrought is analogized both with the confusion of tongues wrought by the Lord at Babel (Genesis, 11) and with the horrible destruction of both the historical and symbolic Babylons as prophesied in Isaiah, 13, Jeremiah, 51, and Revelation, 18."[21] As St. Augustine observes of Babel, "This city named 'Confusion' was none other than Babylon, to whose marvellous construction pagan history also pays tribute. For Babylon means 'Confusion.'"[22] The biblical accounts of both Babel and Babylon are stories of human presumption and divine punishment. So, too, in *The Spanish Tragedy* is the account of Balthazar and Lorenzo, whose crimes invite retribution by the same "heavens."

Hieronimo's allusion to the fall of Babylon evokes divine judgment and the written word in another way as well, for one of the most famous kings of that ancient city was Belshazzar, whose name is given as Balthasar in the Bishops' Bible.[23] Kyd's audience might well recall that this Old Testament king, having ordered the use of vessels taken from the temple in Jerusalem, watched as a hand mysteriously wrote the words "Mene, Mene, Tekel, Upharsin" on the wall of his palace (Daniel 5:25). Unable to decipher the inscription, he summons first his wise men and then Daniel, who explains it as a divine warning in response to the sacrilege; and that very night the king is slain. In *The Spanish Tragedy* the similarly named character has a close association with the written word: he woos Bel-imperia by letter; he gains knowledge of his rival's identity through

Horatio's letters (perused by Pedringano); he suffers the disclosure of his guilt through the letters of Bel-imperia and Pedringano; he hangs up the title-board before the performance of "Soliman and Perseda"; and he dies while enacting a script. The parallel between biblical narrative and play, while hardly exact, is suggestive, particularly in regard to the play-within-the-play. As the king of Babylon found himself unable to comprehend the language of divine warning, so is Balthazar oblivious to the real purpose of Hieronimo's play. As Daniel interpreted the meaning of the inscription for the king of Babylon, so Hieronimo explains the true meaning of his script for the courtiers of Spain and Portugal (4.4.76–152). And as God brought about the demise of Bablyon's king after a great feast, so supernatural forces, working through Hieronimo, bring about the death of Balthazar at a festive occasion.

As "Soliman and Perseda" nears its performance, Hieronimo looks ahead to the realization of his scheme wherein the actual and the theatrical will be indistinguishable: "The plot is laid of dire revenge: / On then, Hieronimo, pursue revenge, / For nothing wants but acting of revenge" (4.3.28–30). As he moves toward revenge, he extends the language of the theater to himself. Thus, replying to Bel-imperia's reproach for being slack, he says, "Let me entreat you grace my practices; / For why, the plot's already in mine head" (4.1.50–51). Hieronimo's realization that he, along with others, plays a "role" in a larger drama helps account for his bizarre mutilation. Captured by the courtiers, he is ordered to explain why he has done what he has done. In refusal he bites out his tongue, whereupon an enraged Castile says, "Yet can he write"; a pen is brought to him, along with writing paper, so that he can "write the troth" (4.4.195, 200). Hieronimo deliberately breaks the quill pen and, according to the stage directions, *Then he makes signs for a knife to mend his pen.* Given the knife, he promptly uses it to stab Castile and himself. The stubborn refusal to say anything—or to write—is perplexing, for Hieronimo has already said a great deal about his purpose (4.4.73–152). Perhaps his theatrical language provides an explanation for his silence. By his revenge he has not only satisfied the impulse to avenge Horatio's death, he has also fulfilled what he has come to regard as his destiny. With the completion of revenge, his destiny is simultaneously complete. Like an actor at the end of a performance, he finds further words superfluous.

The Spanish Tragedy concludes in a maelstrom of violence and confusion. Communication breaks down as, in rapid succession, several languages are used in "Soliman and Perseda," the courtiers fail to comprehend what Hieronimo tells them about his purpose, he refuses to speak or write further, and finally he bites out his tongue. Modern readers of the play are apt to conclude that the incidents dramatize the fundamental unreliability of language in the play. Carol McGinnis Kay regards these events as the culmination of a play concerning "the deceptiveness of words" and "the invalidity of words": "In *The Spanish Tragedy* man's word is but a hollow sham, and it seldom contains what it purports to contain."[24] Similarly, Jonas A. Barish notes that from the "*Vindicta mihi*" soliloquy onward even Hieronimo "must turn language into something opaque and deceptive, instead of revelatory and transparent."[25] Language indeed appears suspect throughout the play. As early as the induction, Kyd suggests its inadequacy when Andrea reports his progress through the underworld: "I saw more sights than thousand tongues can tell, / Or pens can write" (1.1.57–58). The varying reports of Andrea's death in battle lead us to wonder what trust can be placed in any single account. Nevertheless, although the spoken word frequently misrepresents the actual state of things, the written word suffers no comparable devaluation.

Throughout the play characters manifest an impulse to express in writing the truth about themselves and others. Thus the love letters that pass between Bel-imperia and Horatio reveal their feelings for one another,[26] Bel-imperia's letter to Hieronimo accurately names the murderers of Horatio, and Pedringano's letters to Lorenzo disclose the latter's involvement in murder. The petitioners' documents are genuine pleas for justice. The letters that pass between Spain and Portugal are sincere expressions by king and viceroy, even if it seems increasingly doubtful to the audience that a royal marriage between Bel-imperia and Blathazar will ever take place. The playbook of "Soliman and Perseda," while the fruit of literary invention, has a basis in historical record. And the book that Hieronimo carries during his "*Vindicta mihi*" speech, while similarly a work of imagination, is treated as a repository of sage advice; the Knight Marshal assumes that what he reads applies to him.

The impulse to trust in the written word has no more vivid embodiment than old Bazulto. A minor character who appears in a single scene, he nonetheless provides one of the most affecting moments of the play in performance. He is a taciturn figure, initially not even noticed by Hieronimo, who sees three other petitioners carrying documents—a declaration, a bond, and a lease. Instead of speaking, Bazulto proffers a piece of paper, as though it had the power to accomplish what eloquent speech could not. In answer to Hieronimo's inquiry, the old man says:

> could my woes
> Give way unto my most distressful words,
> Then should I not in paper, as you see,
> With ink bewray what blood began in me.
>
> (3.13.74–77)

Here is a man whose pain, anger, and hope of redress are all reduced to ink on paper. Even before Hieronimo hears the contents of the petition, his interest is piqued. The juxtaposition of the words "ink" and "blood" must remind him of Bel-imperia's letter. Eagerly but apprehensively, he takes the document, saying, "What's here? 'The humble supplication / Of Don Bazulto for his murder'd son'" (ll. 78–79). No sooner does he read the words than his grief comes flooding back, and Hieronimo gives way to rage and despair: "Though on this earth justice will not be found, / I'll down to hell, and in this passion / Knock at the dismal gates of Pluto's court" (ll. 108–10). The speaker cannot know how ironic his words are: the Ghost of Andrea, watching and listening, has already visited Pluto's court. Hieronimo even names the very power whose decision permits Andrea to witness the Knight Marshal's outcry: "Then sound the burden of thy sore heart's grief, / Till we do gain that Proserpine may grant / Revenge on them that murdered my son: / Then will I rent and tear them thus and thus, / Shivering their limbs in pieces with my teeth" (ll. 119–23). Speaking the last line, Hieronimo tears up the petitioners' documents, as though he were sundering the limbs of his antagonists. But frenzied though he may be, Hieronimo has not lost faith in what the written word can accomplish. He knows that he must have recourse to another sort of writing than that represented by legal documents. The writing he turns to, as we have seen, is his own—the play of "Soliman and Perseda."

If Hieronimo does not initially trust the written word, he comes to rely upon it, and the more trusting he becomes, the closer he moves to accomplishing revenge. By placing such confidence in writing, the Knight Marshal emulates the gods themselves, who issue passports and who read leaves containing written accounts of men's lives. When Hieronimo makes use of the written word—in the form of letters, book, and script—he advances divine purpose, exemplifying the continuity in action between this world and the other. Hieronimo as revenger demonstrates that writing has an awesome cumulative force, with implications that extend beyond death. That writing could possess such power must have seemed natural to a playwright who was himself the son of a scrivener.

3

In *The Duchess of Malfi,* as in *The Spanish Tragedy,* knowledge is power: the characters seek information with special urgency because their well-being depends upon it. For the virtuous in a menacing world, information offers the prospect of safety: the more they know, the better they can estimate present peril and design a course of future action. For the villainous, information affords a way of gaining their ends: they foil others by staying a step ahead of them and capitalizing on their enemies' jeopardy. Both groups, so disparate morally, make a common discovery: that the avenue to knowledge lies chiefly through the written word. In Webster's tragedy that word takes a variety of forms: letters, books, a horoscope, a will, and even a handkerchief bearing the owner's initials. Although these have a reassuring physicality (they can be closely examined and pondered), they prove challenging as well as helpful, for they cannot always be taken at face value. The words contained in written materials may be equivocal or even deceptive, and the price of misinterpretation can be death.[27] The problematic aspects of reading become especially acute when the written word involves something other than words on paper. More elusive than a devious sentence in a letter or an inconclusive passage in a book is writing of another kind altogether—that in the stars. Metaphoric rather than literal, such writing presents formidable, sometimes insuperable, difficulties: the characters sense that the stars are sources of compulsion, but they lack the capacity to comprehend them. Whether metaphoric or literal, the written word in *The Duchess of Malfi* dramatizes the characters' bafflement at the world they inhabit and their vulnerability to those forces that imperil, compel, and eventually destroy even the most resolute among them.

When first we see the Duchess in a private moment with Antonio Bologna, the two are separated not only by their unequal social status but also by their different knowledge. The Duchess has arrived at a momentous decision involving her steward, but although she intends to woo him and take him for her husband, she presents, initially, a bland exterior. Her command is altogether ordinary: "sit down: / Take pen and ink, and write" (1.1.361–62).[28] While Antonio prepares to do her bidding, she explains her purpose, though in oblique fashion: "I am making my will" (l. 376). The word "will" has special significance in this context, expressing her characteristically strong volition and equally strong sexuality.[29] If she is wary of declaring her intentions publicly, she is nevertheless determined to carry them out privately. Antonio, however, has no sense of the direction his life is about to take. Nor can he guess that her word "will"—in the sense of legal instrument—has a premonitory force, for in pursuing her desires, the Duchess provokes her brothers' wrath, which leads eventually to her demise and to Antonio's as well. The writing of the will is never finished, so far as we know, but from the moment she tells Antonio, pen and paper in hand, that she is preparing her will, the written word becomes identified with danger and death.

Another kind of writing enlarges upon this identification: the horoscope that Antonio casts after the birth of his son. According to this document, which is read aloud, the configuration of the stars "signifies short life" and "doth threaten a violent death" (2.3.61, 63). The action that occurs in this scene underscores the portent. Bosola, hired by the Arragonian brothers to spy on their sister, sees Antonio unwittingly drop the horoscope, whereupon Bosola picks it up, reads it, and finds that he now has evidence to prove his suspicions about the Duchess. Although the child himself may be a minor character, who never speaks a word in the play, his horoscope assumes considerable importance in the development of the plot. As a result of Bosola's discovery, the Duchess's pretense is stripped away, leaving her increasingly vulnerable; both she and her husband move a step closer to death.

Bosola's use of the horoscope illustrates the power of the written word to engender a perilous hostility. He decides to take advantage of a courtier's journey the following day: "by him I'll send / A letter, that shall make her brothers' galls / O'erflow their livers" (2.3.73–75). Subsequently, the audience watches as the letter achieves the effect that Bosola predicts. By the next scene, word reaches Delio that Duke Ferdinand has received a disturbing "letter sent from Malfi" (2.4.79). In the following scene, the letter itself appears when the anguished Ferdinand hands it to his brother: "Read there—a sister damn'd" (2.5.3). As the letter passes from Bosola to Ferdinand and then to the Cardinal, it comes to seem ever more menacing. The delight of Bosola gives way to the apoplectic response of the Duke and the displeasure of the Cardinal. By confirming the brothers' worst suspicions, the letter focuses their anger and thus contributes to the fury that culminates in the Duchess's murder.

Even if the Duchess knows nothing directly of Bosola's letter, certain rumors lead her to suspect, sometime later, that her efforts to conceal marriage and children have failed. To fend off her brothers' antipathy, she decides to seek out Ferdinand and decry "a scandalous report" concerning her honor. Outwardly the Duke professes unconcern: "Let me be ever deaf to't: / One of Pasquil's paper bullets" (3.1.48–49). By this allusion to a fifteenth-century schoolmaster whose statue in the Piazza Navona was adorned with topical lampoons, Ferdinand would conceal both knowledge of his sister's deeds and the depth of his enmity toward her. He may succeed in this, but the Duchess recognizes the risk in another kind of "paper bullet" when, not long after divulging to Bosola the identity of her husband, she receives from Ferdinand a letter purporting to require Antonio's presence on a matter of business. She reads the letter aloud, commenting on the double meaning:

> *(Reads) Send Antonio to me; I want his head in*
> *a business:—*
> A politic equivocation!
> He doth not want your counsel, but your head;
> That is, he cannot sleep till you be dead.
>
> (3.5.28–31)

As the Duchess surmises, the letter seeks to hide deadly purpose beneath a guise of solicitude. Only her shrewd analysis of the letter's true intent saves Antonio from death. After her murder, Antonio is the target of another "paper bullet" when he receives written assurances from the Arragonian brothers. This time it falls to Delio to warn his friend: "though they have sent their letters of safe conduct / For your repair to Milan, they appear / But nets to entrap you" (5.1.3–5).

The potentially fatal influence of the written word has a yet more startling, and successful, demonstration when the Cardinal discloses to his mistress his part in the Duchess' murder. Appalled, Julia tells him, "It lies not in me to conceal it," and he replies, "No? / Come, I will swear you to't upon this book" (5.2.274–75). Obligingly she kisses the book, usually assumed to be a Bible,[30] whereupon the Cardinal reveals his purpose:

> thou'rt poison'd with that book;
> Because I knew thou couldst not keep my counsel,
> I have bound thee to't by death.
>
> (ll. 278–80)

The Cardinal's language suggests that he is as verbally sly as his brother: by using the word "bound," he puns on the instrument of death—a book—whose cover is as closely connected to its contents as is Julia's life to her knowledge.

All these manifestations of the written word have something in common: they are Webster's invention. A review of the story in Painter's *Palace of Pleasure* reveals no will, no horoscope, no letter from Bosola to Ferdinand, no letter from Ferdinand to the Duchess, and no poisoned book. These properties allow for development of the plot, of course, in that information is imparted from one character to another onstage, thereby providing motivation for ensuing action. Even more important, however, the properties involving the written word create a certain theatrical effect—one of surprise or puzzlement. Antonio, for instance, is taken aback when the Duchess announces her intention to compose a will; he was expecting to draw up a simple account of revenue and expense. Similarly, Bosola's letter shocks the Duke; although Ferdinand must have had his suspicions all along, the letter converts surmise into fact and thereby intensifies his distress. The Cardinal's poisoned book produces even greater astonishment in his victim: Julia apparently has no idea what the Cardinal intends when he bids her to kiss the book. She, in turn, uses her final moments of life to take the Cardinal unawares, telling him that their conversation is being overheard by Bosola.

What permits such surprise is the characters' ignorance: they lack knowledge of others, even those close to them. Their discernment is, of course, inhibited by the widespread subterfuge: in public the Duchess strives not to appear a wife, nor Antonio a husband, nor Bosola a spy. There exists, however, a reciprocal relationship between misrepresentation and misperception. In order for the deceiver to succeed, the deceived must suffer from a certain credulousness, a willingness to accept the appearance of things. That trait manifests itself in abundance. The Duke and Cardinal, for all their ruthlessness, are obtuse; on their own they fail to discover the truth about their sister's private life. Depending on Bosola for their information, they glean little but rumor without him. Even Bosola, despite his wiliness, proves somewhat inefficient at the task of discovery. He ascertains the Duchess's motherhood, in 2.3, not chiefly because of his own ingenuity, but rather because evidence, in the form of the horoscope, practically falls at his feet. He also learns the identity of the Duchess's husband when she, disarmed by his praise of Antonio, simply divulges the information.

Because their knowledge is so imperfect, the characters are subject to the machinations of others. When, for example, Ferdinand receives Bosola's letter, he is not only the recipient of information but also the victim of emotional trauma, which Bosola gleefully inflicts. The Duke, in turn, uses his knowledge to formulate a fearsome plan of arrest, torture, and murder. Julia's failure to guess her lover's intent renders her prey to the murderous scheme of the poisoned book. The earnest but dull Antonio would likely succumb to the Duke's letter requesting his head, were it not for his wife's shrewd surmise. She, however, proves less perceptive when she allows herself to be reassured by Ferdinand's airy dismissal of scandalous reports as "paper bullets." What she doesn't know gives her brother an advantage in their test of wills. His curiosity about her private life is not mere prurience but a means to power; the more he knows about her, the more securely he can dominate her.

If knowledge constitutes a source of control, ignorance betokens vulnerability. Even the most determined and resourceful characters find themselves thwarted by fragmentary information, particularly when they confront a kind of writing more difficult to interpret than words on paper.

> *Ferdinand.*   Now Bosola,
>   How thrives our intelligence?
> *Bosola.*   Sir, uncertainly:
>   'Tis rumour'd she hath had three bastards, but
>   By whom, we may go read i'th'stars.
> *Ferdinand.*   Why some
>   Hold opinion, all things are written there.
> *Bosola.* Yes, if we could find spectacles to read them—
>   (3.1.57–62)

This conversation points to the vulnerability of Ferdinand and Bosola—not so much to other schemers at court as to the celestial powers whom they so casually invoke. Although at this point Bosola scarcely imagines that his ignorance of the stars could have untoward consequences for him, he is already subject to their manipulation, for his discovery of the horoscope seems contrived—so much so that the incident might actually appear comic were the result not so serious: "What's here? a child's nativity calculated!" (2.3.55). We feel that someone or something has put Bosola in the right place at the right time to make his discovery, and the nature of the paper he finds supports this impression.[31] After all, a horoscope such as Antonio casts posits a connection between the configuration of celestial bodies and the course of human lives. In short, a horoscope presupposes astral determinism, and if the life of Antonio's son is subject to external control, so, too, may be the life of Bosola.

Bosola would be the last person to concede such vulnerability. When he speaks to Ferdinand about reading the stars, he seems flippant. Admittedly, Bosola speaks portentously when, later, he replies to the Duchess's expression of despair ("I could curse the stars"), saying, "Look you, the stars shine still" (4.1.100). However, even though this line has been interpreted as "the completest assertion in Jacobean drama of man's impotence, of the remoteness, the impersonality of the cosmic powers,"[32] Bosola's personal attitude is difficult to determine. If we interpret the stars as symbolic of fate, and fate as a principle of design (however menacing) in the cosmos, then his observation may be construed as an effort to buoy the Duchess's spirits, an endeavor in keeping with his response of "O fie!" and "O fearful!" to her utterance of despair.[33] Whatever Bosola's intention, it is unclear in the Duchess' imprisonment scene whether the stars have any personal significance for him; not till later does Bosola express a deeply felt conviction about them. Following the Duchess' murder, the Duke's unexpected betrayal of him, and his own unintentional killing of Antonio, Bosola formulates this conclusion: "We are merely the stars' tennis-balls, struck and banded / Which way please them" (5.4.54–55). All along other characters have used Bosola to perpetrate their schemes; and he has rationalized his role as hireling, accepting their money and enacting a caustic isolation. Now as events force him to recognize a more profound lack of autonomy, his gruff belligerence collapses into sententious fatalism.

Bosola, of course, has not set out to conduct a philosophic inquiry. His has been a pragmatic endeavor: to seek information about the Duchess's private life. But this gentleman-felon—variously described as intelligencer, spy, malcontent, fantastical scholar, and speculative man—has the capacity, common in Webster's dramatic world, for extracting far-reaching conclusions from personal experience. One inquiry, the pragmatic, has in effect led the way to another, more reflective inquiry, and although seemingly disparate, the two enterprises have this in common: both depend on writing. In the one instance, Bosola's investigation of the Duchess's life is advanced by literal reading (of the horoscope); in the other, his inquiry culminates in a figurative reading (of the stars). One foreshadows the other, though in a way that Bosola fails to anticipate. When he discovers the horoscope, asserting the thralldom of Antonio's son to the stars, Bosola is elated; he feels that his efforts at intelligence gathering have been crowned with success. When, in an abrupt reversal as unexpected as the discovery of the horoscope, Bosola comes to see himself as one of the stars' tennis balls, he is dejected, recognizing at last his own subjection to destiny.

Like Bosola, other characters confront writing in various forms, and they, too, experience the difficulty of interpretation. Consider Antonio, who develops a nosebleed while perusing the horoscope and staunches the blood with a handkerchief. To his alarm he discovers that his initials, stitched on the handkerchief, have become bloodstained: "Two letters, that are wrought here for my name, / Are drown'd in blood!" (2.3.44–45). Antonio has no more difficulty reading the initials than Bosola has reading the horoscope (both actions occur in the same scene), and he proves just as obtuse. Antonio, sensing that there may be a connection between the handkerchief and the will of those powers ultimately responsible for this incident, entertains two possibilities: determinism and contingency. Quickly he settles on the less threatening: "One that were superstitious would count / This ominous;—when it merely comes by chance" (ll. 42–43). He resists the obvious inference—that the bloody initials portend danger and death; instead, he attributes the incident to "Mere accident" (l. 46). His reasoning would carry greater conviction had he not, only moments earlier, eagerly read the horoscope, signifying belief in astral determinism. The conclusion he arrives at seems an act of desperation, a perhaps unconscious avoidance of the fearsome implications of those bloody initials.

The conundrum that Antonio faces when he ponders the initials recurs later as he seeks to distill meaning from his experience. Once again he oscillates between a conviction that his destiny is fixed and a belief that he is subject to mere contingency. In the echo scene he complains, "Necessity compels me" (5.3.32); and the echo itself, "*O, fly your fate!*" has the force of a premonition. But in this very scene he also evokes the familiar embodiment of chance: "Though in our miseries Fortune have a part, / Yet in our noble suff'rings she hath none" (ll. 56–57). In his wavering Antonio enacts a dualism that Muriel Bradbrook notices throughout the play, characterizing the Duchess no less than Antonio.[34] In keeping with the enigmatic nature of Webster's dramatic world, that dualism is never resolved. Although most of the characters issue sweeping generalizations upon their demise, their opinions are not congruent. If the interpretation of events varies from one character to another within the play and, within a single character, from circumstance to circumstance, the characters are at one in their conviction that they are buffeted by forces that they have not fully understood.

Although typically they envisage the source of that buffeting as external agency of one kind or another, the characters are not insensible of compulsion within. The Arragonian brothers, for example, sense their sister's drive toward a second marriage; hence their vehement admonitions. For her part the Duchess senses the urgency within her brothers leading them to oppose her remarriage so insistently; hence the impassive face she turns to them. The conjunction of internal and external forces impinging on the characters is suggested when the Duke pays a nocturnal visit to this sister's chamber and speculates about the cause of her behavior: "Virtue, where art thou hid? what hideous thing / Is it that doth eclipse thee?" (3.2.72–73). His language has an oddly oblique quality. Instead of addressing his sister directly, Ferdinand personifies an inner quality of hers, apostrophizes it as though it had an existence independent of the Duchess, and then describes it as though it were subject to external influence. Ferdinand's terminology of "eclipse" may have its genesis in the way he learns of his sister's motherhood—through Bosola's letter recounting (and possibly even enclosing) the horoscope.[35] Ferdinand, however, has already applied that same language of astrology to himself: "Till I know who leaps my sister, I'll not stir: / That known, I'll find scorpions to string my whips, / And fix her in a general eclipse" (2.5.77–79). His identification of himself with an astrological event has the effect of blurring a distinction between external and internal compulsion. That distinction is obscured even further when he describes his sister's heart by means of the same metaphor that he has applied to the stars: reading. Imagining her making love, Ferdinand abandons scrutiny of her conduct: "Curse upon her! / I will no longer study in the book / Of another's heart" (4.1.15–17). The metaphor of reading presupposes the existence of meaning and intent capable of discovery. But Ferdinand and others find knowledge of the heart as difficult to attain as knowledge of the stars; and the characters seem unsure which of these forces is chiefly responsible for the menace they feel.

When other characters confront the heart's mysteries, they also use the metaphor of reading, and they do so with much the same feeling of exasperation that we hear in the Duke's voice. The Duchess's maid, for instance, accused by Antonio of complicity in admitting the Duke to his sister's chamber, protests her guiltlessness: "when / That you have cleft my heart, you shall read there / Mine innocence" (3.2.144–46). Although the audience may instinctively trust Cariola's protestation, Antonio appears to have no such surety, which is all the more remarkable when we consider how long he has known her. Cariola is undoubtedly as innocent as she claims. Antonio's problem is that he cannot "read"—cannot know—with certainty what is in her heart; like any other person he can know with confidence only what is in his own. Bosola manages to learn what lies within the Duchess's heart when she divulges the identity of her husband. He pledges, "I will wear [the secret] on th' inside of my heart" (3.2.302). But his betrayal of her and his later remorse culminate in an image expressing the same isolation that Cariola must feel:

> a guilty conscience
> Is a black register, wherein is writ
> All our good deeds and bad, a perspective
> That shows us hell!
>
> (4.2.356–59)

His metaphor of the book of conscience suggests the clarity of words neatly recorded, yet whatever appears in that register is readable by Bosola alone. Who else in the play would guess that he has come to possess such moral sensitivity?

Frustrated by efforts to read both the heart and the stars, the characters turn to seemingly more accessible sources of knowledge: conventional books printed with ink on paper. But even here their endeavor proves disappointing. The Cardinal, for instance, epitomizes a sense of futility when, near the end of the play, he enters with a book in his hand.[36]

> I am puzzled in a question about hell:
> He says, in hell there's one material fire
> And yet it shall not burn all men alike.
>
> (5.5.1–3)

Whatever theological treatise this may be, it fails to resolve the Cardinal's doubts. For him books are no longer a source of knowledge to which he can confidently resort; they have become merely insubstantial accouterments of daily life. Hence when he explains to Pescara his brother's "distraction," he says that "One night, as the prince sat up late at's book," a figure appeared to him (5.2.95). By this mention of a book, the speaker means to create verisimilitude; it is the kind of detail that gives credence to his account of the vision. But the book is merely a verbal prop, concocted by the Cardinal to make his story the more plausible. For Bosola, too, books have a dubious intrinsic value. He speaks of them almost casually when he bids the Duke to cease torturing the Duchess and, instead, to "furnish her / With beads and prayer-books" (4.1.120–21). Here Bosola evokes the common association of books with piety, but he has no more religious feeling than does Shakespeare's Richard, Duke of Gloucester, when he contrives to appear in public holding a prayer book. As for the Duchess herself, the act of reading provides no solace; if reading offers her enlightenment, it is of a most melancholy and unspecified sort: "all our wit / And reading brings us to a truer sense / Of sorrow" (3.5.69–71). She may not know precisely what the future holds, but she senses that loss and destruction are imminent.

The Duchess's sentiment about reading is one that other characters must share, for even when they manage to read successfully, they are likely to be dissatisfied or unsettled. When they confront writing within or without—in hearts or stars—comprehension proves exceedingly difficult. Surrounded by writing of divers kinds, they are mocked by its plenitude. They lack spectacles (in Bosola's expression) to read with understanding,[37] and this contributes to their sense of being manipulated by someone or something only dimly discerned.

Given Webster's concern with the written word and its elusive meaning, the play's final image, articulated by Delio, seems especially apt:

> These wretched eminent things
> Leave no more fame behind 'em than should one
> Fall in a frost, and leave his print in snow;
> As soon as the sun shines, it ever melts,
> Both form, and matter. . . .
>
> (5.5.113–17)

Delio's word "print," which can, of course, have a range of meanings, appeared earlier in a speech by Ferdinand. Giving his sister a hand bearing a ring, the Duke had said, "bury the print of it in your heart" (4.1.46). The context of Delio's remark is hardly the same as Ferdinand's; one character uses the image to describe an external phenomenon; the other, internal. But the images point to the larger treatment of the written word, whether literal or metaphoric, in Webster's play. First, both speeches associate the word "print" with death: Delio is reflecting on the demise of many people, while the Duke specifically uses the word "bury," and the hand he presents ostensibly belongs to a dead man. Second, both suggest the difficulty of asserting one's will upon another individual or upon the world at large; Delio's image is one of gradual but certain obliteration; Ferdinand's entreaty proves ineffectual. Third, the remarks point to the difficulty of perceiving whatever is "printed." Delio imagines a circumstance where the observer is likely to find only indistinct traces or none at all. Ferdinand imagines a print within—in the Duchess's heart—but neither he nor anyone else will be able to discern it, even if it exists. Like the other characters of Webster's play, Delio and Ferdinand come to share a sense of fatality born of this conviction: that their destinies are shaped by that which is printed, and that they themselves are unable to exploit that printing in order to comprehend, much less forestall, their ruin.

4

When students encounter Antonio in *The Duchess of Malfi* or Gloucester in *King Lear,* they tend to view the characters as excessively credulous for attributing influence to the stars. Despite the proliferation of horoscopes in newspapers and magazines today, the stars are no longer mysterious or menacing in an age when telescopes and spacecraft explore the galaxy. Most of us are dismissive of a fatalism that denies the confidence we place in ourselves: we are, we like to think, what our choices have made us. We instinctively credit Cassius's advice—"The fault, dear Brutus, is not in our stars, / But in ourselves, that we are underlings"— and we scorn a fatalism that leaves little room for self-determination. Four centuries ago, however, a theatrical audience would almost certainly have looked more indulgently upon Webster's Antonio or Shakespeare's Gloucester. Astral influence had a history that could be traced back to ancient Babylon. Those who looked at the stars and discerned invisible rays of influence were more numerous than are their modern counterparts. And adherents of astrology, with its implied fatalism, included people of genuine intellectual sophistication. In the age of Kyd, Shakespeare, and Webster, the issue was far from settled.

That issue played a part in the running battle that pitted Thomas Nashe and Robert Greene against the Harvey brothers in the 1580s and early 1590s. Today that clash is chiefly remembered for the savagely funny diatribes written by Nashe and Greene, and for Gabriel Harvey's vivid story of a debauched Greene succumbing to death after a meal of Rhine wine and pickled herring. If it was fueled by personal pique and if it took on a powerful momentum due to the personal nature of the attacks, the dispute also had an ideological dimension. Looked at from this perspective, the feud assumes a somewhat different shape from that which it usually has in modern accounts, and it reveals something important about attitudes toward astrology and fatality during the time that Kyd, Marlowe, and their successors were writing for the London stage.

When he was disparaged by Richard Harvey in *A Theologicall Discourse of the Lamb of God and His Enemies* (1590), a book containing a response to Nashe's 1589 preface to Greene's *Menaphon,* Thomas Nashe responded with *A Wonderfull, strange and miraculous, Astrologicall Prognostication for this yeer of our Lord God. 1591. Discovering such wonders to happen this yeere, as never chaunced since Noes floud* (London, [1591]). The title might be taken at face value as advertising a bona fide book of astrological prediction were it not for the author's pen name: *By Adam Fouleweather, Student in Asse-tronomy*. The work that follows announces its satirical purpose by applying the most high-sounding astrological jargon to the most humble of phenomena, and it does so in a relentlessly singleminded way. Nashe establishes his comical tone in his address to the reader, wherein he recounts his thoughts at Dover, as he watched storm and tide and began his astrological conjectures: "I betook me to my Ephimerides, and, erecting a figure, have found such strange accidents to fall out this yeere, Mercury being Lord and predominate in the house of Fortune, that many fooles shall have full cofers, and wise men walke up and downe with empty pursses; that if Jupiter were not joyned with him in a favourable aspect, the Butchers of East-cheape should doo little or nothing all Lent but make prickes: seeing therefore the wonders that are like to fall out this present yeere, I have for the benefit of my Countrymen taken in hand to make this Prognostication, discoursing breefelye on the Eclipses both of Sunne and Moone. . . ."[38] Nashe's work might be construed as a general satire on astrology rather than a specific attack on particular writers were it not for these facts: he was engaged in a dispute with the Harvey family; two of the three Harvey brothers had published treatises setting forth claims for astrology; and Nashe in *Pierce Pennilesse* specifically alludes to Richard Harvey's *Astrological Discourse* of 1583. The Harvey brothers clearly presented a tempting target for Nashe's verbal skewer.

From our perspective today there is a tendency to see the Harvey brothers as united in their opinions, concerted in their stance against Nashe and Greene. Richard Harvey's book on astrology, however, had its beginnings in an atmosphere of familial contention. In *An Astrological Discourse upon the great and notable Conjunction of the two superiour Planets, Saturne & Jupiter, which shall happen the 28 day of April, 1583* (London, 1583), Richard, addressing his brother Gabriel, explains how the book came to be written: "Good Brother, I have in some part done my endevour to satisfie your late request, wherein you advertise mee either not so much to addict my selfe to the studie, and contemplation of Judiciall Astrologie, or else by some evident and sensible demonstration, to make certaine & infallible proofe what general good I can do my countrie thereby, or what speciall fruite I can reape thereof unto my selfe" (3). It appears that Gabriel had adopted a skeptical attitude, having first investigated the issue for himself; addressing Gabriel directly, Richard writes: "that Judiciall Astrologie is neither any vaine and idle studie, nor forbidden and unlawful Arte, your self having long since, taken some reasonable paines therein, and being able to say so much in the defence therof, out of many olde and new histories of approved authoritie and credit, can sufficiently (I know) and wil readily (I thinke) testifie" (4).

The argument that Richard deploys takes a form that we should expect: a heavy reliance upon authorities, ancient and modern, who embraced astrology. Having surveyed the continental experts, he turns to the English masters: "these of fresh memorie have bene none of the basest scholers in England: M. D. Batte, principal Phisition to king Henry the eight. Sir Thomas Eliot, Sir Thomas Smyth, who as you best knowe, and have both truely and honourably testified in your *Musarum lachrymae*, excelled therin: M. D. Recorde, both the Digges, M. Dee, whome hir majestie vouchsafeth the name of hyr Philosopher . . ." (5). Richard Harvey's rhetorical strategy does not consist solely of creating a roll call of names. He also argues that medical practice depends for its efficacy on the timing of treatment and that such timing must depend upon the stars and planets: "If we shall consider duly of the highest courses and beeings, we shall finde that Astrologie is not the least portion of Phisicke, for it behooveth the Phisition to know the Moone, and the signe of heaven wherein the Moone is, when any patient beginneth to fall sicke, & so forth" (7). Presumably Harvey bases this contention on direct observation or on the experience of others (his brother John was a physician), and he even appends to this work on astrology a complementary treatise on medicine: *A Compendious Table of Phlebotomie, or bloud-letting, setting downe by division the generall and speciall considerations thereunto belonging*.

Although modern readers may assume that a belief in astrology has as a necessary corollary an unrelenting pessimism, Richard Harvey sees his conviction about the stars as consistent not only with fighting disease but also with preparing for adversity of all kinds. Discussing the anticipated events of 1583, Harvey examines the effects wrought by the respective planets and draws certain inferences:

> The conclusion and summe of all must needes be this, that the vehement hatred, despite and malice of the unlucky planet Saturne, hath by his mischievous importunitie overcome and vanquished the good, wholsome, & sweete nature of the benevolous and favourable planet Jupiter, which victorie (I fear me) and I thinke I am too sure thereof, will cause great aboundance of waters, and much cold weather, much unwonted mischiefes & sorow, much envie, debate, quarelling, hatred and strife, many grievous and bitter contentions, muche going to lawe one with another for deade mens goodes, and olde reckonings, manifold troubles, and sodaine uproares, much violent oppression, extreame povertie, hunger and miserie to the needie and impotent sort of people . . .
>
> (15–16)

Such knowledge allows the individual to take whatever measures may lessen the deleterious effects of the heavenly conjunction. Although Harvey's prediction sounds much like the fretting of Gloucester in *King Lear,* Harvey differs from Shakespeare's character in connecting his vision with divine providence. Indeed, Harvey invokes biblical precedent and prophecy: "What is now the conclusion? Truly that the second comming of the sonne of man draweth nigh, whyche shall be as were the dayes of Noah, for as in the dayes whiche were before the floud, they were eating, and drinking, marrying, and giving in marriage, untill the daye that Noah entred into the Arke, and perceived nothyng, til the floud came, and overwhelmed them all, so shall the comming of the sonne of man be" (48). From this it follows that people must mend their ways; their destruction may be at hand: "let us now at the last, speedily and carefullye call upon our merciful God, least he consume us in the heat of his heavie wrath, and indignation: let us humbly sue for grace, and hartilye crave pardon and favour at his handes, least sodaine destruction overwhelme us: let us with penitent and obedient hartes fal downe before the throne of his celestial majestie, asking remission of our manifold sinnes and villanies, and with a contrite affection, earnestly and unfainedly imbrace the gladsome tidings of his holy Gospell" (48–49). Harvey's confidence in astrology, then, is aligned with Christian providentialism—the belief that all events in this world may be traced back to the will of God. Predicting the future, he contends, is a prudent course for any Christian, since it enhances our knowledge of the divine plan.

If Richard's *Astrological Discourse,* published in January 1583, was intended to convince Gabriel and other doubters, it did not entirely succeed, for in the spring of the same year John Harvey, Richard's younger brother, felt obliged to issue his own work, *An Astrologicall Addition, or supplement to be annexed to the late Discourse upon the great Conjunction of Saturne, and Jupiter. Wherin are particularly declared certaine especiall points before omitted, as well touching the elevation of one Planner above another, with theyr severall significations: as touching Oeconomicall and houshold provision: with some other Judicials, no less profitable* (London, 1583). As the title announces, this was intended to buttress Richard's already published arguments. Like Richard's, John's treatise appears to have been written in an atmosphere of controversy. In his dedication to Justice Thomas Meade, John Harvey, alluding to Richard, enumerates his purposes:

> First, to satisfie the demaunds and desires of those his [Richard's] lerned friendes: then, to stoppe the mouthes of his envious & carping enemies: thirdly, to benefit such of our Countrey generally, as by providence are desirous to worke their owne commoditie and safetie: and last of all, to practise my selfe

particularlie in such an exercise, as was so profitable for an Universitie man, so convenient for a Student in *Philosophy,* & the *Mathematicks,* and finally, so agreeable to that studie and profession, whereunto partly by my naturall disposition I was inclyned, and partly upon farther advise of my friendes, and some private consultation of mine owne, I had wholy betaken, and as it were betroathed my selfe.

(sig. A2^v)

Observing that his brother Gabriel favors mathematics as offering a surer means of attaining his goals, John is convinced that Gabriel fails to appreciate the results that astrology can offer. John has, after all, authorities from antiquity to modern times on his side: "*Melancthon* is not afraide to condemne them even for *Epicures,* and *Atheistes,* that condemne this most goodly and godly Science. And as for our secundarie Authors and founders, what two more famous Princes amongst the auncient *Aegyptians,* and *Romanes,* then Hermes Trismegistus, and *Numa Pompilius?* Or what two more excellent kinges amongst the later *Aegyptians* and *Aragonians,* then *Ptolomey,* and *Alphonsus?*" (sigs. A3^v–A4). For the reader of Richard Harvey's earlier book, the arguments here have a familiar ring. John contends that astrology, like other arts, both glorifies God and aids humankind: "The divine or common ende, is the glorie of God; the humane, or proper ende, to do good in the world, by such predictions, and divinations, as the principles and rules of this Art truly delivered, and rightly understoode, doo afford: first, in forewarning what evils and mischiefes are like to ensue: and then in foretelling, what goods and commodities may be reaped by timely provision . . ." (sig. A4^v). To the extent that a study of astrology allows him to accomplish these goals, it is eminently pragmatic. By recording observations of the planets and stars and by making appropriate predictions, he renders valuable service, spiritual and practical, to his nation.

There is virtually nothing in John Harvey's treatise of 1583 that will surprise the reader of Richard's work, published earlier the same year. But there is something quite astonishing about John's subsequent book, *A Discoursive Probleme concerning Prophesies. How far they are to be valued, or credited, according to the surest rules, and directions in Divinitie, Philosophie, Astrologie, and other learning,* published in 1588. In contrast to his stance five years earlier, John Harvey now scoffs at the very notion of prediction: "Did the world, or the divell, ever want impostors, falsaries, coseners, hypocrites, or false prophets? Is it so difficult, or impossible a matter to cast mists before the eies of the simple sort, and ignorant people?" (2). Little escapes the attack. Harvey seems to repudiate almost every kind of prediction, whether based on the configuration of the stars or that of written words:

Were it not a needles, or booteles labor, to make a special Analysis, either of their Abcedary and Alphabeticall Spels, or of their Characteristicall, and Polygraphical suttelties, or of their Steganographicall, and Hieroglyphicall mysteries, or of their hyperbolicall metaphors, phantasticall allegories, and heraldicall illusions, or of their ambiguous aequivocations, interdeux amphibologies, and aenigmaticall ridles, or finally of any their other colourable glosses, & hypocriticall subornations, in some like prestigiatory, and sophisticall veine? What more ludicrous, or ridiculous spectacle can you imagine, than to see a wretched company of such woofull wights, and miserable creatures, scarsely woorth the ground they treade upon, and hardly deserving their daily bread: sodainly presented on a Theater, or comicall stage, in their thredbare liveries, and stale gaberdines, of antique shape, and forlorne fashion? Is not their whole habite, and gesture too notorious? Doth not every childe perceive in what humor they abounde?

(65–66)

Harvey does concede some validity to predictions of a practical nature made by navigators, farmers, and physicians. He also allows the truth of Old Testament prophets and other instances of what he calls "credible authority." But he comes closest to endorsing astrology when he frames this rhetorical question: "who in learning can deny the lawful and warrantable use of philosophie, the mathematiques, astrologie and physique, even in such prenotions and premonitions, so far, as with modest discretion, and without curious search above their naturall, artificiall, or practicable reach, they may providently and reasonably foresee the consequence of Naturall or Morall effects, by deepe and due consideration of the antecedent causes, or apparent signes, either Naturall or Morall" (77). For the most part Harvey exudes an attitude of contempt toward the kind of prediction he had made just a few years earlier. In 1589 John Harvey would publish *An Almanacke, or annual Calender, with a compendious Prognostication thereunto appendyng, servyng for the yeere of our Lord. 1589*. But here he limits his prognosticating chiefly to medical matters: "the knowledge of many thynges by Astronomie, doth much good to many, and specially to the professors of Phisicke and Chirurgerie" (sig. Bii). He offers, rather cautiously, what amounts to an apology in advance: "unperfect judgementes, errours, oversyghtes, and faultes, may be, and are committed in all other sciences dyvers tymes: and therefore no marveyle, yf the auctors of Astronomie, and those that folowe them, fall into errours sometymes: for nothyng in this transitorie worlde is certayne, nothyng true, permanent, and unfallible, but onely the worde of God . . ." (sig. Bii^v). Talk of astrology has been replaced by astronomy, confident prediction by a declaration of fallibility.

What accounts for the transformation of John Harvey? The most obvious explanation is the failure of his—and brother Richard's—predictions for 1583. There were no great floods or civil disorders; the second coming was not at hand after all. The Harveys, consequently, were ridiculed mercilessly for their utterly erroneous warnings, as Thomas Nashe recounts in *Pierce Penniless,* published in August 1592: "Gentlemen, I am sure you have hearde of a ridiculous Asse that many yeares since sold lyes by the great, and wrote an absurd *Astrologicall Discourse* of the terrible Conjunction of *Saturne* and *Jupiter.*"[39] Nashe proceeds to detail the humiliation that befell the Harveys, especially Richard: "his Astronimie broke his day with his creditors and *Saturne* and *Jupiter* prov'd honester men then all the World took them for: whereupon the poore Prognosticator was ready to runne himselfe through with his *Jacobs Staffe,* and cast himselfe headlong from the top of a Globe (as a mountaine) and breake his necke. The whole Universitie hyst at him, [Richard] *Tarlton* at the Theator made jests of him, and [William] *Elderton* consumed his ale-crummed nose to nothing, in bearbayting him with whole bundles of ballets."[40] Such ridicule was more than sufficient to undermine the Harvey brothers' confidence in astrology. No wonder John's *Almanak* of 1589 is hedged about by qualification and disclaimer. Although Gabriel came to his brothers' defense by writing his *Foure Letters* of 1592, he did so out of fraternal loyalty, not out of any newfound trust in astrology.

Whatever John Harvey's motives for so drastically changing his mind about astrology and then announcing that change to the world, this turnabout has something useful to tell us about astrological determinsm and fatality in the late sixteenth century. We tend to imagine that the debate over astrology was clearly defined, as though adherents and detractors were neatly arranged on either side of some line of demarcation. This impression is fostered by our experience of Renaisssance plays, which, for sound dramaturgical reasons, juxtapose sharply opposed viewpoints: Gloucester vs. Edmund, Brutus vs. Cassius, Roderigo vs. Iago. The experience of the Harvey brothers, by contrast, suggests a less certain configuration. As we have seen, there was contention within the Harvey family, pitting Richard and John against Gabriel. And within John's mind the issue that may have seemed secure in 1583 became a lot less so when his prognostications failed to materialize. The battle lines in the controversy over astrology were anything but fixed: combatants could and did change sides. Moreover, an individual could apparently harbor conflicting views simultaneously. John Harvey, in his *Discoursive Probleme concerning Prophesies,* cites the work of Henry Cornelius Agrippa: "my meaning or intention is not to continue, or inlarge Agrippaes invectius Declamation, *De vanitate scientiarum*" (76). Harvey alludes to a book translated into English as *Of the vanitie and uncertaintie of Artes and Sciences* (London, 1575). Agrippa's work, written in 1526, is among the most powerful attacks on judicial astrology in the sixteenth century: "this

Arte is nothing els but a false conjecture of superstitious persons, which through long practise have made a Science of things uncertayne, whereby they deceive the simple sort, to the end to spoile them of their monie, and they themselves are deceyved also" (fol. 45ᵛ). What makes Agrippa's argument so remarkable is that he was also the author of *De Occulta Philosophia,* the first part of which was published in 1531 and the rest in 1533, but written much earlier (begun ca. 1510); this book posits, among other things, the influence of the stars and the dependence of magicians on that influence.[41] This inconsistency has never been satisfactorily explained: "Why Agrippa published first a book on the vanity of the sciences, including the occult sciences, whilst reserving for future publication his already written book on the occult sciences, is one of the many problems of his life and work."[42]

The example of Agrippa, together with the experience of the brothers Harvey, suggests how vexing and uncertain was the issue of determinism, whether that issue was couched in the language of astral bodies or of the book of fate. The energy of the antagonists, moreover, suggests that for them the issue was not merely a topos providing for a display of erudition or wit. The efficacy of astrology was fiercely contested. When it finds expression on the stage, we need to interpret the concern with fatality as something more than mood music deemed suitable to tragedy. Fundamental assumptions about the extent to which people shape their destiny were at stake in Elizabethan and Jacobean England.

The controversy pitting the Harvey family against Nashe and Greene may have ceased when "on 1 June 1599 an order was issued by Archbishop John Whitgift and Bishop Richard Bancroft who had had their fill of scurrilous and vituperative satires. The order included the stipulation that 'all Nasshes and Doctor Harvyes bookes be taken wheresoever they maye be found and that none of theire bookes bee ever printed hereafter.'"[43] But the argument over autonomy and destiny persisted. Near the end of Queen Elizabeth's reign, John Chamber wrote *A Treatise against Judiciall Astrologie* (London, 1601). Two years later Sir Christopher Heydon wrote a spirited riposte, *A Defence of Judiciall Astrologie, in Answer to a Treatise lately published by M. John Chamber* (Cambridge, 1603). Heydon's book appeared exactly twenty years after Richard Harvey's treatise on astrology. Nothing had finally been resolved. And so it went.

Conclusion

"To be a well-favor'd man is the gift of fortune, but to write and read comes by nature." Dogberry's remark in *Much Ado About Nothing* (3.3.14–16) makes us smile because this earnest constable has things backward. Far from being natural, reading and writing are the product of invention and convention, as anyone knows who has ever watched a child confront the written word. In the long evolution of the human species, the written word is a relative latecomer, having had to await the development of a system of signs, a material on which to inscribe those signs, and an instrument suitable for inscription. Once invented, however, writing became so useful for recording ownership, debt, taxes, and other kinds of information that it became indispensable. So widespread and so necessary is the written word for our civilization that it can almost seem "natural," as Dogberry tells us. To gauge its significance, all we need do is try to imagine our lives without the written word.

Following the invention of sign systems in antiquity, the most profound change in the status of the written word occurred during the Renaissance, for it was then that the written word, previously the preserve of the few, became the tool of the many. Even the son of a bricklayer now had access to books. Ben Jonson, before going on to success in the theater, plied his stepfather's trade while reading constantly: "He help'd in the building of the new structure of *Lincolns-Inn,* when having a *Trowell* in his hand, he had a *book* in his pocket."[1] Jonson would later assemble a sizeable personal library, part of which still survives.[2]

Those who experienced the proliferation of books and the exponential rise in literacy knew that something extraordinary was happening. We can almost feel the excitement over what the written and printed word can accomplish when Galileo writes, "surpassing all stupendous inventions, what sublimity of mind was his who dreamed of finding means to communicate his deepest thoughts to any other person, though distant by mighty intervals of place and time! Of talking with those who are in India; of speaking to those who are not yet born and will not be born for a thousand or ten thousand years; and with what facility, by the different arrangements of twenty characters upon a page!"[3] The invention of the printing press, with its limitless capacity to duplicate written words, set in motion a fundamental shift: Europe changed from a culture in which the spoken word was dominant to one in which the written and printed word began to achieve ascendancy.

The dramatists whose plays we have examined were beneficiaries of this metamorphosis. Marlowe, Kyd, Shakespeare, Heywood, and Webster had available to them a plethora of books providing stories that would become the basis of their plots; the variety and sheer number of these materials would have been unavailable a century earlier. The plays themselves would almost certainly have been irretrievably lost had not print been available to preserve in the form of scripts the "two hours' traffic" of the stage. The playwrights had another advantage too: they belonged to an era when the printing press was just beginning to effect the vast changes that Elizabeth Eisenstein and others have traced. Shakespeare and his contemporaries participated in an older oral culture, one in which the spoken word retained considerable prestige and authority: the spoken oath and the curse, for example, must have had a force that they lack today. At the same time writers participated in a culture of writing; the written and especially the printed word were beginning to make an unprecedented claim on people's lives and minds. Elizabethan and Jacobean plays, filled with figurative language and theatrical properties involving writing, express the sense of novelty and importance felt by people for whom writing was creating a range of limitless possibilities.

Today the excitement experienced by Galileo and Shakespeare has largely vanished. So accustomed have we become to easy access to written and printed materials—paperback books, magazines, and newspapers are available everywhere—that we no longer perceive the phenomenon of printing as remarkable. Our speech, however, still occasionally contains metaphors related to reading and writing: take a page out of his book; turn over a new leaf; read him like a book; throw the book at him; rewrite the rules. And we occasionally resort to metaphors of reading and writing when we seek to express something unusual, especially public events of importance: a new chapter is being opened; it's time to close that book. Such a use of metaphoric language increased as we witnessed the collapse of communism in eastern Europe and the breakup of the Soviet Union. Ironically, these events, described in language of books, chapters, and pages, were fostered by the advent of a new technology—instantaneous, worldwide television under the auspices of CNN. As journalists sought to assess the meaning of events that everyone saw, they enlisted, perhaps unconsciously, language of the written and printed word. An article on Ted Turner, *Time* magazine's Man of the Year for 1991, for instance, reported: "The very definition of news was rewritten—from something that *has happened* to something that *is happening* at the very moment you are hearing of it."[4] Similarly, a journalist on *Washington Week in Review,* 20 February 1992, reported that leaders of the former Soviet republics asked Secretary of State James Baker how they could gain access to CNN; the journalist, Thomas Friedman of the *New York Times*, called CNN "their library card." In such usage we witness the effort to relate new technology to a more familiar technology, the unknown to the known. It was just such an effort that helped give powerful impetus to the metaphoric book four centuries ago.

It seems unlikely that the metaphoric book will enjoy similar popularity again, for the book as we know it is undergoing as profound a change as it did in the time of Gutenberg. The development of the personal computer and its near ubiquity have begun to affect the way we conceive of books. No longer will they necessarily be tactile objects, composed of paper and ink and possessed of an aesthetic appeal. Instead, they will consist of words formed by digital electronic impulses and read on a screen. The very concept of a page as having a certain stability is changing as it becomes possible to alter the contents and format of a page by means of a few keystrokes. As one scrolls up or down on a computer screen, the page as a unit of space ceases to have much meaning. The concept of libraries is changing, too. No longer are they likely to be impressive architectural monuments made of stone and brick. Increasingly such buildings will lose their raison d'etre as easy access to all sorts of material becomes available through computer networks. Electronic publication will replace the customary ink and paper. R. Howard Bloch and Carla Hesse do not exaggerate when they say: "We live at a threshold moment in the history of libraries and the forms of knowledge they imply—a moment comparable to that of early antiquity when the clay tablets of the pre-Christian era were replaced by papyrus rolls; or when these rolls gave way, in the fourth century A.D., to parchment leaves bound in codex; comparable, finally, to the transformation of the great monastic libraries of the Middle Ages, where manuscripts were chained to desks, into the Renaissance humanist libraries in which the numerous books made available by printing came to be stacked along the walls, configuring the library as we know it."[5]

The changes we are experiencing today will affect the ways in which we conceptualize the world around us. The more we become familiar with computers and the more we come to depend upon them, the less likely we shall be to use metaphors of conventional books when we wish to describe something either ordinary or extraordinary. A new metaphoric language will be required, and we can see it beginning to take shape in newspapers and magazines. Writing about the 1994 World Cup in the *Times* of London, a journalist comments on the extraordinary hype surrounding the event: "When we come to the question of soccer, it is hardly surprising that Americans are registering a 'disk full' signal on the screen of their minds."[6] And a *Time* cover story on Cuba quotes a communist anticipating the collapse of Castro's regime: "There is no way you can take away the achievements of the revolution. They are installed on the hard disk of my generation."[7] A new metaphoric language, based on today's technology, is already emerging.

Appendix 1
Elizabethan Literacy

It seems logical to assume that the prevalence of reading and writing on the sixteenth-century stage is related to the cultural climate of Elizabethan England. However problematic the relationship between theater and society, dependence upon the written word was growing in both. People did not need to be told that literacy brought practical benefits. There was an advantage in being able to read and write, for illiteracy meant dependence on those who possessed the skills of reading and writing. Illiteracy, therefore, entailed expense, inconvenience, and, possibly, exploitation by others. Such disadvantage provided an impetus to the achievement of literacy, which was fostered by a plethora of newly founded schools and by the increased availability of books which printing made possible.

How many Elizabethans achieved literacy? The question admits of no conclusive answer, for, as Eric Havelock observes, "Of all the activities of mankind which we now take to be ordinary, reading is historically the one which is most sparsely recorded."[1] Even the definition of literacy remains unsettled. It may be defined as the ability to read whatever materials are necessary for one's occupation or the ability to read any sort of material. For some scholars literacy denotes only the ability to read, while for others it denotes the ability both to read and to write (a more difficult skill to master). The ability to make one's mark on a document constitutes evidence of literacy to some, while others require the ability to sign one's name, and still others require the ability to copy a set text. Complicating an estimate of literacy was the existence, in Renaissance England, of different forms of script (secretary hand, italic, legal hand) and print (black letter, roman). As Keith Thomas explains, "it was perfectly possible in the Tudor and early Stuart period for someone to be able to read print fluently, but to be quite incapable of deciphering a written document. For the only people who could easily read script were the privileged minority who had themselves learned to write it."[2] As for writers, only people of considerable attainment were able to shift back and forth between different kinds of script.[3]

Such indirect indicators of literacy as number of schools, production and sale of books, and inventories of possessions, may seem to offer hard evidence, but according to R. A. Houston, all of these yield equivocal results. We cannot be certain, for instance, whether "a growing number of schools provided by church and state produced more literate people or whether a more literate and informed population demanded better education."[4] "It is also possible," notes R. S. Schofield, "that informal instruction, whether by parents, parish officers or friends, was as important as the formal structure of education in the diffusion of elementary literary skills."[5] Knowing the number of books produced at any given time does not tell us precisely who bought them or how many people read them: "There is no necessary relationship between the volume of production and the size of the readership, because the number of readers per copy cannot be assumed to be constant either over time or between publications."[6] The books owned by a person at the time of death may or may not be listed in inventories, which sometimes fail to record items deemed of little financial value or items simply given away before death.

Whatever the rate of literacy in Elizabethan England, some people were clearly more adept at reading than others. The survival of books and broadsides combining picture and text suggests, like comic books today, a limited ability to comprehend the written word and, perhaps, a desire to read even on the part of the relatively unschooled. Single-leaf woodcuts, accompanied by an explanation in words, enjoyed considerable popularity in the Elizabethan era, and those that survive hint at a vast original number: "Since no Englishman of this generation thought to preserve in any systematic fashion the ephemeral woodcuts of the age, very few survive: as few as 300 examples out of perhaps 3000 titles, representing as many as 3 million copies, a survival rate of one in ten thousand."[7] Almanacs, which combined a farrago of astrological, meteorological, and other information, were capable of being understood by the literate (through words) and by the illiterate (through the symbols that appeared in tables). Other works, too, appearing as unbound octavo pamphlets and quartos, suggest that there existed a market for printed materials that made only modest demands on the reader: "Such works have no literary pretensions, but were calculated to catch the attention of those who could read but did not want to involve themselves with anything too long or too difficult of understanding."[8] These materials, dealing with crimes and adventures, sensational deeds and curiosities, must have had much the same appeal that tabloid newspapers have today, and they were readily available from street peddlers, who complemented the more conventional booksellers of the kind who marketed their wares near St. Paul's in London.

Despite the survival of a vast array of miscellaneous printed materials, some scholars believe that only a small portion of the population could actually read and write. David Cressy, for example, maintains that "Evidence from the seventeenth century . . . shows that England was massively illiterate despite an epoch of educational expansion and a barrage of sermons. More than two-thirds of the men and nine-tenths of the women were so illiterate at the time of the civil war that they could not even write their own names."[9] H. S. Bennett, however, believes that literacy was far more prevalent. He cites a proclamation from Henry VIII, the Act for the Advancement of True Religion (1543), which forbade various classes of people from reading the Bible in English; included were artificers, apprentices, husbandmen, laborers, and journeymen serving of the degree of yeoman and under. According to Bennett, "The range of social classes indicated in this Act . . . shows clearly that the authorities recognized that the ability to read was widespread."[10] On the basis of this same proclamation, Rudolf Hirsch similarly argues that "the ability to read was widespread in the English realm."[11]

Although Cressy is dubious about such claims, he concedes that "Contemporary opinion, book production, book ownership and the history of education all point to an increasingly literate population in the late sixteenth and early seventeenth centuries."[12]

Whatever its extent, literacy was far more prevalent in towns and cities than in the countryside because of the number of people involved in the skilled crafts (as opposed to agriculture), the clustering of those crafts in urban areas, and the concentration of people engaged in divinity, law, medicine, and education.[13] Literacy was not merely an asset in the urban workplace but even a requirement for some types of employment. Steve Rappaport points to the role of livery companies in fostering the literacy of Londoners: "For many young men, arriving in London in their late teens and early twenties, their years at home were spent learning to read and write. A degree of functional literacy was expected of apprentices in many companies, especially those associated with the city's retail, wholesale, and overseas trades, since an apprentice often ran the shop in his master's absence."[14] From the requirement in some trades that an apprentice write his oath swearing obedience during his seven years of apprenticeship, Rappaport concludes:

> Over a period of seven decades a total of 823 oaths were enrolled by Ironmongers and the rate of literacy among their apprentices was very high indeed. From the 1520s through the 1540s, 72 per cent of 294 apprentices were able to write the entire 58-word oath, 19 per cent signed their names and probably wrote the oath as well, and only 25 (9 per cent) of the apprentices subscribed their oaths with marks. During the following decades the proportion of written oaths increased substantially, reflecting an increase in the rate of literacy among England's people during the first two decades of Elizabeth's reign: as many as 98 per cent of 529 apprentices could write the entire oath and only 10 were unable even to sign their names.[15]

Based on his careful study of the London trades, Rappaport argues that "with the exception of certain occupational groups, from two-thirds to three-quarters of London's men possessed basic literacy skills during the second half of Elizabeth's reign."[16]

Even those people whose literacy was rudimentary or non-existent were affected by the written word, for the written culture of the sixteenth century coexisted in complex ways with the oral. Harvey J. Graff notes that "Western literacy was *formed, shaped,* and *conditioned* by the oral world that it penetrated."[17] Brian Stock observes: "There is in fact no clear point of transition from a nonliterate to a literate society. For, even at the high point of oral usage, let us say, in the medieval context, continental Europe during the tenth century, writing was not by any means absent from everyday transactions; and, when literate norms were firmly re-established in law and government, that is, by the mid-twelfth, the spoken word did not cease to play a large cultural role. The change . . . was not so much from oral *to* written as from an earlier state, predominantly oral, to various combinations of oral *and* written."[18] In the sixteenth century, too, the written word was a part of the oral world. Tessa Watt notes that "The spread of petty chapmen selling ballads in this period [1550–1640] is a measure of how far print was infiltrating the oral culture."[19]

People also experienced the written word indirectly when they listened to sermons or heard proclamations. Roger Chartier explains: "the written word lies at the very heart of the most concrete and the most 'oralized' forms of traditional cultures. This was true of rituals, which were often intensified by the physical presence of a central text, actually read aloud during the ceremony. It was also true in urban festivals, where inscriptions, banners, and signs bore a profusion of mottoes and slogans."[20] Natalie Zemon Davis recounts an ingenious use of the written word in one such celebration: "In the Lyon festivals of the 1570s through the 1590s, the Lord of Misprint tossed printed verses to the spectators and subsequently published the scenarios, with their complaints about the high cost of bread and paper, about the fluctuations in the value of currency, and especially about the folly of war in France."[21] The rapidly increasing prominence of the written word in a culture still pervasively affected by an older oral culture (in the form of festivals, sermons, memorized Scripture, recited stories, and so forth) generated a significant change in European society. As Richard G. Cole observes, "The combination of oral methods with printed materials as sources of information created a new 'cultural mix' that was essentially a new force in the sixteenth century."[22] Walter J. Ong identifies one such "mix" in his examination of adages, apothegms, and other sayings that were printed in huge quantities during the Renaissance: "It would appear that the glut of collections from classical authors which flooded the Renaissance—and gave it further continuity with the Middle Ages and their passion for florilegia—fed an appetite which was still largely created by a residual oralism in expression. The oral performer favors use of a well-known phraseology. The humanists' insistence on imitation and the typographer's ability to multiply lists of cullings effectively and cheaply combined for the moment to give the orally oriented mind a new lease on life, although ultimately typography was to spell its doom."[23]

The Elizabethan stage furnishes a glimpse of a culture in which the "mix" of spoken and written words has begun to tip in the direction of the latter. Scenes involving the swearing of oaths suggest that the spoken pledge needs to be reinforced by writing in order to be effective. In Marlowe's *Tamburlaine, Part 2*, Christians and Moslems, having sworn an oath of peace, supplement the pact with writing; the King of Natolia tells the King of Hungary:

> By sacred Mahomet, the friend of God,
> Whose holy Alcaron remains with us,
> Whose glorious body, when he left the world
> Closed in a coffin, mounted up the air
> And hung on stately Mecca's temple roof,
> I swear to keep this truce inviolable;
> Of whose conditions and our solemn oaths
> Signed with our hands, each shall retain a scroll
> As memorable witness of our league.

(1.1.137–45)[24]

Similarly, in Shakespeare's *King John,* Lewis, the Dolphin of France, speaks of confirming an oath by setting it down in writing, copies of which are kept by each of the parties:

> My Lord Melune, let this be copied out,
> And keep it safe for our remembrance.
> Return the president to these lords again,
> That having our fair order written down,
> Both they and we, perusing o'er these notes,
> May know wherefore we took the sacrament,
> And keep our faiths firm and inviolable.
>
> (5.2.1–7)

Without that "order written down" and the individually retained copies, the oath would apparently be insufficient to guarantee future behavior.

Sixteenth-century writers provide suggestive, if imprecise, information about the prevalence of the written word in daily life. Raphael Holinshed makes this comment about palaces belonging to the prince: "everie office hath either a bible, or the bookes of the acts and monuments of the church of England, or both, beside some histories and chronicles lieng therein, for the exercise of such as come into the same: whereby the stranger that entereth into the court of England upon the sudden, shall rather imagine himselfe to come into some publike schoole of the universities, where manie give eare to one that readeth, than into a princes palace, if you conferre the same with those of other nations."[25] Sir Thomas Elyot describes the "apparel" belonging to a governor or counselor: "his plate & vessaile wolde be ingraved with histories, fables, or quicke and wise sentences, comprehending good doctrine or counsailes: wherby one of these commodities may happen, either that they which do eate or drinke, havyng those wisdomes ever in sighte, shall happen with the meate to receive some of them: or by purposinge them at the table may sussitate some disputation or reasonynge: wherby some parte of tyme shall be saved, which els by supfluouse eatyng and drinkyng wolde be idely consumed."[26] And George Puttenham in *The Arte of English Poesie* discusses the prevalence of epigrams, noting their appearance on almost every surface: "this *Epigramme* is but an inscription or writting made as it were upon a table, or in a windowe, or upon the wall or mantell of a chimney in some place of common resort, where it was allowed every man might come, or be sitting to chat and prate, as now in our tavernes and common tabling houses, where many merry heades meete, and scrible with ynke with chalke, or with a cole such matters as they would every man should know, & descant upon."[27] Although Puttenham makes this observation while discussing the poetry of Martial in ancient Rome, he clearly sees a parallel with his own experience in Elizabethan London; he speaks of what happens in "our tavernes." When he discusses epigrams that appear in food, he again seems to be describing practices that are as much of his own time as of antiquity: "There be also other like Epigrammes that were sent usually for new yeares giftes or to be Printed or put upon their banketting dishes of suger plate, or of march paines, & such other dainty meates as by the curtesie & custome every gest might carry from a common feast home with him to his owne house, & were made for the nonce, they were called *Nenia* or *apophoreta,* and never contained above one verse, or two at the most, but the shorter the better, we call them Posies, and do paint them now a dayes upon the backe sides of our fruite trenchers of wood, or use them as devises in rings and armes and about such courtly purposes."[28] Although reviewing ancient customs, here, too, Puttenham indicates the survival of certain practices in contemporary London, explicitly mentioning the writing that appears in "our fruite trenchers." A casual remark in *Arden of Faversham* about "a verse or two stolen from a painted cloth" (1.153)[29] indicates that imitation tapestries of the kind owned by middle-class families were at least sometimes embellished with descriptive verses. People of modest means also used cheap printed materials to decorate their walls: "broadside ballads were a widespread, lowly form of ornament, used in cottages, nurseries and alehouses."[30] In Jonson's *Bartholomew Fair* Cokes asks, "O sister, do you remember the ballads over the nursery-chimney at home o' my own pasting up? There be brave pictures" (3.5.45–47).[31]

The presence of written words on windows and walls, in plate and vessels, in food and jewelry, in civic festivals and religious rites, in tapestries and painted cloth, as well as in books and broadsides, imprese and funerary monuments, presupposes a sizeable number of readers. Their literacy, in turn, was fostered by the schools that Jay P. Anglin has studied in Elizabethan London.[32] Of the opportunities for education Ann Jennalie Cook observes: "Between meeting the needs of its own citizenry and supplying specialized training for the whole of England, London supported an immense educational complex, attracting the privileged for training of every sort at every level. Over half the male population were literate, and a truly astonishing number were men of intellectual, cultural, or social sophistication."[33] Cook's investigation leads her to conclude that audiences at the large, popular theaters were more "privileged"—socially, economically, and educationally—than Alfred Harbage recognized when he made his study of London theatergoers.[34] Martin Butler, however, sharply challenges that conclusion. He cites contemporary remarks to demonstrate the presence of comparatively unsophisticated people at theatrical performances.[35] Butler also points out that the range of admission fees suggests a diverse clientele: "the playwrights knew that in different parts of the audiences they were addressing different groups of spectators."[36] Butler sees in the eclecticism and diversity of the plays themselves abundant evidence of a heterogeneous audience.

He does not, however, treat one important feature of the plays relating to the sophistication and literacy of the audience: the prevalence of reading and writing on the stage. Those activities might seem to support Cook's argument, as may the actual sale of books in the theaters; in 1616 William Fennor wrote, "I suppose this Pamphlet will hap into your hands before a Play begin, with the importunate clamour of 'Buy a new Booke!' by some needy companion that will be glad to furnish you with worke for a turned teaster."[37] It is tempting to posit a relationship between reading and writing onstage and those activities in the lives of the audience. But we need to be cautious in making too absolute a correlation, for instances of reading and writing in plays do not in themselves provide anything like conclusive evidence of the spectators' literacy. After all, the presence of a police investigator or cryptographer on the modern stage need not imply the capacity for criminal detection or cryptography on the part of the audience today. Moreover, the extent of literacy in the general population of Elizabethan London, even if it could be determined precisely, is not in itself a sure indication of the literacy of theatrical audiences, for, as Andrew Gurr points out, "Playgoing must have had a special appeal as a leisure activity to the illiterate, since the playgoer's involvement with the written word need have gone no further than the playbills posted to advertise performances."[38]

Appendix 2
Written and Printed Words on the Stage

If the proportion of literate spectators in Elizabethan theaters remains a contentious issue, there is less controversy over the impact of literacy and of the printing press on dramatic language and incident. Plays contain numerous incidental references to the written word in daily life. For example, in *The Spanish Tragedy* Hieronimo gestures for a knife so that he can sharpen the quill pen in his hand (4.4.198.s.d.).[1] In *Much Ado About Nothing,* Dogberry asks Verges to fetch Francis Seacole and "bid him bring his pen and inkhorn" (3.5.58)—a reference to the horns used for storing ink. The contrast in color between dark ink and quill pen is suggested by an extravagant letter-writer in *Love's Labor's Lost,* who speaks of the "most prepost'rous event that draweth from my snow-white pen the ebon-colored ink which here thou viewest" (1.1.241–43).

The legibility of the written word becomes an issue in Brome's *The Antipodes* when a Lawyer says: "I cannot read your hand; your character / Is bad, and your orthography much worse" (3.2.19–20).[2] Plays also contain references to various kinds of script. In Middleton's *Michaelmas Term* when Easy asks, "How like you my Roman hand, i'faith?" Dustbox the scrivener replies, "Exceeding well, sir, but that you rest too much upon your / R's, and make your E's too little" (2.3.346–48)—a reference to the roman, or italic, style in contrast to the native English, or secretary, hand.[3] (The name Dustbox, incidentally, refers to the little box of fine sand or powder which scriveners used for blotting ink.) The imitation of another person's handwriting becomes the focus of a confrontation in Webster's *Appius and Virginia* when Appius accuses Clodius: "Did I not yesterday, no longer since, / Surprize thee in thy Study counterfeiting / Our hand?" (3.2.273–75).[4]

Accouterments of writing sometimes appear onstage alongside pens and paper. When in Beaumont and Fletcher's *The Woman-Hater* Lucio directs his servant to fetch "the Standish I answer French letters with" (5.1),[5] he is asking for an object containing "ink, pens and other writing materials and accessories" (*OED*). A character in Middleton's *Michaelmas Term* refers to the way that letters were folded and sealed with hot wax into which a signet, often fixed in a ring, was pressed: "Now the letter's made up and all; it wants but the print of a seal, and away it goes" (3.5.1–2). To read a letter, one needed first to break that seal, as does the Duke in *The Two Gentlemen of Verona* when he seizes a letter written by Valentine: "I'll be so bold to break the seal for once" (3.1.139). A different kind of seal, consisting of a device impressed in wax and attached by cords or parchment slips, was used to authenticate legal and financial documents. Shylock refers to such a seal when he says, "Till thou canst rail the seal from off my bond, / Thou but offend'st thy lungs to speak so loud" (4.1.139–40). A similar seal is used to authenticate a quasilegal document in *1 Henry IV* when the rebels devise "indentures tripartite" (the plans for dividing the kingdom they envision): Glendower says, "we'll but seal, / And then to horse immediately" (3.1.265–66).

Paper is the surface upon which almost all words are inscribed in Renaissance plays. In *The Noble Spanish Soldier,* however, Onaelia produces her marriage contract, written on a more valuable and durable material: "Here, as the dearest Jewell of my fame, / Lock'd I this parchment from all viewing eyes" (1.2.165–66).[6] Similarly, in Chapman's *All Fools* the Notary prepares a document of divorce, saying, "it has taken me a whole skin of parchment" (4.1.284).[7] In *Sir John Oldcastle, Part 1,* a legal document, a process, is made of parchment and has a wax seal attached; Harpoole tells the Sumner, "If this be parchment, and this wax, eat you this parchment and this wax, or I will make parchment of your skin and beat your brains into wax" (4.42–44).[8]

Paper is, of course, the normal surface for printing; and the books that appear onstage would have looked familiar to sixteenth-century eyes even when the historical setting of a play might suggest a different format. In *Cymbeline* Imogen, growing tired as she reads the story of Tereus and Philomela, directs her servant to "Fold down the leaf where I have left" (2.2.4). This direction suggests the paper leaf of a printed book even though the play is set in ancient times when the story would have been read in a manuscript scroll or, less likely, a codex. Similarly, *Titus Andronicus* is set in an era before the invention of printing, and so the copy of Ovid's *Metamorphoses* that Lavinia uses (4.1.41–42) would, historically speaking, exist in the same form as Imogen's book, but this would probably occur to few people, if anyone, in the Elizabethan audience; Shakespeare's company would probably have used a cheap printed book as the prop.

Like Imogen and Lavinia, characters peruse or refer to literary works with some frequency. In keeping with the classical setting of *Titus Andronicus,* Chiron easily recognizes the source of Latin verses attached to an arrow—"O, 'tis a verse in Horace, I know it well, / I read it in the grammar long ago" (4.2.22–23). Plays with a contemporary setting include allusions to more nearly contemporary books. For instance, in *The Merry Wives of Windsor* Slender says, "I had rather than forty shillings I had my Book of Songs and Sonnets here" (1.1.198–99), almost certainly a reference to Tottel's *Miscellany*. He asks Simple, "You have not the Book of Riddles about you, have you?" (ll. 201–2), referring to another popular book of the late sixteenth century. Harebrain in Middleton's *A Mad World, My Masters* reports that he has removed a woman's reading matter, poems by Marlowe and Shakespeare: "I have convey'd away all her wanton pamphlets, as *Hero and Leander, Venus and Adonis*" (1.2.43–44).[9] In Ford's *'Tis Pity She's a Whore,* Soranzo enters carrying a copy of Sannazaro, which he proceeds to quote and then rewrite: "To work then, happy Muse, and contradict / What Sannazar hath in his envy writ: / 'Love's measure is the mean, sweet his annoys, / His pleasures life, and his reward all joys'" (2.2.8–11).[10]

Plays that feature doctrinal controversy necessarily include works of a theological nature. Thus the Sumner in *Sir John Oldcastle, Part 1*, carries several books onstage, identifying their Lollard origins by their language: "here's not a Latin book, no, not so much as Our Lady's Psalter. Here's the Bible, the Testament, the Psalms in metre, *The Sickman's Salve, The Treasure of Gladness,* and all in English . . ." (13.145–47). But when another character, offended by the Lollard nature of the books, cries, "Now, fie upon these upstart heretics! / All English! Burn them, burn them quickly, Clun!" (ll. 150–51), a reader of vernacular books protests: "But do not, Sumner, as you'll answer it, for I have there English books, my lord, that I'll not part with for your bishopric: *Bevis of Hampton, Owlglass, The Friar and the Boy, Ellen of Rumming, Robin Hood,* and other such godly stories, which if ye burn, by this flesh I'll make ye drink their ashes in Saint Marg'et's ale" (ll. 152–56).

Sometimes the books that appear onstage are of a pragmatic or financial nature. For example, we watch characters handle books containing handwritten accounts of business transactions. In Dekker and Webster's *Westward Ho,* Tenterhook asks, "What booke is that sweet hart?" and his wife replies, "Why the booke of bonds that are due to you" (3.1.1–2).[11] Similarly, in Brome's *A Jovial Crew* Springlove turns over several books to his master, saying, "You may then be pleas'd / To take here a survey of all your rents, / Receiv'd, and all such other payments as / Came to my hands since my last audit" (1.1.122–25).[12] Another kind of book appears in *2 Henry IV,* when Falstaff is busy recruiting a ragtag force: he tells Shallow, "we have a number of shadows fill up the muster-book" (3.2.134–5); this presumably appears onstage, for during their conversation Shallow checks off names at Falstaff's direction. Pragmatic printed books appearing in the drama also include an almanac in Middleton's *No Wit, No Help Like a Woman's:* Weatherwise cites information gleaned from his almanac—an eclipse visible to "the western inhabitants of Mexicana and California" (2.3.200–1)—and he actually reads aloud from the book (3.1 and 5.1).[13]

Written records in the form of bills for various goods turn up on the stage much as they did in daily life. For instance, in *1 Henry IV* Prince Hal directs Peto to search the pocket of the sleeping Falstaff. Peto discovers "Nothing but papers" and proceeds to read aloud an itemized bill for food and drink (2.4.535–39). In Marston's *Antonio and Mellida,* Felice reads aloud a tailor's bill: "Item, for strait canvas, thirteen pence halfpenny; item, for an ell and a half of taffeta to cover your old canvas doublet, fourteen shillings and three pence" (3.2.100–2).[14] A moment later another character says of the bill, "But 'tis not crossed" (l. 106)—a reference to the practice of writing lines at right angles over a bill, thus marking it paid.

Although some characters on the Renaissance stage are clearly illiterate (witness the servant of the Capulets in *Romeo and Juliet* who cannot read a guest list), those who do read are not limited to the middle class or aristocracy. Even characters of modest social station may demonstrate some familiarity with the written word. Margaret, the maid of Fressingfield in *Friar Bacon and Friar Bungay,* works in a milkhouse, but Greene's embodiment of patient Griselda reads aloud the letter she receives from Lacy (10.123–39).[15] In *The Shoemaker's Holiday* the journeyman Ralph Damport, impressed into the military, gives his wife a pair of shoes "Made up and pinked with letters for thy name" (1.241).[16] Later in this play a suitor tells Jane that her husband has died in the French war; he shows her a letter containing a casualty list, and he asks, "Cannot you read?" Jane replies, "I can" (12.88) and finds Ralph's name. In *A Yorkshire Tragedy* Sam, a servingman, implies his literacy when, asked what he has brought back from London, specifies "an almanac in my pocket, and three ballads in my codpiece" (1.24–25).[17] In *The Knight of the Burning Pestle* Rafe, employed by a grocer, is literate as we learn from this stage direction and the subsequent action: *Enter Rafe, like a grocer in's shop, with two prentices . . . reading Palmerin of England* (1.212.s.d.).[18] Finally, in the sheepshearing scene of *The Winter's Tale*, we find another, but more problematic, reference to the written and printed word. When the Clown asks, "What hast here? Ballads?" Mopsa replies, "Pray now buy some. I love a ballet in print, a-life, for then we are sure they are true" (4.4.259–61). The familiarity of the shepherds with printed materials may suggest a similar familiarity on the part of unsophisticated spectators. But any firm conclusion is made impossible by the pastoral setting, a world unknown to ordinary people. In any event, it is possible that Shakespeare intends there to be a comic disparity between the life of shepherds and the experience of reading.

The frontier between script and print is dramatized in the "news office" that Pennyboy Junior visits in *The Staple of News*. That office contains an array of handwritten materials, the raw material for quarto newsbooks. As Cymbal explains to Pennyboy,

> This is the outer room, where my clerks sit
> And keep their sides; the Register i'the midst;
> The Examiner, he sits private there within;
> And here I have my several rolls and files
> Of news by the alphabet, and all put up
> Under their heads.
>
> (1.5.2–7)[19]

In this same conversation another character refers to the "*coranti* and *gazetti*" (l. 11) that were circulating in Ben Jonson's London. These were single printed sheets containing news of the continent—the counterpart in the 1620s of modern journalism. They were based, in part, on letters about recent events written by correspondents in various European countries and sent to London.

Some characters speak of conventions which printing either brought into existence or fostered. For example, Northumberland in *2 Henry IV* refers to a separate title leaf, or title page, which was rare in manuscripts: "this man's brow, like to a title-leaf, / Foretells the nature of a tragic volume" (1.1.60–61). A feature found in some manuscripts but far more prevalent in the era of printing is an index, which designates (in the context of printing) either "a table of contents prefixed to a book" or "an alphabetical list placed (usually) at the end of a book, of the names, subjects, etc. occurring in it"; the *OED*'s first citation of the word with these meanings is dated 1578. Writers of imaginative literature adopted the usage. In Marlowe's *Hero and Leander* the narrator describes the congruence of a man's face and mind: "even as an Index to a booke, / So to his mind was yoong *Leanders* looke."[20] In Marston's *Insatiate Countess* Isabella asks a servant whether he can detect her mood: "Dost thou not see my face? / Is not the face the index of the mind?" (2.3.4–5).[21] In *The Changeling* Middleton compares emotion to the product of a printing press: "If lovers should mark everything a fault, / Affection would be like an ill-set book, / Whose faults might prove as big as half the volume" (2.1.109–11).[22] These lines can refer only to a printed book in which the type has been badly set by the compositor, resulting in a long list of misprints. In *The Insatiate Countess* Claridiana speaks of "our *quondam* wives, that makes us cry our vowels in red capital letters" (5.2.24–25), a reference to the practice of printing in red capital letters the names of martyrs in Roman calendars. And in *Othello* Iago uses the word "index" to mean a table of contents and also perhaps a hand with an extended index finger of the kind that one finds in printed books; he says to Roderigo of Cassio and Desdemona, "Lechery, by this hand; an index and obscure prologue to the history of lust and foul thoughts" (2.1.257–58).[23] Erasmus, in sixteenth-century translation, puts into words the look and meaning of the gesture that became a symbol in the repertory of printers: "The fore fynger nexte unto the thumbe is called in latin, *index,* as if ye should saye in englyshe, the pointyng fynger, or the shewyng fynger, because that stretchyng forth the same fynger on length wee use to shewe this, or that."[24] Finally, in *The Fatal Dowry* Massinger and Field compare the index, chapter division, and pointing hand of a printed book (all of which assist in designating a book's contents), to a person's clothes, which express that person's inner character: "even as the Index tels us the contents of stories, and directs to the particular Chapters, even so does the outward habit and superficiall order of garments (in man or woman) give us a tast of the spirit, and demonstratively poynt (as it were a manuall note from the margin) all the internall quality, and habiliment of the soule . . ." (4.1.48–53).[25]

Aspects of the writing and printing trade are also discussed onstage. For instance, the practice of dedicating a book to more than one patron so as to procure additional money for the writer is the subject of an exchange in *The Honest Whore, Part 2*. When a scholar presents a book to Hippolito, the recipient says, "tell me, / To how many hands besides hath this bird flowne, / How many partners share with me?" (1.1.168–69).[26] In *The Sun's Darling* by Ford and Dekker, Folly refers to the ingratitude of patrons who refuse to remunerate writers: "you finde fault as Patrons do with books, to give nothing" (3.1.32–33).[27] In *The Staple of News* Cymbal mentions a common deception—the printing of old pamphlets or books with new title pages: "Nor shall the stationer cheat upon the time / By buttering over again—" (1.5.58–59). In Dekker's *Match Me in London* Gazetto refers to the practice of withdrawing books from circulation; he tells a husband, "Come th'art a foole, to grieve that thy wife is taken away by the King to his private bed-chamber, / Now like a booke call'd in, shee'l sell better then ever she did" (4.1.80–82).[28] In Webster's induction to Marston's *The Malcontent,* Henry Condell contrasts the largest size of book with the smallest as he alludes to the play's production history—first performed by a company of boys and now by an adult company: "Why not Malevole in folio with us, as Jeronimo in decimo-sexto with them?" (ll. 78–79).[29]

Language of the printing business even lent itself to the description of amatory experience. In *The Taming of the Shrew* Biondello uses terminology of copyright when he urges Lucentio to elope with Bianca: "Take you assurance of her, *cum privilegio ad imprimendum solum* . . ." (4.4.92–93). As Ann and John O. Thompson observe, "The Latin phrase, meaning 'with exclusive rights to print' was a standard one in the book trade and implies that by marrying Bianca Lucentio will establish his copyright in her body, gaining the sole right to print—copies of himself presumably."[30] Another implicitly sexual allusion is made in *Northward Ho* by Dekker and Webster when the randy Phillip addresses Doll, a whore, and her companions: "Come my little Punke with thy two Compositors to this unlawfull printing house" (3.1.1–2).[31] The impact of the printing press also appears in *The Merry Wives of Windsor,* where Mistress Page finds a curious resemblance between the love letter that she has received from Falstaff and the letter that Mistress Ford has received:

> Letter for letter; but that the name of Page and Ford differs! To thy great comfort in this mystery of ill opinions, here's the twin-brother of thy letter; but let thine inherit first, for I protest mine never shall. I warrant he hath a thousand of these letters, writ with blank space for different names (sure, more!); and these are of the second edition. He will print them, out of doubt; for he cares not what he puts into the press, when he would put us two.
>
> (2.1.70–79)

In Mistress Page's mind, the duplicate letters evoke the printing press, which can make virtually limitless copies of anything written. Presumably this speech would never have been uttered without the invention of printing: the words "edition," "print," and "press," together with the reference to a "thousand" letters, point to the production of words on a machine using movable type (though Mistress Page puns on "press" in a sexual sense too, as the weight of one body on another).

For all the changes wrought by the new technology, the written word remained the written word, whether produced by pen or press. Although we usually discriminate between script and print today, that distinction was sometimes blurred in the Renaissance. Especially when the invention of the press was relatively new, the association of printing and manuscript production could be quite close. Colard Mansion of Bruges, who was a scribe, translator, and illuminator, joined William Caxton for a time in the operation of a press, but later returned to his work as a scribe. Printing, moreover, preserved many features of manuscripts. According to Curt F. Bühler, "the fifteenth century itself made little distinction between hand-written and press-printed books."[32] The materials of production could be the same for both: "many manuscripts were written on paper, many printed books were printed on parchment."[33] Format could be similar, too: early printed books resembled most manuscripts in lacking a title page and (often) pagination; also reminiscent of manuscripts was the placement of important information—a book's place of publication, name of maker, and sometimes the name of author and title—in a colophon at the end of the book. Printers sometimes deliberately sought to make their books resemble manuscripts: "A late fifteenth-century edition of the *Roman de la Rose* . . . was printed on a press and illustrated with woodcuts, but made to look like an illuminated manuscript by the publisher, Antoine Vérard. Vérard's shop added ruled lines in red ink to the printed text to imitate the ruling that was drawn on a manuscript page prior to hand lettering by scribes; the woodcuts were painted with opaque pigments and gold highlights."[34] Manuscript copies were even made of printed books; and manuscripts and printed books were shelved together in libraries as they virtually never are today. So close was the relationship between manuscripts and printed books that "Even the mechanical signs of production in a printed book, such as catchwords, signatures, and line endings, resemble those in manuscripts."[35] Just as scribes used ligatures in their writing, so did printers, who customarily linked the letters *a* and *e, o* and *e, f* and *i, f* and *l, f* and *f*. Of perhaps the single most famous early printed book, Sandra Hindman observes that "in script, decoration, and format the *Gutenberg Bible* resembles manuscripts produced in the same center, Mainz, and of the same date, around 1455."[36] Decades later printers continued to emulate script. For example, the development of italic type, attributed to Aldus Manutius, began as an effort to "make available in type a face comfortable for its readers. They had come to feel at home with humanistic cursive. This was the international norm for writing in Latin—everything from private letters through formal documents to literary editions."[37] Aldus himself boasted of the resemblance between his font and writing: "he strove to reproduce the most fashionable manuscript-styles and so make good a repeated claim that his letters were 'as good, if not better, than any written with a pen.'"[38] Given this continuity of appearance between script and print, it does not surprise us to learn that "an early printer referred to the process as *artificialiter scribere,* or a bogus means of writing, thereby stressing its analogies with the hand-written book."[39] In the first book printed in English, William Caxton suggests that printing is simply a means of compensating for a weary eye and an unsteady hand. In the epilogue to book 3 of *The Recuyell of the Historyes of Troye* (Bruges, ca. 1474),[40] Caxton tells his reader:

> for as moche as in the wrytyng of the same my penne is worn, myn hande wery & not stedfast myn eyen dimmed with overmoche lokyng on the whit paper, and my corage not so prone and redy to laboure as hit hath ben, and that age crepeth on me dayly and febleth all the bodye, and also because I have promysid to dyverce gentilmen and to my frendes to adresse to hem as hastely as I myght this sayd book, Therfore I have practysed & lerned at my grete charge and dispense to ordeyne this said book in prynte after the maner & forme as ye may here see, and is not wreton with penne and ynke as other bokes ben, to thende that every man may have them attones, ffor all the bookes of this storye named the recule of the historyes of troyes thus empryntid as ye here see were begonne in oon day, and also fynysshid in oon day, whiche book I have presented to my sayd redoubtid lady. . . . [41]

More than a hundred years separate Caxton's words about the press and the pen from the beginning of Shakespeare's career, but the difference between printing and writing was not so absolute as we might imagine, for much communication continued to be transacted in script. Such essential records as baptism, marriage, and death remained handwritten, as did records of legal proceedings, rental agreements, bills of sale, contracts, and wills. Similarly, indentures and indictments, warrants and charters, treaties, marriage compacts, and other solemn arrangements between nations were also handwritten. And so, of course, was correspondence, whether personal, professional, or diplomatic. Records and arrangements that today invariably appear in type almost always appeared in script four centuries ago, and the occupation of scrivener existed to satisfy the demand for writing.

Reliance upon the written, rather than the printed, word continued in daily life, much as it had for generations. The written word could be important to anyone who sought to purchase or lease property, draw up a contract, prepare a will, edify the mind, pray to God, or woo a woman. None of these activities, however, requires print. Scriveners and notaries were available to produce the documents necessary for business or law. A person does not need to read a printed book in order to pray; a memorized prayer or an impromptu address to one's God can suffice. The mind may be improved by contemplation of what has been heard or seen, and wooing could presumably be accomplished by means that do not require literacy, much less print.

On the stage, where handwritten materials predominate, the distinction between script and print is scarcely felt. That is, the theatrical effects achieved by a handwritten communication are essentially the same as those achieved by print: a letter in script is capable of producing the theatrical effect created by a printed book. So although the printing press exerted a profound effect on Renaissance life and thought, as Elizabeth L. Eisenstein and others contend, we need to be cautious in making too stark a distinction between script and print on the stage. In the theater printed books, handwritten letters, and legal documents exist as part of a continuum of inscribed words—accessible to many literate people, and recognizable as books, letters, and documents even to others in the audience.

Appendix 3
The Pragmatic Value of Property Letters

Perhaps because they can so swiftly drive a plot forward, letters may have a merely mechanical quality on the stage. For instance, some of the letters that mysteriously appear in *King Lear* seem almost arbitrary. Ann Pasternak Slater observes that Shakespeare "camouflages the influx of letters vital to the plot by making his characters distribute many others whose function and contents are never revealed and are, of course, non-existent. In this respect *Lear* is statistically outstanding; letters appear twelve times functionally and three times as mere camouflage."[1] Slater's point is well taken: a letter that unexpectedly turns up and permits a quick advance or resolution of the dramatic action may seem just as mechanical as the phone call in a TV mystery that imparts information decisive for solving a crime. Nevertheless, the letters or other writings that appear on the stage do not necessarily signal a deficiency in a play's construction, for such letters are eminently practical in serving specifically theatrical ends, as evidenced in some of Shakespeare's earliest plays.[2]

In *1 Henry VI* written materials function in a relatively straightforward way. They help drive the plot by communicating information which motivates characters to action. In the opening scene, where various noblemen are marking the funeral of Henry V, three messengers appear in rapid succession; the first and third declaim their news while the second says, "Lords, view these letters full of bad mischance" (1.1.89). All three bring news of revolt and losses in France, and this, in turn, has the immediate effect of undermining the confidence and cohesion of the English court; it also anticipates future violence by leading Bedford to declare that he will raise an army of 10,000 soldiers to recover the lost lands. The letter (probably a single communication despite the plural form) is not necessary in the sense that the news is summarized orally by all three messengers. Nor is this letter used in an especially interesting manner, since there are no stage directions indicating that it is actually read by anyone; the messenger himself exits after delivering seven brisk lines. The theatrical property, however, is not entirely superfluous. Frances Teague observes that "the device of the letter is practical because it precludes questions about the actions of the French leaders, while the spoken messages allow the court to interrogate those messengers."[3] The property letter, moreover, can be used to generate stage business as it is opened, scrutinized, and possibly even passed from hand to hand. By giving concrete and thus visual form to the news, the property letter objectifies the forces impinging on the English, allowing the French to be felt as a political and military presence.

A more complicated version of this theatrical technique occurs in *3 Henry VI*. At the French court, the Earl of Warwick seeks to arrange the marriage of England's Edward, Duke of York, to Bona, sister-in-law of the French king. The situation is delicate not only because the prospective marriage involves two antagonistic states but also because the formidable Queen Margaret is present, and she fiercely opposes the match; her husband, Henry, has been forced to flee England for Scotland, and her son, Prince Edward, is, she claims, "Henry's heir" (3.3.31). Whatever doubts he may harbor, Lewis consents to the marriage, having been assured that Edward of York is England's "true king." But scarcely has the French monarch agreed and directed that the "articles be drawn" (l. 135) when a messenger enters with letters for Warwick, Lewis, and Margaret. According to the stage direction, *They all read their letters* (l. 166), while other characters observe the readers' reactions. The Earl of Oxford notes, "I like it well that our fair queen and mistress / Smiles at her news, while Warwick frowns at his" (ll. 167–68), and Prince Edward replies, "Nay, mark how Lewis stamps as he were nettled." These varying responses have been precipitated by a single stunning development: Edward IV has married Lady Elizabeth Grey. The shock of the letter-readers promptly gives way to political realignment. King Lewis, who believed that an alliance between his nation and England had been achieved, asks Warwick, "has your king married the Lady Grey? / And now to soothe your forgery and his, / Sends me a paper to persuade me patience?" (ll. 174–76). Of the usurping Edward, an embarrassed Warwick pledges, "I here renounce him and return to Henry"; furthermore, "I will revenge his wrong to Lady Bona, / And replant Henry in his former state" (ll. 194, 197–98). For her part, Margaret revises her opinion of the English embassy: "Warwick, these words have turn'd my hate to love, / And I forgive and quite forget old faults, / And joy that thou becom'st King Henry's friend" (ll. 199–201).

This scene is not without awkwardness: it seems improbable that Margaret and Prince Edward should be present at Warwick's negotiations for marriage, and that Warwick's conversion should be instantaneous. But Shakespeare is conflating events of three different years: 1462 (the arrival of Queen Margaret in France); 1464 (Warwick's embassy to negotiate a marriage for Edward IV); and 1470 (reconciliation between Margaret and the disaffected Warwick). And the letters serve a practical function. By having three letters—all, presumably, saying much the same thing—rather than one, Shakespeare ensures that each recipient will know that the news is not a trick but the truth. Even more important, the letters demonstrate the extent to which the characters—denizens of the French court and English visitors alike—are at the mercy of far-off events. By dramatizing the reading of the letters simultaneously, the playwright shows how abruptly allegiances can be abrogated or forged. And by dramatizing the actual moment of reading, Shakespeare intensifies the effect of the news, giving it emotional urgency through changes in the actors' facial expression, gesture, and body language.

Shakespeare also dramatizes the reception of written materials in *2 Henry VI*, where Gloucester reads aloud the "articles of contracted peace" between England and France. During the recitation, Gloucester drops the document to the floor:

Duke Humphrey lets it fall (1.1.52.s.d.). This, of course, is no accident. Gloucester is indicating what he is reluctant to say publicly—that he is appalled by the terms, especially by the English surrender of Anjou and Maine: "Pardon me, gracious lord, / Some sudden qualm hath struck me at the heart, / And dimm'd mine eyes, that I can read no further" (ll. 53–55). By continuing the recitation, the Bishop of Winchester indicates that he has no such qualms. The playwright uses this stage business to dramatize the antithetical views of Gloucester and Winchester and to fix this antinomy in the mind's eye of the audience.

Rarely in a history play does Sakespeare supply the full text of a missive. In *1 Henry VI*, however, when King Henry directs, "now Lord Protector, view the letter / Sent from our uncle Duke of Burgundy" (4.1.48–49), Gloucester proceeds to read aloud the Duke's announcement of fealty to the French king. Shakespeare's usual reluctance to stage such recitations reflects his pragmatism: he knows that they may prove tedious and so tax the patience of an audience. In this instance he makes a virtue of theatrical necessity by keeping the contents brief and by using that brevity to intensify the conflict:

> What means his Grace, that he hath chang'd his style?
> No more but plain and bluntly "To the King"?
> Hath he forgot he is his sovereign?
> Or doth this churlish superscription
> Pretend some alteration in good will?
> What's here? [*Reads.*] "I have, upon especial cause,
> Mov'd with compassion of my country's wrack,
> Together with the pitiful complaints
> Of such as your oppression feeds upon,
> Forsaken your pernicious faction
> And join'd with Charles, the rightful King of France."
>
> (4.1.50–60)

The curt salutation is matched by the letter's six-line length. The abrasive language makes the English court feel the sting of French arrogance. If Burgundy is not physically present, his letter provides the next best thing to an onstage confrontation of antagonists, with its potential for emotional pyrotechnics: the very words of the enemy, calculated to affront. The letter, which startles the courtiers, causes the English to redouble their efforts and helps generate the fierce anger that leads Talbot into a military engagement that costs him his life.

Written materials are attractive to playwrights not only because they move the plot forward and reveal character but also because they are suited to achieve particular theatrical effects. In *The Merchant of Venice,* for example, a messenger delivers a letter from Antonio to Bassanio, who opens and reads it while a watchful Portia notes the changes in emotional climate: "There are some shrowd contents in yond same paper / That steals the color from Bassanio's cheek" (3.2.243–44). Although the letter is not read aloud even in part, it creates a sharp alteration in mood and tone all the same. Bassanio tells Portia, "Here are a few of the unpleasant'st words / That ever blotted paper!" (ll. 251–52). The letter both communicates the news that Antonio's ships have failed to arrive safely and emphasizes the desperation of the merchant's plight; without the cargo from those ships, Antonio will be unable to pay Shylock's bond, and the exaction of the bond means certain death:

> Here is a letter, lady,
> The paper as the body of my friend,
> And every word in it a gaping wound
> Issuing life-blood.
>
> (ll. 263–66)

By directing our attention to the letter in Bassanio's hands, the playwright invests it with emotional force. By comparing the paper of the letter to human flesh and blood, Shakespeare anticipates Antonio's near-death; through the hand property Antonio's jeopardy becomes palpable.

Like Shakespeare, Marlowe, too, uses written materials to enhance the emotional impact of a character's plight. In *Edward II* Leicester reports that he must surrender his charge of the captive king. Berkeley brings the news in an order which the king studies for a moment: "By Mortimer, whose name is written here. / Well may I rend his name that rends my heart!" (5.1.139–40).[4] As he reads, Edward's anger is converted into action. He *Tears the paper:* "This poor revenge hath something eased my mind. / So may his limbs be torn, as is this paper!" (ll. 141–42). What Edward does to the paper he wishes he could do to his enemy. The paper, representing the vehicle by which the king's anger is externalized, comes to stand for Edward's nemesis. Without the paper, Edward might simply splutter or whine; the hand property supplies a tactile target for his rage. What might otherwise seem a very minor incident—the transfer of custody from Leicester to Berkeley—becomes an occasion for dramatizing Edward's helplessness and fury.

These examples indicate the nature of the theatrical appeal that can be provided by property letters. Through them a playwright conveys a feeling or attitude more quickly and memorably than by the spoken word alone. He also can achieve economy in another way. A hand prop involving the written word has the advantage of costing a company of players next to nothing. Apparently because letters, books, and pieces of paper suitable for use onstage as properties could have cost very little, none of these is listed in the inventory of properties belonging to the Admiral's Men on 10 March 1598.[5] The same piece of paper or book, moreover, could serve in dozens of plays. There is another advantage too. A book, letter, or document is easily portable, brought onstage in a player's hand, where it is instantly recognized by the audience.

Appendix 4
Books and Written Materials as Symbols

Props that involve print and writing have a significance that sets them apart from such other objects as swords, lanterns, goblets, and the like, for the use of props containing words is colored by the attitudes toward written words that developed during the Renaissance and intensified following the invention of the press. In theatrical production the written or printed word may possess an exceptionally wide range of symbolic associations.

In the opening scene of *Doctor Faustus,* the title character in his study takes up and then puts down four books. One of these is a Latin Bible, a book possessing powerful symbolic importance. For a culture that found its religious truth in a book, the written word has a natural connection with divinity. In George Wapull's *The Tide Tarrieth No Man* the personification of Christianity carries a sword on one side of which is inscribed "God's word" (line 1341.s.d.).[1] In *Clyomon and Clamydes* Providence, having descended from heaven, hands "verses" to a maiden who mistakenly thinks that her beloved is dead (ll. 1550–54).[2] Later plays, set in an indeterminate or pre-Christian world, also associate writing with the divine will. In *The Winter's Tale* when emissaries of Leontes return from Delphos, a court officer asks them to swear that they "have brought / this seal'd up oracle, by the hand deliver'd / Of great Apollo's priest" (3.2.126–28); the seals are then broken and the divine oracle read aloud. In Ford's *The Broken Heart* a sealed box containing a scroll is brought onto stage, sent by the King: "It is the health of Sparta, the king's life, / Sinews and safety of the commonwealth, / The sum of what the oracle delivered, / When last he visited the prophetic temple / At Delphos" (3.1.66–70).[3]

To live in accord with Christian teaching is to pay particular attention to the written word, with its precepts for behavior.[4] This association is made clear by what characters say as well as what they do. The saintliness of Shakespeare's King Henry VI, for instance, is inseparable from his reading; his fretful wife complains, "His weapons [are] holy saws of sacred writ, / His study is his tilt-yard" (*2 Henry VI,* 1.3.58–59). Books may signify innocence, as in *Richard III* when Tyrrel learns from the murderers of two children that "A book of prayers on their pillow lay" (4.3.14). In *The Merchant of Venice* Bassanio asks his friend to rein in his "wild behavior," and Gratiano obliges, somewhat facetiously, with a pledge to "Wear prayer-books in my pocket" (2.2.192).

Stage directions make explicit the alliance between books and divinity. A book signals the possibility of redemption in *The True Chronicle History of King Leir* when a messenger comes upon the figures of Leir and the courtier Perillus, who have fallen asleep while reading; he says, "I thinke, they know to what intent they came, / And are provided for another world" (ll. 1464–65), and *He takes their bookes away* (line 1466.s.d.).[5] In Middleton's *A Mad World, My Masters* we find this stage direction: *Enter in his chamber out of his study, Master Penitent Brothel, a book in his hand, reading;* his soliloquy begins: "Ha! Read that place again. 'Adultery / Draws the divorce 'twixt heaven and the soul'" (4.1.1–2).[6] In *The Devil's Law-Case* when the rascally Romelio complains of hunger, a Capuchin, *Offering him a book,* says, "Here's food for you" (5.4.93).[7] In *The Insatiate Countess* Isabella, awaiting execution, asks the Cardinal who *Gives [her] a book,* "You put me to my book, my lord, will not that save me?" (5.1.97).[8] He replies, "Yes madam, in the everlasting world" (l. 98). In *A Warning for Fair Women* as the guilty Anne Sanders prepares to depart this world, she offers her children the means for better life than she will know in the next: "here I give to each of you a booke / Of holy meditations, *Bradfords* workes" (ll. 2702–3).[9]

Unscrupulous characters sometimes make use of this association of the written word with divinity. The potential for manipulating the written word and capitalizing for self-aggrandizement on the associations with divinity is nowhere more blatant than in Shakespeare's *Richard III,* where books become part of a pious charade. Richard of Gloucester appears *between two bishops,* carrying "a book of prayer"—the ornament "to know a holy man" (3.7.96–99). The use of a text to obscure the truth is suggested by Bassanio's comment in *The Merchant of Venice:* "In religion, / What damned error but some sober brow / Will bless it, and approve it with a text, / Hiding the grossness with fair ornament?" (3.2.77–80). Antonio reminds Bassanio that "The devil can cite Scripture for his purpose" (1.3.98). In *Hamlet* Polonius treats a book as though it were a prop in the dramatic scene he is staging for the benefit of Claudius; he tells Ophelia, "Read on this book, / That show of such an exercise may color / Your loneliness. We are oft to blame in this— / 'Tis too much prov'd—that with devotion's visage / And pious action we do sugar o'er / The devil himself" (3.1.43–48). Polonius's observation recalls a theatrical tradition stretching back to the moral interludes. For instance, in *The Comedy of the Most Virtuous and Godly Susanna* by Thomas Garter we find this stage direction: *Sensuality and Voluptas sitteth downe at a Table turning of bokes . . .* (ll. 330–31).[10] On the Jacobean stage as well morally dubious characters continue to regard books as easily manipulated symbols of virtue. In *A Mad World, My Masters,* the Courtesan gives this advice to Mistress Harebrain about the man she desires: "If he chance steal upon you, let him find / Some book lie open 'gainst an unchaste mind, / And coted scriptures, though for your own pleasure / You read some stirring pamphlet, and convey it / Under your skirt" (1.2.86–90).

In addition to Jerome's Bible, Marlowe's Doctor Faustus takes up Aristotle's treatises on logic, pondering what they have to offer. In this and other plays books commonly appear in the hands of characters with a philosophic cast of mind. Consider the conjunction of philosophy and the written word in *The Spanish Tragedy,* when Hieronimo, a student at Toledo in his younger days, ponders the apparent silence of the heavens following the murder of his son. When he comes onstage to consider his course in a seemingly impassive universe, his appearance signals thoughtfulness: *Enter Hieronimo with a book in his hand* (3.13.1.s.d.).[11] Hamlet, trained at the University of Wittenberg, also contemplates the mystery of a world that seems indifferent to his father's death. His appearance reveals an introspective and contemplative nature: *Enter Hamlet reading on a book* (2.2.167.s.d.). Such reading is frequently associated with melancholy, Gertrude commenting, "look where sadly the poor wretch comes reading" (l. 168). Similarly, Shakespeare's Henry VIII, in a deliberative moment, peruses a book: *the King draws the curtain and sits reading pensively* (2.2.61.s.d.); Suffolk comments, "How sad he looks! Sure he is much afflicted" (l. 62).

Although associated with philosophy, scholarship, introspection, and meditation, the written word may be identified with intellectual pursuit of a trivial nature, with self-absorption and folly. In *Love's Labor's Lost,* for example, when Jaquenetta requests that a letter given her by Costard be read aloud, Nathaniel obliges, and Holofernes, ignoring the content, subsequently complains, "You find not the apostraphas, and so miss the accent" (4.2.119–20). When Nathaniel says that he enjoyed the verses, Holofernes takes the opportunity to parade his knowledge: "I will prove those verses to be very unlearned, neither savoring of poetry, wit, nor invention" (ll. 157–59). Here learning has turned to an arid and unproductive analysis of words and rhetorical devices. Nor is the schoolmaster alone in this failing. Later when Nathaniel hears him call Don Armado "peregrinate," the curate says, "A most singular and choice epithet" (5.1.15), and he proceeds to draw out his table-book (notebook) to record the word.

The copy of Galen that Doctor Faustus examines briefly in his study reminds us that those who practice medicine, like those who ponder life's mysteries, depend upon the written word to advance their knowledge and record their observations. Although stage directions rarely specify papers or books in the hands of a physician, the words of those who heal indicate their reliance upon writing and make it likely that such characters, at least sometimes, appear carrying props containing the written word. For instance, Helena, in *All's Well That Ends Well,* explains the source of her power:

> You know my father left me some prescriptions
> Of rare and prov'd effects, such as his reading
> And manifest experience had collected
> For general sovereignty; and that he willed me
> In heedfull'st reservation to bestow them,
> As notes whose faculties inclusive were
> More than they were in note.
>
> (1.3.221–27)

With these prescriptions she is able to cure the king of a fistula, an accomplishment denied to the royal physicians. In *Pericles* Cerimon owes his healing skill to the perusal of books as well as to his own experience: "'Tis known, I ever / Have studied physic; through which secret art, / By turning o'er authorities, I have, / Together with my practice, made familiar / To me and to my aid the blest infusions" (3.2.31–35). And in *The Virgin Martyr* Sapritius bids the Doctor, "O You that are halfe gods, lengthen that life / Their dieties lend us, turne ore all the volumes / Of your mysterious *Aesculapian* science / T'encrease the number of this yong mans dayes" (4.1.1–4).[12] The Renaissance physician, like the modern, not only reads but also writes, recording the particulars of a patient's case. Hence the doctor takes careful note of what he witnesses in Lady Macbeth: "Hark, she speaks. I will set down what comes from her, to satisfy my remembrance the more strongly" (5.1.32–34).

Medicine, however, can turn to quackery, dependent on the written word for an air of legitimacy. Jonson's Volpone disguises himself as Scoto of Mantua and, with a paper in one hand and a potion in the other—*Pointing to his bill and his glass*—tells Sir Politick Would-be, "this is the physician, this the medicine; this counsels, this cures; this gives the direction, this works the effect; and, in sum, both together may be termed an abstract of the theoric and practic in the Aesculapian art" (2.2.116–19).[13] Following an exchange between Sir Politick and Peregrine, Nano (a bastard of Volpone) sings about the most renowned Greek physicians, emphasizing their writings: "Had old Hippocrates, or Galen, / That to their books put med'cines all in, / But known this secret, they had never / (Of which they will be guilty ever) / Been murderers of so much paper" (2.2.125–29). Like the doctor or apothecary of *commedia dell'arte,* Volpone closely identifies himself with writing: "whilst others have been at the *balloo,* I have been at my book" (2.2.174–75). To Celia, Volpone as Scoto defines the efficacy of his potion by reference to the written word: "Here is a powder concealed in this paper of which, if I should speak to the worth, nine thousand volumes were but as one page, that page as a line, that line as a word; so short is this pilgrimage of man (which some call life) to the expressing of it" (2.2.236–41).

A near relation of the medical quack is the alchemist, a figure closely associated with the written word in Renaissance culture. Pieter Brueghel depicts an alchemist poring over books in a cluttered, disorderly study while an assistant conducts experiments.[14] On the stage, too, books are the customary tools of alchemists. In John Lyly's *Gallathea* the Alchemist apparently reads a book in view of the audience, for his boy, Peter, says, "Look how he studies. I durst venture my life he is now casting about how of his breath he may make golden bracelets, for oftentimes of smoke he hath made silver drops" (2.3.85–88).[15] In Jonson's *Alchemist* books provide the knowledge that ostensibly makes alchemy possible. The credulous Mammon at one point asks a skeptical Surly:

> Will you believe antiquity? Records?
> I'll shew you a book where Moses and his sister,
> And Solomon have written, of the art;
> Ay, and a treatise penn'd by Adam—
>
> (2.1.80–83)[16]

Later in the play, when Face announces the arrival of another prospective gull—"The Count is come"—he asks the alchemist how he will keep their visitors, Kastril and Dame Pliant, occupied. Subtle replies, "Why, have 'em up, and shew 'em / Some fustian book, or the dark glass" (4.2.58–59).

For officers of the law, as for physicians, the written word proves an indispensable tool. (During his opening soliloquy Doctor Faustus briefly examines Justinian's *Institutes*.) The entry of a judicial officer in *The Merchant of Venice* is preceded by a letter from Bellario, who explains that he is sending "a young doctor of Rome" in his place; Bellario attests to the youth's expertise by writing that "We turn'd o'er many books together. He is furnish'd with my opinion . . ." (4.1.156–57). Although explicit stage directions are lacking, most modern productions give papers and books to the disguised Portia when she subsequently enters, attired as a doctor of laws; these are perhaps the "notes" which she requested from Bellario (3.4.51). At the proceeding itself, Portia repeatedly defers to the written law, observing, "there is no power in Venice / Can alter a decree established" (4.1.218–19). Portia almost certainly handles the document when she acknowledges the claims inherent in Shylock's bond: "For the intent and purpose of the law / Hath full relation to the penalty, / Which here appeareth due upon the bond" (ll. 247–49).

The written word also serves as the basis of judgment in Shakespeare's *2 Henry VI*, where the king, confronting the Duchess of Gloucester, invokes the book of Exodus and its prohibition of witchcraft: "Receive the sentence of the law for sins / Such as by God's book are adjudg'd to death" (2.3.3–4). In another form the written word becomes part of her punishment for consorting with demonic spirits; she appears *barefoot, in a white sheet, and verses written on her back and pinned on* (2.4.16.s.d.). The penitent herself refers to this inscription when she speaks of being "Mail'd up in shame, with papers on my back" (l. 31). Labeling a malefactor is envisaged in *Macbeth* as well, when Macduff predicts the king's future, should he survive combat: "We'll have thee, as our rarer monsters are, / Painted upon a pole, and underwrit, / 'Here may you see the tyrant'" (5.8.25–27).

Props involving the written word have a multitude of judicial purposes. For example, Shakespeare's King Henry V delivers arrest warrants to the traitors at Southampton (2.2.66–69). A prop may also serve as the record of judicial examination: Dogberry in *Much Ado About Nothing* tells the clerk, "Write down Prince John a villain" (4.2.41). Or it may constitute a bill of particulars: Northumberland urges King Richard II to read "These accusations, and these grievous crimes / Committed by your person and your followers" (4.1.223–24). Written materials may be supplied as evidence. In Massinger's *Believe as You List*, for instance, Antiochus defends himself by presenting his own writing: "in this scrowle / writ with my royall hande you may peruse / a true memoriall of all circumstances / answers, despatches, doubts, & difficulties, / betwene my selfe, and your embassadors / sent to negotiate with mee" (ll. 1106–11).[17] Amilcar then orders: "fetch the records," and a stage direction follows: *Enter Rowland: with the booke of records*. Most often the written word functions as evidence of guilt. In Webster's *Appius and Virginia,* Icilius produces letters "full of violent Lust," proof of Appius's indecent proposals: "see here they are" (4.1.268).[18] The written word may also provide proof of treason, as in Shakespeare's *Richard II* when York notices a seal affixed to a paper sticking out of his son's clothes: "What seal is that, that hangs without thy bosom? / Yea, look'st thou pale? Let me see the writing" (5.2.56–57). Aumerle's inattention to the seal and document he carries has the look of nonchalance, but the power of the written word to bring about justice may also be seen as providential. In *Henry VIII* Cardinal Wolsey's fall is triggered when he inadvertently transmits to the king an inventory of his private wealth: *Enter King, reading of a schedule* (3.2.104), and Henry exclaims, "What piles of wealth hath he accumulated / To his own portion!" (ll. 107–8). The incriminating information is included in a "packet" of letters meant for the pope concerning the royal divorce. Norfolk comments about the manner of Wolsey's undoing: "It's heaven's will! / Some spirit put this paper in the packet, / To bless your eye withal" (3.2.128–30).

Legal process, however, can be misapplied. In *The Merchant of Venice,* Bassanio reflects on the prevalence of law subverted: "In law, what plea so tainted and corrupt / But, being season'd with a gracious voice, / Obscures the show of evil?" (3.2.75–77). Written materials become a means of subverting righteousness in *The Devil's Law-Case:* Sanitonella offers a legal brief to Ariosto, an honorable attorney, who reads and then *Tears the brief* (4.1.45.s.d.) in disgust. Ariosto explains: "Such vild suits / Disgrace our courts, and these make honest lawyers / Stop their own ears whilst they plead" (ll. 64–66). Undeterred, Sanitonella subsequently offers the "foul copy" of the brief (Webster's pun intended) to an advocate with fewer scruples and more greed. At times written evidence counts for nothing in a legal proceeding. In *Appius and Virginia,* Icilius is appalled to discover that the letters he presents are ignored: "Will no man view these papers? What not one?" (4.1.280).

Written materials may, of course, provide merely the appearance of justice. In *Richard III,* a scrivener surveys his handiwork—the indictment of Lord Hastings which he has written "That it may be to-day read o'er in Paul's" (3.6.3). The scrivener marvels over the lack of what we would call due process: "within these five hours Hastings liv'd / Untainted, unexamin'd, free, at liberty. / Here's a good world the while!" (ll. 8–10). The black humor of this episode resembles that of an incident in *Enough is as Good as a Feast.* There the feckless Ignorance performs as a scribe: "Here is ink and paper. What shall I write?" (l. 1400).[19] He begins to write the will of a dying Worldly Man, who expires before more than a few words of the will have been written. T. W. Craik comments: "Along with the solemn satisfaction that God will not permit his name to be used in a wicked will, there goes a derisive satisfaction that Worldly Man's sins have recoiled upon him."[20]

Such hand properties and accompanying speeches demonstrate that although the written and printed word may be associated with philosophy and pensive introspection, with physical healing, with the adjudication of disputes and the imposition of legal judgment, with a saintly and austere life, the written and printed word can also be associated with the opposite qualities. Writing may constitute a repository of truth, a source of healing knowledge, a bulwark against lawlessness, a route to salvation. But it may also function as the instrument of pedantry, quackery, iniquity, and hypocrisy.

Although books and letters may help characters to achieve some worthy end, those written materials may also prove suspect, dangerous, even lethal. As their careers suggest, ambitious and manipulative malefactors perceive books—when they are not busy using them hypocritically—as irrelevant to, if not incompatible with, effective action. They look upon reading as symptomatic of an inability to cope with everyday demands, and to some extent they are right. In Shakespeare's *2 Henry VI*, Richard Plantagenet, Duke of York, sees King Henry's bookishness as fecklessness, with disastrous consequences for the kingdom: "I'll make him yield the crown, / Whose bookish rule hath pull'd fair England down" (1.1.258–59). York's complaint correctly anatomizes Henry's character, for even when faced with the danger of a peasant rebellion, Henry hesitates—so that he might further study the rebels' supplication:

> And I myself,
> Rather than bloody war shall cut them short,
> Will parley with Jack Cade their general.
> But stay, I'll read it over once again.
>
> (4.4.11–14)

The impulse to reread betrays the fateful habit of mind that prevents Henry from acting expeditiously, rendering him vulnerable to his enemies. Later, broken in power and on the run, he alters his appearance but not his nature: he carries a tell-tale accouterment, a book. In *3 Henry VI*, Richard, soon to be Duke of Gloucester, caustically jibes at Henry's preoccupation: "Good day, my lord. What, at your book so hard?" (5.6.1).

Richard's attitude finds a counterpart in other plays, too. In *Othello*, Iago asserts the divorce of reading and action when he scoffs at Michael Cassio's "bookish theoric" (1.1.24), the lieutenant's "prattle, without practice." In *Romeo and Juliet*, Mercutio exclaims at the irony of receiving his death's wound from Tybalt, a stylish fencer attentive to the formal rules presented in manuals: "a braggart, a rogue, a villain, that fights by the book of arithmetic!" (3.1.101–2). In *Julius Caesar*, Brutus, who proves politically inept when he appears before the citizens of Rome and militarily inept when he commands troops at Philippi, demonstrates a pronounced bookishness. On the eve of battle, Brutus expresses joy at finding a misplaced book: "Look, Lucius, here's the book I sought for so; / I put it in the pocket of my gown" (4.3.252–53). It is difficult, if not impossible, to imagine Brutus's formidable adversary, Octavius, expressing such a sentiment. In *The Tempest*, Prospero's absorption in books proves to have been his greatest liability, one that others were quick to exploit. Reflecting on his past, Prospero confesses his bookishness, with concomitant inattention to practical matters. Even after his deposition Prospero continued to prize his books. He recounts what the faithful Gonzalo provided: "Knowing I lov'd my books, he furnish'd me / From mine own library with volumes that / I prize above my dukedom" (1.2.166–68). This aspect of the magician's character provides the inspiration for Peter Greenaway's cinematic adaptation, *Prospero's Books;* indeed the books themselves are perhaps the most interesting part of this eccentric production.

Villains express their scorn of the written word not only by what they say but also by what they do. In Shakespeare's *1 Henry VI* when the duke of Gloucester seeks to present a list of accusations, the Bishop of Winchester snatches and tears it. Winchester contemptuously addresses the duke, singling out his reliance on the written word: "Com'st thou with deep premeditated lines, / With written pamphlets studiously devis'd?" (3.1.1–2). The Bishop implies that the written word, because the product of deliberation rather than of spontaneity, may represent some intended treachery. The beleaguered duke has to justify his use of the written word, as though it were generally regarded as untrustworthy and suspect: "Think not, although in writing I preferr'd / The manner of thy vile outrageous crimes, / That therefore I have forg'd, or am not able / Verbatim to rehearse the method of my pen" (ll. 10–13). Overt hostility toward the written word is also expressed through physical action in *2 Henry VI* when petitioners seek to deliver supplications to the lord protector. The queen demands to see the papers, and Suffolk reads one that complains of his misdeeds. Outraged, the queen tears the supplication, saying, "Away, base cullions!" (1.3.40). Marlowe's Tamburlaine, who epitomizes the active life at its extreme, cutting down opposing warriors and innocent virgins with equal relish, caps his career with a bonfire of books: "where's the Turkish Alcaron / And all the heaps of superstitious books / Found in the temples of that Mahomet / Whom I have thought a god? They shall be burnt" (*Part 2*, 5.1.172–75). Tamburlaine orders: "Casane, fling them in the fire" (l. 185), and *They burn the books.*[21]

Scorn of the written word does not prevent the unscrupulous from using it when it suits their purpose. In *Lusty Juventus,* the Vice Hypocrisy counsels the protagonist to adopt books as protective camouflage: "Let your book at your girdle be tied, / Or else in your bosom that he may be spied, / And then it will be said both with youth and age, / Yonder fellow hath an excellent knowledge" (ll. 687–90).[22] The written word can also function more aggressively. In Skelton's *Magnificence,* Counterfeit Countenance forges a letter (ostensibly written by Sad Circumspection) that is given to Magnificence by Fancy: "To you recommendeth Sad Circumspection, / And sendeth you this writing closed under seal" (ll. 311–12).[23] Similarly, in *The Marriage between Wit and Wisdom* Fancy gives Wit a counterfeit letter of introduction: "Here is the letter which she bade me unto you to take" (l. 561).[24] In *Julius Caesar,* Cassius contrives bogus letters in order to influence Brutus:

> Good Cinna, take this paper,
> And look you lay it in the praetor's chair,
> Where Brutus may but find it; and throw this
> In at his window; set this up with wax
> Upon old Brutus' statue.
>
> (1.3.142–46)

The letter thrown in at Brutus's window is later found by Lucius and delivered to its intended reader.[25] This theatrical tradition undoubtedly helped to shape the dramaturgy of *King Lear,* in which Edmund forges a letter designed to serve as the instrument of his brother's destruction (1.2). Significantly, that letter is not found in Shakespeare's chief source for the subplot: the story of the Paphlagonian King in Sidney's *Arcadia.* However, the anonymous play that served as Shakespeare's chief source, *The True Chronicle History of King Leir,* does contain such letters. Gonorill has in her possession letters that falsely represent Leir as slandering Ragan. Gonorill, who directs a messenger to take them to Ragan, means for her sister to become so incensed at the letters that she will order her father's execution: "Instead of carrying the Kings letters to my father, carry thou these letters to my sister, which contayne matter quite contrary to the other: there shal she be given to understand, that my father hath detracted her, given out slaundrous speaches against her; and that hee hath most intollerably abused me . . ." (ll. 1032–37).

The written word proves a convenience to the wicked in sundry ways, some devious, some direct. For example, Aaron in *Titus Andronicus* enlists Tamora in his schemes: "Seest thou this letter? take it up, I pray thee, / And give the King this fatal-plotted scroll" (2.3.46–47); at the denouement Aaron confesses to Lucius, "I wrote the letter that thy father found, / And hid the gold within that letter mentioned" (5.1.106–7). In *King Lear*, Goneril and Regan use letters to collaborate and plot strategy; one appears as a hand prop at 4.2.82. Later, by means of a letter Goneril seeks to arrange the killing of her husband and to foster her hoped-for liaison with Edmund; this letter is read aloud at 4.6.262–70. Edmund, in writing, condemns Lear and Cordelia: "captain; hark. / Take thou this note [*giving a paper*]; go follow them to prison" (5.3.26–27).[26] In *The Duchess of Malfi*, the written word proves deadly when Julia kisses a poisoned book (5.2.276) and perishes.[27]

More subtle but no less lethal is Mortimer's unpunctuated letter in Marlowe's *Edward II*. Written in Latin, the letter is capable of two different interpretations, thus giving Mortimer deniability in the matter of the king's murder:

> "*Edwardum occidere nolite timere, bonum est;*
> Fear not to kill the king, 'tis good he die."
> But read it thus, and that's another sense:
> "*Edwardum occidere nolite, timere bonum est*";
> Kill not the king, 'tis good to fear the worst."
>
> (5.4.8–12)[28]

The deliberate ambiguity here is caused by the absence of a comma following "*nolite*" (in the beneficent sense), or following "*timere*" (in the maleficent sense). In *Julius Caesar* the written word functions as an instrument to rouse the rabble, when the fortunes of the conspirators are precarious, immediately following the assassination. At his oration over Caesar's body, Mark Antony seizes the opportunity to produce a document: "here's a parchment with the seal of Caesar, / I found it in his closet, 'tis his will" (3.2.128–30). Antony does not actually read the will; he gives the gist of it in his own words. But the will proves to be a devastating weapon against the assassins. As Antony correctly predicts of the document, "It will inflame you, it will make you mad" (line 144). Again, in Jonson's *Sejanus* the contents of a long letter from Tiberius to the Roman senate receives a word-for-word presentation, exposing the self-serving corruption of the title character, the emperor's surrogate. During the lengthy recitation, the auditors gradually realize that Tiberius is announcing his estrangement from his erstwhile favorite. Although Sejanus seeks to stop the reading, even claiming that the letter is "forged" (5.634),[29] he cannot frustrate the emperor's purpose.

As these instances suggest, for every person who uses the written word to ponder, heal, judge, or save, there is another who uses it for selfish or pernicious ends; the written word may be manipulated by the unscrupulous, the ambitious, and the vengeful. The very appearance of a hand property involving the written word can be a silent signal to the audience that mischief is in the making; the mere reference to reading may constitute a sign of danger, as when Caesar says of Cassius, "He reads much" (1.2.201). The act of writing actually seems sinister when Mark Antony coolly consigns to death his sister's son: "look, with a spot I damn him" (4.1.6). Depending on circumstance, then, the written word may prove powerfully effective or altogether ineffectual. Properties containing the written or printed word display an extraordinary versatility. To a large extent this was a legacy of the mixed, even antithetical, attitudes that took shape in the Renaissance and intensified in European culture following the invention of the printing press.

Although the shaping forces of sixteenth-century cultural history could induce a sharply defined attitude toward certain kinds of writing, written materials offer an exceptionally wide range of possibilities for deployment as props. They possess this capacity because the dramatic meaning and emotional aura generated by a book, document, or letter onstage are not inherent in the object alone; rather, they reside in the combination of written (or printed) artifact and specific theatrical circumstance. A book in one scene may evoke an ideal of justice while, in another, it may convey to an audience the most flagrant iniquity. The dramatic context makes the difference.

Notes

Introduction

1. Baldassare Castiglione, *The Book of the Courtier,* trans. Charles S. Singleton (Garden City, N.Y.: Doubleday, Anchor Books, 1959), 14.

2. Quoted by Gordon Kipling, *The Triumph of Honour: Burgundian Origins of the Elizabethan Renaissance* (Leiden: Leiden University Press for the Sir Thomas Browne Institute, 1977), 32.

3. Simon Thurley, *The Royal Palaces of Tudor England: Architecture and Court Life, 1460–1547* (New Haven and London: Yale University Press for The Paul Mellon Centre for Studies in British Art, 1993), 141.

4. "The Quene's Majestie's passage through the citie of London to westminster the daye before her coronacion," in *Elizabethan Backgrounds: Historical Documents of the Age of Elizabeth I,* ed. Arthur F. Kinney (Hamden, Conn.: Archon Books, 1975), 39.

5. Raphael Holinshed, *The Description of England* in *The First and Second Volumes of Chronicles* (London, 1587), 197.

6. Julian Roberts and Andrew G. Watson, *John Dee's Library Catalogue* (London: The Bibliographical Society, 1990), 22.

7. The impact of print on sixteenth-century England has been examined by Arthur J. Slavin, "Printing and Publishing in the Tudor Age," in *William Shakespeare: His World, His Work, His Influence,* ed. John F. Andrews, 3 vols. (New York: Charles Scribner's Sons, 1985), 1 : 129–42.

8. Jonas Barish, "'Soft, here follows prose': Shakespeare's Stage Documents," in *The Arts of Performance in Elizabethan and Early Stuart Drama: Essays for G. K. Hunter,* ed. Murray Biggs et al. (Edinburgh: Edinburgh University Press, 1991), 47.

9. The difficulties inherent in estimating the extent of a society's literacy have been examined by R. S. Schofield, "The Measurement of Literacy in Pre-Industrial England," in *Literacy in Traditional Societies,* ed. Jack Goody (Cambridge: Cambridge University Press, 1968), pp. 311–25; and Wyn Ford, "The Problem of Literacy in Early Modern England," *History* 78 (February 1993): 22–37. For a survey of opinion on this vexing topic, see Appendix 1: Elizabethan Literacy.

10. John Marston, *The Malcontent,* ed. George K. Hunter, The Revels Plays (London: Methuen, 1975), 5–6.

11. Ben Jonson, *The New Inn,* ed. Michael Hattaway, The Revels Plays (Manchester: Manchester University Press, 1984), ll. 1–2.

12. John Webster, *The White Devil,* ed. John Russell Brown, The Revels Plays, 2d ed. (1966; reprint, London: Methuen, 1968), 2.

13. In *The Collected Works of Erasmus* (Toronto, Buffalo, and London: University of Toronto Press, 1974–   ), 31 : 161.

14. John Marston, *Parasitaster, or The Fawn,* ed. David A. Blostein, The Revels Plays (Manchester: Manchester University Press; Baltimore: Johns Hopkins University Press, 1978), 68.

15. In *The Complete Works of John Webster,* ed. F. L. Lucas, 4 vols. (London: Chatto & Windus, 1927), 4:42.

Chapter 1. Erasmus, Luther, and the Scriptural Word

1. Quoted by Walter L. Strauss, *The Complete Drawings of Albrecht Dürer,* 6 vols. (New York: Abaris Books, 1974), 4:1993.

2. Ibid., 1994.

3. For a detailed discussion of the print, see Andrée Hayum, "Dürer's Portrait of Erasmus and the *Ars Typographorum,*" *Renaissance Quarterly* 38 (Winter 1985): 650–87.

4. All quotations of Erasmus are from *The Collected Works of Erasmus* (Toronto, Buffalo, and London: University of Toronto Press, 1974–). Abbreviated *CWE* and hereafter cited parenthetically.

5. B. Hall, "Erasmus: Biblical Scholar and Reformer," in *Erasmus,* ed. T. A. Dorey (Albuquerque: University of New Mexico Press, 1970), 84. According to Rudolf Pfeiffer, in *History of Classical Scholarship: from 1300 to 1850* (Oxford: Clarendon Press, 1976), the preface to Valla's *Elegantiae* "contains the highest praise of the Latin language ever written. This language is eternal like Rome itself; indeed, the empire is lost, while the language still lives" (35).

6. Erasmus's edition of Valla's work is known by several titles: *Collatio Novi Testamenti, In Novi Testamenti Interpretationem ex Collatione Graecorum Exemplarium Adnotationes,* or *Adnotationes in Novi Testamenti.* See R. J. Schoeck, *Erasmus of Europe: The Making of a Humanist, 1467–1500* (Edinburgh: Edinburgh University Press, 1990), 156.

7. J. H. W. G. Liebeschuetz, *Continuity and Change in Roman Religion* (Oxford: Clarendon Press, 1979), 249.

8. William V. Harris, in *Ancient Literacy* (Cambridge and London: Harvard University Press, 1989), notes Constantine's important role in fostering the production and distribution of scriptural books: "After the foundation of Constantinople in 324, the emperor wrote to Eusebius to order fifty parchment volumes *(somatia)* of scripture for the churches of the new capital. His action had no kind of classical precedent, and it stemmed from an important cultural change, the rise of a state-sponsored religion which relied heavily on the written word" (285).

9. Erika Rummel, in *Erasmus as a Translator of the Classics* (Toronto, Buffalo, and London: University of Toronto Press, 1985), observes: "He had come to realize that linguistic skills were more than optional gear: they were essential equipment" (12).

10. According to Henk Jan de Jonge, in "Novum Testamentum a Nobis Versum: The Essence of Erasmus' Edition of the New Testament," *Journal of Theological Studies,* n.s., 35 (October 1984): 394–413, "Erasmus chose the word *Instrumentum* in the title because it conveyed better than *Testamentum* the idea of a decision put down in writing: *testamentum* could also mean an agreement without a written record. He knew of the alternative wording from Jerome and Augustine . . ." (396, n. 5).

11. The Latin was actually Erasmus's revised version of the Vulgate. In the second and subsequent editions of *Novum Instrumentum,* Erasmus provided his

entirely new translation of the Vulgate. In all of these editions the Latin and the Greek are set forth in parallel columns.

12. Actually, the Complutensian Bible, named for Complutum (the Latin version of Alcalá), the city in Spain where it was prepared, included what was technically the first printed New Testament in Greek. As Jerry H. Bentley observes, in *Humanists and Holy Writ: New Testament Scholarship in the Renaissance* (Princeton: Princeton University Press, 1983), "The Complutensian editors were unable to obtain a license to bind and distribute their work until 1520; by then Erasmus was already at work on his third edition of the Greek New Testament. But the Complutensian New Testament emerged from the press almost two years before printing began on Erasmus' first edition" (70).

13. Quoted by Rummel, *Erasmus as a Translator of the Classics*, 91. The words appear in *Contra Morosos*, an essay that appeared in the second edition of *Novum Instrumentum* (1519), which bore the traditional title *Novum Testamentum*.

14. Erasmus, *Preparation to Deathe, A boke as devout as eloquent, compiled by Erasmus Roterodame* (London, 1538), sig. A8.

15. Reproduced by Lacey Baldwin Smith, *The Horizon Book of the Elizabethan World* (New York: American Heritage, 1967), 44–45.

16. *Luther's Works,* ed. Jaroslav Pelikan and Helmut T. Lehmann, 55 vols. (St. Louis: Concordia Publishing House; Philadelphia: Fortress Press, 1955–86). Abbreviated *LW* and hereafter cited parenthetically.

17. Steven Ozment, *The Age of Reform, 1250–1550: An Intellectual and Religious History of Late Medieval and Reformation Europe* (New Haven and London: Yale University Press, 1980), 230.

18. See Heiko A. Oberman, *Luther: Man between God and the Devil,* trans. Eileen Walliser-Schwarzbart (New Haven and London: Yale University Press, 1989), 42.

19. Johann Froben, in *The Reformation: A Narrative History Related by Contemporary Observers and Participants,* ed. and trans. Hans J. Hillerbrand (New York and Evanston: Harper & Row, 1964), 76.

20. In his *Paraclesis* Erasmus wrote: "I would that even the lowliest women read the Gospels and the Pauline Epistles. And I would that they were translated into all languages so that they could be read and understood not only by Scots and Irish but also by Turks and Saracens." See *Christian Humanism and the Reformation: Selected Writings of Erasmus,* ed. John C. Olin, 3d ed. (New York: Fordham University Press, 1987), 101.

21. Werner Schwarz, *Principles and Problems of Biblical Translation: Some Reformation Controversies and Their Background* (Cambridge: Cambridge University Press, 1955), 186.

22. R. W. Scribner, in *For the Sake of Simple Folk: Popular Propaganda for the German Reformation* (Cambridge: Cambridge University Press, 1981), sees in this print a reference to Erasmus's 1516 edition of the New Testament (105).

23. Schwarz, *Principles and Problems,* 48.

24. W. D. J. Cargill Thompson, "The Problems of Luther's 'Tower Experience' and Its Place in His Intellectual Development," in *Studies in the Reformation: Luther to Hooker,* ed. C. W. Dugmore (London: Athlone Press, 1980), 62.

25. Richard Hooker, *Of the Laws of Ecclesiastical Polity,* in The Folger Library Edition of *The Works of Richard Hooker,* gen. ed. W. Speed Hill, 5 vols. (Cambridge and London: Harvard University Press, Belknap Press, 1977–), 1:122.

26. Ibid., 2:92.

27. John Favour, *Antiquitie Triumphing over Noveltie* (London, 1619), 300.

28. Ibid., 277.
29. John Calvin, *Institutes of the Christian Religion,* ed. John T. McNeill, trans. Ford Lewis Battles, The Library of Christian Classics 20, 2 vols. (Philadelphia: Westminster Press, 1960), 1:75.
30. Favour, *Antiquitie triumphing over Noveltie,* 165.
31. *The Sermons of John Donne,* ed. George R. Potter and Evelyn M. Simpson, 10 vols. (Berkeley and Los Angeles: University of California Press, 1953–62), 5:216.
32. Ibid., 216–17.
33. Calvin, *Institutes of the Christian Religion,* 1:75.
34. For example, a painting by Caravaggio depicts a seated St. Matthew writing his gospel while an angel guides his right hand; reproduced by John Pope-Hennessy, *Raphael: The Wrightsman Lectures* (New York: New York University Press, 1970), 229, fig. 215. A drawing by Guercino depicts St. Matthew writing in his book, one side of which is held by an angel; as he writes Matthew looks directly into the angel's face. Reproduced by Denis Mahon and Nicholas Turner, *The Drawings of Guercino in the Collection of Her Majesty the Queen at Windsor Castle* (Cambridge: Cambridge University Press, 1989), fig. 73.
35. Calvin, *Institutes of the Christian Religion,* 1:71.
36. Ibid., n. 5.
37. Gabriel Josipovici, *The World and the Book: A Study of Modern Fiction,* 2d ed. (London: Macmillan, 1979), 48.
38. Michel Foucault, *The Order of Things: An Archaeology of the Human Sciences* (New York: Pantheon Books, 1970), 40.
39. Ibid., 40–41.
40. "Of Experience," in *The Complete Essays of Montaigne,* trans. Donald M. Frame (1958; reprint, Stanford: Stanford University Press, 1968), 818.
41. In *Luther and Erasmus: Free Will and Salvation,* trans. and ed. E. Gordon Rupp and A. N. Marlow, The Library of Christian Classics 17 (Philadelphia: Westminster Press, 1969), 85–86.
42. "Various Outcomes of the Same Plan," in *The Complete Essays of Montaigne,* 93.
43. Norman O. Brown, *Love's Body* (New York: Random House, 1966), 199.

Chapter 2. Written Words and Printed Books

1. A generously illustrated survey of early printed books, including examples by Gutenberg, Fust, and Schöffer, is included in a work by Hans Adolf Halbey et al., *Schrift, Druck, Buch im Gutenberg-Museum: Buchkultur in Mainz* (Mainz am Rhein: Verlag Philipp von Zabern, 1985). See also Eva-Maria Hanebutt-Benz, *Die Kunst des Lesens: Lesemöbel und Leseverhalten vom Mittelalter bis zur Gegenwart,* 2d ed. (Frankfurt am Main: Museum für Kunsthandwerk, 1989).
2. *The Collected Works of Erasmus* (Toronto, Buffalo, and London: University of Toronto Press, 1974–). Abbreviated *CWE* and hereafter cited parenthetically.
3. David R. Carlson makes this point in *English Humanist Books: Writers and Patrons, Manuscript and Print, 1475–1525* (Toronto, Buffalo, and London: University of Toronto Press, 1993), 119.
4. Quoted by Lucien Febvre and Henri-Jean Martin, *The Coming of the Book: The Impact of Printing, 1450–1800,* trans. David Gerard, ed. Geoffrey Nowell-Smith and David Wootton (London: Verso, 1984), 172.
5. Heiko A. Oberman, *Luther: Man between God and the Devil,* trans. Eileen

Walliser-Schwarzbart (New Haven and London: Yale University Press, 1989), 98. R. J. Schoeck, in *Erasmus of Europe: The Making of a Humanist, 1467–1500* (Edinburgh: Edinburgh University Press, 1990), notes the importance of Deventer for the development of printing: "Deventer in the 1480s and 1490s was one of the foremost printing centres in Europe, and certainly the most important in the Low Countries; its decline began only after about 1515, when the lead in printing in the Low Countries was taken by Antwerp. During the 1490s . . . more classical texts came from the presses of Deventer than from Paris" (47).

6. R. R. Post, *The Modern Devotion: Confrontation with Reformation and Humanism,* Studies in Medieval and Reformation Thought 3 (Leiden: E. J. Brill, 1968), 657.

7. R. J. Schoeck, *Erasmus Grandescens: The Growth of a Humanist's Mind and Spirituality,* Bibliotheca Humanistica & Reformatorica 43 (Nieuwkoop: De Graaf Publishers, 1988), 70.

8. Post, *The Modern Devotion,* 628–29.

9. Martin Lowry, *The World of Aldus Manutius: Business and Scholarship in Renaissance Venice* (Ithaca: Cornell University Press, 1979), 94.

10. *The "Adages" of Erasmus: A Study with Translations,* ed. Margaret Mann Phillips (Cambridge: Cambridge University Press, 1964), 185.

11. Were the theses, as originally posted, in the form of script or print? Heiko A. Oberman, in *Luther: Man between God and the Devil,* claims: "Luther affixed a handwritten 'list' to the church door and only then sent a second version of the Latin theses to the printer, first in Wittenberg and then in Nuremberg, Leipzig, and Basel" (191).

12. Friedrich Myconius, *Historia Reformationis,* in *The Reformation: A Narrative History Related by Contemporary Observers and Participants,* ed. and trans. Hans J. Hillerbrand (New York and Evanston: Harper & Row, 1964), 47.

13. Marc Lienhard, "Luther and Europe," in *The Reformation,* ed. Pierre Chaunu (Gloucester, England: Alan Sutton, 1989), 95.

14. Scott H. Hendrix, "Luther's Communities," in *Leaders of the Reformation,* ed. Richard L. DeMolen (Selinsgrove, Penn.: Susquehanna University Press; London and Toronto: Associated University Presses, 1984), 51. Richard Crofts, in "Books, Reform and the Reformation," *Archiv für Reformationsgeschichte* 71 (1980): 21–35, estimates that more than half the religious books published in Germany during the years 1518–20 were written by Luther.

15. Lewis W. Spitz, *The Protestant Reformation, 1517–1559* (New York: Harper & Row, 1985), 89.

16. Steven Ozment, *The Age of Reform, 1250–1550: An Intellectual and Religious History of Late Medieval and Reformation Europe* (New Haven and London: Yale University Press, 1980), 192.

17. Ibid., 199.

18. Lowry, *The World of Aldus Manutius,* 12.

19. *Panegyricus ad Illustrissimum Principem Philippum, Archiducem Austriae* was first printed in Antwerp in 1504.

20. *Luther's Works,* ed. Jaroslav Pelikan and Helmut T. Lehmann, 55 vols. (St. Louis: Concordia Publishing House; Philadelphia: Fortress Press, 1955–86). Abbreviated *LW* and hereafter cited parenthetically.

21. Spitz, *The Protestant Reformation,* 200.

22. John Foxe, *The First Volume of the Ecclesiasticall History, contaynyng the Actes & Monumentes of thinges passed in every kinges time, in this Realme, especially in the Churche of England principally to be noted* (London, 1576), 682.

23. François Furet and Jacques Ozouf, *Reading and Writing: Literacy in France from Calvin to Jules Ferry* (Cambridge: Cambridge University Press, 1982), 59.

24. John Gough Nichols, ed., *Narratives of the Days of the Reformation, Chiefly from the Manuscripts of John Foxe,* Camden Society, ser. 1, no. 77 (1859; reprint, New York and London: Johnson Reprint Corp., 1968), 349–50.

25. Elizabeth L. Eisenstein, *The Printing Press as an Agent of Change: Communications and Cultural Transformations in Early-Modern Europe,* 2 vols. in 1 (1979; reprint, Cambridge: Cambridge University Press, 1980), 319.

26. For treatments of this conflict, see Richard H. Popkin, *The History of Scepticism from Erasmus to Spinoza* (Berkeley, Los Angeles, and London: University of California Press, 1979), chap. 1; Victoria Kahn, *Rhetoric, Prudence, and Skepticism in the Renaissance* (Ithaca and London: Cornell University Press, 1985), chap. 4.

27. J. Kelley Sowards, in *Desiderius Erasmus* (Boston: Twayne Publishers, 1975), observes, "The Greek word *enchiridion* means 'something in the hand'—for such a bookish man as Erasmus, a manual or guidebook surely. But the rest of the title, *militis Christiani,* 'of a Christian soldier,' suggests the more militant reading 'dagger' and in at least one later reference Erasmus uses the word *gladiolus,* 'dagger,' for it" (58). It is interesting that Maarten van Dorp applied the word "dagger" to Erasmus's editorial activity: "I hear you have purged St Jerome's letters of the errors in which they abounded hitherto, killed off the spurious pieces with your critical dagger, and thrown light upon the dark places" (*CWE* 3:20).

28. According to Martin Brecht, in *Martin Luther: Shaping and Defining the Reformation, 1521–1532,* trans. James L. Schaaf (Minneapolis: Fortress Press, 1990), Philip Melanchthon, Luther's close friend and confidant, "regarded the *Hyperaspistes* as extremely sharp. As he had feared, Luther's work had caused the conflict to degenerate into one involving the ugliest accusations" (237).

29. Foxe, *The First Volume of the Ecclesiastical History,* 445.

30. S. H. Steinberg, *Five Hundred Years of Printing,* 3d ed., rev. by James Moran (Harmondsworth, England, and Baltimore: Penguin Books, 1974), 261.

31. *Areopagitica,* in *John Milton: Complete Poems and Major Prose,* ed. Merritt Y. Hughes (New York: Odyssey Press, 1957), 720.

32. Rudolf Hirsch, *Printing, Selling and Reading, 1450–1550* (Wiesbaden: Otto Harrassowitz, 1967), 15, n. 9.

33. Ibid., 105.

34. Febvre and Martin, *The Coming of the Book,* 248.

35. Ibid., 262.

36. Miriam Usher Chrisman, *Lay Culture, Learned Culture: Books and Social Change in Strasbourg, 1480–1599* (New Haven and London: Yale University Press, 1982), 318–19, n. 7.

37. Arthur J. Slavin, "Printing and Publishing in the Tudor Age," in *William Shakespeare: His World, His Work, His Influence,* ed. John F. Andrews, 3 vols. (New York: Charles Scribner's Sons, 1985), 1:141.

38. Ozment, *The Age of Reform, 1250–1550,* 199.

39. Curt F. Bühler, *The Fifteenth-Century Book: the Scribes, the Printers, the Decorators* (Philadelphia: University of Pennsylvania Press, 1960), 42. Bühler here refers to the 42-line Bible.

40. C. S. L. Davies, *Peace, Print and Protestantism, 1450–1558,* The Paladin History of England (London: Hart-Davis, MacGibbon, 1976), 133.

41. *The "Adages" of Erasmus,* 182.
42. Ibid.
43. Ibid., 184.
44. Thomas M. Greene, "Erasmus's 'Festina lente': Vulnerabilities of the Humanist Text," in *Mimesis: From Mirror to Method, Augustine to Descartes,* ed. John D. Lyons and Stephen G. Nichols, Jr. (Hanover, N.H. and London: University Press of New England [for Dartmouth College], 1982), 139.
45. Pierre de la Primaudaye, *The French Academie,* trans. T[homas] B[owes], 2d ed. (London, 1589), 566–67.
46. "Of Vanity," in *The Complete Essays of Montaigne,* trans. Donald M. Frame (1958; reprint, Stanford: Stanford University Press, 1968), 721–22.
47. Godfrey Goodman, *The Fall of Man, or the Corruption of Nature, Proved by the light of our naturall Reason* (London, 1616), 166.
48. Margaret Mann Phillips, "Erasmus and the Art of Writing," in *Scrinium Erasmianum,* ed. J. Coppens, 2 vols. (Leiden: E. J. Brill, 1969), 1:349.
49. "Of the Education of Children," in *The Complete Essays of Montaigne,* 107.
50. Pierre Charron, *Of Wisdome,* trans. Samson Lennard (London, [1612?]), 148–49.
51. "Of Experience," in *The Complete Essays of Montaigne,* 828.
52. Charron, *Of Wisdome,* 134.
53. Henry Peacham, *The Compleat Gentleman* (London, 1622), 54.
54. Robert Burton, *The Anatomy of Melancholy* (Oxford, 1621), 65.
55. Sir Thomas Browne, *"Religio Medici" and Other Works,* ed. L. C. Martin (Oxford: Clarendon Press, 1964), 59.
56. Girolamo Cardano, *Cardanus comforte,* trans. Thomas Bedingfeld (London, 1573), sig. Cii^v.
57. Francis Bacon, *The Twoo Bookes of the Proficience and Advancement of Learning* (London, 1605), fol. 18^v.
58. *The Sermons of John Donne,* ed. George R. Potter and Evelyn Simpson, 10 vols. (Berkeley and Los Angeles: University of California Press, 1953–62), 3:208.
59. *The "Adages" of Erasmus,* 182.
60. Jane O. Newman, "The Word Made Print: Luther's 1522 *New Testament* in an Age of Mechanical Reproduction," *Representations* no. 11 (Summer 1985): 109.
61. John Favour, *Antiquitie Triumphing over Noveltie* (London, 1619), 229.
62. P. S. Allen, ed. (with H. M. Allen and H. W. Garrod), *Opus Epistolarum Des. Erasmi Roterodami,* 12 vols. (Oxford: Clarendon Press, 1906–58), 5:172.
63. Goodman, *The Fall of Man,* [446].
64. Erasmus, *Apophthegmes, that is to saie, prompte, quicke, wittie and sentencious saiynges,* trans. Nicholas Udall (London, 1542), fol. 266.
65. La Primaudaye, *The French Academie,* 76.
66. "Of Experience," in *The Complete Essays of Montaigne,* 851.
67. Roger Ascham, *The Schoolmaster,* ed. Lawrence V. Ryan (Ithaca: Cornell University Press [for The Folger Shakespeare Library], 1967), 55.
68. Ibid., 50.
69. Edward Hall, *The Union of the two noble and illustre famelies of Lancastre & Yorke* (London, 1548), sig. Aii.
70. Owen Felltham, *Resolves, A Duple Century,* [3d ed.] (London, 1628–29), 153.
71. *Areopagitica,* in *John Milton: Complete Poems and Major Prose,* 720.

72. Bacon, *The Twoo Bookes of the Proficience and Advancement of Learning,* fol. 32ᵛ.
73. Ibid., fol. 44ᵛ.
74. Pierre Boaistuau, *Theatrum Mundi, The Theator or rule of the world,* trans. John Alday (London, [1566?]), sigs. Sᵛ -Sij.
75. George Hakewill, *An Apologie of the Power and Providence of God in the Government of the World* (Oxford, 1627), 257.
76. Foxe, *The First Volume of the Ecclesiasticall History,* 682.
77. Ibid.
78. *The Sermons of John Donne,* 5:38.
79. Terence Cave, in *The Cornucopian Text: Problems of Writing in the French Renaissance* (Oxford: Clarendon Press, 1979), comments on the inherent conflict involved in making public a private communication, especially for Erasmus: "The movement of his writing towards *autrui,* whether the addressees of his letters or his polemical adversaries, is an act of self-definition which carries a deep ambiguity. For his whole value-system, based as it is on interiority, on *pectus,* on the plenitude of self, is compromised by the public, exterior nature of writing" (47).
80. Lisa Jardine explores his purposeful self-definition, in *Erasmus, Man of Letters: The Construction of Charisma in Print* (Princeton: Princeton University Press, 1993), chap. 1.
81. On this last point, see W. David Kay, "The Shaping of Ben Jonson's Career: A Reexamination of Facts and Problems," *Modern Philology* 67 (February 1970): 224–37.
82. Richard C. Newton, "Jonson and the (Re-)Invention of the Book," in *Classic and Cavalier: Essays on Jonson and the Sons of Ben,* ed. Claude J. Summers and Ted-Larry Pebworth (Pittsburgh: University of Pittsburgh Press, 1982), 36. A collection of articles dealing with Jonson's use of the printed word has been edited by Jennifer Brady and W. H. Herendeen: *Ben Jonson's 1616 Folio* (Newark: University of Delaware Press; London and Toronto: Associated University Presses, 1991).
83. Thomas Heywood, *The English Traveller, as it hath beene publikely acted at the Cock-pit in Drury-Lane* (London, 1633), sig. A3.
84. David Riggs, *Ben Jonson, A Life* (Cambridge and London: Harvard University Press, 1989), 276. Riggs continues: "Heminge's and Condell's prefatory letter 'To the Great Variety of Readers' echoes Jonson's Induction to *Bartholomew Fair,* his preface to *The Alchemist,* his epigram 'To My Bookseller,' and his *Discoveries.* The prefatory poems by Jonson, Hugh Holland, James Mabbe, and Leonard Digges transform Shakespeare into a specifically literary figure whose works have achieved the status of modern classics; the closest analogue to these tributes are the poems prefixed to Jonson's 1616 folio."
85. Letter to Father Dionigi da Borgo San Sepolcro, in *Letters from Petrarch,* trans. Morris Bishop (Bloomington and London: Indiana University Press, 1966), 50.
86. See Paul Saenger, "Silent Reading: Its Impact on Late Medieval Script and Society," *Viator* 13 (1982), 367–414; and Saenger, "Books of Hours and the Reading Habits of the Later Middle Ages," in *The Culture of Print: Power and the Uses of Print in Early Modern Europe,* ed. Roger Chartier, trans. Lydia G. Cochrane (Cambridge, England: Polity Press, 1989), 141–73.
87. *St. Augustine's Confessions,* trans. William Watts, Loeb Classical Library, 2 vols. (New York: G. P. Putnam's Sons, 1919), 2:465.
88. Ibid.

89. In *Machiavelli: The Chief Works and Others,* trans. Allan Gilbert, 3 vols. (1958; reprint, Durham and London: Duke University Press, 1989), 2:929.

90. "Of Three Kinds of Association," in *The Complete Essays of Montaigne,* 629.

91. Hugo Friedrich would distinguish Montaigne's bookishness from that of other Renaissance figures: "this similarity with the humanists is only a superficial one. Montaigne's occupation with books lacks the passionate, cultish, reverent elements. He does not let them dominate him" (*Montaigne,* trans. Dawn Eng, ed. Philippe Desan, 2d rev. ed. [1967; reprint, Berkeley, Los Angeles, and Oxford: University of California Press, 1991], 42.) My own feeling is that Montaigne's attitude toward his books is one that both Petrarch and Machiavelli would instinctively understand and approve.

Chapter 3. Ideology, Printing Press, and Stage

1. John Foxe, *The Second Volume of the Ecclesiasticall History, conteyning the Actes & Monumentes of Martyrs* (London, 1576), 817. The first and second volumes of this third edition are paged continuously.

2. For an account of how Protestants responded to Erasmus, see Bruce Mansfield, "Protestantism: Erasmus and the Patterns of Reformation," in *Phoenix of His Age: Interpretations of Erasmus, c 1550–1750* (Toronto, Buffalo, and London: University of Toronto Press, 1979), 65–114.

3. For a bibliographic account of Erasmus's *Paraphrases* in English translation, see E. J. Devereux, *Renaissance English Translations of Erasmus: A Bibliography to 1700* (Toronto, Buffalo, and London: University of Toronto Press, 1983), 146–75.

4. C. R. Thompson, "Erasmus and Tudor England," *Actes du Congrès Erasme, Rotterdam 27–29 octobre 1969* (Amsterdam and London: North-Holland Publishing Company, 1971), 54.

5. Nicholas Udall, *The first tome or volume of the Paraphrase of Erasmus upon the newe testamente* (London, 1548), fol. x^v .

6. Raphael Holinshed, *The Third Volume of Chronicles* (London, 1587), 1425.

7. Alan Sinfield, *Literature in Protestant England, 1560–1660* (London and Canberra: Croom Helm; Totowa, N.J.: Barnes & Noble, 1983), 21. Sinfield restates this argument in *Faultlines: Cultural Materialism and the Politics of Dissident Reading* (Berkeley, Los Angeles, and London: University of California Press, 1992), 186ff.

8. Anthony Grafton and Lisa Jardine, *From Humanism to the Humanities: Education and the Liberal Arts in Fifteenth- and Sixteenth-Century Europe* (London: Duckworth, 1986), 141.

9. John Stow, *The Annales of England, Faithfully collected out of the most autenticall Authors, Records, and other Monuments of Antiquitie* (London, 1600), 1309.

10. James Kelsey McConica, *English Humanists and Reformation Politics under Henry VIII and Edward VI* (Oxford: Clarendon Press, 1965), 89.

11. *The Life of the Dutches of Suffolke, As it hath beene divers and sundry times acted, with good applause* (London, 1631), sig. F3^{r-v}.

12. William Baldwin, *The Canticles or Balades of Salomon, phraselyke declared in Englysh Metres* (London, 1549), sig. Aii^v.

13. Sir Thomas Elyot, *The boke named the Governour* (London, 1531), fol. 42.

14. *The laboryouse Journey & serche of Johan Leylande, for Englandes Anti-*

quitees . . . with declaracyons enlarged: by Johan Bale (London, 1549), sig. Diii^v-Diiii.

15. Foxe, *The Second Volume of the Ecclesiasticall History*, 816.
16. Foxe, *The First Volume of the Ecclesiasticall History*, 682.
17. Foxe, *The Second Volume of the Ecclesiasticall History*, 1300.
18. *If You Know Not Me You Know Nobody, Part 1*, ed. Madeleine Doran, Malone Society Reprints (Oxford: Oxford University Press, 1935).
19. Alexander Leggatt, *Jacobean Public Theatre* (London and New York: Routledge, 1992), 169–70.
20. Holinshed, *The Third Volume of Chronicles*, 632. Hereafter cited parenthetically.
21. *"Doctor Faustus," A- and B-Texts (1604, 1616)*, ed. David Bevington and Eric Rasmussen, The Revels Plays (Manchester and New York: Manchester University Press, 1993).
22. David Daniell, in *William Tyndale: A Biography* (New Haven and London: Yale University Press, 1994), observes that "Tunstall had lent Erasmus a Greek New Testament manuscript, had consulted Greek codices for him in cases of doubt, and suggested a number of emendations" (84).
23. For this argumentation, Shakespeare substitutes a more general skepticism on Cade's part: "Will you needs be hang'd with your pardons about your necks?" (4.8.22–23).
24. In "The Practical Impact of Writing," in *A History of Private Life*, vol. 3, *Passions of the Renaissance*, ed. Roger Chartier, trans. Arthur Goldhammer (Cambridge and London: Harvard University Press, Belknap Press, 1989), Roger Chartier comments: "In writing about a rebellion that occurred a century and a half earlier, Shakespeare was able to incorporate into his play the fundamental tension between two cultures: one increasingly based on recourse to the written word in both the public and the private spheres; the other based on nostalgic and utopian esteem for a society without writing, governed by words that everyone could hear and signs that everyone could understand" (123).
25. Michael Keefer, ed., *Christopher Marlowe's "Doctor Faustus": A 1604–Version Edition* (Peterborough, Ontario: Broadview Press, 1991), xxxvii.
26. *"Doctor Faustus": A- and B-Texts*, 4.
27. Johannes Trithemius, quoted by Frank Baron, *Doctor Faustus: From History to Legend*, Humanistische Bibliothek, Abhandlungen 27 (Munich: Wilhelm Fink Verlag, 1978), 29.
28. See Lewis Wager, *The Life and Repentaunce of Marie Magdalene*, ed. Frederic Ives Carpenter, rev. ed. (Chicago: University of Chicago Press, 1904), lines 1027–30.
29. John Skelton, *Magnificence*, ed. Paula Neuss, The Revels Plays (Manchester: Manchester University Press; Baltimore: Johns Hopkins University Press, 1980).
30. *Lusty Juventus*, in *Four Tudor Interludes*, ed. J. A. B. Somerset (London: Athlone Press, 1974).
31. *"Doctor Faustus," A-and B-Texts*. Unless otherwise indicated, all quotations are from the A-text.
32. *The English Faust Book: A Critical Edition Based on the Text of 1592*, ed. John Henry Jones (Cambridge: Cambridge University Press, 1994), 92–93.
33. Ibid., 93.
34. See Martha Tuck Rozett, *The Doctrine of Election and the Emergence of Elizabethan Tragedy* (Princeton: Princeton University Press, 1984), chap. 7.

35. Eric Rasmussen, *A Textual Companion to "Doctor Faustus,"* The Revels Plays Companion Library (Manchester and New York: Manchester University Press, 1993), 85.

36. In *A Textual Companion to "Doctor Faustus,"* Rasmussen reports: "I discovered evidence that the 1604 A1 quarto (the A-text) may, in fact, have been set in type directly from the original authorial manuscript, and that the 1616 quarto (the B-text) almost certainly represents a theatrical version of the play after it had been extensively revised by later hands" (x).

37. Keefer, *Christopher Marlowe's "Doctor Faustus",* xxxvii.

38. *The English Faust Book,* 98.

39. *If You Know Not Me You Know Nobody,* xxxviii.

40. Paul Whitfield White, *Theatre and Reformation: Protestantism, Patronage, and Playing in Tudor England* (Cambridge: Cambridge University Press, 1993), 168.

41. Ibid., 169.

42. For discussions of the playwrights' adventurousness in making a critique of contemporary matters and for discussions of the constraints inhibiting dramatists, see Annabel Patterson, *Censorship and Interpretation: The Conditions of Writing and Reading in Early Modern England* (Madison: University of Wisconsin Press, 1984); Janet Clare, *"Art made tongue-tied by authority": Elizabethan and Jacobean Dramatic Censorship,* The Revels Plays Companion Library (Manchester and New York: Manchester University Press, 1990); and Richard Dutton, *Mastering the Revels: The Regulation and Censorship of English Renaissance Drama* (Iowa City: University of Iowa Press, 1991).

43. Thomas Wilson, *The Arte of Rhetorique, for the use of all suche as are studious of Eloquence* (London, 1553), fol. 118v. For a discussion of gesture in the Renaissance, see Anna Bryson, "The Rhetoric of Status: Gesture, Demeanour and the Image of the Gentleman in Sixteenth-and Sevententh-Century England," in *Renaissance Bodies: The Human Figure in English Culture, c. 1540–1660,* ed. Lucy Gent and Nigel Llewellyn (London: Reaktion Books, 1990), 136–53.

Chapter 4. Writing and Print as Figurative Language

1. *"Doctor Faustus," A- and B-Texts (1604, 1616),* ed. David Bevington and Eric Rasmussen, The Revels Plays (Manchester and New York: Manchester University Press, 1993). All quotations are from the A-text unless otherwise noted.

2. See Manfred Pfister, "Reading the Body: the Corporeality of Shakespeare's Text," in *Reading Plays: Interpretation and Reception,* ed. Hanna Scolnicov and Peter Holland (Cambridge: Cambridge University Press, 1991), 110–22; William W. E. Slights, "Bodies of Text and Textualized Bodies in *Sejanus* and *Coriolanus,*" *Medieval & Renaissance Drama in England* 5 (1991): 181–93.

3. An "abstract" denotes "a summary or epitome of a statement or document"; "brief" usually refers to some sort of writing, often royal or religious, or to a letter of written summary; and "volume" commonly signifies a roll or scroll or book containing words in script or print (*OED*).

4. *Soliman and Perseda,* in *The Works of Thomas Kyd,* ed. Frederick S. Boas (Oxford: Clarendon Press, 1901).

5. The word "character" derives from Greek and means to mark, engrave, impress, or stamp; it need not refer specifically to marking the letters of the alphabet. "Print" can designate any kind of symbolic likeness impressed on a plastic material.

6. *The Honest Whore, Part 2*, in *The Dramatic Works of Thomas Dekker*, ed. Fredson Bowers, 4 vols. (Cambridge: Cambridge University Press, 1953–61), vol. 2.

7. Thomas Lodge, *The Wounds of Civil War*, ed. Joseph W. Houppert, Regents Renaissance Drama Series (Lincoln: University of Nebraska Press, 1969).

8. Christopher Marlowe, *Tamburlaine the Great*, ed. J. S. Cunningham, The Revels Plays (Manchester: Manchester University Press; Baltimore: Johns Hopkins University Press, 1981).

9. Christopher Marlowe, *Edward the Second*, ed. Charles R. Forker, The Revels Plays (Manchester and New York: Manchester University Press, 1994).

10. Richard Brome, *A Jovial Crew*, ed. Ann Haaker, Regents Renaissance Drama Series (Lincoln: University of Nebraska Press, 1968).

11. George Chapman, *All Fools*, ed. Frank Manley, Regents Renaissance Drama Series (Lincoln: University of Nebraska Press, 1968).

12. *The Tragedie of Philip Chabot, Admirall of France*, in *The Plays of George Chapman: The Tragedies with "Sir Gyles Goosecappe,"* gen. ed. Allan Holaday, assisted by G. Blakemore Evans and Thomas L. Berger (Cambridge: D. S. Brewer, 1987).

13. *The Virgin Martyr*, in *The Dramatic Works of Thomas Dekker*, vol. 3.

14. There is a classical precedent for this notion in Lucian's *Hermotimus*. Lucian tells the story of Momus, who was asked to settle a quarrel over who was the best artist—Athena, Poseidon, or Hephaestus. Momus inspected the man created by Hephaestus and made this criticism: "he had not made windows in his chest which could be opened to let everyone see his desires and thoughts and if he were lying or telling the truth." See *Lucian*, trans. A. M. Harmon, K. Kilburn, and M. D. Macleod, Loeb Classical Library, 8 vols. (London: William Heinemann; Cambridge: Harvard University Press, 1913–67), 6:299.

15. Ben Jonson, *Catiline*, ed. W. F. Bolton and Jane F. Gardner, Regents Renaissance Drama Series (Lincoln: University of Nebraska Press, 1973).

16. George Chapman, *The Conspiracy and Tragedy of Charles Duke of Byron*, ed. John Margeson, The Revels Plays (Manchester and New York: Manchester University Press, 1988).

17. *Appius and Virginia*, in *The Complete Works of John Webster*, ed. F. L. Lucas, 4 vols. (London: Chatto & Windus, 1927), vol. 3.

18. Ben Jonson, *The New Inn*, ed. Michael Hattaway, The Revels Plays (Manchester: Manchester University Press, 1984).

19. *The Noble Spanish Soldier*, in *The Dramatic Works of Thomas Dekker*, vol. 4.

20. R. A., *The Valiant Welshman*, ed. Valentin Kreb (Erlangen and Leipzig: A. Deichert [Georg Böhme], 1902).

21. *Westward Ho*, in *The Dramatic Works of Thomas Dekker*, vol. 2.

22. Erasmus, *Apophthegmes*, trans. Nicholas Udall (London, 1542), sig. m.

23. Cyril Tourneur, *The Revenger's Tragedy*, ed. R. A. Foakes, The Revels Plays (1966; reprint, London: Methuen, 1975).

24. Aristotle, *Poetics*, trans. Gerald F. Else (Ann Arbor: University of Michigan Press, 1967), 57. Aristotle's sentence continues, explaining that metaphor works "either (a) from genus to species, or (b) from species to genus, or (c) from species to species, or (d) by proportion."

25. For an overview of metaphor in antiquity and in the Renaissance, see S. K. Heninger, Jr., "'Metaphor' and Sidney's *Defence of Poesie*," *John Donne Journal* 1 (1982): 117–49.

26. George Puttenham, *The Arte of English Poesie,* ed. Gladys Doidge Willcock and Alice Walker (Cambridge: Cambridge University Press, 1936), 154.
27. *De Copia,* in *The Collected Works of Erasmus* (Toronto, Buffalo, and London: University of Toronto Press, 1974–), 24:333.
28. Terence Hawkes, *Metaphor,* The Critical Idiom 25 (London: Methuen, 1972), 1.
29. Roland Barthes, *Arcimboldo,* trans. John Shepley (Milan and Paris: Franco Maria Ricci, 1980), 36.
30. "Of Evil Means employed to a Good End," in *The Complete Essays of Montaigne,* trans. Donald M. Frame (1958; reprint Stanford: Stanford University Press, 1968), 516.
31. Barthes, *Arcimboldo,* 40.
32. Plato, *Timaeus and Critias,* trans. Desmond Lee (1965; reprinted with revisions, Harmondsworth, England: Penguin Books, 1977), 41.
33. Godfrey Goodman, *The Creatures Praysing God: or, The Religion of dumbe Creatures* (London, 1622), 3.
34. *Paracelsus: Selected Writings,* ed. Jolande Jacobi, trans. Norbert Guterman, Bollingen Series 28 (New York: Pantheon, 1951), 196.
35. *Novum Organum,* in *The Works of Francis Bacon,* ed. James Spedding, Robert Leslie Ellis, and Douglas Denon Heath, 7 vols. (London: Longman, 1858), 4:61.
36. Sir Thomas Browne, *"Religio Medici" and Other Works,* ed. L. C. Martin (Oxford: Clarendon Press, 1964), 57.
37. *"A Warning for Fair Women": A Critical Edition,* ed. Charles Dale Cannon (The Hague and Paris: Mouton, 1975).
38. *Paracelsus: Selected Writings,* 198.
39. Ben Jonson, *Every Man in His Humour,* ed. Gabriele Bernhard Jackson (New Haven and London: Yale University Press, 1969). This and other such formulations are discussed by Carroll Camden in his important article, "The Mind's Construction in the Face," *Philological Quarterly* 20 (July 1941): 400–12.
40. Louis LeRoy, *Of the Interchangeable Course, or Variety of Things in the Whole World,* trans. Robert Ashley (London, 1594), fol. 18.
41. Leon Battista Alberti, *On the Art of Building in Ten Books,* trans. Joseph Rykwert, Neil Leach, and Robert Tavernor (Cambridge and London: MIT Press, 1988), 256.
42. Jane Donawerth, *Shakespeare and the Sixteenth-Century Study of Language* (Urbana and Chicago: University of Illinois Press, 1984), 25.
43. Cunningham, ed. *Tamburlaine the Great,* note to 3.5.80 of *Part 2.*
44. Frances A. Yates, *The Occult Philosophy in the Elizabethan Age* (London, Boston, and Henley: Routledge & Kegan Paul, 1979), 118.
45. Jacques Derrida, *Of Grammatology,* trans. Gayatri Chakravorty Spivak (Baltimore and London: Johns Hopkins University Press, 1976), 11.
46. S. K. Heninger, "Socrates and His Versified Aesop: The Subtext of Form," in *The Subtext of Form in the English Renaissance: Proportion Poetical* (University Park: Pennsylvania State University Press, 1994), 46.
47. Richard Mulcaster, *The First Part of the Elementarie* (London, 1582), 72–73.
48. "Of Glory," in *The Complete Essays of Montaigne,* 468.
49. The verb *to read* has many meanings, including "To guess, to make out or tell by conjecture"; "To make out or discover the meaning or significance" of something; "To inspect and interpret in thought (any signs which represent words

or discourse)"; "To make out the character or nature of (a person, the heart, etc.) by scrutiny or interpretation of outward signs" (*OED*).

50. George Peele, *King Edward the First,* ed. W. W. Greg, Malone Society Reprints (London: Oxford University Press, 1911).

51. Michel Foucault, *The Archaeology of Knowledge and The Discourse on Language,* trans. A. M. Sheridan Smith (New York: Pantheon Books, 1972), 23.

52. Robert Scholes, *Protocols of Reading* (New Haven and London: Yale University Press, 1989), 10.

53. George Lakoff and Mark Turner, *More than Cool Reason: A Field Guide to Poetic Metaphor* (Chicago and London: University of Chicago Press, 1989), 50.

54. Suzanne Langer, *Philosophy in a New Key: A Study in the Symbolism of Reason, Rite, and Art* (Cambridge: Harvard University Press, 1957), 141.

55. John Middleton Murry, *Countries of the Mind: Essays in Literary Criticism,* 2d ser. (London: Oxford University Press, 1931), 2.

Chapter 5. The Book of Conscience

1. *Luther's Works,* ed. Jaroslav Pelikan and Helmut T. Lehmann, 55 vols. (St. Louis: Concordia Publishing House; Philadelphia: Fortress Press, 1955–86). Abbreviated *LW* and hereafter cited parenthetically.

2. Reproduced as the frontispiece by Michael G. Baylor, *Action and Person: Conscience in Late Scholasticism and the Young Luther* (Leiden: E. J. Brill, 1977).

3. John Calvin, *Institutes of the Christian Religion,* ed. John T. McNeill, trans. Ford Lewis Battles, Library of Christian Classics 20, 2 vols. (Philadelphia: Westminster Press, 1960), 1:848.

4. Sir Thomas Browne, *Christian Morals,* in *"Religio Medici" and Other Works,* ed. L. C. Martin (Oxford: Clarendon Press, 1964), 238.

5. Camille Wells Slights, *The Casuistical Tradition in Shakespeare, Donne, Herbert, and Milton* (Princeton: Princeton University Press, 1981), 10–11.

6. Richard Carpenter, *The Conscionable Christian: or, the Indevour of Saint Paul, to Have and Discharge a good conscience alwayes towards God, and men* (London, 1623), 41.

7. Ibid., 45.

8. Robert Burton, *The Anatomy of Melancholy* (Oxford, 1621), 776.

9. John Downame, *The Christian Warfare* (London, 1604), 379.

10. George Gascoigne, *The Droomme of Doomes day,* in *The Complete Works of George Gascoigne,* ed. John W. Cunliffe, 2 vols. (1907–10; reprint, New York: Greenwood Press, 1969), 2:273.

11. *The Sermons of John Donne,* ed. George R. Potter and Evelyn M. Simpson, 10 vols. (Berkeley and Los Angeles: University of California Press, 1953–62), 1:249.

12. Patrick Forbes, *An Learned Commentarie upon the Revelation of Saint John* (Middelburg, 1614), 225.

13. Ibid.

14. John Napier, *A Plaine Discovery, of the Whole Revelation of S. John: set down in two treatises* [3d ed.] (Edinburgh, 1611), 290–91.

15. *A Commentarie of M. John Calvine uppon the Epistle to the Philippians,* trans. W. B. (London, 1584), 83. These sentences represent a specific comment on 4:3.

16. St. Augustine, *The City of God against the Pagans,* trans. William Chase

Greene et al., Loeb Classical Library, 7 vols. (Cambridge: Harvard University Press; London: William Heinemann, 1957–72), 6:341–43 (bk. 20, chap. 15).

17. Immanuel Bourne, *The Anatomie of Conscience, or a Threefold Revelation of those three most secret Bookes: 1. The Booke of Gods Prescience, 2. The booke of Mans Conscience, 3. The Booke of Life* (London, 1623), 3.

18. Robert Bolton, *A Discourse about the State of True Happinesse* (London, 1611), 109.

19. George Hakewill, *An Apologie of the Power and Providence of God in the Government of the World* (Oxford, 1627), 459.

20. Ibid.

21. John Donne, *Pseudo-Martyr* (London, 1610), 237.

22. William Ames, *Conscience with the Power and Cases Thereof* ([London], 1639), 1.

23. John Hughes, *St. Pauls Exercise, or, A Sermon of Conscience* (London, 1622), 7–8.

24. William Tyndale, *The Obedience of a Christen Man* (Antwerp, 1528), fol. xxxix.

25. Ames, *Conscience with the Power and Cases Thereof*, 167.

26. Downame, *The Christian Warfare*, 211.

27. Bolton, *A Discourse about the State of True Happinesse*, 102.

28. John Favour, *Antiquitie Triumphing over Noveltie* (London, 1619), 451.

29. *The Sermons of John Donne*, 1:173.

30. Bourne, *The Anatomie of Conscience*, p. 6. Modern scholars explain the etymology somewhat differently. C. S. Lewis, in *Studies in Words*, 2d ed. (Cambridge: Cambridge University Press, 1967), writes of *conscience:* "Greek *oida* and Latin *scio* mean 'I know.' The Greek verb can be compounded with the prefix *sun* or *xun* (*sunoida*), the Latin with *cum* which in composition becomes *con-*, giving us *conscio*. *Sun* and *cum* in isolation mean 'with.' And sometimes they retain this meaning when they become prefixes, so that *sunoida* and *conscio* can mean 'I know together with, I share (with someone) the knowledge that.' But sometimes they had a vaguely intensive force, so that the compound verbs would mean merely 'I know well,' and perhaps finally little more than 'I know'" (181).

31. Baylor, *Action and Person: Conscience in Late Scholasticism and the Young Luther*, 23.

32. Ibid., 172.

33. Jeremy Taylor, *Ductor Dubitantium, or The Rule of Conscience*, in *The Whole Works of the Right Rev. Jeremy Taylor*, ed. Reginald Heber, rev. Charles Page Eden, (vols. 9 and 10, ed. Alexander Taylor), 10 vols (London: Longman, 1847–61), 9:18.

34. *St. Augustine's Confessions*, trans. William Watts, Loeb Classical Library, 2 vols. (London: William Heinemann; New York: G. P. Putnam's Sons, 1922), 1:77 (bk. 2, chap. 4).

35. In *The Whole Works of the Right Rev. Jeremy Taylor*, 9:6–7.

36. Timothy C. Potts, *Conscience in Medieval Philosophy* (Cambridge: Cambridge University Press, 1980), 2.

37. Baylor, *Action and Person*, 23.

38. John Calvin, *A Commentarie upon S. Paules Epistles to the Corinthians*, trans. Thomas Timme (London, 1577), fol. 223^v.

39. Calvin, *Institutes of the Christian Religion*, 1:281.

40. Ames, *Conscience with the Power and Cases Thereof*, 10.

41. Ibid., 5.

42. William Perkins, *The Whole Treatise of the Cases of Conscience* (Cambridge, 1606), 212.
43. Pierre de la Primaudaye, *The French Academie*, trans. T[homas] B[owes], 2d ed. (London, 1589), 562.
44. Richard Greenham, *Godly Treatises of Divers Arguments*, in *The Works of the Reverend and Faithfull Servant of Jesus Christ M. Richard Greenham* (London, 1599), 233.
45. Pierre Charron, *Of Wisdome*, trans. Samson Lennard (London, 1612?), 474.
46. Owen Felltham, *Resolves, A Duple Century* [3d ed.] (London, 1628–29), 184–85.
47. Ilja M. Veldman, *Maarten van Heemskerck and Dutch Humanism in the Sixteenth Century*, trans. Michael Hoyle (Maarssen: Gary Schwartz, 1977), 58, fig. 28.
48. Calvin, *Institutes of the Christian Religion*, 1:367–68.
49. Daniel Cramer, *Emblemata Sacra* (Frankfurt, 1624), emblem 23, 103.
50. Carpenter, *The Conscionable Christian*, 43.
51. Bourne, *The Anatomie of Conscience*, 3.
52. John Calvin, *A Commentarie upon S. Paules Epistles to the Corinthians*, fol. 224.
53. La Primaudaye, *The French Academie*, 83.
54. Charron, *Of Wisdome*, 226–27.
55. *The Sermons of John Donne*, 4:149.
56. Felltham, *Resolves, A Duple Century*, 421.
57. Richard Hooker, *Of the Laws of Ecclesiastical Polity*, in *The Works of Richard Hooker*, gen. ed. W. Speed Hill, 5 vols. (Cambridge and London: Harvard University Press, Belknap Press, 1977-), 1:74.
58. *The Sermons of John Donne*, 2:244.
59. King James I, *Basilicon Doron*, in *Political Writings*, ed. Johann P. Sommerville, Cambridge Texts in the History of Political Thought (Cambridge: Cambridge University Press, 1994), 17.

Chapter 6. Conscience on the Stage

1. Samuel Daniel, *The Civil Wars*, ed. Laurence Michel (New Haven: Yale University Press, 1958), 175.
2. *The Three Ladies of London*, attributed to Robert Wilson, appears in *A Select Collection of Old English Plays*, originally published by Robert Dodsley, ed. W. Carew Hazlitt, 4th ed., 15 vols. (London: Reeves and Turner, 1874), vol. 6. Conscience signs the letter (288), is rebuked as bookish (324), is confronted by the Judge, who sees the incriminating letter (366–67).
3. Camille Wells Slights, *The Casuistical Tradition in Shakespeare, Donne, Herbert, and Milton* (Princeton: Princeton University Press, 1981), 106.
4. John S. Wilks, *The Idea of Conscience in Renaissance Tragedy* (London and New York: Routledge, 1990), 8.
5. Wilks does, however, quote Richard Carpenter, Jeremiah Dyke, and Richard Bernard on conscience as book (39).
6. Ibid., 271, n. 14.
7. Representative of contemporary judgments is that by Laura G. Bromley, in "Domestic Conduct in *A Woman Killed with Kindness*," *Studies in English Literature, 1500–1900* 26 (Spring 1986): 259–76; Bromley observes that although

Heywood's tragedy is universally considered a masterpiece, "it is a seriously flawed play" (259).

8. The relationship between the parts of the double plot was made clear in the brilliant production by the Royal Shakespeare Company (1991–92). In this production, directed by Katie Mitchell, Susan's costume in scene 14 matched that of Anne in scene 1; and Susan's prostration in scene 14 matched that of Anne in the discovery scene (13).

9. Heywood's concerns suggest an indebtedness to fifteenth-and sixteenth-century moral plays. Michael Wentworth, in "Thomas Heywood's *A Woman Killed with Kindness* as Domestic Morality," in *Traditions and Innovations: Essays on British Literature of the Middle Ages and the Renaissance,* ed. David G. Allen and Robert A. White (Newark: University of Delaware Press; London and Toronto: Associated University Presses, 1990), observes: "Whether Thomas Heywood was directly familiar with the morality tradition is impossible to establish. Nevertheless, *A Woman Killed with Kindness* . . . reflects the same instructive impulse, the same emphasis upon the inevitability of sin and the possibility of repentance typical of such morality plays as *Everyman, Mankind,* and *The Castle of Perseverance*" (150).

10. *A Woman Killed with Kindness,* ed. R. W. Van Fossen, The Revels Plays (1961; reprint, London: Methuen, 1970).

11. Jeremiah Dyke, *Good Conscience: or A Treatise Shewing the Nature, Meanes, Marks, Benefit, and Necessity Thereof* (London, 1624), 193–94.

12. Modern judgments of Sir Charles are typified by Diana E. Henderson, in "Many Mansions: Reconstructing *A Woman Killed with Kindness,*" *Studies in English Literature, 1500–1900* 26 (Spring 1986): 277–94. Henderson says, "Nothing can make Charles's behavior quite acceptable to a twentieth-century audience, no matter how well it fits the narrative scheme which develops home, family name, and identity . . ." (287).

13. Catherine Belsey, in *The Subject of Tragedy: Identity and Difference in Renaissance Drama* (London and New York: Methuen, 1985), asks of Wendoll's opening soliloquy, especially the beginning lines, "Who is speaking here? A villain? No, because the speaker repudiates this villain as damned, as foolish. The villain becomes 'thou'—precisely not the speaker. A virtuous man, then? No, because the figure defined in the speech cannot pray but only submit to his own desire" (50). What mystifies Belsey, who argues that the character has no naturalistic existence, is Heywood's handling of a convention. Alexander Leggatt, in *Jacobean Public Theatre* (London and New York: Routledge, 1992), explains: "The convention of having a character describe himself breaks down into confusion, as Wendoll's relationship to himself becomes unstable" (87).

14. August Wilhelm von Schlegel, *A Course of Lectures on Dramatic Art and Literature,* trans. John Black, rev. ed. (London: Henry G. Bohn, 1846), 459.

15. Arthur Melville Clark, *Thomas Heywood: Playwright and Miscellanist* (Oxford: Basil Blackwell, 1931), 231.

16. Kathleen McLuskie, *Renaissance Dramatists,* Feminist Readings Series (New York: Harvester Wheatsheaf, 1989), 135.

17. For the various interpretations of the biblical mark, see Ruth Mellinkoff, *The Mark of Cain* (Berkeley and Los Angeles: University of California Press, 1981).

18. Dyke, *Good Conscience,* 79.

19. John Downame, *The Christian Warfare* (London, 1604), 619.

20. *The Three Ladies of London,* in *A Select Collection of Old English Plays,*

ed. Hazlitt, 6:337–38. T. W. Craik, in *The Tudor Interlude: Stage, Costume, and Acting* (Leicester: Leicester University Press, 1962), comments of Lady Lucre: "As she enumerates Conscience's beauties, she touches each in turn with an inky finger; the degradation of Conscience is emphasized by drawing the audience's attention to (for instance) a forehead white as snow and immediately spotting it with ink. The fact that Lucre's action is in itself a light-hearted practical joke (commonly played, one supposes, by children) brings out by contrast the sinister moral of the incident" (77).

21. Robert Ornstein, "Bourgeois Morality and Dramatic Convention in *A Woman Killed with Kindness*," in *English Renaissance Drama: Essays in Honor of Madeleine Doran and Mark Eccles*, ed. Standish Henning et al. (Carbondale: Southern Illinois University Press, 1976), 131.

22. Waldo F. McNeir, "Heywood's Sources for the Main Plot of *A Woman Killed with Kindness*," in *Studies in the English Renaissance Drama: In Memory of Karl Julius Holzknecht*, ed. Josephine W. Bennett, et al. (New York: New York University Press, 1959), 205.

23. In "The Theme of Forgiveness in the Plot and Subplot of *A Woman Killed with Kindness*," *Renaissance Drama* 2 (1969): 123–41, John Canuteson denies that Christianity has any real meaning to Frankford: "Christian terms are to Frankford little more than bywords with which to measure his faith in his wife" (132). This interpretation confuses Frankford's intellectual determination to be merciful with his emotional inability to forgive fully.

24. Otto Rauchbauer, "Visual and Rhetorical Imagery in Th. Heywood's *A Woman Killed with Kindness*," *English Studies* 57 (June 1976): 209.

25. Lisa Jardine, in *Still Harping on Daughters: Women and Drama in the Age of Shakespeare* (Brighton, Sussex: Harvester Press; Totowa, N.J.: Barnes & Noble, 1983), sees eloquence as a defining feature of Anne's character: "'the woman of fluent speech is never chaste' is a worthy epigram to head *A Woman Killed with Kindness*" (57). It seems to me, however, that Anne is neither especially garrulous nor glib. In the seduction scene she is dumbfounded by Wendoll: "What shall I say? / My soul is wand'ring and hath lost her way" (6.150–51). In the discovery scene (13), she speaks many fewer lines than does her husband.

26. Did Chapman ever write a domestic tragedy? Henry Hitch Adams, in *English Domestic or, Homiletic Tragedy, 1575 to 1642* (New York: Columbia University Press, 1943), notes that Chapman's *The Yorkshire Gentlewoman and Her Son* "was entered as a tragedy in the Stationers' Register on June 29, 1660. It also appears in the list of plays destroyed by Warburton's servant. Nothing further is known of the work, but from its title it seems that it must have been a domestic tragedy" (202).

27. In *The Enchanted Glass: The Elizabethan Mind in Literature* (New York: Oxford University Press, 1936), Hardin Craig juxtaposes a discussion of Heywood's play with Chapman's; Craig sees both dramatists as particularly concerned with psychology (128–38).

28. *Bussy D'Ambois*, ed. Nicholas Brooke, The Revels Plays (1964; reprint, Manchester: Manchester University Press, 1979).

29. In a chapter entitled "The Theater of Conscience," Jonathan Goldberg discusses *Bussy D'Ambois*, relating features of the play to circumstances at King James' court. However, specific discussion of conscience in the play is confined largely to one paragraph (158–59). See *James I and the Politics of Literature: Jonson, Shakespeare, Donne, and Their Contemporaries* (Baltimore and London: Johns Hopkins University Press, 1983), 147–61.

30. *Bussy D'Ambois* exists in two quartos, one printed in 1607–8, the other in 1641. These two lines of Bussy's appear near the beginning of 3.1 in the 1641 quarto. The relationship between the quartos is vexing because we do not know whether Chapman himself was responsible for the revisons in the 1641 quarto. Most editors have credited the claim, on the 1641 title page, that *Bussy D'Ambois* was "much corrected and amended by the Author before his death." Accordingly, such important editions as those by Frederick S. Boas (1905), Thomas Marc Parrott (1910), and Robert J. Lordi (1964) base their texts on the later quarto. However, Nicholas Brooke (1964), who believes that Chapman was responsible for some of the revisions and that Nathan Field was responsible for others, prints the revisions of 1641 (in old spelling) beneath the 1607 text on the relevant pages of his edition. John Hazel Smith, in an edition included in *The Plays of George Chapman: The Tragedies with Sir Gyles Goosecappe*, gen. ed. Allan Holaday (Cambridge: D. S. Brewer, 1987), presents a parallel-text edition of the two versions. The additions that I cite from the 1641 quarto are, I believe, in keeping with the spirit of the 1607 quarto.

31. Tamyra's soliloquy and the thirty-three lines of dialogue that precede it were deleted in the 1641 quarto. Albert H. Tricomi, in "The Revised Version of Chapman's *Bussy D'Ambois:* A Shift in Point of View," *Studies in Philology* 70 (July 1973): 288–305, argues that the effect of the deletion is to diminish Tamyra's stature: "Although in both versions Tamyra remains a good woman torn by internal conflict, the deletion of her protestations of helplessness and guilt before her lascivious passions removes the only sympathetic apology for her adulterous behavior which either version affords" (292). Nicholas Brooke suggests that the omission may reflect "the reviser's apparent distaste for Chapman's attitude to passion. . . . The passage seems to me one of Chapman's most interesting achievements, omitted for quite inadequate reasons; the impossibility of retaining it in a reprint of B [1641] is a strong argument for reverting to A [1607] overall" (lxxiii).

32. Henry Peacham, *Minerva Britanna or a Garden of Heroical Devices* (London, 1612), 7, 26, 134, 40, and 35, respectively.

33. Cesare Ripa, *Iconologia overo descrittione di diverse imagini* (Rome, 1603), 35, 71, 113 (misnumbered as 711), 164, 314, 435, 441, 500, respectively.

34. Nicholas Brooke provides the references: "see *All Fools,* II.i.282–5, and *Monsieur D'Olive,* V.i.190–200."

35. Ripa, *Iconologia,* 200.

36. The 1641 quarto makes clear that Pero sees this letter of Barrisor's when Tamyra presents it to Bussy. In the quarto of 1607, Pero tells Monsieur, "'Tis thus then: this last night my Lord lay forth: and I wondering my Lady's sitting up, stole at midnight from my pallet: and (having before made a hole through the wall and arras to her inmost chamber) I saw D'Ambois and she set close at a banquet" (3.2.190–94). The 1641 quarto replaces the words "she set close at a banquet" with "her selfe reading a letter." Nicholas Brooke comments that the "change is obviously to avoid the obscurity [created by the word 'banquet,' which need not mean food], and refers (as Parrott suggested) to Barrisor's letter" (72, n.).

37. Thomas Marc Parrott, in *The Plays and Poems of George Chapman: The Tragedies* (New York: E. P. Dutton, 1910), says: "Monsieur here offers Montsurry a letter which contains the proof of Tamyra's guilt. Presumably it was a love-letter of Bussy's which Pero had stolen from her mistress and conveyed to Monsieur. It corresponds in the play to the letter which the historical Bussy wrote to Monsieur

boasting of his conquest of Montsurry's wife" (556). Nicholas Brooke disagrees: "Parrott supposes the paper to be a proof of Tamyra's guilt and refers to a letter the historical Bussy wrote to Alençon, boasting of his conquest. This is surely wrong: Chapman is vague about papers in the play, but the implication seems to be that Monsieur has *written* what he has sworn not to *speak* (see l. 196 ['tis a foul heart / That fears his own hand'] and IV.ii.87 ['do not let him / Believe what there the wicked man hath written']). I wonder whether Parrott's suggestion may depend on IV.ii.9a-b ['Your Monsieur hath a paper where is writ / Some secret tokens that decipher it'], which is a later addition adding to the confusion" (94, n.). It is not entirely clear what Nicholas Brooke is referring to when he says of Parrott's interpretation, "This is surely wrong," since two matters are at issue here: (1.) Is the letter in question one that Bussy had written? (2.) Is the letter proof of Tamyra's guilt? There is no way of knowing with certainty the answer to the first question. The letter may have been written by Bussy, as Parrott suggests; or by Monsieur, as Brooke suggests; or by Tamyra, as these lines of the Guise to Montsurry may suggest: "Go home my Lord, and force your wife to write / Such loving stuff to D'Ambois as she us'd / When she desir'd his presence" (4.2.101-3). The second question allows a clearer answer: the paper must contain evidence of Tamyra's guilt. If it did not, why would she be so anxious to retrieve it?

38. I borrow my phrasing from Frederick S. Boas, ed., *Bussy D'Ambois and The Revenge of Bussy D'Ambois,* Belles Lettres Series (Boston: D. C. Heath, 1905): "the last two Acts are spun out with supernatural episodes of a singularly unconvincing type. The Friar's invocation of Behemoth, who proves a most unserviceable spirit, and the vain attempts of this scoundrelly ecclesiastic's ghost to shield D'Ambois from his fate, strike us as wofully crude and mechanical excursions into the occult" (xxi). Similarly, Irving Ribner, in *Jacobean Tragedy: The Quest for Moral Order* (London: Methuen, 1962), sees Chapman as pandering to his audience: "The summoning of the spirits, Behemoth and Cartophylax, at the end of the fourth act provided the Jacobean audience with the kind of sensationalism that it relished, and we must not forget that Chapman, in spite of his philosophical bent and of the strong vein of poetic symbolism in his plays, knew well how to please the cruder tastes of his audience" (32).

39. Robert Greene, *Friar Bacon and Friar Bungay,* ed. Daniel Seltzer, Regents Renaissance Drama Series (Lincoln: University of Nebraska Press, 1963).

40. Barbara Howard Traister, in *Heavenly Necromancers: The Magician in English Renaissance Drama* (Columbia: University of Missouri Press, 1984), appears to believe that no book is actually brought onto stage. In her discussion of Greene's scene, Traister speaks of a devil "bringing the Henley hostesss and her shoulder of mutton to show in the flesh the 'book' that one of the learned academics had been pondering the night before" (80). Admittedly, the stage direction does not specifically mention a book, but immediately before that stage direction Bacon says, "I'll show you but his book" (2.115), and Clement, after the appearance of the devil and hostess, asks, "is this the book / That Burden is so careful to look on?" Bacon answers, "It is" (2.140-42). I suspect that the devil carries the book onto the stage.

41. Boas, ed., *Bussy D'Ambois,* 158.

42. In his edition of *Bussy D'Ambois,* Thomas Marc Parrott was the first to recognize the similarity of staging with that of *Friar Bacon:* "The characters named in the stage direction . . . enter on the balcony. Although they speak and act in the following lines, they are not supposed to be really present, but only

made visible and audible to Bussy and Tamyra by the Friar's art. Two similar situations occur in Greene's *Friar Bacon and Friar Bungay,* II, iii, and IV, iii" (558).

43. Seltzer, ed., *Friar Bacon and Friar Bungay,* xiv–xv.

44. Christopher Marlowe, *"Doctor Faustus," A-and B-Texts (1604, 1616),* ed. David Bevington and Eric Rasmussen, The Revels Plays (Manchester and New York: Manchester University Press, 1993).

45. Maurice Evans, ed., *Bussy D'Ambois,* The New Mermaids (London: Ernest Benn; New York: W. W. Norton, 1965), 99; xxii.

46. Robert Rentoul Reed, Jr., in *The Occult on the Tudor and Stuart Stage* (Boston: Christopher Publishing House, 1965), observes, "the Latin invocation uttered by Friar Comolet differs little in its spirit from that which Faustus had used to raise up Mephistophilis" (145). Similarly, Robert Hunter West, in *The Invisible World* (Athens: University of Georgia Press, 1939), says, "the Friar has promised to raise not an angel, but 'any spirit of earth or air,' that is, a sublunary spirit. Most authorities would take this to mean a fallen spirit" (77). Increasingly, however, readers have tended to see Chapman's magic as morally inoffensive. David Woodman, in *White Magic and English Renaissance Drama* (Rutherford, N.J.: Fairleigh Dickinson University Press, 1973), claims that Friar Comolet is "not specifically allied with evil forces" (65). Woodman concedes, however, that the friar "does raise devils, not Neoplatonic daemons." Barbara Howard Traister also believes that *"Bussy D'Ambois* contains magic that is not clearly evil" (110), and she goes on to say: "Chapman's play presents a world where all values are relative and where even the demonic magic that summons the Prince of Shades offers relief from a corrupt world" (117). Keith Thomas, in *Religion and the Decline of Magic: Studies in Popular Beliefs in Sixteenth and Seventeenth Century England* (London: Weidenfeld and Nicolson, 1971), records three parliamentary statutes concerning the practice of magic—those of 1547, 1563, and 1604: "Conjuring of spirits was a felony in all three Acts" (245).

47. Parrott says of the spirit: "The name, Behemoth, as that of an evil spirit, occurs in the pronouncement of the University of Paris on the visions of Joan of Arc, and in the trial of Urbain Grandier, burnt in 1634" (558). Maurice Evans, in his edition, comments, "The friar's motives are of doubtful virtue and the spirit he invokes, Behemoth, was an extremely evil one. Behemoth was the infernal equivalent of Apollo, the sun" (99).

48. Peter Bement, in "The Imagery of Darkness and of Light in Chapman's *Bussy D'Ambois," Studies in Philology* 64 (April 1967): 187–98, argues that although in act 1 "night is not immediately associated with evil" and although night "is associated with contemplative pursuits," nevertheless "the 'night' referred to in the remaining four acts is an instance of the 'false night' which for Chapman signifies not contemplative virtue or mystical knowledge but Man's moral confusion and his blindness to truth" (187–88).

49. In the scene where Monsieur discloses the existence of the paper, Tamyra seems to refer to it when she says to him, "'tis a foul heart / That fears his own hand" (4.1.195–96). According to Thomas Marc Parrott, "Tamyra insinuates, I think, that the paper which Monsieur had offered her husband was a forgery in Monsieur's own hand" (557). Robert J. Lordi, ed., *Bussy D'Ambois,* Regents Renaissance Drama Series (Lincoln: Univeristy of Nebraska Press, 1964), concurs: "Tamyra implies that Monsieur forged the letter" (p. 80, n.). Nicholas Brooke proposes a different interpretation: "Tamyra evidently supposes the paper is in Monsieur's writing: Parrott supports his conjecture about l. 123 ['I must not

speak my Lord'] by suggesting Tamyra takes the letter to be a forgery: this is not implied by IV.ii.87 ['do not let him / Believe what there the wicked man hath written']" (98, n.). In his discussion of 4.2.87 Brooke contends: "Tamyra again assumes that Monsieur wrote the paper, and does not suggest forgery; the assumption that the paper is evidence, not just accusation, is natural . . ." (105, n.).

50. Note to 4.2.87.

51. The ensuing conversation reinforces Tamyra's guilt, when Monsieur points to the paper and says, "There is a glass of ink wherein you see / How to make ready black-fac'd Tragedy: / You now discern, I hope, through all her paintings / Her gasping wrinkles, and fame's sepulchres" (4.2.90–93). Boas interprets "glass of ink" as meaning "a mirror made of ink, i.e., the paper with the proofs of Tamyra's unfaithfulness" (159). Parrott concurs: "A letter which, like a mirror, reflects Tamyra's unfaithfulness" (558). Brooke glosses the words simply as "written image" (106, n.).

52. Boas, ed., *Bussy D'Ambois*, 158.

53. Tamyra's speech has a distinctly Platonic quality, though I have not found an exact counterpart in the work of Platonic philosophers. For Chapman's indebtedness to Platonism, see Franck L. Schoell, "Les emprunts de George Chapman à Marsile Ficin," in *Etudes sur l'humanisme continental en Angleterre à la fin de la renaissance* (1926; reprint, Geneva: Slatkine Reprints, 1978), 1–20.

54. For Chapman's treatment of the historical events on which he bases his play, see Jean Jacquot, ed., *Bussy D'Amboise*, Collection Bilingue des Classiques Etrangers (Paris: Aubier, 1960), xxii-lviii.

55. In *The Plays of George Chapman*, ed. Holaday, 442.

56. *The first tome or volume of the Paraphrase of Erasmus upon the newe testamente* (London, 1548), fol. lix.

57. *The Chester Mystery Cycle*, ed. R. M. Lumiansky and David Mills, Early English Text Society, supplementary series 3, 9, 2 vols. (London, New York, and Toronto: Oxford University Press, 1974, 1986), 1:229.

58. *The Summoning of Everyman*, ed. Geoffrey Cooper and Christopher Wortham (Nedlands: University of Western Australia Press, 1980).

59. Philippe Ariès, *Western Attitudes toward Death: From the Middle Ages to the Present*, trans. Patricia M. Ranum (Baltimore and London: Johns Hopkins University Press, 1974), 32–33.

60. "The Act of Uniformity," in *The Royal Supremacy in the Elizabethan Church*, ed. Claire Cross (London: Allen & Unwin; New York: Barnes & Noble, 1969), 131.

61. Ibid., 133–34.

62. Quoted by Elliot Rose, *Cases of Conscience: Alternatives Open to Recusants and Puritans under Elizabeth I and James I* (Cambridge: Cambridge University Press, 1975), 38.

63. See *Renaissance Self-Fashioning, From More to Shakespeare* (Chicago and London: University of Chicago Press, 1980), chaps. 1 and 2.

64. Quoted by Rose, *Cases of Conscience*, 41.

65. Queen Elizabeth's expediency in using the language of casuistry when dealing with Mary is explored by Lowell Gallagher, in *Medusa's Gaze: Casuistry and Conscience in the Renaissance* (Stanford: Stanford University Press, 1991), chap. 1.

66. Rose, *Cases of Conscience*, 81.

67. Ibid., 89.

68. Ibid.

69. Raphael Holinshed, *The Third Volume of Chronicles* (London, 1587), 1324. Hereafter cited parenthetically.
70. See Kevin T. Kelly, *Conscience: Dictator or Guide?: A Study in Seventeenth-Century English Protestant Moral Theology* (London: Geoffrey Chapman, 1967).
71. John Bartlett, quoted by Patrick Collinson, *The Elizabethan Puritan Movement* (London: Jonathan Cape, 1967), 115.
72. Ibid., 248.
73. William Cecil, in *The Royal Supremacy in the Elizabethan Church,* ed. Cross, 200–1.
74. John Whitgift, ibid., 202.
75. Calvin, *Institutes of the Christian Religion,* ed. John T. McNeill, trans. Ford Lewis Battles The Library of Christian Classics 21, 2 vols. (Philadelphia: Westminster Press, 1960), 2:1489.
76. C. S. L. Davies, *Peace, Print and Protestantism, 1450–1558,* The Paladin History of England (London: Hart-Davis, MacGibbon, 1976), 185.
77. The different ways in which Puritans and Anglicans conceived of obedience to authority, especially in the seventeenth century, has been explored by J. Sears McGee, *The Godly Man in Stuart England: Anglicans, Puritans, and the Two Tables, 1620–1670* (New Haven and London: Yale University Press, 1976), chap. 4.
78. William Perkins, *A Discourse of Conscience: Wherein is set downe the nature, properties, and differences thereof: as also the way to Get and keepe good Conscience* (Cambridge, 1596), 53–54.
79. Ibid., 54.
80. Collinson, *The Elizabethan Puritan Movement,* 447.
81. For an account of the Hampton Court Conference, see Nicholas Tyacke, *Anti-Calvinists: The Rise of English Arminianism, c. 1590–1640* (Oxford: Clarendon Press, 1987), chap. 1.
82. King James I, quoted by Patrick McGrath, *Papists and Puritans under Elizabeth I* (New York: Walker & Company, 1967), 349.
83. Collinson, *The Elizabethan Puritan Movement,* 461.
84. Paul S. Seaver, *Wallington's World: A Puritan Artisan in Seventeenth-Century London* (Stanford: Stanford University Press, 1985), 185.
85. Ibid., 182.
86. These lines are from the 1641 quarto, near the beginning of 3.1.
87. Nancy A. Gutierrez, "Exorcism by Fasting in *A Woman Killed with Kindness:* A Paradigm of Puritan Resistance?" *Research Opportunities in Renaissance Drama* 33 (1994): 44.
88. Chapman's motto comes from a speech by Aeneas to his mother in the first book of Virgil's *Aeneid:* "mens sibi conscia recti" (l. 604).
89. Peacham, *Minerva Britanna,* 67.
90. Margot Heinemann, *Puritanism and Theatre: Thomas Middleton and Opposition Drama under the Early Stuarts* (Cambridge: Cambridge University Press, 1980), 51. Heinemann provides an extensive summary of Middleton's Puritan connections in Appendix A: "Middleton's Parliamentary Puritan Patrons."
91. Thomas Middleton and William Rowley, *The Changeling,* ed. N. W. Bawcutt, The Revels Plays (1958; reprint, London: Methuen, 1970).
92. John Webster, *The Duchess of Malfi,* ed. John Russell Brown, The Revels Plays (1964; reprint, London: Methuen, 1972).
93. *The Virgin Martyr,* in *The Dramatic Works of Thomas Dekker,* ed. Fredson Bowers, 4 vols. (Cambridge: Cambridge University Press, 1953–61), vol. 3.

94. John Ford, *'Tis Pity She's a Whore,* ed. Derek Roper, The Revels Plays (London: Methuen, 1975).

Chapter 7. The Book of Nature

1. John Milton, *Complete Poems and Major Prose,* ed. Merritt Y. Hughes (New York: Odyssey Press, 1957), 3.45–50.
2. Owen Felltham, *Resolves, A Duple Century* [3d ed.] (London, 1628–29), 45.
3. I have found especially helpful Elizabeth L. Eisenstein's "'The great book of Nature' and the 'little books of men,'" in *The Printing Press as an Agent of Change: Communications and Cultural Transformations in Early-modern Europe,* 2 vols. in 1 (1979; reprint, Cambridge: Cambridge University Press, 1980), 453–88.
4. Sir Thomas Browne, *"Religio Medici" and Other Works,* ed. L. C. Martin (Oxford: Clarendon Press, 1964), 15.
5. Pierre de la Primaudaye, *The Third volume of French Academie: Contayning a notable description of the whole world, and of all the principall parts and contents thereof,* trans. R. Dolman (1601), sig. A2.
6. *The Sermons of John Donne,* ed. George R. Potter and Evelyn M. Simpson, 10 vols. (Berkeley and Los Angeles: University of California Press, 1953–62), 2:253.
7. Richard Baxter, *A Christian Directory: or, A Sum of Practical Theologie* (London, 1673), 301.
8. *The Sermons of John Donne,* 4:128.
9. "On Providence," in *Plotinus,* trans. A. H. Armstrong, 7 vols. (Cambridge: Harvard University Press; London: William Heinemann, 1966–88), 3:133 (*Ennead* 3.3).
10. "On Stilicho's Consulship," in *Claudian,* trans. Maurice Platnauer, Loeb Classical Library, 2 vols. (London: William Heinemann; New York: G. P. Putnam's Sons, 1922), 2:33–35.
11. *St. Augustine's Confessions,* trans. William Watts, Loeb Classical Library, 2 vols. (London: William Heinemann; New York: G. P. Putnam's Sons, 1919), 2:403–5 (bk. 13, chap. 15).
12. Hugh of St. Victor, quoted by Charles S. Singleton, *Commedia: Elements of Structure,* Dante Studies 1 (Cambridge: Harvard University Press, 1954), 25.
13. Alain de Lille, *The Plaint of Nature,* trans. James J. Sheridan (Toronto: Pontifical Institute of Mediaeval Studies, 1980), 156. Sheridan explains: "Nature had an effective and reliable blueprint. If this were followed without any change whatsoever, the continuation of the race would be guaranteed. She gave a special pen and special paper to Venus to copy down this blueprint" (156, n.).
14. Dante, *The Paradiso,* The Temple Classics (London: J. M. Dent & Sons, 1962), canto 28, l. 14; and canto 33, ll. 85–87.
15. Nicholas of Cusa, *The Layman on Wisdom and the Mind,* trans. M. L. Führer, Centre for Reformation and Renaissance Studies, University of Toronto, Translation Series 4 (Ottawa: Dovehouse Editions, 1989), 21.
16. Ibid., 22. Führer comments on the Layman's reference to God's books: "To this standard motif, Cusanus adds a distinction in the *Layman* between an external book of nature that constitutes the sensible world and the internal book of nature that is the human mind. He may have discovered this distinction in St. Bonaventure's *Breviloquium* II.11.2" (34, n. 12).
17. Alfonso Ingegno, "The new philosophy of nature," in *The Cambridge His-*

tory of Renaissance Philosophy, gen. ed. Charles B. Schmitt (Cambridge: Cambridge University Press, 1988), 251.

18. See Valeria Giachetti Assenza, "Bernadino Telesio: Il migliore dei moderni: I riferimenti a Telesio negli scritti di Francesco Bacone," *Rivista critica di storia della filosofia* 35 (1980): 41–78.

19. Giordano Bruno, *The Heroic Frenzies,* trans. Paul Eugene Memmo, Jr., University of North Carolina Studies in the Romance Languages and Literatures 50 (Chapel Hill: University of North Carolina Press, 1964), 223.

20. *The Hermetic and Alchemical Writings of . . . Paracelsus,* trans. Arthur Edward Waite, 2 vols. (1894; reprint, Berkeley: Shambhala, 1976), 2:98.

21. Ibid., 155.

22. *Paracelsus: Selected Writings,* ed. Jolande Jacobi, trans. Norbert Guterman, Bollingen Series 28 (New York: Pantheon Books, 1951), 129.

23. Ibid., 79. Jolande Jacobi comments on the hostility of Paracelsus toward Luther: "In all his relations with authority and tradition he was a 'protester.' But it was perhaps this very peculiarity of his character that prevented him from becoming a follower of Luther, as many others did at that time. His rebellious nature led a number of eminent Protestants to hope that he would fight on their side. It seems that they even vied with one another for his adherence. But Paracelsus avoided all purely denominational concerns" (52).

24. Paracelsus, *The Hermetic and Alchemical Writings,* 2:5.

25. Ibid., 1:96.

26. Paracelsus, quoted by Ernst Robert Curtius, *European Literature and the Latin Middle Ages* (1948), trans. Willard R. Trask, Bollingen Series 36 (1953; reprint, New York and Evanston: Harper & Row, 1963), 322.

27. Francis Bacon, *The Twoo Bookes of the Proficience and Advancement of Learning* (London, 1605), fol. 25.

28. Ibid.

29. Ibid., fol. 31^v.

30. Ibid., fol. 6^v.

31. In *The Gutenberg Galaxy: The Making of Typographic Man* (London: Routledge & Kegan Paul, 1962), Marshall McLuhan writes: "The medieval Book of Nature was for *contemplatio* like the Bible. The Renaissance Book of Nature was for *applicatio* and was like movable types" (185).

32. Although the English poet admired and even visited Galileo, Milton's Raphael would evoke an older and more conventional vision of nature in his words to Adam: "To ask or search I blame thee not, for Heav'n / Is as the Book of God before thee set, / Wherein to read his wond'rous Works, and learn / His Seasons, Hours, or Days, or Months, or Years: / This to attain, whether Heav'n move or Earth, / Imports not, if thou reck'n right; the rest / From Man or Angel the great Architect / Did wisely to conceal, and not divulge / His secrets to be scann'd by them who ought / Rather admire . . ." (*Paradise Lost,* 8.66–75).

33. Galileo, *Dialogue Concerning the Two Chief World Systems—Ptolemaic & Copernican,* trans. Stillman Drake (Berkeley and Los Angeles: University of California Press, 1953), 3.

34. Galileo, "Third Letter on Sunspots," in *Discoveries and Opinions of Galileo,* trans. Stillman Drake (Garden City, N.Y.: Doubleday Anchor Books, 1957), 126–27.

35. Elizabeth L. Eisenstein, *The Printing Press as an Agent of Change,* 475–76.

36. Ibid., 478.

37. In *The Renaissance Drama of Knowledge: Giordano Bruno in England*

(London and New York: Routledge, 1989), Hilary Gatti observes of Marlowe's *Doctor Faustus:* "the Bad Angel sees 'Negromantick Art' as one 'wherein all natures treasury is contain'd.' He is thus placing the book of God or the Scriptures against the symbol of a 'book of nature,' creating a contraposition through which . . . the consciousness of a new more scientific enquiry into the truths of nature would gradually develop" (97). This "contraposition" was foreseen and feared by the clergy.

38. *The Sermons of John Donne,* 3:264.

39. John Calvin, *Institutes of the Christian Religion,* ed. John T. McNeill, trans. Ford Lewis Battles, The Library of Christian Classics 20, 2 vols. (Philadelphia: Westminster Press, 1960), 1:52–53.

40. Ibid., 1:70. The trope of spectacles would later be used in *The Divine Weeks and Works of Guillaume de Saluste Sieur Du Bartas, translated by Josuah Sylvester,* ed. Susan Snyder, 2 vols. (Oxford: Clarendon Press, 1979): "To read this Booke [of the world], we neede not understand / Each Strangers gibbrish; neither take in hand / *Turkes* Caracters, nor *Hebrue* Points to seeke, / *Nyle's Hieroglyphikes,* nor the Notes of *Greeke.* / The wandring *Tartars,* the *Antartikes* wilde, / Th'*Alarbies* fierce, the *Scithians* fell, the Childe / Scarce seav'n yeare old, the bleared aged eye, / Though void of Arte, read heere indifferently. But he that weares the spectacles of *Faith,* / Sees through the Spheares above their highest heigth . . ." (1:116).

41. Calvin, *Institutes of the Christian Religion,* 1:164.

42. Galileo, "Letter to the Grand Duchess Christina," in *Discoveries and Opinions of Galileo,* 182–83.

43. Such theologians as Richard Hooker explicitly term God an author: "that which all men have at all times learned, nature her selfe must needes have taught; and God being the author of nature, her voyce is but his instrument." See *Of the Laws of Ecclesiastical Polity,* The Folger Library Edition of the Works of Richard Hooker, gen. ed. W. Speed Hill, 5 vols. (Cambridge and London: Harvard University Press, 1977–), 1:84.

44. Galileo, "The Assayer," in *Discoveries and Opinions of Galileo,* 237–38.

45. Gerald Bruns, *Inventions: Writing, Textuality, and Understanding in Literary History* (New Haven and London: Yale University Press, 1982), 19.

46. Edwin Jones, *Reading the Book of Nature: A Phenomenological Study of Creative Expression in Science and Painting* (Athens: Ohio University Press, 1989), 22.

47. Browne, *"Religio Medici" and Other Works,* 12.

48. Ibid., 15.

49. For Browne's use of the term, see Thomas C. Singer, "Sir Thomas Browne's 'Emphaticall decussation, or fundamentall figure': Geometrical Hieroglyphs and *The Garden of Cyprus,*" *English Literary Renaissance* 17 (Winter 1987): 85–102.

50. Sir Walter Ralegh, *The History of the World* (London, 1614), 2.

51. In *Phaedrus* Socrates says of Theuth, "He it was who invented numbers and arithmetic and geometry and astronomy, also draughts and dice, and, most important of all, letters." See *Plato,* trans. Harold North Fowler, W. R. M. Lamb, R. G. Bury, Loeb Classical Library, 12 vols. (London: William Heinemann; Cambridge: Harvard University Press, 1914–27), 1:561–63.

52. Lodowick Bryskett, *A Discourse of Civill Life: Containing the Ethike part of Morall Philosophie* (London, 1606), 151.

53. Marsilio Ficino, quoted in *The Hieroglyphics of Horapollo,* trans. George Boas, Bollingen Series 23 (New York: Pantheon Books, 1950), 28.

54. Liselotte Dieckmann, *Hieroglyphics: The History of a Literary Symbol* (St. Louis: Washington University Press, 1970), 17.

55. In Margaret Mann Phillips, *The "Adages" of Erasmus: A Study with Translations* (Cambridge: Cambridge University Press, 1964), 175.

56. In *James I and the Politics of Literature: Jonson, Shakespeare, Donne, and Their Contemporaries* (Baltimore and London: Johns Hopkins University Press, 1983), Jonathan Goldberg, citing a paper by Charles Dempsey, writes: "the Renaissance rediscovery of hieroglyphics developed in two directions: one, neoplatonic, treated the hieroglyphic as an intuitive symbolic statement, nontranslatable; another tradition used hieroglyphics as an alternate mode of inscription (literally, based on the hieroglyphics inscribed on obelisks) in which the symbols were to be assembled by a grammar which the viewer was to provide" (273, n. 44). My impression is that Renaissance writers used the term "hieroglyphic" rather loosely at times and that the distinction that Goldberg draws was not always observed.

57. Thomas M. Greene, "Erasmus's 'Festina lente': Vulnerabilities of the Humanist Text," in *Mimesis: From Mirror to Method, Augustine to Descartes,* ed. John D. Lyons and Stephen G. Nichols, Jr. (Hanover, N.H., and London: University Press of New England [for Dartmouth College], 1982), 137.

58. *Paracelsus: Selected Writings,* 194.

59. Erik Iversen, *The Myth of Egypt and Its Hieroglyphs in European Tradition* (Copenhagen: Gec Gad Publishers, 1961), 72.

60. Don Cameron Allen, *Mysteriously Meant: The Rediscovery of Pagan Symbolism and Allegorical Interpretation in the Renaissance* (Baltimore and London: Johns Hopkins University Press, 1970), 115.

61. Charles Moseley, *A Century of Emblems: An Introductory Anthology* (Aldershot, England, and Brookfield, Vt.: Scolar Press, 1989), 7.

62. Andrea Alciato, quoted by Jerome Schwartz, "Emblematic Discourse and Counter-Discourse in Montaigne's *Essais,*" *Emblematica* 5 (Summer 1991): 60. Chaeremon was a first-century Egyptian.

63. Michel Foucault, *The Order of Things: An Archaeology of the Human Sciences* (New York: Pantheon Books, 1970), 35.

64. Galileo, *Dialogue Concerning the Two Chief World Systems, Ptolemaic & Copernican,* 265.

Chapter 8. Nature on the Stage

1. This topos has been discussed by Edward William Tayler, *Nature and Art in Renaissance Literature* (New York: Columbia University Press, 1964), and by Leonard Barkan, *Nature's Work of Art: The Human Body as Image of the World* (New Haven: Yale University Press, 1975).

2. In "'Tongues in Trees': The Book of Nature in *As You Like It,*" *Modern Language Studies* 18 (Summer 1988): 65–74, Paul J. Willis suggests that Orlando's action represents an abuse not only of trees but also of God's book of nature: "he imposes his own text on the supposedly divine text of the forest. He presumes to write the book of nature. Orlando surpasses the others . . . in perverting the function of natural revelation" (70). This theological interpretation seems a bit heavy-handed.

3. Rensselaer W. Lee, *Names on Trees: Ariosto into Art,* Princeton Essays on the Arts 3 (Princeton: Princeton University Press, 1977), 6.

4. Ibid.

5. Agnes Latham, in her introduction to the New Arden *As You Like It* (London: Methuen, 1975), observes of Shakespeare's dependence on *Rosalynde* (1590), which was reprinted in 1592, 1596, and 1598, "There are . . . enough verbal reminiscences to suggest that he had read or reread it at a time close to the writing of the play" (xxxi).

6. Important discussions of pastoral include: Harry Berger, Jr., "The Renaissance Imagination: Second World and Green World," *The Centennial Review* 9 (Winter 1965): 36–78; Renato Poggioli, *The Oaten Flute: Essays on Pastoral Poetry and the Pastoral Ideal* (Cambridge: Harvard University Press, 1975); Helen Cooper, *Pastoral: Medieval into Renaissance* (1977; reprint, Ipswich, England: D. S. Brewer; Totowa, N.J.: Rowman & Littlefield, 1978); Paul Alpers, "What is Pastoral?" *Critical Inquiry* 8 (Spring 1982): 437–60; Andrew V. Ettin, *Literature and the Pastoral* (New Haven and London: Yale University Press, 1984); Annabel Patterson, *Pastoral and Ideology: Virgil to Valéry* (Berkeley and Los Angeles: University of California Press, 1987); Sukanta Chaudhuri, *Renaissance Pastoral and Its English Developments* (Oxford: Clarendon Press, 1989).

7. Jacopo Sannazaro, *Arcadia & Piscatorial Eclogues*, trans. Ralph Nash (Detroit: Wayne State University Press, 1966), 29. In this same prologue to *Arcadia*, Sannazaro asks, "who has any doubt that a fountain that issues naturally from the living rock, surrounded by green growth, is more pleasing to the human mind than all the others made by art of whitest marble, resplendent with much gold?"

8. *A Critical Edition of Yong's Translation of George of Montemayor's "Diana" and Gil Polo's "Enamoured Diana,"* ed. Judith M. Kennedy (Oxford: Clarendon Press, 1968), 321.

9. Thomas Lodge, *Rosalynde, Euphues golden legacie*, in *Narrative and Dramatic Sources of Shakespeare*, ed. Geoffrey Bullough, 8 vols. (New York: Columbia University Press; London: Routledge & Kegan Paul, 1957–75), 2:183. Hereafter cited parenthetically.

10. For Shakespeare's treatment of pastoral, especially in *As You Like It*, see Geoffrey Bullough's *Narrative and Dramatic Sources of Shakespeare*, 2:143–57; R. W. Draper, "Shakespeare's Pastoral Comedy," *Etudes Anglaises* 11 (1958): 1–17; Mary Lascelles, "Shakespeare's Pastoral Comedy," in *More Talking of Shakespeare*, ed. John Garrett (London: Longmans, 1959), 70–86; Albert R. Cirillo, "*As You Like It*: Pastoralism Gone Awry," *ELH* 38 (March 1971): 19–39; David P. Young, *The Heart's Forest: A Study of Shakespeare's Pastoral Plays* (New Haven and London: Yale University Press, 1972), 38–72; Charles W. Hieatt, "The Quality of Pastoral in *As You Like It*," *Genre* 7 (June 1974): 164–82; Barbara J. Bono, "Mixed Gender, Mixed Genre in Shakespeare's *As You Like It*," in *Renaissance Genres*, ed. Barbara Kiefer Lewalski, Harvard English Studies 14 (Cambridge and London: Harvard University Press, 1986), 189–212. For a very different view, that the Forest of Arden is *not* superior to the world of the court in Shakespeare's play, see A. Stuart Daley, "The Dispraise of the Country in *As You Like It*," *Shakespeare Quarterly* 36 (Autumn 1985): 300–14. Shakespeare's adaptation of Lodge is also examined by Marco Mincoff, "What Shakespeare did to *Rosalynde*," *Shakespeare Jahrbuch* 96 (1960): 78–89; Edward I. Berry, "Rosalynde and Rosalind," *Shakespeare Quarterly* 31 (Spring 1980): 42–52; Paul Salzman, *English Prose Fiction, 1558–1700: A Critical History* (Oxford: Clarendon Press, 1985), 71–76; Brian Gibbons, "Amorous Fictions and *As You Like It*," in *"Fanned and Winnowed Opinions": Shakespearean Essays Presented to Harold Jenkins*, ed. John W. Mahon and Thomas A. Pendleton (London and New York: Methuen, 1987), 52–78.

11. Judy Z. Kronenfeld, in "Social Rank and the Pastoral Ideals of *As You Like It*," *Shakespeare Quarterly* 29 (Summer 1978): 333–48, observes: "Silvius' name, changed from 'Montanus,' echoes the many Silvias (Tasso), Sylvios (Guarini), and Sylvanuses (Montemayor) of Continental pastoral. He is the 'faithful shepherd' (V.ii.81), 'this most faithful shepherd' (V.iv.14), *il pastor fido*" (340, n. 29).

12. In "Shakespeare's Corin, Almsgiver and Faithful Feeder," *English Language Notes* 27 (June 1990): 4–17, A. Stuart Daley argues that "In sharp contrast to the novel's escapism, the play points to actualities of life in the 1590s, and concerns itself with remedies for them that the individual may find in himself" (4). This article never considers that Shakespeare may have had specifically *theatrical* reasons for altering the portrayal of the pastoral (beyond including topical allusions). Daley is so anxious to demonstrate his thesis about "contemporary socio-economic history" that he indulges in fantasy, finding in Corin's dialogue with Silvius (2.4) a criticism for not reading how-to manuals: "The joke is that he [Silvius] has misapplied his literacy to reading Marlowe and the sonneteers instead of some of the many guides to farming for husbandmen, law for laymen, and moral improvement for all" (13).

13. Albert R. Cirillo, in "*As You Like It:* Pastoralism Gone Awry," contends that Rosalind's quality of detachment allows for a critique of the very basis of pastoral: "the name *Rosalind* had become, by the time Shakespeare wrote the play, almost a stock symbol for the loved-one in romantic situations; she was, almost in virtue of her name, the lovely lass for whom poetic shepherds pined, and her name evoked all of the sweet melancholy associated with literary lovers. By making the object of Orlando's youthful ardor a figure with inherent associations of romantic pastoral—a Rosalind who, somewhat paradoxically, acts as a cynical iconoclast towards the standard romantic convention—Shakespeare makes his play and its setting a self-reflective commentary on the unreality of the pastoral convention" (25–26).

14. Thomas G. Rosenmeyer, *The Green Cabinet: Theocritus and the European Pastoral Lyric* (Berkeley and Los Angeles: University of California Press, 1969), 4.

15. In the New Arden *As You Like It,* Agnes Latham notes a similarity and a difference between the pastoral lover of the play and that of Greene's *Orlando Furioso,* which was staged ca. 1591: "Shakespeare's Orlando hangs verses on trees in praise of Rosalind. Greene's Orlando finds the trees already hung with 'roundelayes,' which are the work of a rival, hoping to arouse his jealousy. Rosalind accuses Orlando of abusing young plants (III.ii.351) and Jaques prays him to 'mar no more trees with writing love-songs in their barks' (ll. 255–56). Greene's Orlando inquires 'Who wronged happy Nature so / To spoyle these trees with this Angelica?'" (xxxi).

16. In the Renaissance and later, artists frequently depicted Ariosto's Medoro, carving the name of Angelica on a tree. In *Names on Trees* Rensselaer W. Lee reproduces many of these representations.

17. This is not to say that the forest is without its detractors. Kent T. van den Berg, in *Playhouse and Cosmos: Shakespearean Theater as Metaphor* (Newark: University of Delaware Press; London and Toronto: Associated University Presses, 1985), observes: "Shakespeare's Arden, like Lodge's, is ambivalent. It appears alternately as an idyllic 'golden world' and as a harsh 'desert inaccessible,' mirroring the disposition of the beholder" (89). For example, "When Orlando enters the forest, hungry, desperate, and dispossessed, he finds it 'bleak,' 'uncouth,' and 'savage' (II.vi); but after he has joined the Duke's merry men, he

sees, and would have everyone see, Rosalind's virtue 'witnessed everywhere' . . ." (90).

18. In "'The Place of a Brother' in *As You Like It:* Social Process and Comic Form," *Shakespeare Quarterly* 32 (Spring 1981): 28–54, Louis Adrian Montrose assesses the significance of Orlando's Petrarchan poetry: "The Petrarchan lover 'writes' his mistress or 'carves' her in the image of his own desire, incorporating virtuous feminine ster[e]otypes and scrupulously excluding what is sexually threatening. The lover masters his mistress by inscribing her within his own discourse; he worships a deity of his own making and under his control" (49). In "Diana Described: Scattered Woman and Scattered Rhyme," *Critical Inquiry* 8 (Winter 1981): 265–80, Nancy J. Vickers comments on Petrarch's influence: "Petrarch's figuration of Laura informs a decisive stage in the development of a code of beauty, a code that causes us to view the fetishized body as a norm and encourages us to seek, or to seek to be, 'ideal types, beautiful monsters composed of every individual perfection.' Petrarch's text, of course, did not constitute the first example of particularizing description, but it did popularize that strategy by coming into fashion during the privileged early years of printing, the first century of the widespread diffusion of both words and images. It is in this context that Petrarch left us his legacy of fragmentation" (277).

19. D. J. Palmer, in "Art and Nature in *As You Like It,*" *Philological Quarterly* 49 (January 1970): 30–40, remarks that "In the mock-courtship which is a cure for love, . . . the play finds its central image of the alliance between the artificial and the natural" (39).

20. Ann Pasternak Slater, in *Shakespeare the Director* (Brighton, Sussex: Harvester; Totowa, N.J.: Barnes & Noble, 1982), observes of this description: "Fifteen years earlier, Elizabeth had been entertained by a burlesque marriage at Kenilworth, arranged by the local parishoners, in which the groom appeared with 'a fayr strawn hat . . . on hiz hed: a payr of harvest glovez on hiz hands, az a sign of good husbandry: a pen and inkhorn at his bak. For he woold be knowen to be bookish'" (138). Slater notes that "Montanus' dress is forgotten in *As You Like It*" (139).

21. Gibbons, "Amorous Fictions and *As You Like It,*" 77.

22. Agnes Latham, in her New Arden edition of *As You Like It*, notes that Jonson's masque, *Hymenaei,* describes the god of marriage as having "in his right hand a torch of *pine tree*" (note to 5.4.106).

23. Young, *The Heart's Forest,* 56.

24. Eamon Grennan, "Telling the Trees from the Wood: Some Details of *As You Like It* Re-examined," *English Literary Renaissance* 7 (Spring 1977): 202.

25. Stylized action in *Pericles* takes various forms: the ritual at Antiochus' court; the tournament, with its ceremonial presentation of imprese; the banquet at Pentapolis, with its accompanying dance; the solemn reunion at Diana's temple; and the dumb shows.

26. In "Puzzle and Artifice: The Riddle as Metapoetry in 'Pericles,'" *Shakespeare Survey* 29 (1976): 11–20, Phyllis Gorfain comments: "We may consider the riddle a false artifice, for its end is deception, not revelation" (13). Every riddle, however, may be considered to display "false artifice" in the sense that the riddle seeks to delay recognition of the truth. Moreover, whatever Antiochus' purpose, the riddle does in fact bring about a revelation. Therefore, I think that it would be more accurate to say that the riddle represents true artifice, but that the relationship it represents is, of course, perverted.

27. Elizabeth Archibald, in *Apollonius of Tyre: Medieval and Renaissance*

Themes and Variations (Cambridge: D. S. Brewer, 1991), points out that in earlier versions of the story Pericles (Apollonius) is much concerned with the written word: "A very important theme throughout *HA* [*Historia Apollonii*] is learning, which characterizes the main figures and also plays an important functional role in the plot. Apollonius is presented as an unusually well educated hero. . . . When he wants to check his solution of Antiochus' riddle, he consults his personal library, which consists of 'the riddles of all the authors and the debates of almost all the philosophers and also of all the Chaldaeans'" (22).

28. Gower's *Confessio Amantis* was written ca. 1383–93. David Bevington, in *Shakespeare: The Late Romances* (New York: Bantam, 1988), notes that Lawrence Twine's work was registered in 1576 but exists today "only in two editions from about 1594–1595 and 1607" (115).

29. Douglas L. Peterson, *Time, Tide and Tempest: A Study of Shakespeare's Romances* (San Marino, Calif.: The Huntington Library, 1973), 85.

30. Does this branch appear as a picture or is it a real piece of wood? G. Wilson Knight, in *The Crown of Life: Essays in Interpretation of Shakespeare's Final Plays* (London and New York: Oxford University Press, 1947), suggests that the branch is "probably the actual thing, not merely a device" (47). Mary Judith Dunbar, in "'To the Judgement of Your Eye': Iconography and the Theatrical Art of *Pericles*," in *Shakespeare, Man of the Theater*, ed. Kenneth Muir et al. (Newark: University of Delaware Press; London and Toronto: Associated University Presses, 1983), 86–97, accepts Knight's suggestion: "Having no shield he has had to make his own device, probably from a natural branch" (90). If Knight and Dunbar are correct in their supposition, one wonders where precisely the motto would appear: could it have been written on a piece of paper and then attached to the branch? Whatever the materials, scholars have failed to discover an exact pictorial antecedent for Pericles' device. Henry Green, in *Shakespeare and the Emblem Writers: An Exposition of Their Similarities of Thought and Expression* (1870; reprint, New York: Burt Franklin, n.d.), comments: "The sixth knight's emblem is very simple, natural, and appropriate; and I am most of all disposed to regard it as invented by Shakespeare himself to complete a scene, the greater part of which had been accommodated from other writers" (182). F. D. Hoeniger, editor of the New Arden *Pericles* (1963; reprint, London: Methuen, 1969), agrees with Henry Green: "No source for this motto has been found; it may well have been invented by the playwright" (p. 56, n.). However, Alan R. Young, in "A Note on the Tournament Impresas in *Pericles*," *Shakespeare Quarterly* 36 (Winter 1985): 453–56, proposes that Shakespeare may have turned for this detail "to an impresa that Sidney had invented for one of his own appearances at a Whitehall tournament" (454). For analogues of Pericles' branch in the visual arts, see Gerhart B. Ladner, "Vegetation Symbolism and the Concept of Renaissance," *Essays in Honor of Erwin Panofsky*, ed. Millard Meiss, De Artibus Opuscula 40, 2 vols. (New York: New York University Press, 1961), 1:303–22.

31. F. David Hoeniger, "Gower and Shakespeare in *Pericles*," *Shakespeare Quarterly* 33 (Winter 1982): 473.

32. P. Goolden, in "Antiochus's Riddle in Gower and Shakespeare," *Review of English Studies*, n.s., 6 (July 1955): 245–51, observes that the playwright departs from his sources by having the "I" of the riddle refer to the daughter instead of the father.

33. James O. Wood, in "The Running Image in *Pericles*," *Shakespeare Studies* 5 (1969): 240–52, observes that Simonides' book metaphor "led the author to invent the indispensable bibliographical term (surprisingly, not recorded by the

OED), *title-page*." Wood comments, "This matches happily Shakespeare's invention (see *OED*) of the companion term, *title-leaf* (*2H4*, I.i.60)" (243).

34. Joan Hartwig, in *Shakespeare's Tragicomic Vision* (Baton Rouge: Louisiana State University Press, 1972), observes: "Gower's explanation of all the dumb shows in *Pericles* is so extensive that one wonders why the first two are necessary. Since the letters' contents are explained anyway, the visual elaboration seems excessive. Ostensibly they present little more than the reading of a letter, which hardly merits the attention of this special dramatic form. For example, Simonides enters reading a letter in II.iv, the content of which he makes known in a soliloquy (15 ff.). The pantomime, on the other hand, removes the scene from the realistic level and insists on its symbolic potentials" (37).

35. In *The Secular Scripture: A Study of the Structure of Romance* (Cambridge and London: Harvard University Press, 1976), Northrop Frye comments, "*Pericles* . . . seems to be a deliberate experiment in presenting a traditional archetypal sequence as nakedly and baldly as possible" (51).

36. To these three sets of fathers and daughters we may add Cleon and Philoten. This daughter does not actually appear as a character onstage, but she is described by Gower (act 4 chorus, ll. 15–40).

37. For evidence that Wilkins' narrative was based upon a dramatized account of Pericles' story, performed by Shakespeare's company, see Nancy C. Michael, "The Relationship between the 1609 Quarto of *Pericles* and Wilkins' *Painful Adventures*," *Tulane Studies in English* 22 (1977): 51–68. The Shakespearean quality of the words spoken by Pericles when he sees his daughter was first noted by John Payne Collier, in *Shakespeare's Library: A Collection of the Plays, Romances, Novels, Poems and Histories Employed by Shakespeare in the Composition of His Works*, 2d ed. (London: Reeves and Turner, 1875), 4:240. The suggestion has been widely accepted. In his edition of Wilkins' *Painfull Adventures of Pericles Prince of Tyre* (Liverpool: University Press of Liverpool, 1953), Kenneth Muir says that the passage beginning with the words, "Poore inch of Nature," "seems to preserve a Shakespearean phrase, omitted by accident from Q" (xii). Similarly, J. C. Maxwell, in his edition of *Pericles* (Cambridge: Cambridge University Press, 1956), says that the words "belong to the Shakespeare original" (146). James G. McManaway concurs in his Pelican edition of *Pericles* (Baltimore: Penguin Books, 1961), 121. Philip Edwards, in the New Penguin *Pericles* (Harmondsworth, England: Penguin Books, 1976), restores the four words to the text (at 3.1.34 of his edition), but places them within square brackets. The "reconstructed text" of *Pericles*, included in *William Shakespeare: The Complete Works*, gen. ed. Stanley Wells and Gary Taylor (Oxford: Clarendon Press, 1986), restores Pericles' four words (scene 11, l. 34) and omits brackets.

38. David M. Bergeron, in "Reading and Writing in Shakespeare's Romances," *Criticism* 33 (Winter 1991): 91–113, comments on Pericles' action: "Like an artist, Pericles tries by writing to impose some order on his chaos, and to understand it. In the presence of death, he writes to show that he is alive. [Michel] De Certeau says that 'writing plays the role of a burial rite, in the ethnological and quasi-religious meaning of the term; it exorcises death by inserting it into discourse'" (97).

39. George Wilkins, *The Painfull Adventures of Pericles Prince of Tyre*, in *Narrative and Dramatic Sources of Shakespeare*, ed. Geoffrey Bullough, 6:522. G. Blakemore Evans, in the Riverside edition of *Pericles*, writes of Cerimon's statement about Egyptians, "eds. have felt that the text here is corrupt and that Wilkins preserves something close to the original" (1514). Evans then quotes the

words that Wilkins ascribes to Cerimon, and he concludes, "the blank verse movement of Wilkins' prose is obvious."

40. George Puttenham, *The Arte of English Poesie,* ed. Gladys Doidge Willcock and Alice Walker (Cambridge: Cambridge University Press, 1936), 303.

41. The comparison has a precedent in Plato's *Phaedrus,* wherein Socrates says, "The method of the art of healing is much the same as that of rhetoric." When Phaedrus asks, "How so?" Socrates answers, "In both cases you must analyse a nature, in one that of the body and in the other that of the soul. . . ." See *Plato,* trans. Harold North Fowler, W. R. M. Lamb, R. G. Bury, Loeb Classical Library (London: William Heinemann; Cambridge: Harvard University Press, 1914–27), 1:547–49.

42. A pictorial rendering of Mercury's connection with the written word appears in an anonymous Florentine engraving of about 1460. In the lower section of the print, the artist illustrates various human activities over which Mercury, who rides across the sky in his chariot, presides. In the foreground two seated scholars examine books piled on a table. See *Children of Mercury: The Education of Artists in the Sixteenth and Seventeenth Centuries* (Providence, R.I.: Brown University Press, 1984), 8.

43. Those jewels in the coffin may remind some spectators of the powerfully restorative effects which gems were believed to exert on the human body. Paracelsus, for instance, speaks of "the first entities of gems, which, indeed, by their primal essence most powerfully reinstate the whole body in its pristine powers, cleanse it from all its impurities, and renovate and restore it none otherwise than the fire changes lead into purest glass." See *The Hermetic and Alchemical Writings of . . . Paracelsus the Great,* trans. Arthur Edward Waite, 2 vols. (1894; reprint, Berkeley: Shambhala, 1976), 2:132.

44. In *Touches of Sweet Harmony: Pythagorean Cosmology and Renaissance Poetics* (San Marino, Calif.: The Huntington Library, 1974), S. K. Heninger, Jr., writes: "Music is capable of increasing or diminishing the passions of the human soul by affecting its harmony, and there are numerous examples of the emotional effects of music, Biblical as well as classical. David calmed the anguish of Saul by playing on the lyre and singing, and Timotheus by his music aroused Alexander from feasting to warfare. The source of this tradition for music's power is likely to have been Pythagoras' school made popular through Plato" (103). In a discussion of Marsilio Ficino's interest in the occult, John S. Mebane (*Renaissance Magic and the Return of the Golden Age: The Occult Tradition and Marlowe, Jonson, and Shakespeare* [Lincoln and London: University of Nebraska Press, 1989]), suggests the efficacy of music as a restorative to the human body and soul: "music imprints itself on the air, and consequently it can mingle freely with the *spiritus* which lies within the human ear. The harmoniously ordered forms are in motion, as are actual celestial influences, and they communicate that patterned movement, through the *spiritus,* to the soul" (31).

45. Richard Hosley has suggested to me that the action preceding Helicanus' words, "Behold him" (5.1.36), may have consisted of the drawing back of a curtain, revealing Pericles recumbent on a chaise longue, or day bed. The chaise may then have been either thrust or carried out onto the stage from the discovery space. That Pericles is probably behind a curtain is suggested by Lysimachus' question, "May we not see him?" (l. 31), and by Helicanus' ensuing remark, "Behold him." That Pericles is probably reclining is suggested both by the overall situation—he has been incommunicado for three months and has eaten little—and by his words to Marina later in the scene, "Come sit by me" (l. 141). Still

later, as Pericles hears the music of the spheres, he says, "Let me rest" (l. 235), and Lysimachus adds, "A pillow for his head" (l. 236).

46. Godfrey Goodman, *The Creatures Praysing God: or, The Religion of dumbe Creatures* (London, 1622), 22.

47. Phyllis Gorfain observes that Marina's reply, at 5.1.103–5, "encapsulates her autobiography in the form of an oppositional riddle" (15), which "contains at least two comments on a hidden referent; they oppose each other by contradicting laws of logic, natural form, or causality" (15, n. 1).

48. In the New Arden *Pericles,* Hoeniger notes: "The goddess is referred to only twice in Gower and in Twine, but about a dozen times in the play, which may be significant" (4). Marion Lomax, in *Stage Images and Traditions: Shakespeare to Ford* (Cambridge: Cambridge University Press, 1987), writes of Hoeniger's remark: "This would seem to be an enormous understatement," and Lomax goes on to observe, "it seems that Shakespeare carefully deprived the play of an active mother-figure. Until the end, none of the characters have such a guardian—the role is supplied by Diana, who plays a central part throughout" (82). Lomax provides an extensive and insightful analysis of Diana in the play.

49. For the conflation of Diana and Lucina, see Cicero, *De Natura Deorum,* trans. H. Rackham, Loeb Classical Library (1933; reprint, Cambridge: Harvard University Press; London: William Heinemann, 1961), 189–91. I am grateful to Michelle Keller for this reference.

50. In *1 Henry IV,* Falstaff alludes to Diana's familiar associations when he tells Prince Hal, "Let us be Diana's foresters, gentlemen of the shade, minions of the moon, and let men say we be men of good government, being govern'd, as the sea is, by our noble and chaste mistress the moon . . ." (1.2.25–29).

51. Reproduced by Barbara von Barghahn, *Age of Gold, Age of Iron: Renaissance Spain and Symbols of Monarchy,* 2 vols. (Lanham, Md., New York, London: University Press of America, 1985), 2: fig. 290. Such representations are based on classical statues. The Palazzo dei Conservatori, on the Capitoline hill in Rome, contains an ancient statue of the multibreasted Diana of Ephesus, whose body is decorated with the heads of various animals and whose head is surmounted by a tower.

52. *Le vere e nove imagini de gli dei delli antichi* (1615), ed. Stephen Orgel (New York and London: Garland, 1979), 109. Similarly, a ceiling decoration in the Palazzina Marfisa d'Este (Ferrara), painted at the end of the sixteenth century, depicts Diana as a symbol of fertility, her front covered with the same assemblage of breasts. Reproduced by Ranieri Varese, *Ferrara: Palazzina Marfisa* (Bologna: Calderini, 1980), 21, fig. 95.

53. Giordano Bruno, *The Heroic Frenzies,* trans. Paul Eugene Memmo, Jr., University of North Carolina Studies in the Romance Languages and Literatures 50 (Chapel Hill: University of North Carolina Press, 1964), 225.

54. In his *Adages* Erasmus observes: "They say that the Ephesians possessed certain magic characters and words, by the use of which they emerged successful in business of every kind. Our authority is Diogenianus. Eustathius on *Odyssey* 19 tells us that Croesus used these letters on his funeral pyre. They were, he says, certain obscure words very much like riddles, which made absolutely no continuous sense, and were inscribed on the feet, girdle, and crown of Diana" (*The Collected Works of Erasmus* [Toronto, Buffalo, and London: University of Toronto Press, 1974–   ], 34:67–68).

55. Lawrence Twine, *The Patterne of Painefull Adventures,* in *Narrative and Dramatic Sources of Shakespeare,* ed. Bullough, 6:481.

56. Robert Grams Hunter, in *Shakespeare and the Comedy of Forgiveness* (New York and London: Columbia University Press, 1965), observes that "In this use of the theophany, Shakespeare is returning to a romance tradition older than that of his immediate predecessors in the romantic drama" (138). Hunter cites *The Rare Triumphs of Love and Fortune* and *Sir Clyomon and Sir Clamydes.* Interestingly, the written word figures in the theophanies of both plays. Divine intervention in *Pericles, Cymbeline,* and other late romances is usefully discussed by Richard Paul Knowles, "'The More Delay'd, Delighted': Theophanies in the Last Plays," *Shakespeare Studies* 15 (1982): 269–80. Finally, Stephen Dickey, in "Language and Role in *Pericles*," *English Literary Renaissance* 16 (Autumn 1986): 550–66, notes that the intersection of art and nature "often makes for a supernatural moment in the romances" (561). Dickey makes this remark in a paragraph dealing with the invocation of Diana's name in *Pericles.*

57. In "'Deep clerks she dumbs': The Learned Heroine in *Apollonius of Tyre* and *Pericles*," *Comparative Drama* 22 (Winter 1988–89): 289–303, Elizabeth Archibald claims that Marina's skills, including her "writing poetry to Diana," are "stereotypically feminine" (295). Although weaving and needlework, also ascribed to Marina, may fall under this rubric, and although devotion to Diana may be more commonly feminine than masculine, I can find no justification in this or any other Renaissance play for calling writing a specifically feminine activity. The men in *Pericles* who write include Pericles, Helicanus, and, presumably, Cleon, author of the inscription on Marina's tomb. We may add Antiochus to this list, if he is the author of the riddle. Moreover, both Pericles and Simonides use figurative language involving the written word.

58. Hoeniger, "Gower and Shakespare in *Pericles*," 463.

59. See Katherine Duncan-Jones, *Sir Philip Sidney: Courtier Poet* (New Haven and London: Yale University Press, 1991), 115–17.

60. Peter J. French, *John Dee: The World of an Elizabethan Magus* (London: Routledge & Kegan Paul, 1972), 17.

61. In *Actes and Monuments of these latter and perillous dayes* (London, 1563), John Foxe refers to "Doctor Dee the great Conjurer" (1427).

62. John Dee, quoted by C. H. Josten, in "A Translation of John Dee's 'Monas Hieroglyphica' (Antwerp, 1564), with an Introduction and Annotations," *Ambix* 12 (June & October 1964): 88.

63. Ibid., 89.

64. Julian Roberts and Andrew G. Watson, ed., *John Dee's Library Catalogue* (London: The Bibliographical Society, 1990), 69. Roberts and Watson note that Dee once "claimed that his library contained about 3,000 printed volumes and 1,000 manuscripts" (22).

65. Richard Harvey, *An Astrological Discourse upon the great and notable Conjunction of the two superiour Planets, Saturne & Jupiter* (London, 1583), 5.

66. John Dee, *The Mathematicall Praeface to the Elements of Geometrie of Euclid of Megara (1570),* ed. Allen G. Debus (New York: Science History Publications, 1975), sig. *j.

67. Ibid., sigs. bi^v-bij

68. Ibid., sig. biij.

69. "A Translation of John Dee's 'Monas Hieroglyphica,'" 123.

70. Ibid., 127.

71. Martin Elsky, *Authorizing Words: Speech, Writing, and Print in the English Renaissance* (Ithaca and London: Cornell University Press, 1989), 138.

72. "A Translation of John Dee's 'Monas Hieroglyphica,'" 135.

73. Ibid., 121.

74. Nicholas H. Clulee, *John Dee's Natural Philosophy: Between Science and Religion* (London and New York: Routledge, 1988), 86–87.

75. In *The Occult Philosophy in the Elizabethan Age* (London, Boston, and Henley: Routledge & Kegan Paul, 1979), Frances A. Yates writes: "In *The Tempest,* written after Dee's death and during the period of 'the Elizabethan revival within the Jacobean age,' Dee is shadowed through Prospero in this most daring play . . ." (77). Robert Rentoul Reed, Jr., in *The Occult on the Tudor and Stuart Stage* (Boston: Christopher Publishing House, 1965), remarks: "Even within Elizabethan times, Dr. John Dee, as he tells us in his diary, employed his magic to conjure the archangel Raphael, not once but on a dozen occasions. Prospero, although an unparalleled magician, is a product of the Elizabethan-Jacobean conception of sorcery" (125).

76. Clulee, *John Dee's Natural Philosophy,* 217.

Chapter 9. The Book of Fate

1. "An Entertainment of King James and Queene Anne, at Theobalds," in *Ben Jonson,* ed. C. H. Herford, Percy and Evelyn Simpson, 11 vols. (Oxford: Clarendon Press, 1925–52), 7:155.

2. Allan H. Gilbert, in *The Symbolic Persons in the Masques of Ben Jonson* (Durham: Duke University Press, 1948), observes of Cartari: "In his illustration he shows paper and pen and ink bottle on a stone slab in their midst, because they were the chancellors of the gods, whose office it was to understand the will of Jove and the decisions of the heavenly senate and to put them in writing, so that they could be kept until the time of execution" (185).

3. *B. Jon: His Part of King James his Royall and Magnificent Entertainement through his Honorable Cittie of London, Thurseday the 15. of March. 1603,* in *Ben Jonson,* 7:92.

4. In *Martianus Capella and the Seven Liberal Arts,* trans. William Harris Stahl, Richard Johnson, and E. L. Burge, 2 vols. (New York: Columbia University Press, 1977), 2:24–25.

5. *Virgil,* trans. H. Rushton Fairclough, rev. ed., Loeb Classical Library, 2 vols. (London: William Heinemann; Cambridge: Harvard University Press, 1938), 1:259 (bk. 1, ll. 261–62).

6. Abraham Fraunce, *The Third Part of the Countesse of Pembrokes Yvychurch: Entituled, Amintas Dale* (London, 1592), fol. 5ᵛ.

7. *The Myths of Hyginus,* trans. and ed. Mary Grant, University of Kansas Humanistic Studies 34 (Lawrence: University of Kansas Publications, 1960), 178.

8. Jean Bottéro, *Mesopotamia: Writing, Reasoning, and the Gods,* trans. Zainab Bahrani and Marc Van De Mieroop (Chicago and London: University of Chicago Press, 1992), 101.

9. Although Varro identifies the Roman as Tarquinius Priscus (534–510 B.C.), others identify him as Tarquinius Superbus (616–579 B.C.).

10. See J. H. W. G. Liebeschuetz, *Continuity and Change in Roman Religion* (Oxford: Clarendon Press, 1979), 83.

11. *Virgil,* 1:509 (bk. 6, ll. 42–44).

12. Ibid., 1:379 (bk. 3, ll. 443–46).

13. H. W. Parke, *Sibyls and Sibylline Prophecy in Classical Antiquity,* ed. B. C. McGing (London and New York: Routledge, 1988), 91.

14. Ibid., 155.

15. Tertullian, in *Apologetical Works and Minucius Felix Octavius*, trans. Rudolph Arbesmann, O.S.A., Sister Emily Joseph Daly, C.S.J., and Edwin A. Quain, S.J., The Fathers of the Church, A New Translation 10 (New York: Fathers of the Church, 1950), 58.

16. Lactantius, *The Divine Institutes*, trans. Sister Mary Francis McDonald, O.P., The Fathers of the Church, A New Translation 49 (Washington, D.C.: The Catholic University of America Press, 1964), 34, 256, 282, and 530.

17. St. Augustine, *The City of God against the Pagans*, trans. Eva Matthews Sanford and William McAllen Green et al., Loeb Classical Library, 7 vols. (Cambridge: Harvard University Press; London: William Heinemann, 1957–72), 5:441, 447 (bk. 18, chap. 23).

18. John of Salisbury, *Frivolities of Courtiers and Footprints of Philosophers, Being a Translation of the First, Second, and Third Books and Selections from the Seventh and Eighth Books of the Policraticus of John of Salisbury*, trans. Joseph B. Pike (1938; reprint, New York: Octagon Books, 1972), 77.

19. Reproduced by Enzo Carli, *Il Duomo di Siena* (Genoa: SAGEP, 1979), plates 252–55. The pavements were designed by Benvenuto di Giovanni, Matteo di Giovanni, Neroccio di Bartolommeo, Guidoccio Cozzarelli, Urbano da Cortona, Giovanni di Stefano, and Antonio Federighi.

20. Reproduced by Cesare Brandi, *Il Tempio Malatestiano* (Rimini: Edizioni Radio Italiana, 1956), 108–15.

21. See Ellen S. Jacobowitz and Stephanie Loeb Stepanek, eds., *The Prints of Lucas van Leyden & His Contemporaries* (Washington, D.C.: National Gallery of Art, 1983), 228–31.

22. Reproduced by Corrado Ricci, *Pintoricchio (Bernardino di Betto of Perugia): His Life, Work, and Time*, trans. Florence Simmonds (London: William Heinemann; Philadelphia: J. B. Lippincott, 1902), 158.

23. Ricci reproduces the Erythraean Sibyl between pages 224 and 225; the Delphic Sibyl between pages 228 and 229.

24. One of these is reproduced by Ricci, 128.

25. The Sibyls are reproduced by Edgar Wind, "Michelangelo's Prophets and Sibyls," *Proceedings of the British Academy* 51 (1965): 47–84: plates xxvii (Delphic), xxx (Erythraean), xxxiii (Cumaean), xxxvi (Persian), xliii (Libyan).

26. John Napier, *A Plaine Discovery of the whole Revelation of Saint John: set downe in two treatises: The one searching and proving the true interpretation thereof: The other applying the same paraphrastically and Historically to the text* (Edinburgh, 1593), sig. T.

27. Sir John Floyer, *The Sibylline Oracles Translated from the Best Greek Copies, And compar'd with the Sacred Prophesies, Especially with Daniel and the Revelations, and With so much History as plainly shews, That many of the Sibyls Predictions are exactly fulfill'd* (London, 1713).

28. Matthew Gwinn, *Vertumnus sive Annus Recurrens*, in *Narrative and Dramatic Sources of Shakespeare*, ed. Geoffrey Bullough, 8 vols. (London: Routledge & Kegan Paul; New York: Columbia University Press, 1957–75), 7:470–71.

29. Bernard McElroy, in *Shakespeare's Mature Tragedies* (Princeton: Princeton University Press, 1973), argues persuasively that the background from which Othello came, "fraught with sibyls, magic, and arcane knowledge," helps to explain why the Moor believes in "a malignant fate" (124).

30. *Plotinus*, trans. A. H. Armstrong, Loeb Classical Library, 7 vols. (Cambridge: Harvard University Press; London: William Heinemann, 1966–88), 2:69 (*Ennead*, 2.3). In this same section Plotinus recalls the Platonic notion of fatality:

"now we should call to mind the Spindle, which according to the ancients the Fates spin; but for Plato the Spindle is the wandering and the fixed parts of the heavenly circuit, and the Fates and Necessity, who is their mother, turn the spindle and spin a thread at the birth of each one of us, and what is born comes to birth through Necessity" (2:73).

31. *"The Cosmographia" of Bernardus Silvestris*, trans. Winthrop Wetherbee (New York and London: Columbia University Press, 1973), 76.

32. Ibid., 115.

33. John of Salisbury, *Frivolities of Courtiers and Footprints of Philosophers [Policraticus]*, 98–99.

34. D. C. Allen, *The Star-Crossed Renaissance: the Quarrel about Astrology and Its Influence in England* (1941; reprint, New York: Octagon Books, 1973), 51.

35. See Paolo d'Ancona, *The Schifanoia Months at Ferrara*, trans. Lucia Krasnik ([Milan]: Edizioni del Milione, ca. 1954).

36. Reproduced by Rodolfo Signorini, *Lo Zodiaco di Palazzo d'Arco in Mantova*, 3d ed. (Mantua: Amministrazione Provinciale di Mantova, 1989).

37. Reproduced by Giuseppe Maria Sesti, *The Glorious Constellations: History and Mythology*, trans. Karin H. Ford (New York: Harry N. Abrams, 1991), 122–23.

38. Keith Thomas, in *Religion and the Decline of Magic: Studies in Popular Beliefs in Sixteenth and Seventeenth Century England* (London: Weidenfeld and Nicolson, 1971), observes that "there were four main branches to the practice of judicial astrology (to give it its full title, for the term 'astrology' by itself was often used as synonymous with 'astronomy'). First, there were the *general predictions,* based on the future movements of the heavens, and taking note of such impending events as eclipses of the sun and moon, or the conjunction of the major planets in one sign of the zodiac"; "Secondly, there were *nativities,* maps of the sky at the moment of a person's birth, either made on the spot at the request of the infant's parents, or reconstructed for individuals of mature years who could supply the details of their time of birth"; third, there were *"elections,* or choosing the right moment for the right action"; "Finally, there were *horary questions,* the most controversial part of the astrologer's art, and one which had only been developed after the days of Ptolemy by the Arabs. Its optimistic assumption was that the astrologer could resolve any question put to him by considering the state of the heavens at the exact moment when it was asked . . ." (286).

39. Johannes Kepler, quoted by Arthur Koestler, *The Sleepwalkers: A History of Man's Changing Vision of the Universe* (New York: Macmillan, 1959), 243.

40. Ibid.

41. Eugenio Garin, *Astrology in the Renaissance: The Zodiac of Life*, trans. Carolyn Jackson and June Allen, rev. Clare Robertson (London and Boston: Routledge & Kegan Paul, 1983), 68.

42. *The Collected Works of Erasmus* (Toronto, Buffalo, and London: University of Toronto Press, 1974–).

43. *Luther's Works*, ed. Jaroslav Pelikan and Helmut T. Lehmann, 55 vols. (St. Louis: Concordia Publishing House; Philadelphia: Fortress Press, 1955–86).

44. J. D. North, "The Reluctant Revolutionaries: Astronomy after Copernicus," in *The Universal Frame: Historical Essays in Astronomy, Natural Philosophy and Scientific Method* (London and Ronceverte, W.V.: Hambledon Press, 1989), 24.

45. *"The Cosmographia" of Bernardus Silvestris*, 92.

46. Garin, *Astrology in the Renaissance*, 69.

47. *The Hermetic and Alchemical Writings of . . . Paracelsus,* trans. Arthur Edward Waite, 2 vols. (1894; reprint, Berkeley: Shambhala, 1976), 2:165.
48. Robert Burton, *The Anatomy of Melancholy* (Oxford, 1621), 74.
49. Owen Felltham, *Resolves, A Duple Century* [3d edition] (London, 1628–29), 245.
50. Ibid.
51. Ibid., 302.
52. George Chapman, *The Conspiracy and Tragedy of Charles Duke of Byron,* ed. John Margeson, The Revels Plays (Manchester: Manchester University Press, 1988).
53. Thomas Middleton, *No Wit, No Help Like a Woman's,* ed. Lowell E. Johnson, Regents Renaissance Drama Series (Lincoln: University of Nebraska Press, 1976).
54. See Frederick Kiefer, *Fortune and Elizabethan Tragedy* (San Marino, Calif.: The Huntington Library, 1983), 61, 63, 78 n. 6, 79 n. 9, 183–84.
55. The quarto of 1600 gives the line as: "Will Fortune never come with both hands full, / But wet her faire words still in foulest termes?" (sig. H3). The folio has "write" for "wet," and "Letters" for "termes." The New Arden *2 Henry IV,* ed. A. R. Humphreys (London: Methuen, 1966), and the Pelican, ed. Allan G. Chester (Baltimore: Penguin Books, 1970), adopt the folio version. The New Penguin, ed. P. H. Davison (New York: Penguin Books, 1977), preserves the quarto version. The New Cambridge edition, ed. Giorgio Melchiori (Cambridge: Cambridge University Press, 1989), gives the lines as: "Will Fortune never come with both hands full, / But whet her fair words still in foulest terms?" (ll. 103–4).
56. Fraunce, *The Third part of the Countesse of Pembrokes Yvychurch,* fol. 59. Richard Linche, in *The Fountaine of Ancient Fiction* (London, 1599), says that Fortune "is alwaies flying from destiny, seeking all means to avoid her company, for that indeed these two can never accord or agree together; for so much as where Destiny sets hir foot, Fortune is there as it were inchanted & conjured, as having no power, efficacie, or vertue" (sig. Ccij). Linche's book is a partial translation of Vincenzo Cartari's *Imagini de i dei de gli antichi* (1580 edition).
57. Plutarch's *Life of Julius Caesar,* in Sir Thomas North's translation, makes explicit the cautionary nature of Artemidorus' suit: "Artemidorus . . . a Doctor of Rethoricke in the Greeke tongue, who by meanes of his profession was verie familliar with certaine of Brutus confederates, and therefore knew the most parte of all their practises against Caesar: came and brought him a little bill wrytten with his owne hand, of all that he ment to tell him" (in *Narrative and Dramatic Sources of Shakespeare,* ed. Bullough, 5:84–85). In the play Artemidorus reads aloud (to himself) the contents of the paper he would have Caesar read (2.3.1–10).
58. Robert S. Knapp, in *Shakespeare—The Theater and the Book* (Princeton: Princeton University Press, 1989), comments on the King's speech about fate and Warwick's response: "Turned though they are to psychological purposes, the terms of both complaint and consolation draw larger meanings in their train, for in the book, its figures, and such prophecy as gives figure an embodied form rest all those implications of authored and providential history that motivate Christian exegesis, whether practiced on the Bible, the sixth age, or the Tudor myth in Shakespeare" (21–22).

Chapter 10. Fate on the Stage

1. T. S. Eliot, introduction to *Seneca His Tenne Tragedies Translated into English* (1927; reprint, Bloomington and London: Indiana University Press, 1966), xxv.

2. Philip Edwards, ed., *The Spanish Tragedy*, The Revels Plays (1959; reprint, London: Methuen, 1969), lv.

3. For a useful survey of the theatrical properties (including letters and books), see Eleanor M. Tweedie, "'Action is Eloquence': The Staging of Thomas Kyd's *Spanish Tragedy*," *Studies in English Literature, 1500–1900* 16 (Spring 1976): 223–39.

4. *The Spanish Tragedy*, ed. Edwards.

5. C. F. Tucker Brooke and Nathaniel Burton Paradise, eds., *English Drama, 1580–1642* (Lexington, Mass.: D. C. Heath, 1933), 99.

6. Although Andrea's description of the underworld is indebted to book 6 of the *Aeneid*, Virgil makes no mention of a passport, which seems to be Kyd's invention.

7. Precisely because he is so histrionic, Balthazar's evocations of destiny (2.1.118 and 132) have less import than they would if spoken by another character.

8. Commenting on "structural precision in the play," Ernest William Talbert, in *Elizabethan Drama and Shakespeare's Early Plays: An Essay in Historical Criticism* (Chapel Hill: University of North Carolina Press, 1963), observes: "Hieronimo's reading of two letters . . . frames Kyd's emphasis upon Lorenzo's concatenated plots and may well have been conceived of as a structural device" (73).

9. The hangman brings the letter to Hieronimo, saying, "O lord sir, he went the wrong way, the fellow had a fair commission to the contrary. Sir, here is his passport" (3.7.22–23). The word "passport" recalls Andrea's repeated use of the same term in the induction. Its use in this context may be meant to suggest the connection between what happens in this world and in the next.

10. A production of *The Spanish Tragedy* at the National Theatre, London, adopted an ingenious staging of Hieronimo's speech. In this production directed by Michael Bogdanov and first staged on 22 September 1982, Hieronimo entered carrying a small black book, the gold crucifix on the cover suggesting a New Testament. When he said, "*Vindicta mihi*," he was reading aloud the words in Romans which lay open on the page before him. Having spoken the subsequent lines in English, Hieronimo turned upstage, where his glance fell upon a second book, placed on a chair by Revenge. Hieronimo picked up this book, evidently a collection of Seneca's tragedies, while Revenge, who functioned as a sort of stage manager, pocketed the New Testament. Although this staging is unlikely to have been adopted in Kyd's day, it not only accounted for the diverse sources of the Latin quotations in Hieronimo's speech but also skillfully externalized the conflicting impulses within his mind. For discussions of this production, see Elizabeth Maslen, "The Dynamics of Kyd's 'Spanish Tragedy,'" *English* 32 (Summer 1983): 111–25; Richard Proudfoot, "Kyd's *Spanish Tragedy*," *Critical Quarterly* 25 (Spring 1983): 71–76; and the reviews by Emrys Jones, *Times Literary Supplement* (15 October 1982), 1131; and by G. M. Pearce, *Cahiers élizabéthains* no. 26 (October 1984): 101–3.

11. Fredson Bowers, in "A Note on *The Spanish Tragedy*," *Modern Language Notes* 53 (December 1938): 590–91, observes: "Certainly on hearing *Vindicta mihi* from his lips the Elizabethan audience would inevitably recall not Seneca but the Bible, for this was the standard and familiar text quoted in sermons and tracts against private revengefulness" (591). Geoffrey Aggeler, in "The Eschatological Crux in *The Spanish Tragedy*," *Journal of English and Germanic Philology* 86 (July 1987): 319–31, argues of Hieronimo: "The Christian commonplaces he utters initially are maxims he has accepted all his life, even up to the moment he

cried aloud to his king for justice, but the rage within him will not permit Christian patience. He does not rationalize. The lines from Seneca are not arguments to counter the Biblical injunctions but *sententiae* he finds expressive of his own vengeful resolution and his readiness to accept whatever consequences 'destiny' decrees" (327).

12. Long before Bowers wrote his note of 1938, Frederick S. Boas, editor of *The Works of Thomas Kyd* (Oxford: Clarendon Press, 1901), had argued that the words "*Vindicta mihi*" were "From Seneca's *Octavia*: '*Vindicta debetur mihi*'" (408).

13. In "The Book of Seneca in *The Spanish Tragedy*," *Studies in English Literature, 1500–1900* 14 (Spring 1974): 201–8, Scott McMillin seeks to buttress the argument first put forward by William Empson that Hieronimo, in the "*Vindicta mihi*" speech, twists the meaning of Seneca's words: "The three Senecan passages have nothing to do with revenge, and wrenching them to prove the case for vengeance seems to be a piece of desperate logic" (202). Even if one were to accept this claim, it is difficult to see what significance it could have for the play in performance. The argument assumes that an audience has read the three Senecan plays, recalls what character speaks each passage in each play, remembers the precise context of the Latin lines, and has the time to compare mentally the original context of the lines with that in Hieronimo's soliloquy. Few Elizabethans (or moderns), I believe, could have accomplished this. For the original argument by Empson, see "*The Spanish Tragedy*," *Nimbus* 3 (Spring 1956): 16–29; reprinted in *Elizabethan Drama: Modern Essays in Criticism,* ed. R. J. Kaufmann (New York: Oxford University Press, 1961), 60–80.

14. In the "*Vindicta mihi*" soliloquy (ll. 14–19), Hieronimo speaks of both "destiny" and "heaven" without drawing any clear distinction between them. Were the world of the play unambiguously Christian, this might suggest inconsistency if not confusion. But the world that Kyd creates owes as much to the ancients as it does to contemporary belief. Thus while the characters may speak of "heaven," "hell," and "saints," the induction locates the Ghost of Andrea in a classical underworld, where he is subject to the judgment of Minos, Aeacus, and Rhadamanth, not Christ. The playwright, like many other writers of his time, conflates the classical and the modern. Gordon Braden, in *Renaissance Tragedy and the Senecan Tradition: Anger's Privilege* (New Haven and London: Yale University Press, 1985), observes, "The pagan hell that Hieronimo keeps invoking is not systematically the opposite of a Christian heaven; Kyd's own frame scenes vouch for the authority of the judges Hieronimo here names, as they also vouch for the concern of the dead with having their deaths avenged, and indeed for the blessed reward that Hieronimo will eventually receive for his actions" (204).

15. G. K. Hunter, "Ironies of Justice in *The Spanish Tragedy*," *Renaissance Drama* 8 (1965): 93.

16. Geoffrey Whitney, *A Choice of Emblemes* (Leiden, 1586), 183.

17. The significance of writing in Shakespeare's *Hamlet* has been explored by Margaret W. Ferguson, in "*Hamlet:* letters and spirits," in *Shakespeare and the Question of Theory,* ed. Patricia Parker and Geoffrey Hartman (New York and London: Methuen, 1985), 292–309.

18. Alan C. Dessen, in *Elizabethan Stage Conventions and Modern Interpreters* (Cambridge: Cambridge University Press, 1984), observes of Hamlet's speech: "Generations of actors playing Hamlet have carried and used tablets here, but the repeated emphasis upon memory and forgetting throughout the play could

suggest (as in 'the table of my memory' in l. 98) that the tragic hero's 'tables' are not literal but rather imaginary or metaphoric" (68).

19. Henry Peacham, *Minerva Britanna* (London, 1612), 140.

20. The 1592 quarto of *The Spanish Tragedy* gives all the speeches in English, with this explanation: "Gentlemen, this play of Hieronimo in sundry languages, was thought good to be set down in English more largely, for the easier understanding to every public reader" (4.4.10 s.d.). Philip Edwards believes that "Kyd originally intended the play to be in English, but that, when abridgement of an over-long play was required, a mime was substituted, a mime accompanied, for the sake of 'drama,' with a few well-chosen lines in gibberish or 'sundry languages,' and references to these languages were inserted before and after the mime" (xxxvii). However, Michael Bogdanov, for his National Theatre production, had the English lines translated into the four languages and the device worked surprisingly well. Although the audience may not have understood the foreign words, that audience thoroughly enjoyed the outlandish costumes, the exaggerated enunciation, and the posturing of Balthazar and Lorenzo while they were "in character." The comic effect enhanced the grotesque quality of a scene that evokes the biblical account of Babel.

21. S. F. Johnson, "*The Spanish Tragedy,* or Babylon Revisited," in *Essays on Shakespeare and Elizabethan Drama in Honor of Hardin Craig,* ed. Richard Hosley (Columbia: University of Missouri Press, 1962), 24.

22. St. Augustine, *The City of God against the Pagans,* trans. Eva Matthews Sanford, William McAllen Green, et al., Loeb Classical Library, 7 vols. (Cambridge: Harvard University Press; London: William Heinemann, 1957–72), 5:27 (bk. 16, sec. 4).

23. This spelling was first pointed out by Peter Goodstein in "Hieronimo's Destruction of Babylon," *English Language Notes* 3 (March 1966): 173, n. 5.

24. Carol McGinnis Kay, "Deception Through Words: A Reading of *The Spanish Tragedy,*" *Studies in Philology* 74 (January 1977): 30.

25. Jonas A. Barish, "*The Spanish Tragedy,* or the Pleasures and Perils of Rhetoric," in *Elizabethan Theatre,* Stratford-upon-Avon Studies 9 (London: Edward Arnold, 1966), 79.

26. Carol McGinnis Kay, in "Deception through Words," contends: "we never know whether Pedringano's claim that Bel-imperia has written love letters to Horatio is fact or fiction" (29). Although this is technically accurate, no evidence to contradict the servant's statement ever appears in the play. (In the National Theatre production, described above, the audience witnessed Pedringano actually carrying a letter from Bel-imperia to Horatio.)

27. See Susan McCloskey, "The Price of Misinterpretation in *The Duchess of Malfi,*" in *From Renaissance to Restoration: Metamorphoses of the Drama,* ed. Robert Markley and Laurie Finke (Cleveland, Ohio: Bellflower Press, 1984), 34–55.

28. John Webster, *The Duchess of Malfi,* ed. John Russell Brown, The Revels Plays (1964; reprint, London: Methuen, 1972).

29. Kathleen McLuskie, in "Drama and Sexual Politics: the Case of Webster's Duchess," in *Drama, Sex and Politics,* ed. James Redmond, Themes in Drama 7 (Cambridge: Cambridge University Press, 1985), pp. 77–91, notes how unusual is this characterization: "In terms of the stated ideologies of Webster's own day, *The Duchess of Malfi* seems a remarkable play. There was little in the contemporary discussion of women which could have prefigured Webster's sympathetic portrayal of the Duchess's strong-willed sexuality . . ." (88). Similarly, Theodora A.

Jankowski, in "Defining/Confining the Duchess: Negotiating the Female Body in John Webster's *The Duchess of Malfi*," *Studies in Philology* 87 (Spring 1990): 221–45, remarks, "The Duchess is represented as being radically different from the traditional picture of the Renaissance wife in this scene. Not only is she a woman who is capable of commanding her husband specifically as regards his sexual desires (III.2.4–6), and refusing him—'you get no lodging here tonight, my lord' (2). But she is also a woman who thoroughly enjoys her sexuality—'Alas, what pleasure can two lovers find in sleep?' (10)—and the products of it, her children" (235–36).

30. Peter B. Murray, in *A Study of John Webster* (The Hague and Paris: Mouton, 1969), 137, and Arthur C. Kirsch, in *Jacobean Dramatic Perspectives* (Charlottesville: University Press of Virginia, 1972), 106, both suggest that the Cardinal's book is a Bible. This may well be the case, although in *The White Devil*, ed. John Russell Brown, The Revels Plays, 2d ed. (1966; reprint, London: Methuen, 1968), Lodovico speaks of a prayer book that is poisoned (5.1.69).

31. William Archer, in *The Old Drama and the New: An Essay in Re-valuation* (New York: Dodd, Mead, 1929), complained: "What should we say of a modern dramatist who should bring about the revelation of a deadly secret through the inconceivable folly of a leading character, who first composes a compromising document, and then drops it in the actual presence of a man whom he knows to be a spy!" (54). Christopher Ricks, in "The Tragedies of Webster, Tourneur and Middleton: Symbols, Imagery and Conventions," a chapter in *The Sphere History of English Literature*, vol. 3, *English Drama to 1710*, ed. Ricks (1971; reprint, New York: Peter Bedrick Books, 1987), finds Archer's comment "somewhat too fierce" (356), though he seems to share essentially the same feeling. Ricks, however, suggests a way of accounting for the incident psychologically: "My own view is that Webster's Antonio is indeed accident-prone, oppressed by the sense that he will never get away with it, half-happy to slump into the only anxiety-free state of mind available to him: death" (357). Jonathan Dollimore, in *Radical Tragedy*, 2d ed. (New York and London: Harvester Wheatsheaf, 1989), quotes Ricks and goes on to argue: "Alternatively it would be possible to reply that the episode is not intrinsically implausible: the play makes it clear that it is night and that Antonio and Bosola are in darkness (the servant exits at line 42 to fetch a lanthorn)—and so on" (66).

32. Clifford Leech, *John Webster: A Critical Study* (London: The Hogarth Press, 1951), 83.

33. Joan Lord Hall, in *The Dynamics of Role-Playing in Jacobean Tragedy* (London: Macmillan, 1991), comments of Bosola: "His impulse of compassion towards the Duchess is genuine enough in 'Now, by my life, I pity you' (IV.i.88). And when she curses the stars along with her brothers, Bosola's rejoinder, 'Look you, the stars shine still' (l. 99) need not be a cruel reminder of cosmic indifference; rather it is his way of fostering in her that stern impassivity he now sees mirrored in the universe" (161).

34. See Muriel Bradbrook, "Fate and Chance in 'The Duchess of Malfi,'" *Modern Language Review* 42 (July 1947): 283–91. Reprinted in *Aspects of Dramatic Form in the English and the Irish Renaissance: The Collected Papers of Muriel Bradbrook*, 3 vols. (Brighton, Sussex: Harvester Press; Totowa, N.J.: Barnes & Noble, 1983), 3:73–88.

35. The idea that Bosola sends the actual horoscope to Ferdinand is based on the Duke's reaction to the news: "here's the cursed day / To prompt my memory, and here 't shall stick / Till of her bleeding heart I make a sponge / To wipe it

out" (2.5.13–16). John Russell Brown, in his edition of the play, observes: "[F. L.] Lucas suggested that Ferdinand refers to the horoscope which Bosola has sent to Rome, and at 'here 't shall stick' thrusts it back into his bosom. But this gesture might be too difficult for an actor to effect quickly enough for this 'wild' scene" (64). In any event, says Brown, Ferdinand's words about the bleeding heart "are highly figurative . . . and he may be speaking so already: like Hamlet, he may allude to the 'table of his memory' and the 'book and volume of his brain' (*Ham.*, I. v.97–104)."

36. Elmer Edgar Stoll, in *John Webster* (Boston: printed by A. Mudge & Son; Cambridge: sold by the Harvard Cooperative Society, 1905), notes Webster's dependence upon dramatic tradition: "From Kyd or from Marston come[s] the appearance of the hero in black, book in hand, to meditate . . ." (115). Stoll refers to the entrance of Hieronimo in *The Spanish Tragedy* (3.13), and to the entrance of Antonio in *Antonio's Revenge* (2.3). F. L. Lucas, in *The Complete Works of John Webster*, 4 vols. (London: Chatto & Windus, 1927), 2:198, also observes a similarity with the entrance of Govianus in *The Second Maiden's Tragedy* (4.4). To these precedents John Russell Brown adds the protagonist of *Hamlet* (2.2).

37. In the National Theatre production of 1985, directed by Philip Prowse, Bosola (played by Ian McKellen) sometimes wore spectacles, giving him a scholarly appearance.

38. *A Wonderfull, strange and miraculous, Astrologicall Prognostication*, in *The Works of Thomas Nashe*, ed. Ronald B. McKerrow, 5 vols. (London: A. H. Bullen, 1905), 3:381.

39. Thomas Nashe, *Pierce Pennilesse, His Supplication to the Divell (1592)*, ed. G. B. Harrison, Elizabethan and Jacobean Quartos (1924; reprint, New York: Barnes & Noble, 1966), 63.

40. Ibid., 63–64.

41. Charles G. Nauert, Jr., in *Agrippa and the Crisis of Renaissance Thought*, Illinois Studies in the Social Sciences 55 (Urbana: University of Illinois Press, 1965), observes that *De Occulta Philosophia* "became and long remained the most comprehensive, the most widely used and respected of all books on the magical arts" (229). According to Nauert, Agrippa's magician utilizes astral influence "to do things which he could not accomplish by merely terrestrial powers" (269).

42. Frances A. Yates, *The Occult Philosophy in the Elizabethan Age* (London, Boston and Henley: Routledge & Kegan Paul, 1979), 40.

43. Virginia F. Stern, *Gabriel Harvey: His Life, Marginalia and Library* (Oxford: Clarendon Press, 1979), 129.

Conclusion

1. Thomas Fuller, *The History of the Worthies of England* (London, 1662), sig. Hhh4.

2. David McPherson, in "Ben Jonson's Library and Marginalia: An Annotated Catalogue," *Studies in Philology* 71, no. 5 (December 1974): 1–103, observes: "In 1614 Jonson's personal library was called 'well-furnisht' by the great scholar John Selden, who would not use the term lightly" (5).

3. *Dialogue Concerning the Two Chief World Systems—Ptolemaic & Copernican*, trans. Stillman Drake (Berkeley and Los Angeles: University of California Press, 1953), 105.

4. *Time*, 6 January 1992, 23.

5. Introduction to *Future Libraries,* a special issue of *Representations* no. 42 (Spring 1993): 1.
6. *Times,* 17 June 1994.
7. *Time,* 6 December 1993, 48.

Appendix 1

1. Eric A. Havelock, *Origins of Western Literacy,* Monograph Series 14 (Toronto: The Ontario Institute for Studies in Education, 1976), 20.
2. Keith Thomas, "The Meaning of Literacy in Early Modern England," in *The Written Word: Literacy in Transition,* ed. Gerd Baumann (Oxford: Clarendon Press, 1986), 100.
3. See Jonathan Goldberg, *Writing Matter: From the Hands of the English Renaissance* (Stanford: Stanford University Press, 1990), 240–41.
4. R. A. Houston, *Literacy in Early Modern Europe: Culture and Education, 1500–1800* (London and New York: Longman, 1988), 117.
5. R. S. Schofield, "The Measurement of Literacy in Pre-Industrial England," in *Literacy in Traditional Societies,* ed. Jack Goody (Cambridge: Cambridge University Press, 1968), 315.
6. Ibid.
7. Patrick Collinson, *The Birthpangs of Protestant England: Religious and Cultural Change in the Sixteenth and Seventeenth Centuries* (London: Macmillan, 1988), 119.
8. H. S. Bennett, *English Books & Readers, 1603 to 1640* (Cambridge: Cambridge University Press, 1970), 85.
9. David Cressy, *Literacy and the Social Order: Reading and Writing in Tudor and Stuart England* (Cambridge: Cambridge University Press, 1980), 2.
10. H. S. Bennett, *English Books & Readers, 1475 to 1557* (Cambridge: Cambridge University Press, 1952), 27.
11. Rudolf Hirsch, *Printing, Selling and Reading, 1450–1550* (Wiesbaden: Otto Harrassowitz, 1967), 94.
12. Cressy, *Literacy and the Social Order,* 53.
13. Miriam Usher Chrisman, in *Lay Culture, Learned Culture: Books and Social Change in Strasbourg, 1480–1599* (New Haven and London: Yale University Press, 1982), concludes of literacy in the city of Strasbourg, "If one puts all the evidence together—the production of books for the different reader-markets, the professional libraries, the teaching of reading and writing to adults, the testamentary inventories—it is clear that reading was not limited to the scholars and the educated. There was probably a fairly high literacy rate among the urban population, and these readers seem to have read a surprising variety of books" (75).
14. Steve Rappaport, *Worlds within Worlds: Structures of Life in Sixteenth-Century London* (Cambridge: Cambridge University Press, 1989), 298.
15. Ibid., 298–99.
16. Ibid., 301.
17. Harvey J. Graff, *The Legacies of Literacy: Continuities and Contradictions in Western Culture and Society* (Bloomington and Indianapolis: Indiana University Press, 1987), 5.
18. Brian Stock, *The Implications of Literacy: Written Language and Models of Interpretation in the Eleventh and Twelfth Centuries* (Princeton: Princeton University Press, 1983), 9.
19. Tessa Watt, "Publisher, pedlar, pot-poet: The changing character of the

broadside trade, 1550–1640," in *Spreading the Word: The Distribution Networks of Print, 1550–1850*, ed. Robin Myers and Michael Harris (Winchester: St Paul's Bibliographies; Detroit: Omnigraphics, 1990), 62.

20. Roger Chartier, *The Cultural Uses of Print in Early Modern France*, trans. Lydia G. Cochrane (Princeton: Princeton University Press, 1987), 6.

21. Natalie Zemon Davis, "Printing and the People," in *Society and Culture in Early Modern France* (Stanford: Stanford University Press, 1975), 218.

22. Richard G. Cole, "The Dynamics of Printing in the Sixteenth Century," in *The Social History of the Reformation*, ed. Lawrence P. Buck and Jonathan W. Zophy (Columbus: Ohio State University Press, 1972), 97.

23. Walter J. Ong, *Rhetoric, Romance, and Technology: Studies in the Interaction of Expression and Culture* (Ithaca and London: Cornell University Press, 1971), 42.

24. Christopher Marlowe, *Tamburlaine the Great*, ed. J. S. Cunningham, The Revels Plays (Manchester: Manchester University Press; Baltimore: Johns Hopkins University Press, 1981).

25. Raphael Holinshed, *The Description of England* in *The First and Second Volumes of Chronicles* (London, 1587), 197.

26. Sir Thomas Elyot, *The boke named the Governour* (London, 1531), fol. 111.

27. George Puttenham, *The Arte of English Poesie*, ed. Gladys Doidge Willcock and Alice Walker (Cambridge: Cambridge University Press, 1936), 54.

28. Ibid., 58.

29. *The Tragedy of Master Arden of Faversham*, ed. M. L. Wine, The Revels Plays (London: Methuen, 1973).

30. Tessa Watt, *Cheap Print and Popular Piety, 1550–1640* (Cambridge: Cambridge University Press, 1991), 221.

31. Ben Jonson, *Bartholomew Fair*, ed. E. A. Horsman, The Revels Plays (Cambridge: Harvard University Press, 1960).

32. Jay P. Anglin, "The Expansion of Literacy: Opportunities for the Study of the Three Rs in the London Diocese of Elizabeth I," *Guildhall Studies in London History* 4 (April 1980): 63–74.

33. Ann Jennalie Cook, *The Privileged Playgoers of Shakespeare's London, 1576–1642* (Princeton: Princeton University Press, 1981), 73.

34. See Alfred Harbage, *Shakespeare's Audience* (New York: Columbia University Press, 1941). Cook's thesis has been accepted by Michael Hattaway, in *Elizabethan Popular Theatre: Plays in Performance* (London and Boston: Routledge & Kegan Paul, 1982). Hattaway concludes his examination of audiences by saying, "It seems therefore that the majority of the audience was, as Ann Jennalie Cook has argued recently, 'privileged'" (49). That thesis, however, has been attacked by Andrew Gurr, in *Playgoing in Shakespeare's London* (Cambridge: Cambridge University Press, 1987). He writes of Cook: "She replaced Harbage's stereotype of the idle artisan with the equally oversimplifying stereotype of the idle rich" (4). Gurr observes: "Over the years between the 1560s, when the first purpose-built playhouses were established, and 1642, when the playhouses were closed, well over fifty million visits were made to playhouses. Even by Cook's very generous definition of the privileged as including 350,000 of the London population they could not have provided more than a small part of that total."

35. Martin Butler, Appendix II: "Shakespeare's unprivileged playgoers, 1576–1642," in *Theatre and Crisis, 1632–1642* (Cambridge: Cambridge University Press, 1984), 305.

36. Ibid., 305.
37. William Fennor, quoted by E. K. Chambers, *The Elizabethan Stage*, 4 vols. (Oxford: Clarendon Press, 1923), 2:549.
38. Gurr, *Playgoing in Shakespeare's London*, 55.

Appendix 2

1. Thomas Kyd, *The Spanish Tragedy*, ed. Philip Edwards, The Revels Plays (London: Methuen, 1959).
2. Richard Brome, *The Antipodes*, ed. Ann Haaker, Regents Renaissance Drama Series (Lincoln: University of Nebraska Press, 1966).
3. Thomas Middleton, *Michaelmas Term*, ed. Richard Levin, Regents Renaissance Drama Series (Lincoln: University of Nebraska Press, 1966).
4. *Appius and Virginia*, in *The Complete Works of John Webster*, ed. F. L. Lucas, 4 vols. (London: Chatto & Windus, 1927), vol. 3.
5. *The Woman-Hater*, in *The Works of Francis Beaumont and John Fletcher*, ed. Arnold Glover and A. R. Waller, The English Classics, 10 vols. (1905–12; reprint, New York: Octagon Books, 1969), 10:126.
6. *The Noble Spanish Soldier*, in *The Dramatic Works of Thomas Dekker*, ed. Fredson Bowers, 4 vols. (Cambridge: Cambridge University Press, 1953–61), vol. 4.
7. George Chapman, *All Fools*, ed. Frank Manley, Regents Renaissance Drama Series (Lincoln: University of Nebraska Press, 1968).
8. *Sir John Oldcastle, Part 1*, in *The Oldcastle Controversy*, ed. Peter Corbin and Douglas Sedge (Manchester: Manchester University Press, 1991).
9. Thomas Middleton, *A Mad World, My Masters*, ed. Standish Henning, Regents Renaissance Drama Series (Lincoln: University of Nebraska Press, 1965).
10. John Ford, *'Tis Pity She's a Whore*, ed. Derek Roper, The Revels Plays (London: Methuen, 1975).
11. *Westward Ho*, in *The Dramatic Works of Thomas Dekker*, vol. 2.
12. Richard Brome, *A Jovial Crew*, ed. Ann Haaker, Regents Renaissance Drama Series (Lincoln: University of Nebraska Press, 1968).
13. Thomas Middleton, *No Wit, No Help Like a Woman's*, ed. Lowell E. Johnson, Regents Renaissance Drama Series (Lincoln: University of Nebraska Press, 1976).
14. John Marston, *Antonio and Mellida*, ed. W. Reavley Gair, The Revels Plays (Manchester and New York: Manchester University Press, 1991).
15. Robert Greene, *Friar Bacon and Friar Bungay*, ed. Daniel Seltzer, Regents Renaissance Drama Series (Lincoln: University of Nebraska Press, 1963).
16. Thomas Dekker, *The Shoemaker's Holiday*, ed. R. L. Smallwood and Stanley Wells, The Revels Plays (Manchester: Manchester University Press; Baltimore: Johns Hopkins University Press, 1979).
17. *A Yorkshire Tragedy*, ed. A. C. Cawley and Barry Gaines, The Revels Plays (Manchester: Manchester University Press, 1986).
18. Francis Beaumont, *The Knight of the Burning Pestle*, ed. Sheldon P. Zitner, The Revels Plays (Manchester: Manchester University Press, 1984).
19. Ben Jonson, *The Staple of News*, ed. Anthony Parr, The Revels Plays (Manchester and New York: Manchester University Press, 1988).
20. "Hero and Leander," in *The Complete Works of Christopher Marlowe*, ed. Fredson Bowers, 2 vols. (Cambridge: Cambridge University Press, 1973), 2:448, 2d sestiad, ll. 129–30.

21. John Marston and others, *The Insatiate Countess,* ed. Giorgio Melchiori, The Revels Plays (Manchester: Manchester University Press, 1984).
22. Thomas Middleton and William Rowley, *The Changeling,* ed. N. W. Bawcutt, The Revels Plays (1958; reprint, London: Methuen, 1970).
23. The hand with extended finger had been a feature of manuscripts, too. M. T. Clanchy, in *From Memory to Written Record: England, 1066–1307* (London: Edward Arnold, 1979), observes, "Such signs are not essentially different from the rubrics, capital letters, running titles, introductory paragraph flourishes and other aids to the reader which are usual in medieval manuscripts" (142).
24. Erasmus, *Apophthegmes, that is to saie, prompte, quicke, wittie and sentencious saiynges* (London, 1542), fol. 86^v-87. Erasmus continues: "And the middlemust fynger was emong menne of olde tyme rekened slaundreous, for a cause at this present not to bee rehersed."
25. Massinger and Field, *The Fatal Dowry,* ed. T. A. Dunn, Fountainwell Drama Texts (Berkeley and Los Angeles: University of California Press, 1969).
26. *The Honest Whore, Part 2,* in *The Dramatic Works of Thomas Dekker,* vol. 2.
27. *The Sun's Darling,* in *The Dramatic Works of Thomas Dekker,* vol. 4.
28. Dekker, *Match Me in London,* ibid., vol. 3.
29. *The Malcontent,* ed. George K. Hunter, The Revels Plays (London: Methuen, 1975).
30. Ann Thompson and John O. Thompson, *Shakespeare: Meaning & Metaphor* (Iowa City: University of Iowa Press, 1987), 179. The authors make this comment in their chapter entitled, "Meaning, 'Seeing,' Printing," an insightful treatment of Shakespeare's figurative language.
31. *Northward Ho,* in *The Dramatic Works of Thomas Dekker,* vol. 2.
32. Curt F. Bühler, *The Fifteenth-Century Book: the Scribes, the Printers, the Decorators* (Philadelphia: University of Pennsylvania Press, 1960), 40.
33. James Douglas Farquhar, "The Manuscript as a Book," in *Pen to Press: Illustrated Manuscripts and Printed Books in the First Century of Printing,* ed. Sandra Hindman and James Douglas Farquhar ([College Park]: University of Maryland Art Department, 1977), 12.
34. Virginia Tuttle Clayton, *Gardens on Paper: Prints and Drawings, 1200–1900* (Washington, D.C.: National Gallery of Art, 1990), 35.
35. Sandra Hindman, Introduction to *Pen to Press,* ed. Hindman and Farquhar, 2.
36. Ibid., 1.
37. Harry George Fletcher III, *New Aldine Studies: Documentary Essays on the Life and Work of Aldus Manutius* (San Francisco: Bernard M. Rosenthal, 1988), 5–6.
38. Martin Lowry, *The World of Aldus Manutius: Business and Scholarship in Renaissance Venice* (Ithaca: Cornell University Press, 1979), 131.
39. Introduction to *Pen to Press,* ed. Hindman and Farquhar, 1.
40. Lotte Hellinga, in *Caxton in Focus: The Beginning of Printing in England* (London: The British Library, 1982), writes: "The *Recuyell* was probably printed on two presses working concurrently. The fifteen months between the beginning of 1473 and the end of March 1474 would therefore be a realistic length of time for Caxton to have started his enterprise and produced the first two books . . ." (48).
41. *The Prologues and Epilogues of William Caxton,* ed. W. J. B. Crotch, Early English Text Society, no. 176 (London: Oxford University Press, 1928), 7–8.

Appendix 3

1. Ann Pasternak Slater, *Shakespeare the Director* (Brighton, Sussex: Harvester Press; Totowa, N.J.: Barnes & Noble, 1982), 179.

2. Mark Taylor, in "Letters and Readers in *Macbeth, King Lear,* and *Twelfth Night,*" *Philological Quarterly* 69 (Winter 1990): 31–53, suggests a possible reason for the use of so many letters in Shakespeare's plays: the publication in Elizabethan and Jacobean England of guides to letter writing. Among these are Angel Day's *The English Secretary* (1586), Abraham Fleming's *A Panoplie of Epistles* (1576), and Thomas Gainsford's *The Secretaries Studie* (1616). Julian Hilton, in "Reading Letters in Plays: Short Courses in Practical Epistemology?" in *Reading Plays: Interpretation and Reception,* ed. Hanna Scolnicov and Peter Holland (Cambridge: Cambridge University Press, 1991), pp. 140–60, sees in property letters Shakespeare's "keen interest in the nature of the relationship between epistemology and reading" (141).

3. Frances Teague, *Shakespeare's Speaking Properties* (Lewisburg: Bucknell University Press; London and Toronto: Associated University Presses, 1991), 43.

4. Christopher Marlowe, *Edward II,* ed. Charles R. Forker, The Revels Plays (Manchester and New York: Manchester University Press, 1994).

5. That inventory includes a wide variety of items, including a hatchet, a lion skin, a bridle, a pair of gloves, and a pope's miter. See *Henslowe's Diary,* ed. R. A. Foakes and R. T. Rickert (Cambridge: Cambridge University Press, 1961), 319–21.

Appendix 4

1. *The Tide Tarrieth No Man,* in *English Morality Plays and Moral Interludes,* ed. Edgar T. Schell and J. D. Shuchter (New York: Holt, Rinehart & Winston, 1969).

2. *Clyomon and Clamydes,* ed. W. W. Greg, Malone Society Reprints (Oxford: Oxford University Press, 1913).

3. John Ford, *The Broken Heart,* ed. T. J. B. Spencer, The Revels Plays (Manchester: Manchester University Press; Baltimore: Johns Hopkins University Press, 1980).

4. In Renaissance portraits the presence of a book sometimes indicates a concern with Christian values. Ivan Gaskell, in *Seventeenth-century Dutch and Flemish Painting* (London: Sotheby's Publications, 1990), explains the significance of a book in the hands of a woman whose portrait was painted in 1594: "The sitter's attribute of a prayer book, a place held by a finger between the leaves, was a formulaic indication of piety" (112).

5. *The History of King Leir 1605,* ed. W. W. Greg and R. Warwick Bond, Malone Society Reprints (London: Oxford University Press, 1907).

6. Thomas Middleton, *A Mad World, My Masters,* ed. Standish Henning, Regents Renaissance Drama Series (Lincoln: University of Nebraska Press, 1965).

7. John Webster, *The Devil's Law-Case,* ed. Frances A. Shirley, Regents Renaissance Drama Series (Lincoln: University of Nebraska Press, 1972).

8. John Marston and others, *The Insatiate Countess,* ed. Giorgio Melchiori, The Revels Plays (Manchester: Manchester University Press, 1984).

9. *"A Warning for Fair Women": A Critical Edition,* ed. Charles Dale Cannon (The Hague and Paris: Mouton, 1975). Of John Bradford, Cannon explains, "Among his many works are *Godlie Meditations upon the Lordes Prayer, the Beleefe, and Ten Commandements* . . . published in 1562 and reprinted in 1578, 1604, and later" (195).

10. *The Most Virtuous & Godly Susanna,* ed. B. Ifor Evans and W. W. Greg, Malone Society Reprints (London: Oxford University Press, 1937).

11. Thomas Kyd, *The Spanish Tragedy,* ed. Philip Edwards, The Revels Plays (1959; reprint, London: Methuen, 1969).

12. *The Virgin Martyr,* in *The Dramatic Works of Thomas Dekker,* ed. Fredson Bowers, 4 vols. (Cambridge: Cambridge University Press, 1953–61), vol. 3.
13. *Volpone or, the Fox,* ed. R. B. Parker, The Revels Plays (Manchester: Manchester University Press, 1983).
14. Reproduced by Louis Lebeer, *Catalogue raisonné des estampes de Bruegel l'ancien* (Brussels: Bibliothèque Royale Albert Ier, 1969), [81].
15. John Lyly, *Gallathea and Midas.* ed. Anne Begor Lancashire, Regents Renaissance Drama Series (Lincoln: University of Nebraska Press, 1969). The verb "study," however, does not necessarily signify the perusal of the written word. The *OED* gives as the first meaning of the verb "study": "To apply the mind to the acquisition of learning, whether by means of books, observation, or experiment." The study of Lyly's alchemist could, of course, be more efficiently and cheaply indicated by putting a book in his hands than by bringing equipment onstage.
16. Ben Jonson, *The Alchemist,* ed. F. H. Mares, The Revels Plays (1967; reprint, London and New York: Methuen, 1974).
17. Philip Massinger, *Believe as You List,* ed. Charles J. Sisson, Malone Society Reprints (London: Oxford University Press, 1927).
18. *Appius and Virginia* in *The Complete Works of John Webster,* ed. F. L. Lucas, 4 vols. (London: Chatto & Windus, 1927), vol. 3.
19. William Wager, *Enough is as Good as a Feast,* in *English Morality Plays and Moral Interludes,* ed. Edgar T. Schell and J. D. Shuchter (New York: Holt, Rinehart & Winston, 1969).
20. T. W. Craik, *The Tudor Interlude: Stage, Costume, and Acting* (Leicester: Leicester University Press, 1962), 108.
21. Marjorie Garber, in "'Here's Nothing Writ': Scribe, Script, and Circumscription in Marlowe's Plays," *Theatre Journal* 36 (October, 1984): 301–20, discusses the significance of Tamburlaine's action.
22. *Lusty Juventus,* in *Four Tudor Interludes,* ed. J. A. B. Somerset (London: Athlone Press; New York: Humanities Press, 1974).
23. John Skelton, *Magnificence,* ed. Paula Neuss, The Revels Plays (Manchester: Manchester University Press; Baltimore: Johns Hopkins University Press, 1980).
24. *The Marriage between Wit and Wisdom,* in *English Moral Interludes,* ed. Glynne Wickham (London: Dent; Totowa, N.J.: Rowman & Littlefield, 1976).
25. For a discussion of this and other props in the play, see Frances Teague, "Letters and Portents in *Julius Caesar* and *King Lear,*" *Shakespeare Yearbook* 1 (Spring 1990): 87–104.
26. For a close examination of the letters in this play, see David M. Bergeron, "Deadly Letters in *King Lear,*" *Philological Quarterly* 72 (Spring 1993): 157–76.
27. John Webster, *The Duchess of Malfi,* ed. John Russell Brown, The Revels Plays (1964; reprint, London: Methuen, 1969). For the connection between writing and death in Renaissance plays, see Marion Lomax, "The Letter of Death in Elizabethan and Jacobean Drama," *Swansea Review* 1 (1986): 14–26.
28. Christopher Marlowe, *Edward the Second,* ed. Charles R. Forker, The Revels Plays (Manchester and New York: Manchester University Press, 1994).
29. Ben Jonson, *Sejanus His Fall,* ed. Philip J. Ayres, The Revels Plays (Manchester and New York: Manchester University Press, 1990).

Select Bibliography

Primary Works

Alberti, Leon Battista. *On the Art of Building in Ten Books*. Translated by Joseph Rykwert, Neil Leach, and Robert Tavernor. Cambridge and London: MIT Press, 1988.

Ames, William. *Conscience with the Power and Cases Thereof.* London, 1639.

Ascham, Roger. *The Schoolmaster.* Edited by Lawrence V. Ryan. Ithaca: Cornell University Press [for the Folger Shakespeare Library], 1967.

Bacon, Francis. *The Twoo Bookes of the Proficience and Advancement of Learning.* London, 1605.

———. *The Works of Francis Bacon.* Edited by James Spedding, Robert Leslie Ellis, and Douglas Denon Heath. 7 vols. London: Longman, 1857–59.

Baldwin, William. *The Canticles or Balades of Salomon, phraselyke declared in Englysh Metres.* London, 1549.

Baxter, Richard. *A Christian Directory: or, A Sum of Practical Theologie.* London, 1673.

Bernardus Silvestris. *"The Cosmographia" of Bernardus Silvestris.* Translated by Winthrop Wetherbee. New York and London: Columbia University Press, 1973.

Bolton, Robert. *A Discourse about the State of True Happinesse.* London, 1611.

Bourne, Immanuel. *The Anatomie of Conscience.* London, 1623.

Browne, Sir Thomas. *"Religio Medici" and Other Works.* Edited by L. C. Martin. Oxford: Clarendon Press, 1964.

Bruno, Giordano. *The Heroic Frenzies.* Translated by Paul Eugene Memmo, Jr. University of North Carolina Studies in the Romance Languages and Literatures 50. Chapel Hill: University of North Carolina Press, 1964.

Bryskett, Lodowick. *A Discourse of Civill Life: Containing the Ethike part of Morall Philosophie.* London, 1606.

Bullough, Geoffrey, ed. *Narrative and Dramatic Sources of Shakespeare.* 8 vols. New York: Columbia University Press; London: Routledge & Kegan Paul, 1957–75.

Burton, Robert. *The Anatomy of Melancholy.* Oxford, 1621.

Calvin, John. *A Commentarie of M. John Calvine upon the Epistle to the Philippians.* Translated by W. B. London, 1584.

———. *A Commentarie upon S. Paules Epistles to the Corinthians.* Translated by Thomas Timme. London, 1577.

———. *Institutes of the Christian Religion.* Edited by John T. McNeill. Translated by Ford Lewis Battles. The Library of Christian Classics 20. 2 vols. Philadelphia: Westminster Press, 1960.

Carpenter, Richard. *The Conscionable Christian.* London, 1623.

Castiglione, Baldassare. *The Book of the Courtier.* Translated by Charles S. Singleton. Garden City, N.Y.: Doubleday, Anchor Books, 1959.

Chapman, George. *Bussy D'Ambois.* Edited by Nicholas Brooke. The Revels Plays. 1964. Reprint, Manchester: Manchester University Press, 1979.

―――. *Bussy D'Ambois.* Edited by Maurice Evans. The New Mermaids. London: Ernest Benn; New York: Norton, 1965.

―――. *Bussy D'Ambois and The Revenge of Bussy D'Ambois.* Edited by Frederick S. Boas. The Belles Lettres Series. Boston: Heath, 1905.

―――. *The Conspiracy and Tragedy of Charles Duke of Byron.* Edited by John Margeson. The Revels Plays. Manchester and New York: Manchester University Press, 1988.

―――. *The Plays and Poems of George Chapman.* Edited by Thomas Marc Parrott. New York: Dutton, 1910.

Charron, Pierre. *Of Wisdome.* Translated by Samson Lennard. London, 1612?

Cramer, Daniel. *Emblemata Sacra.* Frankfurt, 1624.

Daniel, Samuel. *The Civil Wars.* Edited by Laurence Michel. New Haven: Yale University Press, 1958.

Donne, John. *Pseudo-Martyr.* London, 1610.

―――. *The Sermons of John Donne.* Edited by George R. Potter and Evelyn M. Simpson. 10 vols. Berkeley and Los Angeles: University of California Press, 1953–62.

Downname, John. *The Christian Warfare.* London, 1604.

Dyke, Jeremiah. *Good Conscience: or a Treatise Shewing the Nature, Meanes, Marks, Benefit, and Necessity Thereof.* London, 1624.

Erasmus, Desiderius. *Apophthegmes.* Translated by Nicholas Udall. London, 1542.

―――. *The Collected Works of Erasmus.* Toronto, Buffalo, and London: University of Toronto Press, 1974–.

―――. *The first tome or volume of the Paraphrase of Erasmus upon the newe testamente.* London, 1548.

―――. *Panegyricus ad Illustrissimum Principem Philippum, Archiducem Austriae.* Antwerp, 1504.

―――. *Preparation to Deathe, A boke as devout as eloquent.* London, 1538.

Favour, John. *Antiquitie Triumphing over Noveltie.* London, 1619.

Felltham, Owen. *Resolves, A Duple Century.* [3d ed.] London, 1628–29.

Floyer, Sir John. *The Sibylline Oracles Translated from the Best Greek Copies, And compar'd with the Sacred Prophesies.* London, 1713.

Forbes, Patrick. *An Learned Commentarie upon the Revelation of Saint John.* Middelburg, 1614.

Foxe, John. *Actes and Monuments of these latter and perillous dayes.* London, 1563.

―――. *The First Volume of the Ecclesiasticall History, contaynyng the Actes & Monumentes of thinges passed in every kinges time.* London, 1576.

Fraunce, Abraham. *The Third part of the Countesse of Pembrokes Yvychurch: Entituled, Amintas Dale.* London, 1592.

Fuller, Thomas. *The History of the Worthies of England.* London, 1662.

Galileo Galilei. *Dialogue Concerning the Two Chief World Systems —Ptolemaic and Copernican.* Translated by Stillman Drake. Berkeley and Los Angeles: University of California Press, 1953.

———. *Discoveries and Opinions of Galileo.* Translated by Stillman Drake. Garden City, N.Y.:Doubleday Anchor Books, 1957.

Goodman, Godfrey. *The Creatures Praysing God: or, The Religion of dumbe Creatures.* London, 1622.

———. *The Fall of Man, or the Corruption of Nature, Proved by the light of our naturall Reason.* London, 1616.

Greene, Robert. *Friar Bacon and Friar Bungay.* Edited by Daniel Seltzer. Regents Renaissance Drama Series. Lincoln: University of Nebraska Press, 1963.

Greenham, Richard. *The Works of the Reverend and Faithfull Servant of Jesus Christ M. Richard Greenham.* London, 1599.

Hakewill, George. *An Apologie of the Power and Providence of God in the Government of the World.* Oxford, 1627.

Hall, Edward. *The Union of the two noble and illustre famelies of Lancastre & Yorke.* London, 1548.

Harvey, John. *An Almanacke, or annual Calender, with a compendious Prognostication thereunto appendyng.* London, 1589.

———. *An Astrologicall Addition, or supplement to be annexed to the late Discourse upon the great Conjunction of Saturne, and Jupiter.* London, 1583.

———. *A Discoursive Probleme concerning Prophesies.* London, 1588.

Harvey, Richard. *An Astrological Discourse upon the great and notable Conjunction of the two superiour Planets, Saturne & Jupiter.* London, 1583.

Heywood, Thomas. *The English Traveller, as it hath beene publikely acted at the Cock-pit in Drury-Lane.* London, 1633.

[Heywood, Thomas]. *If You Know Not Me You Know Nobody, Part 1.* Edited by Madeleine Doran. Malone Society Reprints. Oxford: Oxford University Press, 1935.

———. *A Woman Killed with Kindness.* Edited by R. W. Van Fossen. The Revels Plays. 1961. Reprint, London: Methuen, 1970.

Hillerbrand, Hans J., ed. and trans. *The Reformation: A Narrative History Related by Contemporary Observers and Participants.* New York and Evanston: Harper & Row, 1964.

Holinshed, Raphael. *The Chronicles of England, Scotland, and Ireland.* 3 vols. in 2. London, 1587.

Hooker, Richard. *The Works of Richard Hooker.* General editor W. Speed Hill. 5 vols. Cambridge and London: Harvard University Press, 1977–.

Hughes, John. *St. Pauls Exercise, or, A Sermon of Conscience.* London, 1622.

Jones, John Henry, ed. *The English Faust Book: A Critical Edition Based on the Text of 1592.* Cambridge: Cambridge University Press, 1994.

Jonson, Ben. *Ben Jonson.* Edited by C. H. Herford, Percy and Evelyn Simpson. 11 vols. Oxford: Clarendon Press, 1925–52.

———. *Catiline.* Edited by W. F. Bolton and Jane F. Gardner. Regents Renaissance Drama Series. Lincoln: University of Nebraska Press, 1973.

———. *The New Inn.* Edited by Michael Hattaway. The Revels Plays. Manchester: Manchester University Press, 1984.

———. *The Staple of News.* Edited by Anthony Parr. The Revels Plays. Manchester and New York: Manchester University Press, 1988.

———. *Volpone or, the Fox.* Edited by R. B. Parker. The Revels Plays. Manchester: Manchester University Press, 1983.

Josten, C. H. "A Translation of John Dee's 'Monas Hieroglyphica' (Antwerp, 1564), with an Introduction and Annotations." *Ambix* 12 (June & October 1964): 84–221.

Kennedy, Judith M., ed. *A Critical Edition of Yong's Translation of George of Montemayor's "Diana" and Gil Polo's "Enamoured Diana."* Oxford: Clarendon Press, 1968.

Kinney, Arthur F., ed. *Elizabethan Backgrounds: Historical Documents of the Age of Elizabeth I.* Hamden, Conn.: Archon Books, 1975.

Kyd, Thomas. *The Spanish Tragedy.* Edited by Philip Edwards. The Revels Plays. 1959. Reprint, London: Methuen, 1969.

———. *The Works of Thomas Kyd.* Edited by Frederick S. Boas. Oxford: Clarendon Press, 1901.

LeRoy, Louis. *Of the Interchangeable Course, or Variety of Things in the Whole World.* Translated by Robert Ashley. London, 1594.

Lille, Alain de. *The Plaint of Nature.* Translated by James J. Sheridan. Toronto: Pontifical Institute of Mediaeval Studies, 1980.

Linche, Richard. *The Fountaine of Ancient Fiction.* London, 1599.

Luther and Erasmus: Free Will and Salvation. Translated and edited by E. Gordon Rupp and A. N. Marlow. The Library of Christian Classics 17. Philadelphia: Westminster Press, 1969.

Luther, Martin. *Luther's Works.* Edited by Jaroslav Pelikan and Helmut T. Lehmann. 55 vols. St. Louis: Concordia Publishing House; Philadelphia: Fortress Press, 1955–86.

Machiavelli, Niccolò. *Machiavelli: The Chief Works and Others.* Translated by Allan Gilbert. 3 vols. 1958. Reprint, Durham and London: Duke University Press, 1989.

Marlowe, Christopher. *"Doctor Faustus": A- and B-Texts (1604, 1616).* Edited by David Bevington and Eric Rasmussen. The Revels Plays. Manchester and New York: Manchester University Press, 1993.

———. *Edward the Second.* Edited by Charles R. Forker. The Revels Plays. Manchester and New York: Manchester University Press, 1994.

———. *Tamburlaine the Great.* Edited by J. S. Cunningham. The Revels Plays. Manchester: Manchester University Press; Baltimore: Johns Hopkins University Press, 1981.

Martianus Capella. *Martianus Capella and the Seven Liberal Arts.* Translated by William Harris Stahl, Richard Johnson, and E. L. Burge. 2 vols. New York: Columbia University Press, 1971–77.

Martin, L. C., ed. *"Religio Medici" and Other Works.* Oxford: Clarendon Press, 1964.

Milton, John. *Complete Poems and Major Prose.* Edited by Merritt Y. Hughes. New York: Odyssey Press, 1957.

Montaigne, Michel de. *The Complete Essays of Montaigne.* Translated by Donald M. Frame. Stanford: Stanford University Press, 1958.

Mulcaster, Richard. *The First Part of the Elementarie.* London, 1582.

Napier, John. *A Plaine Discovery of the whole Revelation of Saint John.* Edinburgh, 1593.

Nashe, Thomas. *A Wonderfull, strange and miraculous, Astrologicall Prognostication for this yeer of our Lord God. 1591.* London, [1591].

Nicholas of Cusa. *The Layman on Wisdom and the Mind.* Translated by M. L. Führer. Centre for Reformation Studies, University of Toronto, Translation Series 4. Ottawa: Dovehouse Editions, 1989.

Paracelsus. *The Hermetic and Alchemical Writings of . . . Paracelsus.* Translated by Arthur Edward Waite. 2 vols. 1894. Reprint, Berkeley: Shambhala, 1976.

―――. *Paracelsus: Selected Writings.* Edited by Jolande Jacobi. Translated by Norbert Guterman. Bollingen Series 28. New York: Pantheon, 1951.

Peacham, Henry. *The Compleat Gentleman.* London, 1622.

―――. *Minerva Britanna or a Garden of Heroical Devices.* London, 1612.

Perkins, William. *A Discourse of Conscience.* Cambridge, 1596.

―――. *The Whole Treatise of the Cases of Conscience.* Cambridge, 1606.

Petrarch, Francesco. *Letters from Petrarch.* Translated by Morris Bishop. Bloomington and London: Indiana University Press, 1966.

Puttenham, George. *The Arte of English Poesie.* Edited by Gladys Doidge Willcock and Alice Walker. Cambridge: Cambridge University Press, 1936.

Ralegh, Sir Walter. *The History of the World.* London, 1614.

Ripa, Cesare. *Iconologia overo descrittione di diverse imagini.* Rome, 1603.

Shakespeare, William. *The Riverside Shakespeare.* Edited by G. Blakemore Evans. Boston: Houghton Mifflin, 1974.

―――. *William Shakespeare: The Complete Works.* Edited by Stanley Wells, Gary Taylor, et al. Oxford: Clarendon Press, 1986.

Stow, John. *The Annales of England, Faithfully collected out of the most autenticall Authors, Records, and other Monuments of Antiquitie.* London, 1600.

The Summoning of Everyman. Edited by Geoffrey Cooper and Christopher Wortham. Nedlands: University of Western Australia Press, 1980.

Taylor, Jeremy. *The Whole Works of the Right Rev. Jeremy Taylor.* Edited by Reginald Heber. Revised by Charles Page Eden. 10 vols. London: Longman, 1847–61.

Tyndale, William. *The Obedience of a Christen Man.* Antwerp, 1528.

Webster, John. *The Duchess of Malfi.* Edited by John Russell Brown. The Revels Plays. 1964. Reprint, London: Methuen, 1972.

―――. *The White Devil.* Edited by John Russell Brown. The Revels Plays. 2d ed. 1966. Reprint, London: Methuen, 1968.

Whitney, Geoffrey. *A Choice of Emblemes.* Leiden, 1586.

Wilson, Thomas. *The Arte of Rhetorique.* London, 1553.

Secondary Works

Adams, Henry Hitch. *English Domestic or, Homiletic Tragedy, 1575 to 1642.* New York: Columbia University Press, 1943.

Allen, Don Cameron. *Mysteriously Meant: The Rediscovery of Pagan Symbolism and Allegorical Interpretation in the Renaissance*. Baltimore and London: Johns Hopkins University Press, 1970.

———. *The Star-Crossed Renaissance: The Quarrel about Astrology and Its Influence in England*. 1941. Reprint, New York: Octagon Books, 1973.

Archibald, Elizabeth. *Apollonius of Tyre: Medieval and Renaissance Themes and Variations*. Cambridge: D. S. Brewer, 1991.

Ariès, Philippe. *Western Attitudes toward Death: from the Middle Ages to the Present*. Translated by Patricia M. Ranum. Baltimore and London: Johns Hopkins University Press, 1974.

Barkan, Leonard. *Nature's Work of Art: The Human Body as Image of the World*. New Haven: Yale University Press, 1975.

Baron, Frank. *Doctor Faustus: From History to Legend*. Humanistische Bibliothek, Abhandlungen 27. Munich: Wilhelm Fink, 1978.

Barthes, Roland. *Arcimboldo*. Translated by John Shepley. Milan and Paris: Franco Maria Ricci, 1980.

Baylor, Michael G. *Action and Person: Conscience in Late Scholasticism and the Young Luther*. Leiden: E. J. Brill, 1977.

Belsey, Catherine. *The Subject of Tragedy: Identity and Difference in Renaissance Drama*. London and New York: Methuen, 1985.

Bennett, H. S. *English Books & Readers, 1475 to 1557*. Cambridge: Cambridge University Press, 1952.

———. *English Books & Readers, 1603 to 1640*. Cambridge: Cambridge University Press, 1970.

Bentley, Jerry H. *Humanists and Holy Writ: New Testament Scholarship in the Renaissance*. Princeton: Princeton University Press, 1983.

Berg, Kent van den. *Playhouse and Cosmos: Shakespearean Theater as Metaphor*. Newark: University of Delaware Press; London and Toronto: Associated University Presses, 1985.

Bergeron, David M. "Deadly Letters in *King Lear*." *Philological Quarterly* 72 (Spring 1993): 157–76.

———. "Reading and Writing in Shakespeare's Romances." *Criticism* 33 (Winter 1991): 91–113.

Bloch, R. Howard, and Carla Hesse. Introduction to *Future Libraries* a special issue of *Representations* no. 42 (Spring 1993): 1–12.

Bottéro, Jean. *Mesopotamia: Writing, Reasoning, and the Gods*. Translated by Zainab Bahrani and Marc Van de Mieroop. Chicago and London: University of Chicago Press, 1992.

Braden, Gordon. *Renaissance Tragedy and the Senecan Tradition: Anger's Privilege*. New Haven and London: Yale University Press, 1985.

Bradley, Jennifer, and W. H. Herendeen, ed. *Ben Jonson's 1616 Folio*. Newark: University of Delaware Press; London and Toronto: Associated University Presses, 1991.

Brown, Norman O. *Love's Body*. New York: Random House, 1966.

Bruns, Gerald. *Inventions: Writing, Textuality, and Understanding in Literary History*. New Haven and London: Yale University Press, 1982.

Bühler, Curt F. *The Fifteenth-Century Book: the Scribes, the Printers, the Decorators*. Philadelphia: University of Pennsylvania Press, 1960.

Butler, Martin. *Theatre and Crisis, 1632–1642*. Cambridge: Cambridge University Press, 1984.
Carlson, David R. *English Humanist Books: Writers and Patrons, Manuscript and Print, 1475–1525*. Toronto, Buffalo and London: University of Toronto Press, 1993.
Cave, Terence. *The Cornucopian Text: Problems of Writing in the French Renaissance*. Oxford: Clarendon Press, 1979.
Chambers, E. K. *The Elizabethan Stage*. 4 vols. Oxford: Clarendon Press, 1923.
Chartier, Roger. *The Cultural Uses of Print in Early Modern France*. Translated by Lydia G. Cochrane. Princeton: Princeton University Press, 1987.
———. *The History and Power of Writing*. Translated by Lydia G. Cochrane. Chicago and London: University of Chicago Press, 1994.
———. *The Order of Books: Readers, Authors, and Libraries in Europe between the Fourteenth and Eighteenth Centuries*. Translated by Lydia G. Cochrane. Cambridge, England: Polity Press, 1994.
———. "The Practical Impact of Writing" in *A History of Private Life*, vol. 3: *Passions of the Renaissance*. Edited by Roger Chartier. Translated by Arthur Goldhammer. Cambridge and London: Harvard University Press, 1989.
Chaudhuri, Sukanta. *Renaissance Pastoral and Its English Developments*. Oxford: Clarendon Press, 1989.
Chrisman, Miriam Usher. *Lay Culture, Learned Culture: Books and Social Change in Strasbourg, 1480–1599*. New Haven and London: Yale University Press, 1982.
Clanchy, M. T. *From Memory to Written Record: England, 1066–1307*. London: Edward Arnold, 1979.
Clare, Janet. *"Art Made Tongue-Tied by Authority": Elizabethan and Jacobean Dramatic Censorship*. Revels Plays Companion Library. Manchester and New York: Manchester University Press, 1990.
Clulee, Nicholas H. *John Dee's Natural Philosophy: Between Science and Religion*. London and New York: Routledge, 1988.
Collinson, Patrick. *The Birthpangs of Protestant England: Religious and Cultural Change in the Sixteenth and Seventeenth Centuries*. London: Macmillan, 1988.
———. *The Elizabethan Puritan Movement*. London: Jonathan Cape, 1967.
Cook, Ann Jennalie. *The Privileged Playgoers of Shakespeare's London, 1576–1642*. Princeton: Princeton University Press, 1981.
Craik, T. W. *The Tudor Interlude: Stage, Costume, and Acting*. Leicester: Leicester University Press, 1962.
Cressy, David. *Literacy and the Social Order: Reading and Writing in Tudor and Stuart England*. Cambridge: Cambridge University Press, 1980.
Curtius, Ernst Robert. *European Literature and the Latin Middle Ages*. Translated by Willard R. Trask. Bollingen Series 36. 1953. Reprint, New York and Evanston: Harper & Row, 1963.
Daniell, David. *William Tyndale: A Biography*. New Haven and London: Yale University Press, 1994.
Davies, C. S. L. *Peace, Print and Protestantism, 1450–1558*. The Paladin History of England. London: Hart-Davis, MacGibbon, 1976.
Davis, Natalie Zemon. *Society and Culture in Early Modern France*. Stanford: Stanford University Press, 1975.

Derrida, Jacques. *Of Grammatology*. Translated by Gayatri Chakravorty Spivak. Baltimore and London: Johns Hopkins University Press, 1976.

Dessen, Alan C. *Elizabethan Stage Conventions and Modern Interpreters*. Cambridge: Cambridge University Press, 1084.

Devereux, E. J. *Renaissance English Translations of Erasmus: A Bibliography to 1700*. Toronto, Buffalo, and London: University of Toronto Press, 1983.

Dieckmann, Liselotte. *Hieroglyphics: The History of a Literary Symbol*. St. Louis: Washington University Press, 1970.

Dollimore, Jonathan. *Radical Tragedy*. 2d ed. New York and London: Harvester Wheatsheaf, 1989.

Donawerth, Jane. *Shakespeare and the Sixteenth-Century Study of Language*. Urbana and Chicago: University of Illinois Press, 1984.

Dutton, Richard. *Mastering the Revels: The Regulation and Censorship of English Renaissance Drama*. Iowa City: University of Iowa Press, 1991.

Eisenstein, Elizabeth L. *The Printing Press as an Agent of Change: Communications and Cultural Transformations in Early-Modern Europe*. 2 vols. in 1. 1979. Reprint, Cambridge: Cambridge University Press, 1980.

Elsky, Martin. *Authorizing Words: Speech, Writing, and Print in the English Renaissance*. Ithaca and London: Cornell University Press, 1989.

Ettin, Andrew. *Literature and the Pastoral*. New Haven and London: Yale University Press, 1984.

Febvre, Lucien, and Henri-Jean Martin. *The Coming of the Book: The Impact of Printing, 1450–1800*. Translated by David Gerard. Edited by Geoffrey Nowell-Smith and David Wootton. London: Verso, 1984.

Ford, Wyn. "The Problem of Literacy in Early Modern England." *History* 78 (February 1993): 22–37.

Foucault, Michel. *The Archaeology of Knowledge and the Discourse on Language*. Translated by A. M. Sheridan Smith. New York: Pantheon Books, 1972.

———. *The Order of Things: An Archaeology of the Human Sciences*. New York: Pantheon Books, 1970.

French, Peter J. *John Dee: The World of an Elizabethan Magus*. London: Routledge & Kegan Paul, 1972.

Frye, Northrop. *The Secular Scripture: A Study of the Structure of Romance*. Cambridge and London: Harvard University Press, 1976.

Furet, François, and Jacques Ozouf. *Reading and Writing: Literacy in France from Calvin to Jules Ferry*. Cambridge: Cambridge University Press, 1982.

Gallagher, Lowell. *Medusa's Gaze: Casuistry and Conscience in the Renaissance*. Stanford: Stanford University Press, 1991.

Gatti, Hilary. *The Renaissance Drama of Knowledge: Giordano Bruno in England*. London and New York: Routledge, 1989.

Goldberg, Jonathan. *James I and the Politics of Literature: Jonson, Shakespeare, Donne, and Their Contemporaries*. Baltimore and London: Johns Hopkins University Press, 1983.

———. *Writing Matter: From the Hands of the English Renaissance*. Stanford: Stanford University Press, 1990.

Graff, Harvey J. *The Legacies of Literacy: Continuities and Contradictions in Western Culture and Society*. Bloomington and Indianapolis: Indiana University Press, 1987.

Grafton, Anthony, and Lisa Jardine. *From Humanism to the Humanities: Education and the Liberal Arts in Fifteenth-and Sixteenth-Century Europe.* London: Duckworth, 1986.

Green, Henry. *Shakespeare and the Emblem Writers.* 1870. Reprint, New York: Burt Franklin, n.d.

Greenblatt, Stephen. *Renaissance Self-Fashioning, from More to Shakespeare.* Chicago and London: University of Chicago Press, 1980.

Guerin, Eugenio. *Astrology in the Renaissance: The Zodiac of Life.* Translated by Carolyn Jackson and June Allen. Revised by Clare Robertson. London and Boston: Routledge & Kegan Paul, 1983.

Gurr, Andrew. *Playgoing in Shakespeare's London.* Cambridge: Cambridge University Press, 1987.

Halbey, Hans Adolf, et al. *Schrift, Druck, Buch im Gutenberg-Museum: Buchkultur in Mainz.* Mainz am Rhein: Philipp von Zabern, 1985.

Hannebutt-Benz, Eva-Maria. *Die Dunst des Lesens: Lesemöbel und Leseverhalten vom Mittelalter bis zur Gegenwart.* 2d ed. Frankfurt am Main: Museum für Kunsthandwerk, 1989.

Harbage, Alfred. *Shakespeare's Audience.* New York: Columbia University Press, 1941.

Harris, William V. *Ancient Literacy.* Cambridge and London: Harvard University Press, 1989.

Hartwig, Joan. *Shakespeare's Tragicomic Vision.* Baton Rouge: Louisiana State University Press, 1972.

Havelock, Eric A. *Origins of Western Literacy.* Monograph Series 14. Toronto: The Ontario Institute for Studies in Education, 1976.

Hawkes, Terence. *Metaphor.* The Critical Idiom 25. London: Methuen, 1972.

Heinemann, Margot. *Puritanism and Theatre: Thomas Middleton and Opposition Drama under the Early Stuarts.* Cambridge: Cambridge University Press, 1980.

Heninger, S. K. *The Subtext of Form in the English Renaissance: Proportion Poetical.* University Park: Pennsylvania State University Press, 1994.

———. *Touches of Sweet Harmony: Pythagorean Cosmology and Renaissance Poetics.* San Marino, Calif.: The Huntington Library, 1974.

Hillerbrand, Hans J., ed. and trans. *The Reformation: A Narrative History Related by Contemporary Observers and Participants.* New York and Evanston: Harper & Row, 1964.

Hirsch, Rudolf. *Printing, Selling and Reading, 1450–1550.* Wiesbaden: Otto Harrassowitz, 1967.

Hoeniger, F. David. "Gower and Shakespeare in *Pericles.*" *Shakespeare Quarterly* 33 (Winter 1982): 461–79.

Horapollo. *The Hieroglyphics of Horapollo.* Translated by George Boas. Bollingen Series 23. New York: Pantheon Books, 1950.

Houston, R. A. *Literacy in Early Modern Europe: Culture and Education, 1500–1800.* London and New York: Longman, 1988.

Iversen, Erik. *The Myth of Egypt and Its Hieroglyphs in European Tradition.* Copenhagen: Gec Gad Publishers, 1961.

Jardine, Lisa. *Erasmus, Man of Letters: The Construction of Charisma in Print.* Princeton: Princeton University Press, 1993.

———. *Still Harping on Daughters: Women and Drama in the Age of Shakespeare.* Brighton, Sussex: Harvester Press; Totowa, N.J.: Barnes & Noble, 1983.

Jones, Edwin. *Reading the Book of Nature: A Phenomenological Study of Creative Expression in Science and Painting.* Athens: Ohio University Press, 1989.

Josipovici, Gabriel. *The World and the Book: A Study of Modern Fiction.* 2d ed. London: Macmillan, 1979.

Kahn, Victoria. *Rhetoric, Prudence, and Skepticism in the Renaissance.* Ithaca and London: Cornell University Press, 1985.

Kelly, Kevin T. *Conscience: Dictator or Guide?: A Study in Seventeenth-Century English Protestant Moral Theology.* London: Geoffrey Chapman, 1967.

Kennedy, Judith M., ed. *A Critical Edition of Yong's Translation of George of Montemayor's "Diana" and Gil Polo's "Enamoured Diana."* Oxford: Clarendon Press, 1968.

Kiefer, Frederick. *Fortune and Elizabethan Tragedy.* San Marino, Calif.: The Huntington Library, 1983.

Kipling, Gordon. *The Triumph of Honour: Burgundian Origins of the Elizabethan Renaissance.* Leiden: Leiden University Press for the Sir Thomas Browne Institute, 1977.

Knapp, Robert S. *Shakespeare—The Theater and the Book.* Princeton: Princeton University Press, 1989.

Knight, G. Wilson. *The Crown of Life: Essays in Interpretation of Shakespeare's Final Plays.* London and New York: Oxford University Press, 1947.

Koestler, Arthur. *The Sleepwalkers: A History of Man's Changing Vision of the Universe.* New York: Macmillan, 1959.

Lakoff, George, and Mark Turner. *More than Cool Reason: A Field Guide to Poetic Metaphor.* Chicago and London: University of Chicago Press, 1989.

Langer, Suzanne. *Philosophy in a New Key: A Study in the Symbolism of Reason, Rite, and Art.* Cambridge: Harvard University Press, 1957.

Lee, Rensselaer W. *Names on Trees: Ariosto into Art.* Princeton Essays on the Arts 3. Princeton: Princeton University Press, 1977.

Leggatt, Alexander. *Jacobean Public Theatre.* London and New York: Routledge, 1992.

Lewis, C. S. *Studies in Words.* 2d ed. Cambridge: Cambridge University Press, 1967.

Liebeschuetz, J. H. W. G. *Continuity and Change in Roman Religion.* Oxford: Clarendon Press, 1979.

Lowry, Martin. *The World of Aldus Manutius; Business and Scholarship in Renaissance Venice.* Ithaca: Cornell University Press, 1979.

McConica, James Kelsey. *English Humanists and Reformation Politics under Henry VIII and Edward VI.* Oxford: Clarendon Press, 1965.

McElroy, Bernard. *Shakespeare's Mature Tragedies.* Princeton: Princeton University Press, 1973.

McGee, J. Sears. *The Godly Man in Stuart England: Anglicans, Puritans, and the Two Tables, 1620–1670.* New Haven and London: Yale University Press, 1976.

McGrath, Patrick. *Papists and Puritans under Elizabeth I.* New York: Walker, 1967.

McLuhan, Marshall. *The Gutenberg Galaxy: The Making of Typographic Man.* London: Routledge & Kegan Paul, 1962.

McLuskie, Kathleen. *Renaissance Dramatists.* Feminist Readings Series. New York: Harvester Wheatsheaf, 1989.

Mansfield, Bruce. *Phoenix of His Age: Interpretations of Erasmus, c 1550–1750.* Toronto, Buffalo, and London: University of Toronto Press, 1979.

Moseley, Charles. *A Century of Emblems: An Introductory Anthology.* Aldershot, England, and Brookfield, Vt.: Scolar Press, 1989.

Murry, John Middleton. *Countries of the Mind: Essays in Literary Criticism.* 2d series. London: Oxford University Press, 1931.

Newman, Jane O. "The Word Made Print: Luther's 1522 *New Testament* in an Age of Mechanical Reproduction." *Representations* no. 11 (Summer 1985): 95–133.

Newton, Richard C. "Jonson and the (Re-)Invention of the Book." In *Classic and Cavalier: Essays on Jonson and the Sons of Ben,* edited by Claude J. Summers and Ted-Larry Pebworth. Pittsburgh: University of Pittsburgh Press, 1982, 31–55.

North, J. D. *The Universal Frame: Historical Essays in Astronomy, Natural Philosophy and Scientific Method.* London and Ronceverte, W.V.: Hambledom Press, 1989.

Oberman, Heiko A. *Luther: Man between God and the Devil.* Translated by Eileen Walliser-Schwarzbart. New Haven and London: Yale University Press, 1989.

Olin, John C., ed. *Christian Humanism and the Reformation: Selected Writings of Erasmus.* 3d ed. New York: Fordham University Press, 1987.

Ong, Walter J., S.J. *Rhetoric, Romance, and Technology: Studies in the Interaction of Expression and Culture.* Ithaca and London: Cornell University Press, 1971.

Ozment, Steven. *The Age of Reform, 1250–1550: An Intellectual and Religious History of Late Medieval and Reformation Europe.* New Haven and London: Yale University Press, 1980.

Parke, H. W. *Sibyls and Sibylline Prophey in Classical Antiqutity.* Edited by B. C. McGing. London and New York: Routledge, 1988.

Patterson, Annabel. *Censorship and Interpretation: The Conditions of Writing and Reading in Early Modern England.* Madison: University of Wisconsin Press, 1984.

———. *Pastoral and Ideology: Virgil to Valéry.* Berkeley and Los Angeles: University of California Press, 1987.

Peterson, Douglas L. *Time, Tide and Tempest: A Study of Shakespeare's Romances.* San Marino, Calif.: The Huntington Library, 1973.

Pfeiffer, Rudolf. *History of Classical Scholarship: from 1300 to 1850.* Oxford: Clarendon Press, 1976.

Pfister, Manfred. "Reading the Body: the Corporeality of Shakespeare's Text." In *Reading Plays: Interpretation and Reception,* edited by Hanna Scolnicov and Peter Holland. Cambridge: Cambridge University Press, 1991.

Phillips, Margaret Mann, ed. *The "Adages" of Erasmus: A Study with Translations.* Cambridge: Cambridge University Press, 1964.

Popkin, Richard H. *The History of Scepticism from Erasmus to Spinoza.* Berkeley, Los Angeles, and London: University of California Press, 1979.

Post, R. R. *The Modern Devotion: Confrontation with Reformation and Humanism.* Studies in Medievgal and Reformation Thought 3. Leiden: E. J. Brill, 1968.

Potts, Timothy C. *Conscience in Medieval Philosophy.* Cambridge: Cambridge University Press, 1980.

Rappaport, Steve. *Worlds within Worlds: Structures of Life in Sixteenth-Century London.* Cambridge: Cambridge University Press, 1989.

Rasmussen, Eric. *A Textual Companion to "Doctor Faustus."* Revels Plays Companion Library. Manchester and New York: Manchester University Press, 1993.

Riggs, David. *Ben Jonson, A Life.* Cambridge and London: Harvard University Press, 1989.

Roberts, Julian, and Andrew G. Watson, eds. *John Dee's Library Catalogue.* London: The Bibliographical Society, 1990.

Rose, Elliot. *Cases of Conscience: Alternatives open to Recusants and Puritans under Elizabeth I and James I.* Cambridge: Cambridge University Press, 1975.

Rosenmeyer, Thomas G. *The Green Cabinet: Theocritus and the European Pastoral Lyric.* Berkeley and Los Angeles: University of California Press, 1969.

Rozett, Martha Tuck. *The Doctrine of Election and the Emergence of Elizabethan Tragedy.* Princeton: Princeton University Press, 1984.

Rummel, Erika. *Erasmus as a Translator of the Classics.* Toronto, Buffalo, and London: University of Toronto Press, 1985.

Rupp, E. Gordon, and A. N. Marlow, ed. and trans. *Luther and Erasmus: Free Will and Salvation.* The Library of Christian Classics 17. Philadelphia: Westminster Press, 1969.

Sannazaro, Jacopo. *Arcadia and Piscatorial Eclogues.* Translated by Ralph Nash. Detroit: Wayne State University Press, 1966.

Schoeck, R. J. *Erasmus Grandescens: The Growth of a Humanist's Mind and Spirituality.* Bibliotheca Humanistica & Reformatorica 43. Nieuwkoop: De Graff, 1988.

———. *Erasmus of Europe: The Making of a Humanist, 1467–1500.* Edinburgh: Edinburgh University Press, 1990.

Schofield, R. S. "The Measurement of Literacy in Pre-Industrial England." In *Literacy in Traditional Societies,* edited by Jack Goody. Cambridge: Cambridge University Press, 1968.

Scholes, Robert. *Protocols of Reading.* New Haven and London: Yale University Press, 1989.

Schwarz, Werner. *Principles and Problems of Biblical Translation: Some Reformation Controversies and Their Background.* Cambridge: Cambridge University Press, 1955.

Scribner, R. W. *For the Sake of Simple Folk: Popular Propaganda for the German Reformation.* Cambridge: Cambridge University Press, 1981.

Seaver, Paul S. *Wallington's World: A Puritan Artisan in Seventeenth-Century London.* Stanford: Stanford University Press, 1985.

Sinfield, Alan. *Faultlines: Cultural Materialism and the Politics of Dissident Reading.* Berkeley, Los Angeles, and London: University of California Press, 1992.

———. *Literature in Protestant England, 1560–1660.* London and Canberra: Croom Helm; Totowa, N.J.: Barnes & Noble, 1983.

Slater, Ann Pasternak. *Shakespeare the Director.* Brighton, Sussex: Harvester; Totowa, N.J.: Barnes & Noble, 1982.

Slavin, Arthur J. "Printing and Publishing in the Tudor Age." In *William Shakespeare: His World, His Work, His Influence.* Edited by John Andrews. 3 vols. New York: Charles Scribner's Sons, 1985, vol. 1.

Slights, Camille Wells. *The Casuistical Tradition in Shakespeare, Donne, Herbert, and Milton.* Princeton: Princeton University Press, 1981.

Sowards, J. Kelley. *Desiderius Erasmus.* Boston: Twayne Publishers, 1975.

Spitz, Lewis W. *The Protestant Reformation, 1517–1559.* New York: Harper & Row, 1985.

Steinberg, S. H. *Five Hundred Years of Printing.* 3d ed. Revised by James Moran. Harmondsworth, England, and Baltimore: Penguin Books, 1974.

Stern, Virginia F. *Gabriel Harvey: His Life, Marginalia and Library.* Oxford: Clarendon Press, 1979.

Tayler, Edward William. *Nature and Art in Renaissance Literature.* New York: Columbia University Press, 1964.

Teague, Frances. "Letters and Portents in *Julius Caesar* and *King Lear.*" *Shakespeare Yearbook* 1 (Spring 1990): 87–104.

———. *Shakespeare's Speaking Properties.* Lewisburg: Bucknell University Press, 1991.

Thomas, Keith. *Religion and the Decline of Magic: Studies in Popular Beliefs in Sixteenth and Seventeenth Century England.* London: Weidenfeld & Nicolson, 1971.

Thompson, Ann, and John O. Thompson. *Shakespeare: Meaning & Metaphor.* Iowa City: University of Iowa Press, 1987.

Traister, Barbara Howard. *Heavenly Necromancers: The Magician in English Renaissance Drama.* Columbia: University of Missouri Press, 1984.

Watt, Tessa. *Cheap Print and Popular Piety, 1550–1640.* Cambridge: Cambridge University Press, 1991.

White, Paul Whitfield. *Theatre and Reformation: Protestantism, Patronage, and Playing in Tudor England.* Cambridge: Cambridge University Press, 1993.

Wilks, John S. *The Idea of Conscience in Renaissance Tragedy.* London and New York: Routledge, 1990.

Woodman, David. *White Magic and English Renaissance Drama.* Rutherford, N.J.: Fairleigh Dickinson University Press, 1973.

Yates, Frances A. *The Occult Philosophy in the Elizabethan Age.* London, Boston and Henley: Routledge & Kegan Paul, 1979.

Young, David P. *The Heart's Forest: A Study of Shakespeare's Pastoral Plays.* New Haven and London: Yale University Press, 1972.

Index

Abraham, 134
Account book, 113, 122–23, 155
Act for the Advancement of True Religion, 269
Adam, language of, 99, 215, 290
Adams, Henry Hitch, 314 n. 26
Admiral's Men, 286
Aggeler, Geoffrey, 336 n. 11
Agrippa, Henry Cornelius, 262–63
Alain de Lille, 166
Albert of Brandenburg, 66
Alberti, Leon Battista, 100, 223
Albi, fresco at, 155
Alciato, Andrea, 177–78
Allen, Don Cameron, 226, 323 n. 60
Allen, P. S., 62
Almanacs, 56, 269, 277, 278
Alpers, Paul, 324 n. 6
Alphabet, 88, 100, 173, 204, 215, 217, 219, 278; invention of, 322 n. 51
Ambrose, Saint, 27, 62
Amerbach brothers, 47
Ames, William, 115–16, 118, 161
Andrelini, Fausto, 58, 81
Anglin, Jay P., 273
Apius and Virginia, 124
Apollo, 210, 222, 234, 287, 317 n. 47
Apollonius of Tyre, 316 n. 27
Archer, William, 339 n. 31
Archibald, Elizabeth, 326 n. 27, 331 n. 57
Arcimboldo, Giuseppe, 96–98
Arden of Faversham, 138, 273
Areopagus, 112
Ariès, Philippe, 155
Ariosto, 325 n. 16
Aristotle, 74, 81, 103, 171, 288; *Poetics:* 96
Art-nature topos, 180, 184, 185, 195, 196, 198, 203–8
Ascensian press, 48, 49
Ascham, Roger, 64

Assenza, Valeria Giachetti, 321 n. 18
Astrology, 13, 101, 215, 221, 225–29, 251–63, 334 n. 38.
Astronomy, 101, 163, 170–74, 178, 215, 226, 229, 261. *See also* Astrology, Stars
Audience, theatrical, 14, 15–16, 79, 273–74, 278, 282
Augustine, Saint, 27, 39, 117, 223, 243. Works: *Confessions:* 68, 166; *City of God:* 114, 298 n. 10
Augustus Caesar, 176, 222
Avicenna, 168

Babel, 243, 338 n. 20
Babylon, 243–44, 256
Babylonia, 221
Bacon, Sir Francis, 59, 63, 99, 167, 171; *The Advancement of Learning:* 64–65, 169–70
Bade, Josse, 46, 61
Baker, James, 266
Baldwin, William, 75
Bale, John, 75
Ballads, 278
Bancroft, Richard, 263
Barish, Jonas, 13, 245
Barkan, Leonard, 323 n. 1
Baron, Frank, 306 n. 27
Bartas, Seigneur Guillaume Du, 322 n. 40
Barthes, Roland, 98
Bartlett, John, 158
Basel, 47, 168
Baxter, Richard, 165
Baylor, Michael G., 116
Beaumont, Francis: *The Knight of the Burning Pestle:* 278
Beaumont and Fletcher: *The Woman-Hater,* 275
Behemoth, 147, 148, 151, 317 n. 47
Belsey, Catherine, 313 n. 13

361

Belshazzar, 243
Bement, Peter, 317 n. 48
Bennett, H. S., 269
Bentley, Jerry H., 299 n. 12
Berger, Harry, 324 n. 6
Bergeron, David M., 328 n. 38, 346 n. 26
Bernard, Saint, 116–17
Bernardus Silvestris, 225, 228
Berry, Edward I., 324 n. 10
Bevington, David, 81
Bible, 116; access to, 22, 31–32, 63; authenticity of, 37, 38; Bishops', 243; cited by the devil, 288; and classical literature, 25, 37, 39; Complutensian, 299 n. 12; divine inspiration of, 38; doctrinal controversy about, 41, 50, 70; in English, 11–12, 73, 76, 77, 80, 269, 272, 277; and English churches, 73, 74; and the English stage, 87; Geneva, 243; in German, 44, 47, 62; glosses of, 34, 60, 120; of Gutenberg, 48, 56, 281; interpretation of, 38–40, 41, 42, 76, 171, 179, 218; in Latin, 25, 26, 34, 36, 82, 287; and literary convention, 37; and music, 329 n. 44; original languages of, 22, 30, 43, 53, 73; and philology, 26, 27–28, 33–34, 36, 37, 39, 43; and printing, 22; private responsibility for interpretation of, 36, 40–43, 76, 171; as prop, 77, 82, 83, 84, 237–38, 249, 287, 339 n. 30; and Queen Elizabeth, 11, 77; and reason, 39–40; sale of, 47, 56; and rebuilding Christianity, 28; and salvation, 12, 28, 35, 40, 52, 165; as source of information, 163–65, 169, 172, 217; textual corruption of, 36, 37, 218; translation of, 22, 26–27, 31, 36, 44, 74, 173, 218; and unwritten tradition, 36; and the vernacular, 36; and words versus spirit, 119. Individual books: Daniel, 243–44; Esther, 37; Exodus, 291; Ezekiel, 117; Genesis, 37, 98, 243; Isaiah, 243; Jeremiah, 117, 243; Job, 37; Proverbs, 118; Psalms, 226, 277; Song of Solomon, 75; John's Gospel, 27, 83, 98–99, 135, 154–55; Corinthians, 117, 120, 130; Hebrews, 172; James, epistle of, 37; Philippians, 114, 135; Romans, 29, 34, 68–69, 83, 112, 115–16, 118, 134–35, 237, 238, 336 n. 10; Revelation, 113–14, 115–16, 120, 135, 243. *See also* New Testament, *Novum Instrumentum,* Old Testament
Billingsley, Henry, 215
Bishop of Liège, 22
Bloch, R. Howard, 266
Blood as ink, 84–85, 89, 105, 114, 124, 144, 153, 162, 235, 246
Boaistuau, Pierre, 65
Boas, Frederick S., 152, 315 n. 30, 316 n. 38, 318 n. 51, 337 n. 12
Boccaccio, Giovanni, 188
Boethius, 222
Bogdanov, Michael, 336 n. 10, 338 n. 20
Boleyn, Anne, 28
Boleyn, Thomas, 28
Bolton, Robert, 115, 116, 161
Bono, Barbara J., 324 n. 10
Book(s): of accounts, 113, 155, 161; of adamant, 219; affordable, 65; and alchemy, 290; and bookishness, 81, 124, 292–93; about books, 41; burning of, 52–55, 70, 79–80, 85, 168, 294; censorship of, 54–55, 70, 76, 80; clasps of, 77, 92, 224, 229; as codex, 266, 276; collation of, 25, 114, 119; colophon of, 280; of Common Prayer, 158; and compositors, 48, 49, 61, 62, 63; and computers, 266; of conscience, 12, 111–23, 124–62, 254; of creatures, 163, 164–65, 166, 169, 172; dedication of, 279; of deeds, 124, 197, 200; of destiny, 230; of the devil, 95; and the dissemination of ideas, 44; and divinity, 287–88; and faith, 142; of fate, 12, 219–31, 263; and fecklessness, 292–93; of the firmament 101, 102, 165, 166, 174, 225, 228–29; and folly, 289; of foreknowledge, 115; and Fortune, 230; given to sovereign, 122; and glosses, 34, 41, 60, 120; of the heart, 253–54, 255; in heaven, 133, 135; and heresy, 53, 76–77, 277; and hypocrisy, 144, 288; index of, 93, 278–79; of infamy, 94; internal, 91–94; inventories of, 269; and knowledge, 142, 163; and the law, 64, 82, 115, 290–92; and law misapplied, 292; and learning, 63, 144; of life, 113–15, 120, 135–36, 155; and

magic, 82–83, 102, 147–52; manipulated by the unscrupulous, 288, 292, 294–96; margins of, 25, 67, 93, 105; and medicine, 82, 168, 289–90; of memory, 94, 128; of misfortune, 229, 230; as model, 95; of nature, 163–79, 180–82, 197, 204, 213, 217–18; and necromancy, 82, 149, 151; obscure the Bible, 60–61; in paintings, 43; and patrons, 279; and philosophy, 82, 142, 288–89; and piety, 43, 255, 288, 345 n. 4; pirating of, 62; pocket size, 25; poisoned, 249, 250, 295; in portraits, 22–23, 29, 43; of praises, 197, 198; of prayer, 56, 77, 255, 287, 288, 339 n. 30, 345 n. 4; production of, 12, 47–48, 55–63, 76, 106, 269; as prop, 13, 77, 81–86, 101–2, 107, 124, 141–45, 147–51, 211, 234, 237–38, 242–43, 246, 247, 249, 254, 276–78, 287–96; and quackery, 290; and reason, 128; of rebellion, 105; of records, 291; of remembrance, 128; and sadness, 255, 288–89; of the saints, 27; sale at theaters, 273; and salvation, 12, 106, 114; and scholars, 59; of secrecy, 178; and sex, 143–44; sizes of, 165, 279; sold at St. Paul's, 269; and spirituality, 43, 63, 79; of sport, 88; and strife, 31, 41, 50–54, 70, 75, 76; of time, 104; and trees, 181–82, 186–87, 189, 323 n. 2; and truth, 65, 144; and virtue, 64–65; winged, 241; and wisdom, 142; and witchcraft, 82; withdrawn from circulation, 279. *See also* Bible, Metaphoric books, Manuscripts, Pen, Print, Reading, Writing
Bottéro, Jean, 221
Bourne, Immanuel, 114–15, 116, 120
Bowers, Fredson, 238
Bradbrook, Muriel, 252
Braden, Gordon, 337 n. 14
Bradford, John, 288, 345 n. 9
Brecht, Martin, 302 n. 28
Brethren of the Common Life, 45–46
Broadside, 269, 273
Brome, Richard: *The Antipodes,* 275; *A Jovial Crew,* 90–91, 277
Bromley, Laura G., 312 n. 7
Brooke, C. F. Tucker, 336 n. 5

Brooke, Nicholas, 151–52, 315 nn. 30, 31 and 36, 316 n. 37, 317 n. 49
Brown, John Russell, 340 n. 35
Brown, Norman O., 42
Browne, Sir Thomas, 59, 99, 112, 164, 165, 171, 174
Brueghel, Pieter, 290
Bruno, Giordano, 151, 167–68
Bruns, Gerald, 173
Bryskett, Lodowick, 175
Bryson, Anna, 307 n. 43
Budé, Guillaume, 31, 50, 69
Bühler, Curt F., 280
Bullough, Geoffrey, 324 n. 10
Buondelmonti, Cristoforo, 174
Burton, Robert, 59, 113, 228
Butler, Martin, 273

Cabala, 215–16, 217
Cade, Jack, 15, 78–80, 87, 293
Caesar, Julius, 64
Cain, 130, 131–32
Calvin, John, 162; and the Bible, 36, 38, 120, 172; and conscience, 112, 117–18, 119–20; and obedience to authorities, 159; and predestination, 84, 114
Cambridge, 53; University of, 73, 74, 158, 213
Camden, Carroll, 309 n. 39
Campanella, Tommaso, 167
Campion, Edmund, 157–58
Canuteson, John, 314 n. 23
Cardano, Girolamo, 59
Carpenter, Richard, 113, 120
Carlson, David R., 300 n. 3
Caravaggio, 300 n. 34
Cargill Thompson, W. D. J., 299 n. 24
Cartari, Vincenzo, 219, 220
Cartophylax, 148, 316 n. 38
Cartwright, Thomas, 158
Cassiodorus, 24
Castiglione, Baldassare: *Book of the Courtier,* 11, 64
Castle of Perseverance, 313 n. 9
Casuistry, 156
Cave, Terence, 304 n. 79
Caxton, William, 280–81
Cecil, William, 156, 158, 213
Censorship, 54–55, 70, 76, 88
Certeau, Michel de, 328 n. 38
Chaeremon, 178, 323 n. 62

Chamber, John, 263
Chapman, George, 271. Works: *All Fools*, 144, 276; *Bussy D'Ambois*, 112–13, 125, 138–54; *Chabot, Admiral of France*, 91; *The Conspiracy of Charles Duke of Byron*, 92, 94, 229; *Monsieur D'Olive*, 144; *Ovid's Banquet of Sense*, 161; *The Revenge of Bussy D'Ambois*, 154; *The Shadow of Night*, 151; *The Yorkshire Gentleman*, 314 n. 26
Chapmen, 271
Character: definition of, 307 n. 5; as genre, 14, 106; as letter, 82, 90, 92, 101, 102, 104, 113, 137, 153, 171, 181, 187, 193, 207, 208, 225, 228, 229, 264, 275, 320 n. 54, 322 n. 40
Charles V (emperor), 35
Charron, Pierre, 58–59, 119, 120–21
Chartier, Roger, 271, 306 n. 24
Chaucer, Geoffrey, 127
Chaudhuri, Sukanta, 324 n. 6
Cheke, Sir John, 213
Chiromancy, 99
Chrisman, Miriam Usher, 56, 341 n. 13
Christianity, personified, 287
Chrysostom, Saint John, 44, 132
Cicero, 24; *De Officiis*, 25
Cirillo, Albert, 324 n. 10, 325 n. 13
Clanchy, M. T., 344 n. 23
Clare, Janet, 307 n. 42
Clark, Arthur Melville, 130
Clasps (book), 77, 92, 224, 229
Claudian, 24, 165–66
Clement VIII (pope), 55
Clulee, Nicholas H., 217–18
Clyomon and Clamydes, 287, 331 n. 56
Codex, 266, 276
Cole, Richard G., 271
Colet, John, 25, 41, 53, 59
Collier, John Payne, 328 n. 37
Collinson, Patrick, 319 n. 80, 341 n. 7
Colonna, Francesco, 177
Colophon, 280
Commedia dell'arte, 290
Compositors, 45, 48, 49, 61, 62, 63, 279, 280
Computers, metaphors of, 266–67
Condell, Henry, 67
Conscience, 34; and Act of Uniformity, 155–56; and Articles of Religion, 158–59; book of, 12, 111–23, 124–62, 254; and equivocation, 157; and feeling guilty, 116; and John Ford, 162; formation of, 118–19; and the heart, 115–20, 126, 130, 155, 162; and introspection, 112–15; and mental reservation, 157; and metaphor of punctuation, 122; and Thomas Middleton, 161–62; personified, 112, 124, 134; and Puritans, 139, 158–61; as sergeant, 126; and John Webster, 162, 254
Constance, Council of, 53–54
Constantine (emperor), 25–26, 298 n. 8
Cook, Ann Jennalie, 273
Cooper, Helen, 324 n. 6
Cossa, Francesco del, 226
Coverdale, Miles, 80
Craig, Hardin, 314 n. 27
Craik, T. W., 292, 314 n. 20
Cramer, Daniel, 120, 121
Cranach, Lucas, 29
Cressy, David, 269–70
Crofts, Richard, 301 n. 14
Cromwell, Thomas, 74
Cumae (Italy), 62, 222, 223, 224
Cuneiform, 221
Curtius, Ernst Robert, 321 n. 26

Daley, A. Stuart, 324 n. 10, 325 n. 12
Daniel, Samuel, 124
Daniell, David, 306 n. 22
Dante, 166
Davies, C.S.L., 56, 159
Davis, Natalie Zemon, 271
Day, Angel, 345 n. 2
Dee, John: and astrology/astronomy, 215, 258; conception of nature, 213, 215, 217–18; his library, 12, 214, 331 n. 64; and Queen Elizabeth, 12, 211, 213–14, 215; and navigation, 214–15; *Monas Hieroglyphica*, 214, 215, 216–18
Dekker, Thomas: *The Honest Whore, Part 2*, 90, 92, 93, 279; *Match Me in London*, 279; *The Noble Spanish Soldier*, 93, 95, 276; *Northward Ho* (with Webster), 280; *The Shoemaker's Holiday*, 277–78; *The Sun's Darling* (with Ford), 279; *The Virgin Martyr*, 92, 94, 162, 289–90; *Westward Ho* (with Webster), 93, 277

Derrida, Jacques, 102–3
Descartes, René, 173
Desk, writing, 152–53
Dessen, Alan C., 337 n. 18
Destiny. *See* Fate
Deventer, 45, 46, 301 n. 5
Devereux, E.J., 305 n. 3
Diana, 209–11, 330 nn. 48–52, 54, 331 n. 57
Dickey, Stephen, 331 n. 56
Dieckmann, Liselotte, 176
Diocletian (emperor), 25
Dioscorides, 168
"Divine Mill, The," 32, 33
Documents in drama: *All Fools* (divorce), 276; *Believe as You List* (record of communication with ambassadors), 291; *The Broken Heart* (an oracle), 287; *Cymbeline* (Jupiter's tablet), 100–101; *The Devil's Law-Case* (legal brief), 292; *Doctor Faustus* (contract with devil), 84–85, 89; *Edward II* (transfer of custody), 286; *Enough is as Good as a Feast* (will), 292; *Hamlet* (execution order), 242; *1 Henry IV* (indentures of rebels), 276; *2 Henry IV* (list of complaints), 105; *Henry V* (arrest warrants), 291; *2 Henry VI* (articles of peace), 284–85; *3 Henry VI* (marriage articles), 284; *A Jovial Crew* (rent receipts), 277; *Julius Caesar* (will), 295; *King John* (a written oath), 272; *King Lear* (execution order), 295; *The Merchant of Venice* (Shylock's bond), 276, 291; *Much Ado About Nothing* (judicial interrogation), 291; *The Noble Spanish Soldier* (marriage contract), 276; *Richard II* (accusations of crime), 291; *Richard III* (indictment), 292; *Sir John Oldcastle, Part 1* (a process); *The Spanish Tragedy* (declaration, bond, lease), 245–46; *Tamburlaine, Part 2* (a truce), 271; *Westward Ho* (bonds), 277; *The Winter's Tale* (an oracle), 287
Dollimore, Jonathan, 339 n. 31
Donation of Constantine, 30
Donawerth, Jane, 101
Donne, John, 37, 60–61, 114, 115, 116, 122, 164–65, 172

Dorp, Maarten van, 27, 38, 302 n. 27
Downame, John, 113, 116, 132, 161
Drake, Sir Francis, 214
Draper, R. W., 324 n. 10
Drue, Thomas: *The Life of the Duchess of Suffolk,* 74
Duccio, Agostino di, 223
Dudley, Robert, 211, 213
Dunbar, Mary Judith, 327 n. 30
Duncan-Jones, Katherine, 331 n. 59
Dürer, Albrecht, 21, 22, 23, 29, 43, 54
D'Urfey, Thomas, 139
Dustbox, 275
Dutton, Richard, 307 n. 42
Dyer, Sir Edward, 211, 214, 217
Dyke, Jeremiah, 126, 132, 161

Eck, Johann, 34, 111
Edward IV (king of England), 11, 213
Edwards, Philip, 328 n. 37, 338 n. 20
Egypt, 93, 100, 175, 177, 203, 260, 323 n. 62
Eisenstein, Elizabeth L., 50, 171, 265, 282, 320 n. 3
Elderton, William, 262
Electronic publication, 266
Eliot, T. S., 232
Elizabeth I (queen of England), 76, 88, 263, 270; and the Bible, 11, 77; and books, 12; and conscience, 155–60, 318 n. 65; coronation procession of, 11, 77; and John Dee, 12, 211, 213, 214, 215, 217
Elsky, Martin, 331 n. 71
Elyot, Sir Thomas, 75, 258, 272
Emblems, 177–78
Empson, William, 337 n. 13
Enchiridion, 51, 302 n. 27
Enough Is as Good as a Feast, 292
Ephesus, 210, 330 n. 51
Epistles, Pauline, 25, 50. *See also* Bible
Erasmus, Desiderius, 93, 106, 168; and astrology, 227; and Josse Bade, 46; and the Bishop of Liège, 22; bookish upbringing of, 24; and the Brethren of the Common Life, 45–46; and Guillaume Budé, 31, 69; and Cicero, 25; and classical authors, 24, 25, 26, 57; and John Colet, 25, 41, 53, 59; criticizes printers, 61–62; defines metaphor, 96; and Doctor Faustus, 81; and Maarten van Dorp, 27, 38; as

editor, 14, 25, 26, 27, 42, 44, 51, 73, 302 n. 27; English reception of, 73–76; and his father, 44–45; and free will, 42, 51–52; and Johann Froben, 31, 47, 61, 62; and Saint Jerome, 26, 27, 47, 51; and Wolfgang Lachner, 61; and Johann Lang, 31; laments book production, 56–57; laments deference to the written word, 58; laments printing errors, 61; and William Latimer, 61; and Edward Lee, 50; and Jacques Lefèvre d'Etaples, 27, 50, 51; letters of, 22, 31, 66; and Martin Luther, 21–22, 32, 33, 34, 36, 41, 42, 46, 51–52, 66, 75, 76, 79, 82, 84, 87, 168, 173, 218; and Aldus Manutius, 46, 47, 61; and metaphors of editing, 51; as monk, 46; and New Testament, 14, 22, 26–27; and *Novum Instrumentum*, 26–28, 31, 32, 34, 47, 50–51, 76, 80, 168, 298 nn. 10 and 11; and Konrad Peutinger, 44; and Pope Leo X, 28; portrait of, 22, 23; praise of Luther, 31; praises printing, 65; praises libraries, 11, 64; and printing, 15, 22, 45, 76; and the reformers, 73–76; and Johann Reuchlin, 53; and sale of his books, 56, 74; and Georgius Spalatinus, 31; statue of, 73–74; and style, 24, 51, 52, 69, 81; temperament of, 29; and Terence, 24; and university curricula, 74; and Lorenzo Valla, 24, 25, 26, 46; visits to England, 73; and William Warham, 27, 70, 73. Works: *Adages*, 13–14, 56, 176, 330 n. 54; *Adagiorum Chiliades*, 46; *Adagiorum Collectanea*, 46, 61; *Annotations*, 44; *Apologia ad Iacobum Fabrum Sapulensem*, 50; *Apothegms*, 64; *Colloquia*, 62; *Compendium Vitae*, 44; *Contra Morosos*, 299 n. 13; *De Conscribendis Epistolis*, 66; *De Copia*, 58; *De Libero Arbitrio*, 42; *De Officiis* (editor), 25; *De Praeparatione ad Mortem*, 28; *Enchiridion Militis Christiani*, 51; *Epistolae ad Diversos*, 66; *Hecuba* (editor), 46, 61; *Hyperaspistes*, 52; *Institutio Principis Christiani*, 31; *Iphegenia in Aulis* (editor), 46, 61; *On the Freedom of the Will*, 51–52;

Panegyricus, 48, 49; *Paraclesis*, 299 n. 20; *Paraphrases of the New Testament*, 73, 74, 75, 155; *Querela Pacis*, 31
Ettin, Andrew V., 324 n. 6
Euripides, 46
Eusebius, 60, 298 n. 8
Evans, G. Blakemore, 328 n. 39
Evans, Maurice, 151
Everyman, 127, 155, 313 n. 9

Falconetto, Giovanni Maria, 226
Farquhar, James Douglas, 344 n. 33
Fate, book of, 12, 219–31, 263; and Christianity, 222–23; and Fortune, 229–30, 252–53; and free will, 228; and prophecy, 222–25
Fates, the, 140, 219, 220, 222, 228, 332 n. 2, 334 n. 30
Fathers of the church, 21, 27, 34, 53, 116
Favour, John, 36, 116
Febvre, Lucien, 55–56
Federico of Montefeltro, 11
Felltham, Owen, 64, 119, 122, 163, 164, 165, 228–29
Fennor, William, 273
Ferguson, Margaret W., 337 n. 17
Ficino, Marsilio, 175, 227, 228, 329 n. 44
Field, Nathan: *The Fatal Dowry* (with Massinger), 279; responsible for revising *Bussy D'Ambois*, 315 n. 30
Figurative langugage, 88–107
Fisher, Christopher, 26
Fisher, John, 73
Fleming, Abraham, 345 n. 2
Fletcher, Harry George, 344 n. 37
Floyer, Sir John, 225
Forbes, Patrick, 114, 119
Ford, John: *The Broken Heart*, 287; *The Sun's Darling* (with Dekker), 275; *'Tis Pity She's a Whore*, 124, 125, 276
Ford, Wyn, 297 n. 9
Foucault, Michel, 40–41, 106, 178
Foxe, John, 54, 75; and John Dee, 213; praise of Erasmus, 74; and printing, 12, 48; *Acts and Monuments*, 12, 65, 74, 76
Frankfurt Fair, 31, 54
Fraunce, Abraham, 219, 230
Frederick of Saxony, 31

Free will, 42, 51–52, 225–26
French, Peter J., 331 n. 60
Friedman, Thomas L., 266
Friedrich, Hugo, 305 n. 91
Froben, Johann, 31, 47, 61, 62, 75, 168
Frobisher, Martin, 214
Frye, Northrop, 328 n. 35
Führer, M. L., 329 n. 16
Fuller, Thomas, 340 n. 1
Furet, François, 302 n. 23
Fust, Johann, 44, 81

Gainsford, Thomas, 345 n. 2
Galen, 81, 168, 289, 290
Galileo, 163, 170–74, 178, 215, 218, 264, 265
Gallagher, Lowell, 318 n. 65
Garber, Marjorie, 346 n. 21
Garin, Eugenio, 227
Garter, Thomas, 288
Gascoigne, George, 113
Gaskell, Ivan, 345 n. 4
Gatti, Hilary, 322 n. 37
Gaurico, Luca, 226
Georgius of Helmstadt, 81
Gibbons, Brian, 324 n. 10
Gilbert, Allan H., 332 n. 2
Goldberg, Jonathan, 314 n. 29, 323 n. 56, 341 n. 3
Goodman, Godfrey, 57, 62–63, 98, 207–8
Goodstein, Peter, 338 n. 23
Goolden, P., 327 n. 32
Gorfain, Phyllis, 326 n. 26, 330 n. 47
Gower, John, 198
Graff, Harvey J., 270
Grafton, Anthony, 74
Greek language, 22, 25, 26, 27, 30, 32, 34, 36, 61, 73, 82–83, 100, 116, 174, 215, 243, 299 n. 11, 306 n. 22, 307 n. 5, 322 n. 40
Green, Henry, 327 n. 30
Greenaway, Peter, 293
Greenblatt, Stephen, 156
Greene, Robert, 256; *Friar Bacon:* 147–51, 277; *Menaphon,* 256
Greene, Thomas M., 57, 176
Greenham, Richard, 118–19, 161
Greenwich, 11, 214, 217
Gregory Nazianzen, 37
Grennan, Eamon, 195–96
Grocyn, William, 73

Groote, Geert, 45, 46
Guercino, 300 n. 34
Gurr, Andrew, 274, 342 n. 34
Gutenberg, Johann, 12, 44, 48, 50, 56, 266, 281
Gutierrez, Nancy A., 319 n. 87
Gwinn, Matthew, 225

Hakewill, George, 65, 115
Halbey, Hans Adolf, 300 n. 1
Hall, B., 298 n. 5
Hall, Edward, 64
Hall, Joan Lord, 339 n. 33
Hammurabi, 111
Hampton Court, 11, 213, 214
Hanebutt-Benz, Eva-Maria, 300 n. 1
Harbage, Alfred, 273
Harris, William V., 298 n. 8
Hartwig, Joan, 328 n. 34
Harvey, Gabriel, 256, 257, 259, 262
Harvey, John, 258, 259–62
Harvey, Richard, 214, 256–63
Havelock, Eric, 268
Hattaway, Michael, 342 n. 34
Hawkes, Terence, 96
Haynum, Andrée, 298 n. 3
Heart, and conscience, 115–20, 126, 130, 155, 162
Hebrew language, 30, 32, 36, 43, 53, 82–83, 117, 215
Heemskerck, Maarten van, 119
Heidelberg, University of, 81
Heinemann, Margot, 319 n. 90
Hellinga, Lotte, 344 n. 40
Heminges, John, 67
Henderson, Diana E., 313 n. 12
Hendrix, Scott H., 301 n. 14
Heninger, S. K., 103, 308 n. 25, 329 n. 44
Henneberg, Berthold von, 54
Henry III (king of France), 138
Henry IV (king of England), 124
Henry VII, 11, 227
Henry VIII, 11, 74, 213, 227, 258, 269
Henslowe's *Diary,* 345 n. 2
Herbert, William, 213
Hermes, 175
Hermetic philosophy, 151
Hesse, Carla, 266
Hendon, Christopher, 263
Heywood, Thomas, 265; attitude toward printing, 67. Works: *The En-*

glish Traveller, 67; If You Know Not Me, 15, 76–77, 78, 87, 88; A Woman Killed with Kindness, 112, 125–38, 140, 144–45, 153, 161
Hieatt, Charles W., 324 n. 10
Hieroglyphics, 174–78, 214–17, 322 n. 40, 322 n. 49, 323 n. 56
Hilary (bishop of Poitiers), 39, 62
Hilton, Julian, 345 n. 2
Hindman, Sandra, 281
Hirsch, Rudolf, 55, 269
Historie of the Damnable Life . . . of Doctor Faustus, 82–83
Hoeniger, F. David, 199, 327 n. 30, 330 n. 48
Holinshed, Raphael: account of Edmund Campion, 157–58; account of Jack Cade, 78–80; books in English palaces, 12, 272; and *Macbeth*, 225
Hooker, Richard, 35, 122, 322 n. 43
Horace, 24, 276
Horapollo Niliacus (Horus Apollo), 174–75, 177, 178
Hosley, Richard, 329 n. 45
Hugh of St. Victor, 166
Houston, R. A., 268
Hughes, John, 115
Hunter, G. K., 239
Hunter, Robert Grams, 331 n. 56
Hus, Jan, 48
Hutten, Ulrich von, 30–31
Hyginus, 219
Hymen, 195–96, 239

Illiteracy, 13, 78–80, 101–2, 194, 268, 277. *See also* Literacy
Impatient Poverty, 124
Indentures, 276
Index of a book, 93, 278–79
Index Librorum Prohibitorum, 55
Ingegno, Alfonso, 320 n. 17
Ink, 77, 89, 105, 117, 144, 153, 186, 190, 235, 246, 247, 254, 266, 272, 275, 318 n. 51; as prop, 104, 124, 134, 202, 219, 247, 292, 314 n. 20
Inkhorn, 78, 275, 326 n. 20
Italic, 268, 275, 281
Iversen, Erik, 323 n. 59

Jacobi, Jolande, 321 n. 23
Jacquot, Jean, 318 n. 54
James I (king of England), 122–23, 219, 225; and John Dee, 213; and Hampton Court Conference, 160; *Basilicon Doron*, 122–23
Jankowski, Theodora A., 338 n. 29
Jardine, Lisa, 74, 304 n. 80, 314 n. 25
Jerome, Saint, 26, 27, 42, 44, 47, 51, 60, 82, 288
John, Saint, 27, 35
John of Salisbury, 223, 225–26
Johnson, S. F., 243
Jones, Edwin, 173
Jones, Emrys, 336 n. 10
Jonge, Henk van de, 298 n. 10
Jonson, Ben, 138, 264; and the Fates, 219, 221; printing of his *Works*, 66–67. Works: *The Alchemist*, 217, 290, 304 n. 84; *An Entertainment of King James and Queen Anne at Theobalds*, 219; *Bartholomew Fair*, 273, 304 n. 84; *Catiline*, 92; *Discoveries*, 304 n. 84; *Every Man in His Humour*, 67, 99; *Hymenaei*, 326 n. 22; *The New Inn*, 13, 92; *Sejanus*, 67, 295; *The Staple of News*, 278, 279; *Volpone*, 290
Josipovici, Gabriel, 40
Judicial astrology. *See* Astrology
Jupiter (Jove), 219, 222, 228
Justinian: *Institutes*, 81, 290–91

Kahn, Victoria, 302 n. 26
Kay, Carol McGinnis, 244–45
Kay, W. David, 304 n. 81
Keefer, Michael, 81, 84
Keller, Michelle, 330 n. 49
Kelley, Edward, 213
Kepler, Johannes, 226–27
Kiefer, Frederick, 335 n. 54
Kipling, Gordon, 297 n. 2
Kirsch, Arthur, 339 n. 30
Knapp, Robert S., 335 n. 58
Knight, G. Wilson, 327 n. 30
Knowles, Richard Paul, 331 n. 56
Koestler, Arthur, 334 n. 39
Kronenfeld, Judy Z., 325 n. 11
Kyd, Thomas, 256, 265. Works: *Soliman and Perseda*, 90, 92; *The Spanish Tragedy*, 144, 221, 232–46, 275, 288–89, 340 n. 36

Lachner, Wolfgang, 61
Lactantius, 221–23

Ladner, Gerhart B., 327 n. 30
Lakoff, George, 106
Lang, Johann, 31, 32
Langer, Suzanne, 107
Language, and materiality, 98–104
Lascelles, Mary, 324 n. 10
Latham, Agnes, 324 n. 5, 325 n. 15
Latimer, William, 61
Latin language, 24, 25, 26, 27, 34, 36, 73, 75, 85, 100, 101, 116, 148, 157, 175, 184, 215, 217, 225, 237–39, 243, 276, 295, 298 n. 11
Lee, Edward, 50
Lee, Rensselaer W., 181, 194
Leech, Clifford, 339 n. 32
Lefèvre, Jacques, 27, 50, 51
Leggatt, Alexander, 77, 313 n. 13
Leicester, earl of, 73
Leipzig, 31
Leo X (pope), 28
LeRoy, Louis, 100
Letters: of alphabet, 82, 103, 104, 165, 166, 173, 174, 175, 219, 252; guides to writing, 345 n. 2; personal, 66, 304 n. 79; as prop, 13, 77, 104, 107, 124, 136, 144–45, 146, 152–53, 154, 162, 199–202, 229, 230–31, 234, 235–37, 243–46, 247, 248–49, 253, 275, 277, 278, 280, 283–86, 294–96, 312 n. 2
Lewis, C. S., 311 n. 30
Leyden, Lucas van, 224
Library: at Alexandria, 65; of Apollonius, 327 n. 27; of creatures, 163, 165; of John Dee, 12, 213, 214; designed by Michelangelo, 11; of Doctor Faustus, 81; of Duke Frederick of Saxony, 31; in England, 11; of the gods, 219; in Italy, 11; of Ben Jonson, 264; less useful than Bible, 61; of Machiavelli, 69–70; as mark of status, 59; monastic, 11, 24, 25, 29, 30, 65, 266; of Montaigne, 70; praise of, 64; of Pericles, 210; of Cardinal Piccolomini, 11; of Prospero, 293; professional, 341 n. 13; and renown, 64; as source of useful information, 168; transformation of, 266; of Johannes Trithemius, 81; Vatican, 11
Liebeschuetz, J.H.W.G., 298 n. 7
Lienhard, Marc, 301 n. 13

Linacre, Thomas, 73
Linche, Richard, 335 n. 56
Link, Wenceslas, 48
Literacy: and aggrievement, 78–80; of audiences, 13, 78–79, 194, 273–74, 275, 278, 282, 342 nn. 34 and 35; and book production, 269; and chapmen, 270–71; in cities, 270, 271, 341 n. 13; definitions of, 268; and Erasmus, 15; estimate of, 269–71, 297 n. 9, 340 n. 13; and forms of script, 268; and founding of schools, 79, 268–69, 273; gradations of, 269; growth of, 56, 75, 85, 264; and interior decoration, 272–73; and inventories of books, 269, 341 n. 13; of London apprentices, 270, 278; and Luther, 15; onstage, 277–78; and oral culture, 270–71; of ordinary people, 277–78; pride in, 78–79; and rituals, 271; and salvation, 12; and single-leaf woodcuts, 269. *See also* Illiteracy
Livy, 68
Lodge, Thomas: *Rosalynde*, 182–96; *The Wounds of Civil War*, 90, 93, 94
Lollards, 277
Lomax, Marion, 330 n. 48, 346 n. 27
London, 11, 53, 77, 78, 79, 270, 272, 273, 278
Lordi, Robert J., 315 n. 30, 317 n. 49
Lowry, Martin, 46, 47–48
Lucas, F. L., 340 n. 36
Lucian, 227, 308 n. 14
Lusty Juventus, 82, 294
Luther, Martin: and astrology, 227–28; and the Brethren of the Common Life, 45–46; burns papal bull, 53; and canon law, 35; and conscience, 111–12, 116; and contract with the devil, 84; and Doctor Faustus, 81; and Johann Eck, 34; and Erasmus, 31–32, 33, 34, 36, 41, 42, 46, 47, 51–52, 66, 75, 76, 79, 82, 84, 87, 168, 173, 218; and fate, 228; and free will, 42, 51–52, 227–28; and Johann Froben, 31; and Ulrich von Hutten, 30, 31; and interpretation of the Bible, 14, 34, 37, 39, 43; and knowledge of languages, 39; laments book production, 59–61; and Johann Lang, 31, 32; as monk, 29, 30; and ninety-five theses, 12, 47, 76,

81; and *Novum Instrumentum*, 32; and Paracelsus, 321 n. 23; portrait of, 29; and praise of Erasmus, 31; and predestination, 228; and printing, 15, 45, 47, 48, 76; and printing errors, 62; and reliance on faith in interpretation of Bible, 39–40; and reliance on reason, 34, 39–40, 111–12; and reliance on Scripture, 34–35, 111–12; report of his death, 21, 29, 43, 54; and sales of his books, 31, 47, 56; and scholasticism, 30; and St. Paul's Epistle to the Romans, 29, 30, 34; and Georgius Spalatinus, 31, 32, 39, 53; and Johann von Staupitz, 53; as translator, 14, 47; his translation of the New Testament, 29, 32, 47, 62; and Lorenzo Valla, 30; and Virgil, 42, 228. Works: *De Servo Arbitrio*, 41, 228; *On the Bondage of the Will*, 51–52; *Sermon on Indulgence and Grace*, 47
Lyly, John, 194, 290, 346 n. 15

Machiavelli, Niccolò, 69–70
Mainz, 12, 44, 54–55, 281
Maldon, William, 48
Mankind, 313 n. 9
Mansfield, Bruce, 305 n. 2
Mansion, Colard, 280
Mantuan, 188
Manuscript(s): belonging to John Dee, 12; chained, 266; discovery by Erasmus, 25, 26; destruction of Luther's, 54; in era of print, 45; and the frontier of print, 278; internal, 92; of nature, 164, 165, 171, 278; production in Middle Ages, 56; and scribal error, 22, 27, 36, 61; and similarity to print, 280–82; written on paper, 280
Manutius, Aldus, 46, 47, 61, 175, 176, 177, 281
Mark, Saint, 44
Marlowe, Christopher, 138, 265. Works: *Doctor Faustus*, 15, 79, 80–87, 88, 89, 101–2, 107, 124, 149, 151, 287, 289, 290; *Edward II*, 90, 104, 107, 286, 295; *Hero and Leander*, 276, 278–79; *Tamburlaine*, 90, 101, 294; *Tamburlaine, Part 2*, 94, 271–72
Marriage between Wit and Wisdom, 294

Marston, John, 138. Works: *Antonio and Mellida*, 277; *Antonio's Revenge*, 340 n. 36; *The Insatiate Countess*, 279, 288; *The Malcontent*, 13, 279; *Parasitaster*, 14
Martianus Capella, 219
Martial, 24, 272
Martin, Henri-Jean, 55–56
Mary I (queen of England), 74, 76–77, 213
Maslen, Elizabeth, 336 n. 10
Massinger, Philip: *Believe as You List*, 291; (with Field), *The Fatal Dowry*, 279
Mathematics, and nature, 173, 214, 215–18, 260
Matthew, Saint, 38, 44, 300 n. 34
Maxwell, J. C., 328 n. 37
McCloskey, Susan, 338 n. 27
McConica, James Kelsey, 305 n. 10
McElroy, Bernard, 333 n. 29
McGee, J. Sears, 319 n. 77
McKellen, Ian, 340 n. 37
McLuhan, Marshall, 321 n. 31
McLuskie, Kathleen, 130–31, 338 n. 29
McManaway, James G., 328 n. 37
McMillin, Scott, 337 n. 13
McNeill, John T., 38
McNeir, Waldo, 135
McPherson, David, 340 n. 2
Mebane, John S., 329 n. 44
Melanchthon, Philip, 54, 260, 302 n. 28
Melito (bishop), 37
Mellinkoff, Ruth, 313 n. 17
Memory: book of, 93–95; and writing, 239–41
Mercator, Gerard, 213
Mercury, 175, 204–5, 215, 257, 329 n. 42
Metaphor(s): and abstractions, 12, 104–7; of computers, 266–67; of conscience, 120; definition of, 96–98, 106–7, 308 n. 25; of editing, 51; and Galileo, 173–74; of nature, 178; of reading and writing, 15, 89–107, 265; of printing, 15, 265
Metaphoric books, 12–13, 15; definition of, 105–7. *See also* Book of conscience, of fate, of nature
Michael, Nancy C., 328 n. 37
Michelangelo, 11, 177, 224
Middleton, Thomas, 161–62. Works:

The Changeling, 162, 279; *A Mad World My Masters,* 276, 288; *Michaelmas Term,* 275; *No Wit, No Help Like a Woman's,* 229, 277
Mignault, Claude, 178
Milton, John, 63, 64, 170. Works: *Areopagitica,* 55; *Paradise Lost,* 163, 164, 321 n. 32
Mincoff, Marco, 342 n. 10
Mind-reading, 93
Misprint, Lord of, 271
Mitchell, Katie, 313 n. 8
Modern Devotion, The, 45
Monasticism, 24, 30, 31, 73, 75, 163. *See also* Erasmus, Libraries, Luther
Montaigne, Michel de, 41, 42, 57, 58, 63, 64, 70, 98, 103
Montrose, Louis Adrian, 326 n. 18
More, Sir Thomas, 156
Moseley, Charles, 323 n. 61
Moses, 32, 35, 37, 111, 119, 290
Motto: in emblems, 178; in imprese, 129, 198–99
Muir, Kenneth, 328 n. 37
Mulcaster, Richard, 103
Murray, Peter B., 339 n. 30
Murry, John Middleton, 107
Muster book, 277
Myconius, Friedrich, 47
Mystery play (Chester), 155

Napier, John, 114, 224–25
Nashe, Thomas, 256, 257, 262, 263
National Theatre (London), 336 n. 10, 338 n. 20
Nature: book of, 12, 163–79, 180–218, 229; and mathematics, 173, 214, 215–18, 260; and pastoral, 180–96; personified, 166, 198, 204–5, 228; subject of observation 166–74
Nauert, Charles G., 340 n. 41
Necromancy, 82, 149, 151, 322 n. 37
Neoplatonism, 149, 175–76, 217, 317 n. 46, 323 n. 56
New Testament, 35, 46, 117, 134–35, 237, 277, 336 n. 10; in English, 48, 50; in German, 31–32, 44, 47; in Greek, 22, 25, 26, 27, 30. *See also* Bible, Erasmus, Luther, *Novum Testamentum*
Newman, Jane O., 303 n. 60
Newton, Richard C., 67

Nicholas of Cusa, 167
Nicholas of Lyra, 34
North, J. D., 228
Notary, 113, 276, 282
Novum Testamentum, 26–28, 31, 32, 34, 47, 50–51, 76, 80, 168, 298 nn. 10 and 11. *See also* Bible, Erasmus

Oberman, Heiko A., 299 n. 18, 300 n. 5, 301 n. 11
Oecolampadius, Johannes, 32
Old Testament, 26, 30, 35, 43, 53, 73, 111, 117, 224, 243, 261. *See also* Bible
Ong, Walter J., 271
Oostsanen, Jacob Cornelisz van, 224
Origen, 42, 44
Ornstein, Robert, 135
Orthography, 166, 229, 275
Ovid, 24, 219, 230, 276
Oxford, 56, 73; University of, 74, 160
Ozment, Steven, 29, 299 n. 17
Ozouf, Jacques, 302 n. 23

Pagan literature, and Christianity, 24, 25, 37
Painter, William, 249
Palazzina Marfisa d'Este (Ferrara), 330 n. 52
Palazzo d'Arco (Mantua), 226
Palazzo Ducale (Mantua), 166
Palazzo Farnese (Caprarola), 226
Palazzo Schifanoia (Ferrara), 226
Palladio, Andrea, 166–67
Palmer, D. J., 326 n. 19
Paper: and book production, 45, 61; bullets, 248, 249; figurative use of, 183; and innocence, 95, 120–21; and manuscripts, 280; mills, 79; mysterious paper in *Bussy D'Ambois,* 145–52; and normal surface for writing, 276; and print, 276; as symbol, 120–22, 286; as prop, 77, 125, 145–47, 202, 244–46, 247, 277, 286
Papyrus, 266
Paracelsus, 99, 168–69, 170, 171, 176–77, 228, 321 n. 23, 329 n. 43
Paradise, Nathaniel Burton, 336 n. 5
Parchment, 35, 38, 56, 90, 266, 276, 280, 295, 298 n. 8
Paris, 81, 169, 317 n. 47
Parke, H. W., 332 n. 13

Parrott, Thomas Marc, 315 nn. 30 and 37, 316 n. 42, 317 nn. 47 and 49
Pasquil, 248
Pastoral, 180–96
Patterson, Annabel, 307 n. 42, 324 n. 6
Paul, Saint, 32, 34, 50, 68, 111, 117
Paul IV (pope), 55
Pauline Epistles, 299 n. 20. *See also* Bible
Paul's, St. (cathedral), 53, 269, 292
Peacham, Henry, 59, 141, 142, 161, 241
Pearce, G. M., 336 n. 10
Peele, George: *Edward I,* 104, 105
Pen: of adamant, 119; of Doctor Faustus, 84–85, 89; of iron, 132; of Julius Caesar, 64; of Luther, 75; of Marina, 211; and printing press, 281–82; of Rosader, 191; of a scholar, 59; sharpened with a knife, 244, 275; of a shepherd, 183; of the Sibyl, 224; of Venus, 166; writes book of conscience, 113; writes history, 95; writes name of Jesus, 120; quill pen as prop, 78, 82, 104, 244, 247, 275; worn, 281. *See also* Book, Reading, Writing
Perkins, William, 118, 159–60, 161
Peterson, Douglas L., 199
Petrarch: and love poetry, 185, 186, 326 n. 18; and Mont Ventoux, 68–69
Peutinger, Konrad and Margarethe, 44
Pfeiffer, Rudolf, 298 n. 5
Pfister, Manfred, 307 n. 2
Phillips, Margaret Mann, 303 n. 48
Physiognomy, 99
Piccolomini, Francesco Todeschini, 11
Pico della Mirandola, 75, 227
Pietrasanta, Sylvester, 204–5
Pinturicchio, 11, 224
Pius II (pope), 11
Plato, 81, 175, 329 n. 44, 333 n. 30; and *Bussy D'Ambois,* 318 n. 53. Works: *Phaedrus,* 175, 322 n. 51, 329 n. 41; *Timaeus,* 98
Pliny, 168
Plotinus, 165, 175, 176, 225, 333 n. 30
Plowden, Edmund, 156
Plutarch, 335 n. 57
Pluto, 233, 246
Poem, as prop, 186–87, 189, 190, 192, 193, 194
Poggioli, Renato, 324 n. 6

Polo, Gaspar Gil, 182, 186
Popkin, Richard H., 302 n. 26
Post, R. R., 301 n. 6
Potts, Timothy C., 117
Predestination, 84, 114–15, 120, 228, 229
Primaudaye, Pierre de la, 57, 64, 118, 120–21, 164
Print: and accessibility of ancient culture, 70; and aggrievement, 79; as anachronism, 80; as artificial writing, 281; and the Bible, 12, 22, 44, 47, 48, 70, 76; and the Brethren of the Common Life, 45–46; and catchwords, 281; causes strife, 50–55, 70, 75, 76; and chapter divisions, 279; and compositors, 45, 48, 49, 61, 62, 63, 279, 280; and copyright, 280; deference to, 45, 58–59, 63; and dedication of books, 279; definition of, 90, 307 n. 5; and dispersal of ideas, 44, 47–48, 171; and England, 73–76, 297 n. 7; errors, 22, 61–63, 76, 93, 279; and the face, 93, 129; forms of, 268; and the Frankfurt Fair, 31; and the Holy Spirit, 32, 65–66; and an index, 278–79; invention of, 12, 44; and ligatures, 281; and literacy, 56; and love experience, 280; and Luther's ninety-five theses, 12, 301 n. 11; makes books affordable, 56, 76, 106; as metaphor, 255–56; and misprints, 61, 62–63, 279; and newsbooks, 278; and operation of a press, 47–48, 49; and oral culture, 265, 270–71, 306 n. 24; on parchment, 280; and playwrights, 13, 76; and a pointing hand, 279; praise of, 12, 65–66; and the preservation of playscripts, 67–68, 265; and production of books, 48, 55–63, 106, 264–65, 268; and proofreaders, 45, 61; and providence, 65–66; and public opinion, 47; and the Reformation, 48, 50, 75, 76; and reputation, 50, 66, 67; in red ink, 279; resembles manuscripts, 280–82; and script, 278, 280–82; and signatures, 281; and size of books, 279; and strife, 50–54, 70, 75, 76; and title page, 278, 279, 327 n. 33; and unscrupulous printers, 62, 76; as vehicle of religious propaganda, 76.

See also Bible, Books, Library, Reading, Writing
Properties: *See* Bible, Book, Documents, Ink, Letters, Pen, Poem, Reading, Scrolls, Seal, Signet, Writing
Property list, 286
Prophecy: and fate, 222; and providence, 222, 223, 224, 225
Proserpine, 233
Proudfoot, Richard, 336 n. 10
Providence, personified, 287
Prowse, Philip, 340 n. 37
Ptolomy Philadelphus, 65
Puritans, 74, 139, 140, 158–61
Puttenham, George: *Arte of English Poesie*, 96, 204, 272–73
Pythagoras, 167, 173, 174, 175, 217, 329 n. 44

Ralegh, Sir Walter, 174
Rappaport, Steve, 270
Rare Triumphs of Love and Fortune, 333 n. 56
Rasmussen, Eric, 81, 84
Rauchbauer, Otto, 136–37
Reading: the Bible, 21–22, 24, 30, 48, 74, 75, 83, 118–19; the body, 88, 89, 99; by Brutus, 64; definition of, 103, 309 n. 49; difficulty of, 38–43, 88, 89, 90, 91, 92, 93, 94, 95–96, 102, 103, 172–73, 174–79, 221, 228–29, 247, 249, 250–55; excessive, 296; the face, 88, 89–93, 95, 98, 99, 101, 103, 129, 131, 132, 133, 137, 209; and fecklessness, 292–93; figurative, 89–107; by God, 113, 119, 125; the heart/mind, 88, 89, 91, 92, 93, 94, 95, 98, 103, 253–54; and ill health, 59; by Julius Caesar, 64; as a kind of writing, 106; and Last Judgment, 113–16, 119, 122–23, 155; learning to read, 122, 264; and melancholy, 289; and memory, 93–95; nature, 163–65, 169–79; pagan literature, 24, 228; psychology of, 68–70; silent, 68, 106, 304 n. 86; with spectacles, 97–98, 172, 250–51, 255, 322 n. 40; as theatrical liability, 14, 194, 285. *See also* Bible, Books, Documents, Letters, Manuscripts, Print, Writing
Recorde, Robert, 211

Red letters, 279
Reed, Robert Rentoul, 317 n. 46, 332 n. 75
Reformation, the, 12, 35–36, 38, 48, 73, 74, 75, 76, 106, 111–12, 118, 158. *See also* Bible, Calvin, Erasmus, Foxe, Luther
Reuchlin, Johann, 53
Ribner, Irving, 316 n. 38
Richmond Palace, 11
Ricks, Christopher, 339 n. 31
Riggs, David, 67
Ripa, Cesare, 142, 143, 144
Roberts, Julian, 297 n. 6, 331 n. 64
Roman de la Rose, 280
Rosenmeyer, Thomas G., 185
Rotterdam, 73–74
Rozett, Martha Tuck, 306 n. 34
Rubens, Peter Paul, 204
Rummel, Erika, 298 n. 9

Sabbioneta, palace of, 166
Saenger, Paul, 304 n. 86
Salmonius, Blasius, 31
Salzman, Paul, 324 n. 10
Sannazaro, Jacopo, 182, 276, 324 n. 7
San Sebastiano, church of, 167
Santeramo, Pietro, 58
Schlegel, August Wilhelm von, 130
Schoeck, R. J., 298 n. 6, 301 nn. 5 and 7
Schoell, Franck L., 318 n. 53
Schöffer, Peter, 44
Schofield, R. S., 268, 297 n. 9, 341 n. 5
Scholes, Robert, 106
Schools, founding of, 15, 75, 79, 268, 273
Schwarz, Werner, 32, 34
Scribal error, 22, 27, 36, 61
Scribe, 26, 27, 36, 45–46, 56, 58, 61, 113, 280–81, 292
Scribner, R. W., 299 n. 22
Script: forms of, 268, 275; similarities to print, 280–82; theatrical effects of, 282
Scrivener, 246, 275, 282, 292
Scrolls, 32, 222, 224, 276; as props, 85, 271, 287, 291, 295
Seal/sealing wax, 125, 192, 291, 275, 276, 294
Seaver, Paul S., 161
Second Maiden's Tragedy, 340 n. 36
Secretary hand, 268, 275

Seltzer, Daniel, 149
Seneca, 51, 237–39, 336 nn. 10 and 11, 337 nn. 12 and 13
Shakespeare: and the First Folio, 67–68; and plots found in printed books, 265; and writing on the stage, 13. Works: *All's Well That Ends Well*, 289; *Antony and Cleopatra*, 95, 178–79; *As You Like It*, 164, 180–96; *The Comedy of Errors*, 90; *Coriolanus*, 91, 94–95; *Cymbeline*, 100–101, 229, 276, 331 n. 56; *Hamlet*, 91, 124, 240–42, 288, 289, 337 n. 18, 340 n. 36; *1 Henry IV*, 276, 277, 330 n. 50; *2 Henry IV*, 230–31, 277, 278; *Henry V*, 291; *1 Henry VI*, 94, 225, 283, 285, 293–94; *2 Henry VI*, 15, 78–80, 87, 95, 104–5, 284–85, 287, 291, 293, 294; *3 Henry VI*, 284, 293; *Henry VIII*, 207, 289, 292; *Julius Caesar*, 91, 124, 230, 256, 262, 293, 294, 295, 296; *King John*, 89–90, 272; *King Lear*, 107, 256, 259, 262, 283, 294, 295; *Love's Labor's Lost*, 289; *Macbeth*, 91, 94, 124–25, 161, 225, 290, 291; *Measure for Measure*, 161; *The Merchant of Venice*, 276, 285–86, 287, 288, 291, 292; *The Merry Wives of Windsor*, 276, 280; *Much Ado About Nothing*, 264, 275, 291; *Othello*, 16, 93, 225, 262, 279, 293, 333 n. 29; *Pericles*, 164, 180, 196–211, 212, 289, 331 n. 56; *Richard II*, 291; *Richard III*, 92, 124, 255, 287, 288, 292; *Romeo and Juliet*, 229–30, 277, 293; *The Taming of the Shrew*, 280; *The Tempest*, 78, 151, 217, 293, 332 n. 75; *Timon of Athens*, 196; *Titus Andronicus*, 88, 230, 239–40, 276, 295; *Troilus and Cressida*, 88; *Twelfth Night*, 92; *The Two Gentlemen of Verona*, 275; *The Two Noble Kinsmen*, 90; *Venus and Adonis*, 276; *The Winter's Tale*, 196, 278, 287
Sheridan, James J., 320 n. 13
s'Hertogenbosch, 46
Sibyls, 221–25, 240
Sidney, Sir Philip, 96, 211, 213, 217, 327 n. 30; *Arcadia*: 182, 294
Siena cathedral, 11, 223
Sinfield, Alan, 74

Singer, Thomas C., 322 n. 49
Sir John Oldcastle, Part 1, 276, 277
Sistine Chapel, 224
Skelton, John: *Magnificence*, 82, 294
Slater, Ann Pasternak, 283, 326 n. 20
Slavin, Arthur J., 297 n. 7, 302 n. 37
Slights, Camille Wells, 112, 124, 125
Slights, William W. E., 307 n. 2
Smith, John Hazel, 315 n. 30
Smyth, Sir Thomas, 258
Socrates, 31, 322 n. 51, 329 n. 41
Soliman and Perseda, story of, 242–43, 245, 246
Solomon, 75 142, 290
Solon, 111
Songs and Sonnets, 276
Sowards, J. Kelley, 302 n. 27
Spalatinus, Georgius, 31, 39, 53, 54
Spitz, Lewis W., 48
Standish, 275
Stars, 99, 174, 215, 225–29, 256–63; and the drama, 229, 247, 250–54, 256, 339 n. 33. *See* also Astrology, Astronomy
Stationers, 56; Register of, 211, 314 n. 26
Staupitz, Johann von, 53
Steinberg, S. H., 302 n. 30
Stern, Virginia, 340 n. 43
Steyn, monastery at, 46
Stock, Brian, 270
Stoll, Elmer Edgar, 340 n. 36
Storm, Claus, 46
Stow, John, 74
Strasbourg, 56
Stylus, 219
Sumer, 221
Sylvester (pope), 30

Table (notebook), 130, 289, 337 n. 18, 340 n. 35
Talbert, Ernest William, 336 n. 8
Tarlton, Richard, 262
Tarquin (king of Rome), 222, 223
Tayler, Edward William, 323 n. 1
Taylor, Gary, 328 n. 37
Taylor, Jeremy, 116–17
Taylor, Mark, 345 n. 2
Teague, Frances, 283, 346 n. 25
Telesio, Bernardino, 167
Tempio Malatestiano (Rimini), 223

Ten Commandments, 82, 111, 119–20, 241
Terence, 24, 37
Tertullian, 223
Theaters, and censorship, 88
Theocritus, 188
Theodoric (king of Ostrogoths), 24
Theuth, 175, 322 n. 51
Thomas, Keith, 268, 317 n. 46, 334 n. 38, 341 n. 2
Thompson, Ann and John O., 280
Thompson, C. R., 305 n. 4
Three Ladies of London, 124, 134
Thurley, Simon, 297 n. 3
Title page, 200, 278, 279, 280, 328 n. 33
Torresani of Asola, Andrea, 47
Tottel's *Miscellany*, 276
Tourneur, Cyril: *The Atheist's Tragedy*, 124; *The Revenger's Tragedy*, 95
Traister, Barbara Howard, 316 n. 40, 317 n. 46
Tricomi, Albert H., 315 n. 31
Trithemius, Johannes, 81
True Chronicle History of King Leir, 287–88, 294–95
Tunstall, Cuthbert (bishop of London), 80
Turner, Mark, 106
Turner, Ted, 265
Tweedie, Eleanor M., 336 n. 3
Twelve Tables, 111
Twine, Lawrence, 198, 210, 211, 327 n. 28
Tyacke, Nicholas, 319 n. 81
Tyndale, William, 115, 156

Udall, Nicholas, 73
Ulm, cathedral of, 223
Urbino, 11

Valeriano Bolzani, Giovanni Pierio, 177, 178, 217
Valiant Welshman, The, 93
Valla, Lorenzo, 36, 46, 75, 106, and the Donation of Constantine, 30. Works: *Collatio Novi Testamenti*, 25, 26, 298 n. 6; *Elegantiae Linguae Latinae*, 24
Van den Berg, Kent T., 325 n. 17
Varro, Terentius, 221–22
Vatican, frescoes at, 224
Veldman, Ilja M., 312 n. 47

Venice, 46, 167
Venus, 166, 182–83, 219
Vérard, Antoine, 281
Veronese, 166–67
Vettori, Francesco, 69
Vickers, Nancy J., 326 n. 18
Villa Barbaro, 167
Villa d'Este, 210
Virgil, 24, 42, 188. Works: *Aeneid*, 219, 222, 228, 319 n. 88, 336 n. 6; *Eclogues*, 39
Visscher, Peter, 112
Vulgate, 27, 116, 237, 298 n. 11. See also Bible

Wager, Lewis, 82
Wager, William, 346 n. 19
Wallington, Nehemiah, 161
Walsingham, Sir Francis, 211, 214, 217
Wapull, George, 287
Warham, William (archbishop of Canterbury), 27, 70, 73
Warning for Fair Women, A, 99, 288
Watt, Tessa, 270
Webster, John, 265. Works: *Appius and Virginia*, 92, 275, 291, 292; *The Devil's Law Case*, 288, 292; *The Duchess of Malfi*, 107, 124, 162, 221, 232, 246–56, 295; induction to *The Malcontent*, 279; *Northward Ho* (with Dekker), 280; *Westward Ho* (with Dekker), 93, 277; *The White Devil*, 13
Wells, Stanley, 328 n. 37
Wentworth, Michael, 313 n. 9
West, Robert Hunter, 317 n. 46
White, Paul Whitfield, 87
Whitehall Palace, 11
Whitgift, John, 158–59, 263
Whitney, Geoffrey, 239–40
Wilkins, George, 202, 203, 211, 212
Wilks, John S., 124, 125
Willis, Paul J., 323 n. 2
Wilson, Thomas: *Arte of Rhetorique*, 88
Wind, Edgar, 333 n. 25
Windesheim Congregation, 46
Wittenberg, 29, 31, 37, 47, 53, 54, 81, 85, 289
Wolsey, Cardinal, 53, 292
Women: characters as readers, 141–44, 187–93, 198–99, 201, 234–35, 248–49, 255, 276, 277–78, 280, 284, 288, 289,

291, 294, 315n. 36; characters as writers, 124, 125, 146, 152–53, 199–200, 211, 235–36, 295, 331n. 57; characters as figurative writers, 131, 133, 137, 197, 279; as readers, 44, 299n. 20; as writers, 221–25, 331n. 57

Wood, James O., 327n. 33

Woodcuts, and words, 269, 280

Woodes, Nathaniel, 124

Woodman, David, 317n. 46

Words: and creation, 98–99; and emblems, 177–78; and identity, 133; and imprese, 129, 198–99; insufficiency of, 137; power of, 101–2. *See also* Bible, Reading, Print, Writing

World and the Child, The, 124

Worms, Diet of, 34, 35, 39, 55, 111

Writing: and an abstract, 307n. 3; and adamant, 219; and aggrievement, 239; and alchemy, 290; ambiguity of, 295; and astrology, 101, 221, 225, 228, 229, 247, 250–56, 260–61; in Babylonia, 221; in blood, 84–85, 89, 105, 114, 124, 144–45, 146, 153, 162, 235, 246; on the body, 88, 89, 90–93, 99, on brass, 219, 240; and a (legal) brief, 292, 307n. 3; and business transactions, 277; and church fathers, 21, 34; collation of, 25, 114, 119; confidence in, 30, 34, 85, 246; and conscience, 124–62; culture of, 265, 270–71; and cuneiform, 221; and daily life, 272–73, 281–82; and dearth of originality, 58–59; and death, 155, 243, 249, 250, 252, 291, 292, 294, 295, 296, 346n. 27; as decoration, 272–73; deficiencies of, 14; and desk, 152–53; and Diana, 210–11, 330n. 54; at the direction of God, 35; and a dustbox, 275; on the earth, 105; and emblems, 178; an epitaph, 95, 137–38, 208–9; and essential documents, 281–82; in Egypt, 100, 175, 177; of Etruscans, 100; on the face, 90, 92–93, 99, 131, 133, 137, 144–45; and fate, 220–25, 228–29, 232–56; in the firmament, 101, 102, 166, 174, 225, 228–29; with food, 272; and forgery, 30, 151, 242, 275, 294, 295, 317n. 49; by Fortune, 230, 335n. 55; by God, 99, 100, 119, 132, 164, 165, 166, 167, 217; in gold, 94, 138, 208; on the ground, 135, 155; on hats, 91; in the heart/mind, 38, 115–20, 130, 194, 253; in heaven, 133, 135; and heresy, 53, 76–77, 277; of a horoscope, 247, 248, 249, 250, 251, 252, 256, 339n. 35; and imprese, 129, 198–99, 273, 327n. 30; inadequacy of, 244–45; of initials, 247, 252; and italic, 268, 275, 281; and journalism, 278; and Last Judgment, 113–16, 119, 122–23, 155; and law, 57, 82, 115–16, 118, 290–92; and leaves of lottery, 233, 234; and leaves of the Sibyl, 222; and Lollards, 27; by Love, 193; and magic, 82–83, 102, 147–51; manipulated by the unscrupulous, 288, 292–96; and manuscript transmission, 36, 82; and the material world, 98–99, 178; and mathematics, 215–18; and medicine, 82, 204, 289–90; and memory, 93–95, 239–41, 340n. 35; and morality, 111–23; and natural law, 118, 166, 172; and nature, 163–79, 180–82, 197, 204, 213, 217–18; and notary, 113, 276, 282; and oaths, 271–72; and oppression, 57, 78–80; and oral culture, 14, 264–65, 270–72, 306n. 24; and pardon, 236; of a passport, 233, 336nn. 6 and 9; and pastoral, 181, 182, 186–95; and philosophy, 82, 288–89; of a physician, 290; and playbills, 274; and playbook (script) as prop, 242–43; posted at St. Paul's, 292; and punishment, 91, 291; and religion, 82, 287–88; and revenge, 232–46, 48; and riddle, 196–97, 199, 200, 202–3; and rituals, 271; and salvation, 12, 113–14, 288, 292; and scribal carelessness, 36, 61; and scrivener, 246, 275, 282, 292; and seal/sealing wax, 192, 275–276, 291, 294; and secretary hand, 268, 275; and Sibyls, 221–25, 240; and signet, 275; similarities to print, 280–82; skill at, 268; on snow, 255; of sonnets, 184, 190, 191, 192, 193, 326n. 18; and a standish, 275; on stone, 111, 117, 120, 239–40; with steel, 240; in Sumer, 221; in a table (notebook), 130, 240, 289, 337n. 18, 340n. 35; and textual corruption, 27; by time, 90; as theatrical liability, 14; on trees, 181, 182, 187, 188, 189, 192, 325 nn. 15 and 16; unread, 230; by Venus, 166, 320 n. 13; and violence, 152–53; and virtue, 64–65; on the wall, 243; of a will, 247, 292, 295. *See also* Bible, Books, Character, Documents, Letters, Library, Literacy, Manuscripts, Paper, Pen, Poem, Print, Reading, Scribe, Script, Scrivener, Scrolls, Stars, Women

Wycliffe, John, 52, 54

Yates, Frances, 217, 332 n. 75
Yorkshire Tragedy, A, 278
Young, Alan R., 327 n. 30
Young, David P., 324 n. 10

Zodiacal symbols, 102, 215–16, 226